CIVIL PROCEDURE

KEYED TO YEAZELL
SIXTH EDITION

John T. Cross

Professor of Law, Louis D. Brandeis School of Law at the University of Louisville

The *Emanuel Law Outlines* Series

PUBLISHERS

111 Eighth Avenue, New York, NY 10011
www.aspenpublishers.com

© 2004 Aspen Publishers, Inc.
A Wolters Kluwer Company
www.aspenpublishers.com

Permissions
Aspen Publishers
111 Eighth Avenue
New York, NY 10011

Printed in the United States of America.

4 5 6 7 8 9 0

ISBN 0-7355-4419-0

This book is intended as a general review of a legal subject. It is not intended as a source of advice for the solution of legal matters or problems. For advice on legal matters, the reader should consult an attorney.

About Aspen Publishers

Aspen Publishers, headquartered in New York City, is a leading information provider for attorneys, business professionals, and law students. Written by preeminent authorities, our products consist of analytical and practical information covering both U.S. and international topics. We publish in the full range of formats, including updated manuals, books, periodicals, CDs, and online products.

Our proprietary content is complemented by 2,500 legal databases, containing over 11 million documents, available through our Loislaw division. Aspen Publishers also offers a wide range of topical legal and business databases linked to Loislaw's primary material. Our mission is to provide accurate, timely, and authoritative content in easily accessible formats, supported by unmatched customer care.

To order any Aspen Publishers title, go to *www.aspenpublishers.com* or call 1-800-638-8437.

To reinstate your manual update service, call 1-800-638-8437.

For more information on Loislaw products, go to *www.loislaw.com* or call 1-800-364-2512.

For Customer Care issues, e-mail *CustomerCare@aspenpublishers.com*; call 1-800-234-1660; or fax 1-800-901-9075.

Aspen Publishers
A Wolters Kluwer Company

Note

This book includes analyses of the facts and holdings of nearly all of the cases treated as principal cases in Yeazell, *Civil Procedure*, Sixth Edition, 2004. The analysis of each Yeazell case is preceded by a ★ symbol.

Summary of Contents

Table of Contents

CHAPTER 1

INTRODUCTION

CHAPTER 2

PERSONAL JURISDICTION

I. OVERVIEW 12

  A. Definition of personal jurisdiction 12

  B. Subject matter jurisdiction distinguished 12

  C. Constitutional requirement 12

CHAPTER 3

VENUE

CHAPTER 4

SUBJECT MATTER JURISDICTION

CHAPTER 5

THE *ERIE* DOCTRINE

CHAPTER 6

LITIGATION AND ITS ALTERNATIVES

CHAPTER 7

PLEADING

CHAPTER 8

DISCOVERY

CHAPTER 9

RESOLUTION BEFORE TRIAL

CHAPTER 10

DETERMINING THE TRIER

CHAPTER 11

THE TRIAL

CHAPTER 12

APPEALS

CHAPTER 13

RESPECT FOR JUDGMENTS

CHAPTER 14

JOINDER OF CLAIMS AND PARTIES

CHAPTER 15
CLASS ACTIONS

Preface

Welcome to the world of Civil Procedure! Although the world may seem strange at first, with patience and diligent effort you will gradually grow comfortable in it. This book is intended to help ease your transition into the realm of Civil Procedure.

Civil Procedure deals with the process by which attorneys conduct civil suits. A civil case, roughly speaking, is any case other than a criminal prosecution. Nevertheless, most Civil Procedure courses do not spend much time on certain specialized types of civil cases, such as divorce and child custody actions or suits against the government. Although many of the general principles of Procedure also govern these cases, you will have to wait until other courses to learn the idiosyncratic rules that apply in these areas.

Most schools offer Civil Procedure in the first-year curriculum. However, the course is different from other traditional first-year courses. First, because Procedure deals primarily with *process* rather than the substantive law, you will deal with claims and defenses involving a number of different areas of substantive law. The same procedural issue can arise in a Contracts, Constitutional Law, or Corporate Law case. You will soon realize that the merits of the underlying dispute is usually not the crucial issue for purposes of Civil Procedure.

Second, unlike other first-year courses such as Torts and Property, the study of Procedure does not focus overwhelmingly on case law. Most systems have codified their rules of procedure. In many situations, your primary source for a legal principle will be a statute or written rule rather than a judicial opinion. During your study of Civil Procedure, you will become very familiar with the Federal Rules of Civil Procedure as well as certain statutes dealing with the authority of the federal courts. Although cases are important, in some situations the case merely illustrates how the statute or rule applies in practice.

Because Procedure differs from state to state, many Procedure professors focus mainly on *federal* procedure. Although many of you may never set foot in federal court, it is nevertheless useful to study how the federal courts conduct cases. The federal procedural system has had a tremendous influence on many states. In fact, a number of states have copied the Federal Rules of Civil Procedure for use in their own courts. Others, while not copying the federal rules, have borrowed many of the underlying concepts. While each state has its own particular rules and interpretations, a study of federal Civil Procedure nevertheless provides a solid grounding for learning the particular rules in force in any U.S. jurisdiction.

Many students claim that Civil Procedure is one of the most difficult courses in law school, especially when it is taught as part of the first-year curriculum. With the benefit of hindsight, I can assure you this is not true. The rules of Procedure are no more numerous or complex than the rules in many of your other courses. And although Procedure has its share of difficult concepts — the *Erie* doctrine, claim and issue preclusion, and the right to a jury spring to mind — other courses deal with concepts that are equally tough to grasp.

Nevertheless, although a law school alumna or alumnus might not list Civil Procedure among the more difficult subjects in law school, there is no doubt that the subject *seems* difficult to the first-year student. This perception stems from the nature of the course. The problem with Procedure is that the subject is almost entirely foreign to the law student. Other mainstream courses, such as Contracts, Torts, Constitutional Law, and Criminal Law, present real-life issues to which students can immediately relate. Because they understand the issue, students more often than not have a ''gut reaction'' as to what the rule of law ought to be. Civil Procedure seems cold and mechanical in comparison. The outcome of a dispute concerning whether an answer is properly framed has no immediately obvious effect on the greater social good. Students therefore have no ''hunch'' as to how the dispute ought be resolved.

Nevertheless, do not assume that Civil Procedure comprises a set of arbitrary rules that must simply be committed to memory. As in all your other courses, there is a philosophy underlying Civil Procedure. Once you accept that there are norms underlying Civil Procedure, and make the effort to understand the "big picture," half of the battle of understanding the subject will be won.

Properly used, this book will help you understand Civil Procedure. Given the nature of the work, the primary focus is the individual rules. Of course, you will need to know those rules in preparation for your course examinations. Nevertheless, the book also attempts to explain *why* certain rules are the way they are. Understanding the policy underlying the rules will help you understand the overall policy underlying Civil Procedure in the United States.

When using this book, approach the different elements in different ways. First, when preparing for class, check the correlation chart to find the section of the book that corresponds to what you are reading. Read this material *before* reading the casebook to give yourself a basic overview of what you are covering. You may also find it helpful to reread the same section of this book after each class to reinforce what you have learned. When you finish a topic or chapter, work through the Quiz Yourself questions to check what you know and where you need work. Make sure that you can apply the rules you have learned. Equally importantly, however, make sure that you can spot the issue being addressed in the problem. Issue spotting can be especially tricky in Civil Procedure.

Second, when preparing your outline, refer again to this work for a summary of the rules. Here, however, you should also consider the general structure of this work. Great care has been taken to organize the material into a useful outline form. Although this outline generally follows the Yeazell *Civil Procedure* casebook, in places it diverges to help the reader make connections between various concepts.

Finally, when preparing for the final examination, study the Exam Tips, which focus on areas that students frequently find confusing. Work again through the Quiz Yourself sections, both to make sure you know the material and to help you practice your writing. Finally, take a stab at the longer essays in the essay section, which mirror the exam format used by many professors.

It should go without saying that this work is meant to complement, *not be a substitute for*, your casebook. You should always read the assigned material in the casebook and any supplementary materials. *Never* go into class having read only the material in this work. In addition, this work is not intended to be a "canned outline." You should always prepare your own outline for the course, at the very least because your professor will have his or her own slant and possibly bring in additional materials.

Good luck with Civil Procedure!

John Cross

March 2004

Casebook Correlation Chart

Material in Yeazell, Civil Procedure, Sixth Edition (by chapter and section heading)	Pages in Yeazell	Pages in Emanuel Law Outline
I. OVERVIEW OF PROCEDURE	1-60	1-10
II. PERSONAL JURISDICTION		
A. Origins	61-75	11-14, 30-32
B. The Modern Constitutional Formulation of Power	76-140	14-21
C. Consent as a Substitute for Power	140-145	21-22
D. The Constitutional Requirement of Notice	145-159	25-29
E. Self-Imposed Restraints on Jurisdictional Power: Long-Arm Statutes, Venue, and Forum Non Conveniens	159-178	26-27, 37-46
III. SUBJECT MATTER JURISDICTION OF THE FEDERAL COURTS		
A. The Idea and Structure of Subject Matter Jurisdiction	179-181	51-52
B. Federal Question Jurisdiction	181-192	52-55
C. Diversity Jurisdiction	192-205	57-65
D. Supplemental Jurisdiction	205-212	73-76
E. Removal	212-219	73-76
IV. THE ERIE PROBLEM		
A. State Courts as Lawmakers in a Federal System	221-231	85-88, 98
B. The Limits of State Power in Federal Courts	231-253	88-98
V. INCENTIVES TO LITIGATE		
A. Litigation in the United States	259-265	not covered
B. Substitutionary Remedies	265-278	103-105
C. Specific Remedies	278-285	105-106
D. Declaratory Relief	285-287	106
E. Financing Litigation	287-312	110-111
F. Provisional Remedies	312-327	106-109
VI. PLEADING		
A. The Story of Pleading	329-377	120-125, 141-144
B. Responding to the Complaint	377-405	127-141
VII. DISCOVERY		
A. Modern Discovery	407-408	152
B. The Possibilities and Limits of Discovery: Relevance and Privilege	408-416	152-154
C. Surveying Discovery: Procedures and Methods	416-427	154-163
D. Discovery and Privacy	427-437	163-164, 166-167
E. Discovery in an Adversary System	438-451	167-170
F. Ensuring Compliance and Controlling Abuse of Discovery	451-464	172-176

Capsule Summary

This Capsule Summary provides a "road map" for the main body of this book. It should be used as a general overview, *not* as a substitute for the more in-depth material in the main body. The bracketed numbers provide cross-references to the page numbers in the main body.

CHAPTER 1

INTRODUCTION

I. CIVIL PROCEDURE GENERALLY

Civil Procedure is the study of how civil cases are resolved. Although it focuses primarily on litigation in the courts, there is also some discussion of alternate means of resolving disputes.

A. Different from other courses: Civil Procedure differs in certain significant ways from the other first-year courses. However, although there is less focus on the substantive law, you should always keep your other courses in mind since the substantive law may affect how the rules of Procedure apply. [1-3]

B. Sources of Civil Procedure: Another difference between Civil Procedure and other courses is that the rules of Procedure are far more likely to come from a statute or written rule than from case law. [3]

    1. Federal Rules of Civil Procedure: The Federal Rules of Civil Procedure are especially important in the study of Procedure. [3]

    2. Cases: Although most of the rules come from statutes and other written rules, cases are also important insofar as they explain and sometimes fine-tune the rules. [3]

II. GENERAL THEMES

A. Multiple court systems: One recurring theme in Civil Procedure is the system of parallel state and federal courts. Unlike in some other federal nations, in the United States it is often possible for both state and federal courts to hear a given dispute. [4]

B. Stages in a civil lawsuit: A typical lawsuit goes through several stages.

    1. Determining where to sue: The plaintiff first determines where to bring the action. This decision requires consideration of *subject matter jurisdiction, personal jurisdiction*, and *venue*. [6]

    2. Pleading the case: Next, the party determines how to plead the case. The *complaint* is the document in which plaintiff sets out her claims. The defendant responds with an answer or a pre-answer motion. [7]

C. Joinder: It is possible for a case to involve more than a single plaintiff and defendant. If so, the parties may file various claims against each other. In addition, it is possible for parties other than plaintiffs and defendants to be joined to a case, or, in some cases, the third parties may join of their own volition. [7-8]

D. Discovery: Although the parties will engage in significant information gathering before the case begins, they may also obtain information from each other and from third-party witnesses. This process of discovery may take several years in large and complex cases. [8]

E. Resolution before trial: Many cases are *settled* before ever going to trial. A party may also *dismiss* her case voluntarily or have her case dismissed for failure to cooperate in the litigation process. Finally, if it becomes clear that one side should prevail, the court may grant a *summary judgment* in that party's favor, which operates like a judgment after a full trial. [8-9]

F. Trial: If a case reaches trial, additional issues arise, primarily involving the *jury*. [9]

G. Post-trial: An unfavorable judgment usually may be *appealed*, although strict rules govern the timing of the appeal. In addition, a final judgment may prevent the litigants or other parties from relitigating the claims and issues in later cases. [9-10]

CHAPTER 2

PERSONAL JURISDICTION

I. OVERVIEW

A. Definition: Personal jurisdiction is a court's power to enter a judgment that binds the parties to the case. [12]

B. Constitutional considerations: The U.S. Constitution sets limits on a court's power to exercise personal jurisdiction over the parties to a case. Several Supreme Court cases set out a test for when the Constitution allows jurisdiction. [12]

C. Two categories: Courts distinguish between two broad categories of personal jurisdiction: *in personam* (jurisdiction over the person) and *in rem* (jurisdiction over property). There are several important distinctions between the two. [12-13]

II. THE CONSTITUTIONAL TEST

The Supreme Court, through a long line of cases spanning well over a century, has set out an analysis for when a court may exercise jurisdiction over a *nonpresent defendant*. This test is commonly referred to as the minimum contacts test. [13]

A. Pennoyer v. Neff (1877): *Pennoyer* was the first case to hold that the Constitution limited jurisdiction. The decision set out a very territorial approach to the issue, under which a state's authority usually was confined to its borders. However, many (but by no means all) of *Pennoyer*'s territorial rules have been supplanted by more recent decisions. [13-14]

B. International Shoe v. Washington (1945): *International Shoe* established the basic *minimum contacts test*, which is still used today to measure jurisdiction. The Court also indicated that the level of contacts necessary to sustain jurisdiction would depend on whether the suit arose out of the contacts ("specific" jurisdiction) or whether it was unrelated to the contacts ("general" jurisdiction). [14-15]

C. **Shaffer v. Heitner (1977):** *Shaffer* held that the minimum contacts test also applied to *in rem* jurisdiction. In addition, the Court held that if the property was the only contact between the defendant and the forum, and the cause of action did not arise directly out of the property, a state ordinarily could not exercise jurisdiction over the owner of that property. [15-16]

D. **World-Wide Volkswagen v. Woodsen (1980):** *World-Wide* fleshed out the minimum contacts test. The Court indicated that the minimum contacts test comprised two distinct elements.

   1. First, there must be one or more contacts between the defendant and the forum. [17]

   2. Second, the exercise of jurisdiction must be fair. [17]

E. **Contract cases:** In McGee v. International Life, Hanson v. Denckla, and Burger King v. Rudzewicz, the Court discussed how the minimum contacts analysis would apply to contract-based claims. These decisions make it clear that a contract can constitute purposeful availment with a state if the contract is negotiated and/or is to be performed in that state. Merely contracting with a citizen of another state, however, is not enough to qualify as a contact by itself. [18-19]

F. **Asahi:** Asahi Metal v. Superior Court deals with the ***stream of commerce*** problem, where a defendant injects a good into commerce through a third party. The decision produced no clear majority opinion. The Court split on whether mere awareness that some of your product would end up in the forum state was enough, or whether other activities specifically directed at the forum, such as advertising, were required. [19-20]

G. **Internet cases:** Because people using the Internet do not necessarily know the location of the people with whom they interact, the Internet poses special difficulties for the minimum contacts test. Although the Supreme Court has not dealt with the issue, the lower courts have often analyzed the nature of the Web site involved. While passive sites usually do not create jurisdiction, active sites, especially those where the Web site owner takes orders, can be a sufficient contact. [20]

H. **Summary:** These cases and others set out a basic analysis to use in determining whether most assertions of personal jurisdiction satisfy the Constitution.

   1. **Two distinct steps:** The contacts and fairness portions of the test are separate steps.

      a. Contacts are always required. Unless there is at least one contact between the defendant and the forum, there will not be jurisdiction.

      b. Once at least one contact is identified, a court will evaluate fairness. Usually, fairness will not make a difference. However, if the exercise of jurisdiction would be extremely unfair, a court might be precluded from exercising jurisdiction even though contacts exist. [17-18]

   2. **Contacts and purposefulness:** The Court has indicated that a contact does not count unless it is the result of ***purposeful availment*** by the defendant of the benefits and protections of the forum. [17]

   3. **Fairness:** When evaluating fairness, one must consider not only the burden on the defendant but also the interests of the plaintiff, the forum state, and the judicial system. However, fairness is not a consideration unless there is at least one purposeful contact. [18]

4. General jurisdiction: The Supreme Court has never clearly held that general jurisdiction — that is, jurisdiction when the claim is unrelated to the contacts — actually exists. Lower courts continue to apply the concept, however. [20]

III. CASES OUTSIDE THE MINIMUM CONTACTS TEST

A. *Pennoyer* **still applies:** Although the minimum contacts test of *International Shoe* replaces the territorial approach of *Pennoyer* in most circumstances, there are still situations in which the *Pennoyer* rules apply. These include:

1. the *domicile* of an individual [21],

2. the *state of incorporation* of a corporate defendant [21],

3. the *physical presence* of the defendant in the forum state at the time of service (illustrated by Burnham v. Superior Court) [21], and

4. when the defendant *consents* to jurisdiction. [21]

B. When jurisdiction challenged: In addition, when a party challenges jurisdiction, a court has the authority to make a binding ruling on the question of its own jurisdiction. [22]

IV. NOTICE

Notice — which usually comprises a summons and complaint — is the other primary prerequisite for exercising personal jurisdiction.

A. Constitutional considerations: The Constitution also places certain restrictions on notice. The Supreme Court held in *Mullane* that notice must be reasonably calculated to give actual notice to the parties being served. [25-26]

B. How notice is provided: State and federal courts differ on the methods of service.

1. Long-arm statute: Service on an out-of-state defendant in a state court action is usually effected by means of a special statute called the long-arm statute. [26-27]

2. Federal courts: Service in a federal action is governed by *Fed. R. Civ. P. 4*.

    a. Methods: A federal court can serve either using the various methods listed in *Fed. R. Civ. P. 4* or by borrowing the law of the state in which the federal court sits or in which service occurs. Special service rules apply to certain types of defendants, such as infants, foreign defendants, and the United States. [27]

    b. Territorial limits: Service alone does not effect jurisdiction. Instead, Fed. R. Civ. P. 4(k) provides that, in most cases, a federal court can exercise jurisdiction only if the courts of the state in which the federal court sits could exercise jurisdiction over that defendant. [27]

        i. Thus, the minimum contacts analysis discussed above applies to the federal courts, albeit indirectly. [27]

        ii. However, there are a few exceptions to the rule of Fed. R. Civ. P. 4(k). [28]

   c. **Waiver of service:** A party suing in federal court may also ask the defendant to waive service. The rule provides incentives to a defendant to encourage waiver. [28-29]

V. CHALLENGES TO PERSONAL JURISDICTION

Personal jurisdiction is a personal defense that can be waived by inaction or by taking inconsistent action.

A. Traditional approach: The traditional approach was very strict. If a defendant participated in the case in any way, she waived the personal jurisdiction defense. [30-31]

B. Modern approach: The modern approach is exemplified by the Federal Rules of Civil Procedure.

   1. Under this approach, a defendant may challenge personal jurisdiction and, if he loses, go ahead and litigate the merits. [32]

   2. However, he must raise personal jurisdiction no later than the answer. Moreover, if he makes certain pre-answer motions, he must include the personal jurisdiction defense in that motion or it is lost. [31-32]

CHAPTER 3

VENUE

I. BASIC PRINCIPLES

Legislatures often prescribe a particular location for litigation, which is called the venue. [37]

II. FEDERAL VENUE

Venue in the state systems varies significantly. In the federal courts, however, venue is specifically defined by 28 U.S.C. §1391 and other statutes. [37]

A. Districts: Federal venue is defined in terms of judicial districts rather than states. Many states have more than one district. [38]

B. Where proper: Under §1391(a) and (b), a plaintiff may bring her action in any district in which a defendant resides (provided that all defendants reside in the same state) or in any district in which a substantial portion of the events or omissions giving rise to the cause of action occurred. If venue is not possible under either of those options, the plaintiff may bring the action in any district in which any defendant is subject to personal jurisdiction. [38-39]

   1. Corporations and aliens: Section 1391 also contains special rules governing corporate and alien defendants.

   a. Pursuant to §1391(c), a corporation is deemed to reside wherever it is subject to personal jurisdiction. [39-40]

   b. Under §1391(d), an alien is deemed to reside in every district in the United States. [40]

    2. Local actions: Certain actions directly affecting land are deemed to be ''local actions.'' Notwithstanding the language of §1391, these actions may be brought only in the district where the land is situated. [40]

    3. Special venue: Special venue statutes apply to certain cases, such as statutory interpleader actions. [40]

III. CHALLENGES TO VENUE

The rules governing challenges to venue are the same as those that apply to challenges to personal jurisdiction. [42]

IV. *FORUM NON CONVENIENS*

Forum non conveniens (FNC) is a court-created doctrine, applicable in both state and federal court, that gives a court **discretion** to dismiss an action even though venue is proper. A court will dismiss a case based on FNC only if:

A. an alternate forum is available to hear the case, [42], and

B. the court determines that the ***private*** and ***public factors*** warrant dismissal. The private factors relate generally to matters of convenience, while the public factors consider choice of law questions and the interests of the judicial system. [42-43]

V. TRANSFER OF VENUE

A case filed in a federal court may be transferred to another federal district. State courts cannot transfer cases to different states or to federal courts.

A. If venue proper: If the original court has venue over the action, any party may ask the court to transfer the case to another federal district where venue would also be proper. 28 U.S.C. §1404. The court will grant the request if the new forum is a more convenient place for litigation. [44]

    1. As in *forum non conveniens*, the court considers both public and private factors. [44-45]

    2. The governing law in the new court is the same as that which would apply in the original court. [45]

B. If venue improper: If venue is improper in the original court, 28 U.S.C. §1406 allows the court to transfer the case to a district where venue would be proper, but only if transferring the case is more just than simply dismissing for lack of venue. Section 1631 sets forth a similar rule that comes into play when the court has no personal jurisdiction. [45-46]

CHAPTER **4**

SUBJECT MATTER JURISDICTION

I. BASIC PRINCIPLES

A. Definition: Subject matter jurisdiction (SMJ) is a court's power to hear a particular dispute. [51]

B. All courts: SMJ is an issue in both state and federal courts.

    1. State courts: State courts have residual jurisdiction; that is, there is at least one court in every state that has SMJ over every claim other than those specifically delegated to another court. [51-52]

    2. Federal courts: Federal courts are courts of limited jurisdiction. The SMJ of federal courts is limited by the Constitution and federal statutes. There are two basic categories of federal SMJ: *federal question* and *diversity*. [52]

C. Challenges: Unlike other defenses, any party may challenge SMJ at any time. A court may also raise the issue *sua sponte*. [52]

II. FEDERAL QUESTION JURISDICTION

28 U.S.C. §1331 gives federal courts SMJ over statutory and constitutional claims, regardless of the amount in controversy. [53]

A. Basics

    1. Exclusive jurisdiction: SMJ under §1331 is usually not exclusive but is instead shared with the state courts. However, the federal courts do have exclusive jurisdiction over certain claims arising under federal law. [53]

    2. Claims "arising under": Section 1331 gives federal courts jurisdiction over claims "arising under" not only federal statutes but also under the U.S. Constitution and treaties. [54]

    3. When claim "arises under": A claim can arise under one of these bodies of law either if the law itself creates the right, or, in some cases, when the law is a necessary element of a claim. [54]

B. Well-pleaded complaint rule: Whether a case involves a federal question is determined using the well-pleaded complaint rule. Under this rule, federal question jurisdiction exists only if the federal issue is necessary to plaintiff's case. [54-55]

III. DIVERSITY JURISDICTION

28 U.S.C. §1332 gives a federal court SMJ based on the citizenship of the parties.

A. Basics

    1. Actions included: The statute grants SMJ over actions that (a) are between citizens of different states and/or foreign citizens, and (b) involve an amount in controversy greater than $75,000. [57]

    2. **Not exclusive:** Diversity jurisdiction is not exclusive. The same action may be filed in state courts. [57]

    3. **Exceptions:** There are certain exceptions to diversity jurisdiction, including domestic relations and probate cases, abstention, and situations of collusive joinder. [57-58]

    4. **Complete diversity required:** Section 1332 requires complete diversity; that is, no plaintiff can be a citizen of the same state as any defendant. [58]

  B. **Determining citizenship:** A "citizen of a state" within the meaning of §1332 is a citizen of the United States who is domiciled within a particular state.

    1. **Domicile:** A person's domicile is determined by residence plus intent to remain. An individual always has only one domicile. [59-60]

    2. **Permanent resident aliens:** Section 1332 also treats permanent resident aliens as citizens of the United States. [59]

    3. **Corporations:** Section 1332(c) provides that a corporation is a citizen of both its state of incorporation and its principal place of business. Thus, a corporation can have two citizenships. [60-61]

    4. **Insurance companies:** Special rules apply to insurance companies and represented parties. [61]

    5. **Foreign citizens:** Although §1332 allows suits between citizens of a state and foreign citizens, suits involving only foreigners are not covered. [62]

  C. **Amount in controversy:** Section 1332 requires an amount in controversy greater than $75,000.

    1. In a case involving damages, the requirement is satisfied as long as plaintiff's complaint states a colorable claim for damages of more than $75,000. [63]

    2. In cases involving nonmonetary relief, courts must ascertain the money value of the relief sought. [63]

    3. Plaintiff may often *aggregate* claims to meet the amount in controversy. [63-64]

  D. **Skirting §1332:** Section 1359 deals with attempts to create diversity by collusive means. [64-65]

IV. SUPPLEMENTAL JURISDICTION

For a federal court to hear a case, SMJ must exist over every claim. However, §1367 allows a federal court to hear claims it could not otherwise hear when those claims are brought along with related claims over which the court has SMJ. [68]

  A. **Basics:** Applying §1367 involves a *two-step process*.

    1. **§1367(a):** First, you determine if the claim in question is sufficiently related to another claim in the case over which the court has diversity or federal question jurisdiction. [68]

      a. To determine if a sufficient relationship exists, courts determine if the two claims arise from a *common nucleus of operative fact*. [68-69]

      b. This analysis often parallels the *same transaction test* used in joinder. [68-69]

2. **§1367(b) & (c):** The second step is to determine if the exceptions in subsections (b) and (c) apply.

    a. Section 1367(b) prevents a federal court from exercising jurisdiction over certain claims *by plaintiffs* against parties *joined under certain rules*, when jurisdiction over the original federal claim is based *solely on diversity*. [69-70]

    b. Section 1367(c) gives a court *discretion* to refuse to hear the nonfederal claim based upon certain criteria set out in the subsection. [70-71]

V. REMOVAL OF CASES FROM STATE COURT TO FEDERAL COURT

In some situations, a case filed in state court may be removed by the defendant to federal court pursuant to §1441.

A. When case is removable: Generally, a case in state court may be removed when it is one that could have been filed originally in federal court. [73]

    1. The federal court to which the case is removed must have diversity, federal question, or supplemental jurisdiction over all claims in the case. [73]

    2. Certain exceptions to the well-pleaded complaint rule apply when removal is based on a federal question. [74]

    3. When removal is based on diversity, special rules apply.

        a. Section 1441(b) prevents a defendant sued in her home state from removing. [74]

        b. Diversity must exist both when the case is filed and at the time of removal. [74-75]

        c. A diversity case cannot be removed more than one year after it was filed. [76]

    4. Section 1441(c) allows removal of certain ''separate and independent'' claims that would not otherwise be removable. [75]

B. Process

    1. Only defendants may remove. [73]

    2. Defendants remove by filing a notice of removal with the federal and state court. [75-76]

    3. Removal must occur within 30 days after defendant receives notice that she is party to a removable state court case. [76]

CHAPTER 5

THE *ERIE* DOCTRINE

I. OVERVIEW

The *Erie* doctrine requires a federal court to apply state law on certain issues.

A. Three categories of cases: Conceptually, there are three basic categories of *Erie* cases:

  1. those in which there is no federal statute or rule on point, and the federal court is considering applying a federal judge-made rule;

  2. those in which the federal rule is a *Federal Rule of Civil Procedure* or similar court rule; and

  3. those in which the federal law is a federal statute. [85-86]

B. Federal statutes underlying *Erie*: Two federal statutes lurk in the background of the *Erie* doctrine:

  1. The *Rules of Decision Act* (RODA) mirrors the basic command of *Erie*. [85]

  2. The *Rules Enabling Act* (REA) requires a different approach to disputes concerning Federal Rules of Civil Procedures, the second category of *Erie* case. [86]

II. MAIN CASES IN THE DEVELOPMENT OF THE DOCTRINE

The *Erie* doctrine developed in a line of Supreme Court cases.

A. *Erie*: Erie R.R. v. Tompkins (1938) is the source of doctrine.

  1. Overruling the 1841 *Swift* case, *Erie* held that a federal court must apply state rules of tort liability instead of determining for itself what the "best" common law tort rule would be. [87]

  2. The Court indicated that the result was mandated by constitutional considerations of judicial federalism. [87-88]

B. *Guaranty Trust*: Guaranty Trust v. York (1945) created a major exception to *Erie*, holding that the doctrine does not apply to *matters of procedure*. However, the Court's test for determining whether a rule was procedural — the so-called outcome determinative test — was to prove problematic. [88]

C. *Byrd*: Byrd v. Blue Ridge Electric (1958) held that a state rule about whether a judge or jury decided a narrow issue in a case was one that federal courts need not follow. The Court suggested a balancing test for determining when state law applies. [89]

D. *Hanna*: Hanna v. Plumer (1965) devised a more workable test for rules of procedure and provided a separate analysis to be used in case of Federal Rules of Civil Procedure and similar rules. Most *Erie* issues will be analyzed under the basic *Hanna* analysis. [89-90]

III. DEALING WITH FEDERAL JUDGE-MADE LAW

In the case of an ordinary federal judge-made rule, the issue is whether the rule is procedural. If so, federal law applies instead of state law.

A. Test: In most cases, a court applies the *Hanna* test to determine if the federal rule is procedural. A rule is procedural under this test if the difference between state and federal law would *not be likely to cause forum-shopping* between state and federal court. [89-90]

B. Exceptions: There are several exceptions to this analysis, including:

  1. Judge-jury determinations are still analyzed under the balancing test used in *Byrd*. [91]

2. Courts have recognized a limited body of purely substantive federal common law, which applies even though it clearly would lead to forum-shopping. [89]

C. **Choice of law:** The Supreme Court has held that state choice of law rules are substantive and must therefore be applied by a federal court. [90]

IV. DEALING WITH FEDERAL RULES OF CIVIL PROCEDURE AND SIMILAR RULES

Hanna held that a different test applied to the Federal Rules of Civil Procedure and similar rules, reflecting the different origins of these rules.

A. **Rules Enabling Act:** In the REA, Congress gave the Supreme Court the power to enact rules of "procedure and evidence." [93]

   1. However, those rules cannot abridge, enlarge, or modify substantive rights. [93]

   2. The REA is the source of the Federal Rules of Civil Procedure, Federal Rules of Evidence, and other rules. [93]

B. **Analysis for Federal Rules of Civil Procedure:** The *Erie* doctrine binds the courts, not Congress. Therefore, because the REA delegates Congress's power, a rule made under it is valid as long as it is truly a rule of procedure or evidence, and does not abridge, enlarge, or modify substantive rights. Whether the rule would cause forum-shopping is not relevant. [94-95]

C. **Limited reading:** However, the courts will sometimes read a rule narrowly to avoid a clash with state law. [93-94]

V. DEALING WITH FEDERAL STATUTES

Congress is not bound by *Erie*. Therefore, if a federal statute is valid and truly applies to the issue at hand, it takes precedence over state law. [96]

CHAPTER 6

LITIGATION AND ITS ALTERNATIVES

I. REMEDIES

The ultimate goal of most civil suits is obtaining an appropriate remedy.

A. **Substitutionary remedies:** Substitutionary remedies attempt to replace what the claimant has lost. [103]

   1. **Compensatory damages:** Damages are a frequently sought remedy. Generally speaking, the victorious plaintiff will recover a sum that equals the value of what she has lost. [104]

   2. **Other forms of damages:** In some circumstances, the law allows for the recovery of *liquidated* (amount is agreed upon ahead of time), *statutory* (amount fixed by statute), and *multiple* (proven damages augmented automatically) damages. [104]

3. Punitive damages: Punitive damages are not compensatory but instead are designed to punish the defendant and thereby deter such behavior in the future. [105]

    a. Punitive damages are available only in certain narrow categories of cases, primarily in tort. [105]

    b. The Supreme Court has recognized constitutional limits on punitive damages. [105]

B. Specific remedies: A specific remedy orders a defendant to act, or to refrain from acting, in a certain way.

    1. Equitable remedies: Many (but not all) specific remedies are equitable. Equitable remedies are subject to certain limitations that do not apply to other sorts of remedies. [105-106]

    2. Injunction: The injunction is the most common specific remedy. When determining whether to grant an injunction, a court will balance the hardships as well as consider the public interest. [106]

C. Provisional remedies: In some cases, a party may be entitled to specific relief, such as a preliminary injunction or temporary restraining order, before the case is resolved.

    1. However, the party must make a very strong showing to obtain such relief. [107]

    2. *Pretrial attachment* of a defendant's assets presents special constitutional concerns. [108-109]

II. ATTORNEYS' FEES

A. Default rule: Under the so-called *American rule*, each side pays its own attorney, regardless of the outcome of the case. Insurance and contingent fee agreements ameliorate this rule. [110]

B. Exceptions: However, shifting of attorneys' fees is increasingly done through private agreements, statutes, and rules. [111]

III. JUDICIAL MANAGEMENT OF LITIGATION

In many systems, courts play an increasingly significant role in speeding up the litigation process. The *discovery conference* and *pretrial conference* are two of the main tools for controlling the process. [111-112]

IV. ALTERNATIVES TO LITIGATION

The judicial system increasingly encourages alternate forms of dispute resolution to relieve the strain on court resources and parties.

A. Settlement: Settlement has long been an encouraged means of resolving disputes. [113-114]

B. Arbitration and mediation

    1. Mediation, although like settlement, uses a third party to facilitate the negotiations. The mediator makes no decisions. [114]

2. Arbitration, by contrast, typically results in the arbitrator deciding the merits of the dispute. However, the procedure differs in many respects from court litigation. [114-115]

CHAPTER 7

PLEADING

I. OVERVIEW

Pleading is the process by which the parties apprise each other and the court of their claims and defenses.

A. Historical development: Pleading has gone through centuries of evolution. At common law, pleading was highly legalistic and formalistic. The trend has been to cut back on formalism and to require more factual assertions. [120]

B. Code pleading: The system of code pleading, which remains in force in several states, requires a party to plead the facts in ordinary and concise language. [120]

C. Federal pleading: The system of notice pleading encapsulated in the Federal Rules of Civil Procedure is also in use in many state systems. [121]

II. FEDERAL PLEADING: OVERVIEW

A. Pleadings allowed: The Federal Rules of Civil Procedure require a complaint, an answer, and, in some cases, a reply by the plaintiff.

   1. All other requests to the court are made by ***motion*** rather than by a pleading. [121, 122]

   2. Additional pleadings occur in cases where additional parties are joined to the suit. [121]

B. Format of pleadings: The Federal Rules of Civil Procedure contain certain requirements involving case information, separation of allegations, and the use of exhibits. [121-122]

III. FEDERAL PLEADING: STATING A CLAIM

The term *notice pleading* describes the flexible rules governing stating a claim.

A. Basic standard: Fed. R. Civ. P. 8(a) requires the claimant to make a "***short and plain statement***" of the claim. [123-124]

   1. As long as the claimant affords the other side notice of what she seeks, this standard is satisfied. Legal conclusions are acceptable. [123-124]

   2. The ***Federal Forms*** provide examples of the minimal detail necessary to satisfy the basic standard. [123]

   3. The Federal Rules of Civil Procedure also contain special rules dealing with pleading formal matters such as capacity. [125]

B. Prayer for relief: The claimant must also ask for relief. [125]

C. Jurisdiction: A plaintiff must include a statement describing the basis for the federal court's subject matter jurisdiction. [123]

D. Elevated pleading standards: For some claims and issues, the Federal Rules of Civil Procedure require more detail than the basic standard set in Rule 8(a).

   1. A party must provide more detail for claims of *fraud* and *mistake*. [124]

   2. Claims for *special damages* must also be set out with particularity. [124]

IV. FEDERAL PLEADING: DEFENDANT'S RESPONSE

A defendant's general response is her *answer*, while she can make specific responses by *motion*. [127]

A. Pre-answer motions: Defendants can use motions to raise both procedural and substantive challenges to the complaint. [127]

   1. *Rule 12(b)* contains a special set of objections that may be made by motion, including challenges to jurisdiction, venue, and the form of the complaint. [127-128]

   2. The *Rule 12(b)(6) motion* allows defendant to assert that the plaintiff's complaint does not state a claim upon which relief can be granted. [128]

   3. *Rule 12* also allows for a motion for a *more definite statement* and a motion to *strike* redundant, immaterial, impertinent, or scandalous material. [128-129]

   4. *Rule 12(g) and (h)* set out certain restrictions on the timing of pre-answer motions.

      a. Defenses relating to *personal jurisdiction*, *service*, and *venue* can easily be waived by omission from the answer or failure to include them in a pre-answer motion. [129-130]

      b. The remaining Rule 12 defenses may be asserted at a later time. [129]

B. Answer: The answer is defendant's general response to the complaint.

   1. The answer must be filed within 20 days, subject to certain exceptions. However, this time period is often extended. [130]

   2. A defendant must *admit or deny* all allegations in the complaint.

      a. Failure to deny is deemed an admission. [131]

      b. An *ineffective denial* — one where the defendant does not address the substance of the claims — is treated like an admission. [131-132]

      c. If a defendant does not have sufficient information to allow him to admit or deny an allegation, he can plead insufficient information, which is treated as a denial. [131]

      d. A defendant need not address each individual allegation, but can admit certain allegations and, in a single statement, deny the remainder of the entire complaint. [132]

   3. Defenses: A defendant may also respond by asserting defenses: reasons why plaintiff is not entitled to the relief it has requested.

      a. There are two basic types of defenses: *ordinary* and *affirmative*. [132-133]

      i.   The *ordinary defense* considers only the complaint and argues that there is a procedural, legal, or pleading defect. [133]

      ii.   The *affirmative defense* introduces additional facts that prevent plaintiff from recovering. Fed. R. Civ. P. 8(c) contains a list of affirmative defenses. [133]

   b.   The issue of who has the *burden of pleading* a particular issue depends on several factors. However, Fed. R. Civ. P. 8(c) and 12(b) make it clear that the burden of pleading certain issues falls on defendant. [133-134]

V. AMENDMENTS TO THE PLEADINGS

Most pleadings can be amended. However, issues can arise as to whether court permission is required and whether the amendments relate back.

  A.   **When permission is required:**   Fed. R. Civ. P. 15 provides a fairly short period in which a party may amend its pleading without court permission. After that, court permission is necessary. [137]

  B.   **Relation back:**   The rules also allow certain amendments to relate back to the date of the original pleading, which is important when the amendment was filed or served after the statute of limitations expired.

   1.   An amendment relates back if it arises from the same transaction or occurrence as the original pleading. [138]

   2.   Additional requirements must be satisfied if the amendment changes the party against whom a claim is asserted. [138-139]

  C.   **Other changes:**   Fed. R. Civ. P. 15 also allows *amendments to conform to the evidence* and *supplemental pleadings*. [139]

VI. MOTION FOR JUDGMENT ON THE PLEADINGS

If the pleadings, taken as a whole, show that one party should prevail as a matter of law, the court may grant a motion for judgment on the pleadings. [140-141]

VII. ETHICAL LIMITATIONS ON PLEADINGS AND MOTIONS

Fed. R. Civ. P. 11 sets out detailed standards designed to ensure honesty and candor in pleadings and motions.

  A.   **Signing requirement:**   The rule requires that all documents submitted to the court be signed by an attorney or the party. [141]

  B.   **Representations:**   Signing constitutes a certification that the signer has conducted background research, that the assertions in the document are supported by law and fact, and that the document has not been filed for an improper purpose. [141-143]

  C.   **Sanctions:**   Violation of Fed. R. Civ. P. 11 may result in sanctions.

1. In many situations, however, the 21-day **safe harbor provision** will afford the signer a chance to correct the problem. [143]

2. Sanctions may be imposed not only on the signer, but also on the entire law firm. [144]

3. Monetary sanctions are usually paid to the court. [144]

CHAPTER 8

DISCOVERY

I. OVERVIEW

A. **Definition:** Discovery is the formalized process by which the parties to a lawsuit obtain information from each other and from third parties. A great deal of informal discovery not covered by the Federal Rules of Civil Procedure also occurs in most cases. [152]

B. **Types:** Discovery falls into two main categories.

1. **Mandatory disclosures:** In the federal courts, parties are required to turn over certain information to the other parties at various stages of the case. [152]

2. **Requests for information:** Each party may also seek information from other parties to the case and from third parties. [152]

C. **Standard for discovery:** A party may discover any information that is **relevant** to the claim or defense of any party and **not privileged**. [152]

1. Information is relevant as long as it helps a party prepare a case in any way. [152-153]

2. The information must be relevant to the claim or defense of any party. [153]

3. The law provides **privileges** for certain types of information, such as attorney-client communications. Privileged information cannot be discovered. [153-154]

D. **Sequence of discovery:** Discovery may occur from a very early stage in the case to the eve of trial. In federal courts, a **discovery conference** will occur very early in the case. Following that conference, the parties engage in the **initial mandatory disclosures** and then may seek information from other parties and third parties. [154-155]

II. DISCOVERY METHODS

The Federal Rules of Civil Procedure provide for a number of different discovery methods.

A. **Mandatory disclosures:** The Federal Rules of Civil Procedure require the parties automatically to turn over certain information to other parties at two stages in the lawsuit. [156-157]

1. Soon after the discovery conference, a party must disclose various forms of evidence that he may use to support his claims or defenses. [157]

2. Prior to trial, the party must disclose all testifying experts and lay witnesses. [157-158]

3. The mandatory disclosure rules have not been adopted by most state systems. [156]

B. Depositions: A deposition resembles the questioning of a witness at trial. The witness is placed under oath, and the parties can object to improper questions. [158]

  1. Depositions are one of the few discovery devices that can be used to force a nonparty to provide information. [158, 159]

  2. The Federal Rules of Civil Procedure limit the number of depositions that may occur in a case and the length of each deposition. [158]

  3. Under certain circumstances, a party may notice the deposition of a corporation, requiring the corporation to produce someone with the information sought. [159]

  4. The Federal Rules of Civil Procedure also allow for alternate forms of depositions, including a deposition prior to the commencement of the action and a deposition on written questions. [160-161]

C. Interrogatories: Interrogatories are written questions to another party that must be answered under oath.

  1. Only 25 questions may be included in a set of interrogatories. [161]

  2. The recipient has a duty to investigate before answering an interrogatory. [161]

D. Documents and things: Fed. R. Civ. P. 34 allows one party to inspect documents and property in the possession of another. [162]

E. Requests for admission: A party may ask another party to admit certain facts. In effect, requests for admission operate like a second round of pleading. [162-163]

F. Physical and mental examinations: Fed. R. Civ. P. 35 allows a party to force another party to submit to a medical examination.

  1. Unlike all other discovery devices, a party must obtain a ***court order*** in order to force the other party to submit to an examination. [163]

  2. A court will grant the request for an order only if the condition is ***in controversy*** and ***good cause*** exists for an examination. [163-164]

    a. While a party may place her own condition in controversy in the pleadings, more is required for one party to place another party's condition into controversy. [164]

    b. Good cause exists when the information is not reasonably available from other sources. [164]

III. POLICY LIMITS ON DISCOVERY

In some situations, a court may limit discovery.

A. Protective orders: A court may issue a protective order to protect a person or party from overly burdensome, embarrassing, or otherwise objectionable discovery. [166]

  1. Before going to court, parties must attempt to resolve the disagreement themselves. [166]

  2. Two common reasons for protective orders are to protect a person's privacy and a business enterprise's trade secrets. [166-167]

B. Work product: Fed. R. Civ. P. 26(b)(3) also places limits on the discovery of work product.

    1. Work product is a document or tangible thing that was prepared by a party or its representative in anticipation of litigation. [168]

    2. Work product may be discovered only if the requesting party can show need. An evaluation of need considers both the importance of the information and whether it is available from other sources. [168-169]

    3. The rule creates an exception for a party's own statement, which can be discovered without showing need. [169]

C. Expert information: Facts known by and opinions of *nontestifying experts* may, like work product, be discovered only by showing need. [169-170]

IV. SUPPLEMENTATION OF DISCOVERY

In some situations, a party is required to supplement her response to an earlier discovery request. [171-172]

V. CONTROLLING DISCOVERY ABUSE

The Federal Rules of Civil Procedure contain a number of different tools to help keep discovery abuse in check.

A. Signing of discovery: Fed. R. Civ. P. 26(g) requires that all discovery documents be signed. Signing constitutes a certification that the discovery is consistent with the rules and conducted in good faith. [172-173]

B. Compelling discovery: If a person refuses to respond to a discovery request, the requesting party may ask the court to intervene.

    1. Sanctions are available against a person who refuses to respond to a proper discovery request. [173]

    2. In addition, the party may obtain an order compelling a response. [173-174]

    3. Violation of the order may result in additional sanctions, including contempt. [174]

    4. Other rules contain specific sanctions that apply to particular discovery issues, such as failure to attend one's own deposition or to supplement discovery. [175-176]

CHAPTER 9

RESOLUTION BEFORE TRIAL

I. SETTLEMENT

Most pending cases are resolved by settlement, which presents few significant issues.

A. Judicial approval: In the vast majority of cases, the court need not approve a settlement. [181]

B. Later actions: Whether a settlement prevents the plaintiff from suing again depends in large part on the terms of the settlement agreement. [182]

II. DEFAULT

A defendant who fails to respond to a complaint may be held in default.

A. Two stages in process

  1. Entry: If a party fails to plead or otherwise defend, the clerk enters default against that party. [182-183]

  2. Judgment: After default is entered, the other party may obtain a default judgment. [183]

  a. Depending on the circumstances, either the court or clerk enters the judgment. [183-184]

  b. If judgment is to be entered by the court, the court may hold a hearing. The defaulting party may be entitled to notice prior to the hearing, allowing it to show up and contest damages. [184]

B. Sanction defaults: A default judgment is sometimes imposed as a sanction against a party who violates the Federal Rules of Civil Procedure. Special rules apply to such defaults. [184]

C. Challenges: A default judgment can be overturned by showing good cause. Default judgments are generally disfavored by the courts. [184-185]

III. DISMISSALS

A case may be dismissed, either involuntarily by the court or voluntarily by the plaintiff.

A. Involuntary dismissal

  1. When available: Involuntary dismissals are granted when the plaintiff fails to prosecute its case or as a sanction against an uncooperative plaintiff. [185]

  2. Effect of dismissal: In many cases, an involuntary dismissal prevents the plaintiff from filing the case again. [185-186]

  a. However, dismissals for lack of jurisdiction or venue do not prevent refiling in a different court. [186]

  b. The effect of an involuntary dismissal in federal court is somewhat uncertain because of the *Semtek* case. [186]

B. Voluntary dismissals: A plaintiff may also dismiss his case voluntarily.

  1. How accomplished: Depending on the timing, a plaintiff may be required to obtain the consent of the defendants or the court in order to dismiss. [186-187]

  2. Effect of dismissal: A voluntary dismissal may prevent the plaintiff from refiling, depending on the wording of the dismissal and whether the plaintiff had previously dismissed the same action. [187]

IV. SUMMARY JUDGMENT

If the facts in the case are undisputed, a court may grant summary judgment to the party who is entitled to prevail under governing law. Fed. R. Civ. P. 56 governs summary judgments. [189]

A. Procedure: The party seeking summary judgment files a motion. Evidence submitted by a party seeking or opposing summary judgment must be admissible at trial. [189-190]

B. Standard: Summary judgment is proper when there is no genuine issue of material fact and the movant is entitled to judgment as a matter of law. [190]

    1. Burdens: The burden of production directly affects how this standard is applied.

        a. It is easier for a party without the burden of production to obtain summary judgment. In this case, the movant need only show that the other side is missing evidence on at least one element of its claim or defense. [192-193]

        b. When the party with the burden moves, by contrast, it must show that it has uncontradicted evidence on every element of its case. [192-193]

    2. Evaluating evidence: The court does not weigh the evidence. If there are questions of credibility, summary judgment should be denied. [190]

    3. Inferences: Determining whether an inference may be drawn from indirect testimony is a crucial question in summary judgment.

        a. Although drawing inferences is usually a question for the jury, a court can consider the likelihood of a given inference in the summary judgment process. [191]

        b. At times, multiple inferences may be drawn from given testimony. Whether summary judgment is appropriate in such a case turns on the burden of production and on whether the inferences all favor one party. [191]

CHAPTER 10

DETERMINING THE TRIER

I. RIGHT TO A JURY TRIAL

In some situations, the Seventh Amendment to the U.S. Constitution gives the parties a right to demand a jury trial.

A. Overview of Seventh Amendment

    1. The amendment applies only in federal courts, not in state courts. [200]

    2. The amendment also places certain restrictions on the size of the jury and on whether a unanimous verdict is required. [200]

    3. A party must file a *timely demand* for a jury. [200]

B. Basic analysis: The amendment ''preserves'' a right to a jury in ''*suits at common law*.''

1. Because the amendment preserves rather than creates a right, courts use a historical analysis in applying it. If an action would have been deemed a suit at common law in 1791, the amendment gives a right to a jury. [200]

2. A suit at common law is an action that traditionally would have been heard in the English courts of common law rather than in the courts of equity, admiralty, or exchequer. [201-202]

3. Distinguishing common law from equity requires a consideration not only of the *remedy* being sought, but also of the underlying cause of action and procedures. [201-202]

C. **Applying analysis to new claims:** Many rights are created by statute and therefore did not exist at common law. Courts analyze these situations using a *two-part test*.

1. The first step is to find the *closest historic analogue* to the new claim and to determine whether that analogous claim would be heard in common law or equity in 1791. [202]

2. The second step is to determine the *nature of the remedy*. [202]

3. The second step prevails over the first in cases where the two point to different conclusions. [202]

D. **Applying analysis to new procedures**

1. **Traditional equitable procedures:** Procedural devices that were historically available only in equity (such as the class action) do not deprive a party of the right to a jury if the underlying substantive claim would qualify as an action at common law. [203]

2. **Merger of law and equity:** Unlike in 1791, both legal and equitable claims may be joined in a single action. A party is entitled to a jury for all issues relevant to all legal claims, even if those same issues arise in the equitable claims. [203-204]

3. **Agency adjudication:** Congress may skirt the Seventh Amendment by assigning cases involving the adjudication of *statutory public rights* to an *agency* rather than to a court. [204]

II. SELECTING JURORS

Selecting jurors involves two main stages.

A. **Selecting the pool:** First, a jury pool is selected at random from the world of qualified jurors. [207-208]

1. Systems differ in what groups they exclude from jury duty. The federal courts exclude relatively few groups. [207-208]

2. The Constitution prevents systematic exclusion of jurors based on certain attributes. [208-209]

B. **Forming the panel:** The pool of jurors is narrowed through the actual panel through *voir dire.*

1. Jurors are asked a wide range of questions to determine bias or other reasons for disqualification. [209]

2. Jurors can be excluded for cause or by use of peremptory challenges.

   a. *Challenges for cause* are based on actual or potential bias, or for other reasons making the juror unfit to serve. [209]

   b. *Peremptory challenges* require no stated reason, but are limited in number. [209]

   c. However, if a party's use of his peremptory challenges exhibits a pattern of excluding jurors of the same race, gender, or other protected attribute, the Constitution requires the party to justify the exclusion based on a reason other than the attribute. [210]

III. DISQUALIFYING JUDGES

A judge can be disqualified for personal bias, a financial or other interest in the amount in controversy, family interests, or in any other situation in which her impartiality might reasonably be questioned. [212-213]

CHAPTER 11

THE TRIAL

I. PREVENTING IMPROPER INFLUENCE ON THE JURY

Courts have a number of tools at their disposal to ensure that the jury considers only the information it is supposed to consider.

   A. Evidence: The Rules of Evidence attempt to prevent the use of unreliable evidence. [219-220]

   B. Juror experimentation: It is grounds for a new trial if a juror conducts her own inspection outside the courtroom. [220]

   C. Attorney misconduct: Attorneys may not provide their own personal opinions concerning the facts or make an improper appeal to the jurors' sympathy. [220]

   D. Instructions: The court instructs the jury in a set of instructions as to the law to be applied. [220-221]

II. JUDGMENT AS A MATTER OF LAW

In certain circumstances, the evidence will be so one-sided that the court can take the case away from the jury and enter judgment as a matter of law (JML).

   A. When available: A JML is available at two points in the case: before the case is submitted to the jury or after the jury returns with a verdict. However, there are strict timing rules that apply to the postverdict JML. [221-222]

   B. Standard: The standard for JML is that no reasonable jury could find for the party opposing the motion. [222]

      1. The standard is similar to the standard for summary judgment, although the judge has slightly more leeway to weigh the evidence. [222]

      2. As with summary judgment, both *inferences* and the *burden of production* are important factors in applying the standard for JML. [222-223]

III. NEW TRIALS

A judge can grant a new trial because the jury verdict is clearly incorrect or to remedy a procedural error.

A. Strict timing rules apply to requests for new trials. [223]

B. New trial to cure erroneous verdict: If a verdict is *against the great weight of the evidence*, the court may grant a new trial. [224]

    1. This standard is significantly easier to satisfy than the standard for a JML. [224]

    2. The party may combine a motion for new trial with a JML motion. In that case, the court must decide both even if the court grants the JML. [224]

C. New trial to cure procedural defects

    1. To obtain a new trial based on procedural errors, the requesting party must demonstrate he was *prejudiced* by the error. [225]

    2. The party must also *object* in timely fashion. [225]

    3. Special rules limit the *use of juror testimony* to prove procedural error. [225-226]

D. Partial and conditional new trials: A court may grant a new trial as to only certain issues. In addition, the court may be able to condition its grant of a new trial on the winning party's refusal to accept a modification of the verdict. [226]

CHAPTER 12

APPEALS

I. WHAT ISSUES MAY BE APPEALED

Not every issue may be appealed.

A. Adversity: The party must show that the ruling is against her interests. This showing is relatively easy to make. [231-232]

B. Need to raise: Except in cases of clear error, the party must usually give the trial judge a chance to consider and rule on the issue. [232]

II. TIMING OF APPEAL

In the federal courts and many states, a party may appeal only a final decision of the trial court.

A. Definition: A final decision is one that completely wraps up the case. All other decisions are deemed interlocutory. [233]

B. Exceptions to rule: There are several exceptions to the final decision rule.

1. **Rule 54(b):** Fed. R. Civ. P. 54(b) allows a party to appeal the final resolution of a discrete ''claim for relief,'' provided the judge makes an express determination that there is no reason to delay entry of judgment. [234-235]

2. **Injunctions:** 28 U.S.C. §1292(a) allows immediate appeal of a decision granting, denying, or modifying an injunction or receivership. [235]

3. **§1292(b) certification:** If the trial judge certifies a ruling on a controlling question of law and the court of appeals agrees to hear the case, a party may appeal the ruling immediately. [235]

4. **Class actions:** A decision granting or denying class certification is immediately appealable under Fed. R. Civ. P. 23(f). [235]

5. **Mandamus/prohibition:** Technically original actions rather than appeals, writs of mandamus and prohibition provide an alternate means of challenging certain decisions of the trial court. However, such writs are rarely granted. [235-236]

6. **Practical finality:** The court-created *collateral order* doctrine allows immediate appeal of a decision that:

   a. involves an important issue of law that is separate from the merits of the case,

   b. has been conclusively settled, and

   c. would be effectively unreviewable if appeal does not occur until after a final decision. This last requirement is very difficult to meet because a new trial will solve most problems. [236-237]

III. SCOPE OF APPELLATE REVIEW

An appellate court is limited in its review of lower court decisions.

A. **Law:** The appellate court need give no deference whatsoever to a lower court's ruling on the law. [239]

B. **Fact:** However, the appellate court can overturn a factual finding only if the finding is *clearly erroneous*: The same standard applies to mixed questions of law and fact. [239-240]

C. **Discretion:** If an issue lies within the discretion of the trial judge, the appellate court may overturn the finding only if there has been an *abuse of discretion*. [240]

CHAPTER 13

RESPECT FOR JUDGMENTS

I. CLAIM PRECLUSION

The doctrine of claim preclusion, or *res judicata*, prevents a party from relitigating claims that he litigated, or should have litigated, in a prior case.

A. **Standard:** A claim is barred if it, or another claim arising from the same basic event, was litigated in a prior suit that ended in a final judgment. [246]

1. A claim is the same as one brought in a prior case if it uses the same legal theory to recover against the same defendant based on the same underlying facts. [246-247]

2. Determining whether two claims arise from the same basic event is more difficult. Courts differ significantly on the test used to determine whether a claim is sufficiently related to be barred by claim preclusion. [247]

   a. Most look to see if the claims share a significant amount of the same relevant evidence. [247]

   b. Other courts use the narrower ''same cause of action'' or ''same primary right'' approaches. [247]

3. Installment contracts are governed by special rules. [248]

B. Defense preclusion: Claim preclusion may bar a claim even though the party asserting it was a defendant in the prior action.

1. The **compulsory counterclaim rule** of Fed. R. Civ. P. 13(a) may bar factually related counterclaims that were omitted from the prior action. [248]

2. In addition, there is a narrow common law compulsory counterclaim rule that applies when Rule 13(a) does not. This rule applies if the omitted counterclaim would have been a defense to the claim in the first suit. [248-249]

C. Other issues: Other issues arise in claim preclusion.

1. **Same parties:** Claim preclusion usually applies only when the parties are the same in the two cases. However, parties who are in *privity* with someone who was a party to the first action are also bound by the judgment. [249-250]

2. **Final judgment on the merits:** Claim preclusion only applies if the first case resulted in a final judgment on the merits. Courts differ concerning whether certain dismissals, such as those based on the statute of limitations or failure to state a claim, are on the merits. [250]

3. **Lack of jurisdiction in first court:** In most cases, claim preclusion does not apply when the first court did not have subject matter jurisdiction over the claim in question. [251]

II. ISSUE PRECLUSION

Issue preclusion, or collateral estoppel, prevents the relitigation of certain issues that were resolved in prior litigation. [253]

A. Basic standard

1. Issue preclusion applies if the two cases involve the *same issue*, that issue was *actually litigated* and *decided* in the first case, and the first court's ruling was *necessary* to the judgment. [253]

2. Unlike claim preclusion, issues that are merely related to issues decided in the first suit are never barred by issue preclusion. [253]

B. Same issue: Determining whether two cases involve the same issue can be difficult in situations involving differences in the burden of proof or when there is a series of related obligations or events. [253-254]

C. Actually decided: Whether an issue was actually decided is an important issue in cases involving multiple claims and/or defenses.

    1. An issue was actually decided a particular way only if the court logically had to decide the issue that way to reach the ultimate conclusion. [254-255]

    2. The above analysis applies when the case is decided by ***general verdict***. In bench trials, the judge sets out her ruling on each claim and/or defense, making the task simpler. [255]

D. Necessary: The issue of whether a ruling was necessary arises both with respect to *dictum* and when the court explicitly relies on alternate bases for its holding. In the latter situation, courts are roughly split as to whether each of the alternate bases is entitled to issue preclusion effect. [255-256]

E. Parties affected: Unlike claim preclusion, people who were not parties to the first case may sometimes take advantage of issue preclusion.

    1. Most courts have abandoned the old requirement of ***full mutuality***, especially in cases involving defensive use of issue preclusion. [256]

    2. ***Offensive use*** is more problematic. Most courts place certain restrictions on offensive use of preclusion. [257]

    3. Issue preclusion may never be used against someone who was ***neither a party nor in privity*** with a party to the first action. [257-258]

III. LIMITS ON PRECLUSION

There are limits to the use of both claim and issue preclusion.

A. Claim preclusion: Exceptions to claim preclusion include suits to enforce a judgment and situations where the first court lacked subject matter jurisdiction. [260]

B. Issue preclusion: Exceptions to issue preclusion include situations where no review of the first suit was available, where there has been an intervening change in the law, where there were procedural disadvantages in the first case, and where use of preclusion would defy the public interest. [260-261]

IV. FULL FAITH AND CREDIT

The constitutional requirement of full faith and credit [FFC] requires courts throughout the nation to honor the judgments of their sister states and federal courts.

A. Basic command: FFC extends both claim and issue preclusion across state lines. If a court in the rendering state would afford either claim or issue preclusion to the judgment, all other courts in the country must ordinarily extend the same preclusive effect. [261-262]

B. Exceptions: Judgments rendered without subject matter jurisdiction or decreeing rights to property in another state usually are not entitled to FFC. [262]

C. Divorce: A state has jurisdiction to grant a divorce if at least one of the spouses is domiciled there. [262]

V. OTHER ISSUES IN PRECLUSION

A. Reopening judgments: Fed. R. Civ. P. 60(b) allows a party to reopen a judgment well after the usual 10-day period for obtaining a new trial has expired. [263]

   1. In some cases, the party must seek relief within a year of the judgment. [263]

   2. Relief under Fed. R. Civ. P. 60(b) is rarely granted. [263]

B. Law of the case: The doctrine of "law of the case" makes certain rulings on law binding for the remainder of a given lawsuit. [263-264]

C. Judicial estoppel: A party may be barred from taking a position contrary to a sworn position taken in a previous case. [264]

CHAPTER 14

JOINDER OF CLAIMS AND PARTIES

I. JOINDER INVOLVING CURRENT PARTIES

Fed. R. Civ. P. 13 and 18 allow the existing plaintiffs and defendants to file additional claims against each other.

A. Adding claim to existing claim: Fed. R. Civ. P. 18 allows a party who already has filed an original claim, counterclaim, cross-claim, or third-party claim against another to add any additional claims he may have against that party. [269]

   1. The additional claims need not be related to the first. [270]

   2. Fed. R. Civ. P. 18 does not give the federal courts jurisdiction over the additional claims. Jurisdiction must be acquired under the jurisdictional statutes. [270]

B. Counterclaims: Rule 13 allows, and in some cases requires, a defendant to file a counterclaim against the plaintiff. [270]

   1. Subject only to jurisdictional considerations, a defendant may file any counterclaim it has against the plaintiff, regardless of whether it is related. [270]

   2. A counterclaim is ***compulsory*** if it arises from the ***same transaction or occurrence*** as the plaintiff's claim. [270]

      a. Failure to file a compulsory counterclaim means that the claim will be barred by claim preclusion. [271]

      b. Rule 13(a) lists several exceptions to the compulsory counterclaim rule. [271]

   3. Same transaction or occurrence: Courts use two main tests to determine if two claims arise from the same transaction or occurrence. [270-271]

      a. The ***logical relationship test*** asks if the facts of the claims are logically related in any meaningful way. [270]

b. The *same evidence test* looks for a significant overlap in the facts giving rise to both claims. [270]

4. Parties other than defendants may also be required to file counterclaims. [271]

C. Cross-claims: Coplaintiffs and codefendants may cross-claim against each other. A cross-claim must arise from the same transaction or occurrence as the original claim or a counterclaim. [271-272]

II. JOINDER OF PARTIES

A. Multiple plaintiffs and defendants: Fed. R. Civ. P. 20 allows a plaintiff to sue multiple defendants, and/or for multiple plaintiffs to join, if three requirements are met.

1. The plaintiffs are suing, or the defendants are being sued, jointly, severally, or in the alternative. [272]

2. The claims arise from the same transaction or occurrence. [272]

3. The claims involve a common question of law or fact. [272-273]

B. Adding parties to cross-claims and counterclaims: A party may add a new party to the case in connection with a cross-claim or counterclaim if the requirements of Fed. R. Civ. P. 20 are satisfied. [273]

C. Impleader: If defendant may demand contribution or indemnity from a third party for all or part of plaintiff's claim, the defendant may be able to join that third party to the suit under Fed. R. Civ. P. 14. [273]

1. Impleader is commonly used by one joint tortfeasor against another or where there is a contractual right to indemnity. [274]

2. The defendant must allege that the third party is liable to defendant, not solely to the plaintiff. [274-275]

3. Special rules deal with service of process on the joined third party. [275]

4. The joined third party and plaintiff may file additional claims in the case. [275]

D. Compulsory joinder: While joinder of parties is usually optional, on occasion it is required. Fed. R. Civ. P. 19 covers compulsory joinder.

1. Compulsory joinder is primarily a *defense* raised by the defendant. [277]

2. Fed. R. Civ. P. 19 sets out a three-part test for dealing with claims of compulsory joinder.

a. Rule 19(a) sets out situations where a party should be joined if feasible. If the absence of the party may pose a significant risk to the rights of either that party or the existing parties, the person should be joined. [278-280]

b. If the party should be joined, then the plaintiff should try to join her. Subject matter and personal jurisdiction may prevent joinder. [280]

c. If the party cannot be joined, the court considers the factors listed in Rule 19(b) to determine whether to dismiss the case or to proceed without the missing party. [280-281]

E. Intervention: A nonparty may also be able to intervene as a party in the action.

    1. Fed. R. Civ. P. 24(a) gives a party a *right to intervene* in certain situations. Although the grounds for intervention by right parallel the necessary party rule, Rule 24 is interpreted more broadly than Rule 19. [282-284]

    2. Even if a party does not have a right to intervene, she may be able to intervene with the court's permission. [282]

F. Interpleader

    1. When available: Interpleader is available when a party is exposed to logically inconsistent claims to the same thing. [284]

    2. Two types: Interpleader is available under both Fed. R. Civ. P. 22 (rule interpleader) and 28 U.S.C. §1335 (statutory interpleader). The two differ significantly with respect to subject matter jurisdiction, personal jurisdiction, and venue. [284]

        a. *Rule interpleader* is subject to the usual rules governing jurisdiction and venue. [285]

        b. The statutes governing *statutory interpleader* make it much simpler for the court to acquire jurisdiction and venue. [285-286]

III. SEVERANCE AND CONSOLIDATION

A. Severance: If joinder of claims and parties makes the lawsuit too unwieldy or confusing, the Federal Rules of Civil Procedure give the court the power to split the case up into several smaller suits. [288]

B. Consolidation: If two separate cases pending in a single district share a common question of law or fact, the court can consolidate them into a single action. [288]

IV. JURISDICTION AND JOINDER

Joinder of claims and parties often raises questions of subject matter and personal jurisdiction.

A. Personal jurisdiction: A court must have personal jurisdiction over all parties other than voluntary plaintiffs. [288]

B. Subject matter jurisdiction: Supplemental jurisdiction often proves very useful in establishing subject matter jurisdiction over claims brought in federal court. [289]

    1. The same transaction or occurrence test used in many of the joinder rules is for all intents and purposes the same as the common nucleus of operative fact test used under 28 U.S.C. §1367(a). Therefore, if joinder is proper under these rules, the requirements of §1367(a) are satisfied also. [289-290]

    2. However, even if joinder satisfies §1367(a), one must still consider subsections (b) and (c). When jurisdiction over the original claim is based on diversity, subsection (b) bars most claims by plaintiffs against nondiverse parties. [290-291]

CHAPTER 15

CLASS ACTIONS

I. OVERVIEW

A class action is a case in which one or more people represent the rights of other similarly situated people. [299]

A. Plaintiff or defendant class: Although class actions usually involve groups of plaintiffs, defendant class actions are also possible. [300]

B. Control: To ensure adequate representation, the court exercises a significant degree of control over the class action. [300]

II. CONSTITUTIONAL CONCERNS

There are constitutional concerns in cases where one private individual represents the rights of others.

A. Due process: The right to sue another person is a property right protected by the Due Process Clause of the U.S. Constitution. [300]

B. Representation: In *Hansberry*, the Supreme Court held that the Due Process Clause prevented the class members from being bound by a judgment when the representative did not adequately represent their interests. [301-302]

C. Personal jurisdiction: However, in *Phillips Petroleum*, the Supreme Court held that the Due Process Clause does not prevent a court from adjudicating the rights of members of a plaintiff class who have no minimum contacts with that state. [302-303]

III. RULE 23

The Federal Rule of Civil Procedure dealing with class actions attempts to meet the constitutional requirements set out in *Hansberry* and *Phillips Petroleum*.

A. Overview: Rule 23 requires the court to certify the case as a class action. There are two general steps in the certification process.

B. Step one: Rule 23(a): Rule 23(a) requires the court to determine if the case is appropriate for a class action. In making this determination, the court considers:

1. numerosity — whether the class is so numerous that ordinary joinder is impracticable [304-305],

2. commonality — whether there are questions of law or fact common to the class [305],

3. typicality — whether the claim of the representative is typical of those of the class [305], and

4. adequacy — whether the representative will adequately represent the interests of the class. [305]

C. **Step two: Rule 23(b):** The court then determines whether the case falls into one of three types of class action.

    1. **Rule 23(b)(1):** Cases where the members of the class would be necessary parties under Fed. R. Civ. P. 19. [306]

    2. **Rule 23(b)(2):** Cases where the class seeks injunctive or declaratory relief pertaining to action that affects them all. [306]

    3. **Rule 23(b)(3):** Cases where the common questions of law or fact predominate over the individual questions and a class action is superior to other methods for resolving the disputes. [306]

        a. In determining predominance, courts consider factors such as any individual defenses the defendant may have toward some members and choice of law considerations. [307]

        b. In determining superiority, the court considers factors such as the size of the individual claims. [307]

D. **Procedure after certification:** Once the case is certified, additional materials may be provided to the class members.

    1. *Notice* is ordinarily provided to all members of the class. Although notice is required only in Rule 23(b)(3) class actions, courts frequently demand it in other types. The representative bears the cost of the notice. [308]

    2. In Rule 23(b)(3) class actions, the members must be afforded an opportunity to *opt out* of the class. [308-309]

E. **Settlement:** A class action cannot be settled without notice to the class members and approval of the court. [309]

IV. OTHER ISSUES PERTAINING TO CLASS ACTIONS

A. **Subject matter jurisdiction:** Special rules apply when determining whether a class action may be brought in federal court using diversity jurisdiction. Supplemental jurisdiction, however, is also an option. [311-312]

B. **Attorneys' fees:** Courts have considerable control over attorneys' fees in class actions. [312-313]

V. OTHER REPRESENTATIONAL LITIGATION

Class actions are not the only form of representational litigation. Shareholder derivative actions and actions involving unincorporated associations present many of the same sorts of issues. [313-314]

CHAPTER 1

INTRODUCTION

ChapterScope ━━━━━━━━━━━━━━━━━━━━━━━━━━━━━━━━

This chapter takes a ''big picture'' look at the subject of Civil Procedure. It demonstrates how the many detailed issues discussed in the remaining chapters are all parts of a cohesive system.

- ■ Although Civil Procedure seems different from the other substantive first-year law school courses, it cannot be understood in isolation from those courses. The underlying substantive rules of Tort, Contract, Property, and other areas of law are always important.

- ■ The rules of Civil Procedure serve two main goals: *fairness* and *efficiency*. In many situations, however, these ends conflict.

- ■ The rules that comprise Civil Procedure come from several different sources, including statutes, court-drafted rules, case law, and, in some cases, the U.S. Constitution.

- ■ The distinction between the *federal and state court* systems is crucial in Civil Procedure. In many cases, the federal and state courts have overlapping authority. Nevertheless, there are often differences between the two systems.

- ■ A civil case may go through several different stages before it is complete. Each of these stages presents its own issues.

I. CIVIL PROCEDURE GENERALLY

The Civil Procedure course focuses on the process by which civil disputes are litigated in the courts. As such, it is a vital counterpart to the other substantive law courses you are taking, such as Torts, Contracts, and Property. Civil Procedure deals with how the various causes of action you study in these other courses are resolved in actual practice.

Note: Most law schools offer Civil Procedure as a first-year course. This book is accordingly written mainly for a first-year audience, one with a limited grasp of the substantive law. If you are taking the course as an upper-level student, you may find that the explanations almost always involve basic issues of Tort, Contract, and Property law. Nevertheless, the discussion of Civil Procedure concepts is equally suited to an upper-level course.

A. How Civil Procedure differs from other courses: Because of the focus on *how* cases are litigated, discussion of cases in a Civil Procedure class often proceeds along different lines than the discussion in other substantive courses.

    1. Procedural issues: The discussion concentrates more heavily on the procedural issues in the case, such as the *procedural posture of the various parties* and who is claiming what against whom.

    2. Jurisdiction: In addition, at many points in the course, it is very important to determine *which court* is hearing the case.

3. **Procedural history:** When reading a Civil Procedure case, it is also important to keep the ***procedural history*** of the case in mind.

4. **Policy:** Finally, and perhaps most importantly, the ***underlying policy concerns*** in Civil Procedure are often quite different from those in your other courses.

   a. **Other first-year courses:** The other courses focus on whether public policy supports making X pay Y for some injury that X has caused.

   b. **Civil Procedure:** Procedure, by contrast, takes that basic question for granted. The policy concerns deal more with questions of ***how a court system should operate***.

      i. **Fairness:** An often-cited policy concern in Procedure is ***fairness***. The system should not only reach the ''right'' result most of the time, but it should also *appear* fair to the litigants. Even if a party's case is weak, fairness dictates that she have a chance to make the claim before a court.

      ii. **Efficiency:** On the other hand, Procedure is also concerned with ***efficiency***. To the extent that the system can minimize the time that courts, the parties, and (especially) their attorneys must spend in the litigation process, it helps reduce these costs of litigation.

      iii. **Fairness vs. efficiency:** These concerns with fairness and efficiency often clash. To the extent that procedural rules hurry the litigation process, they can result in mistakes, which runs counter to the goal of fairness. Similarly, there are limits to the notion that a party is always entitled to a court. If a claim or defense is completely groundless, it wastes the court's and the opponent's time to conduct a full trial on the matter. Thus, the procedure system allows for summary resolution of groundless claims and defenses at several stages of the case.

B. **Common misperceptions in Civil Procedure:** Because Civil Procedure seems so ''different'' from the other substantive courses in the first year of law school, students often come into the course with certain basic misperceptions.

   1. **Procedure is not completely separate from the other courses:** As discussed above, there are significant differences between Procedure and the substantive courses. However, this does not mean that Procedure is unrelated to those courses. Whenever you apply a case, statute, or rule, it is crucial to consider the underlying substantive law.

   2. **Procedure is not more ''straightforward'' than the other courses:** Many students come into Procedure with a sense of false confidence, wrongly assuming that learning Procedure involves nothing more than memorizing a set of technical rules.

      a. **Underlying policy concerns:** Just as in your other substantive courses, ***policy concerns*** underlie the rules of Civil Procedure. In almost every case, a rule makes more sense if you take the time to understand these policy concerns.

      b. **Procedure as a system:** On a broader level, Procedure is more than a collection of arcane rules. It is a system: one designed to strike a fine balance between the goals of efficiency and fairness. However, at first you probably will not appreciate how the various areas of Civil Procedure fit together into a unified whole.

   3. **Procedure is not ''harder'' than the other courses:** A few weeks into Procedure, many students conclude that Procedure is more difficult than the other courses. Again, that is not neces-

sarily true. The problem with Procedure is that the policies and rules that underlie the system are not as immediately obvious to the layman. Unlike their other classes, students often find themselves with no "gut reaction" as to how an issue should be resolved. The rule seems arbitrary at first glance.

4. **Procedure does not deal only with trials:** Certainly, the course in Procedure focuses heavily on the process of litigation. However, the litigation process involves far more than the trial. In fact, only a small portion of the Civil Procedure course deals with trials.

   a. **Pretrial:** The vast majority of an attorney's time in a typical civil case is spent with pretrial matters such as pleading and discovery.

   b. **Out-of-court resolution:** In addition, it is increasingly the case that disputes are resolved without going to court at all. The trend to use arbitration and mediation to resolve civil cases continues to grow.

C. **Sources of Civil Procedure:** One final way in which Procedure differs from other first-year courses is in the source of the legal rules. Although cases are important, they are less important than in other courses. Instead, Procedure relies much more heavily on positive law such as statutes and rules.

   1. **Statutes:** Most of the statutes used in Civil Procedure are codified in title 28 of the U.S. Code.

   2. **Federal rules:** Another important source of positive law is the *Federal Rules of Civil Procedure*, which are promulgated by the U.S. Supreme Court (actually by an Advisory Committee to the Court) pursuant to a delegation of authority by the U.S. Congress.

      a. **Application in state court:** Although the *Federal Rules of Civil Procedure apply only in federal court*, many states have adopted similar rules for use in their own courts. On the other hand, some states — including California, Illinois, and New York, which are the source of many reported decisions — do not follow the Federal Rules of Civil Procedure. The Civil Procedure systems in these states exhibit some important differences from the federal approach.

      b. **Other federal rules:** There are other bodies of federal rules, including the Federal Rules of Appellate Procedure, the Supreme Court Rules, local rules in the various federal districts, and the Federal Rules of Evidence. These rules arise only occasionally in a basic Civil Procedure course.

   3. **Importance of case law:** Although Procedure involves a much larger proportion of positive law than other first-year courses, cases are also important.

      a. **Application:** A case can illustrate how a given statute or rule applies, which can help in understanding the technical wording of statutes and rules.

      b. **Interpretation:** In addition, courts occasionally interpret a statute or rule in a way that is not obvious from the face of the statute or rule. In these cases, the judicial interpretation represents the "law" on that topic.

      c. **Doctrinal sources:** Finally, some Civil Procedure doctrines — such as personal jurisdiction (Chapter 2), the *Erie* doctrine (Chapter 5), and the effect of a decided case on later cases (Chapter 13) — were developed primarily by case law.

II. GENERAL THEMES IN U.S. CIVIL PROCEDURE

Certain basic themes underlie Civil Procedure.

A. Civil vs. Criminal Procedure: The course in Civil Procedure deals exclusively with the litigation process in *civil cases*. It does not deal with the procedure in *criminal cases*, a subject that is taught in a separate course.

    1. *Civil* defined: The easiest way to define a *civil* action is to compare it to criminal proceedings. A *criminal case* is brought by the state against a person committing a crime. The state seeks a conviction, pursuant to which the defendant will be *punished*. By comparison, a civil suit usually seeks compensation or other relief, not punishment.

    2. Civil or criminal? However, it is not always immediately clear whether a case is civil or criminal.

        a. Punishment: First, civil cases can also involve punishment. In an intentional tort case, for example, the plaintiff may be entitled to *punitive damages*. Although the purpose of such damages is to punish, a case involving punitive damages is *always civil* in nature.

        b. Compensation: On the other hand, some criminal cases seek reimbursement for the victim. In many states, the prosecutor can ask for an order of *restitution*.

    3. Terminology: Criminal and civil cases each have some of their own terminology. Avoid using criminal law terms in Procedure (as well as in your other courses). For example, a defendant in a civil case is found *liable, not guilty*. Similarly, when discussing the concept of claim preclusion, do not speak of *double jeopardy*. That concept applies only in criminal cases.

B. Multiple court systems: Another complicating feature of U.S. Civil Procedure is the existence of *multiple court systems*. This feature is one aspect of the United States' own unique brand of *federalism*. Strong federalism overtones exist in some Civil Procedure issues.

    1. State courts: Every state has its own court system, with at least two levels.

        a. Trial courts: Every state has multiple *trial courts*, the courts to which litigants first bring their dispute.

        b. Courts of appeals: Most states follow the federal model and have one or more *courts of appeals*, including a single *high court*. (Note that the high court is not always called the ''supreme'' court. For example, in New York, the ''supreme court'' is a trial court.) These courts review cases heard in the trial courts.

        c. Specialized courts: Most states also have *specialized* courts to hear certain types of cases, such as a *probate court* to deal with wills, a *family court* for family matters, a *court of claims* to hear claims against the state itself, and a *small claims court* that deals with claims involving less than a certain dollar amount.

    2. Federal courts: In addition, the United States operates a separate, nationwide system of federal courts.

        a. Federal courts are main focus of Procedure: A typical first-year course in Civil Procedure focuses on the federal courts. If the procedure in your state differs significantly, your school may offer an upper-level course in state procedure.

    i.   **State procedural rules:** However, many states have procedural rules that *mirror the federal rules*.

    ii.   **Issues for federal courts only:** There are also certain issues that are *unique to the federal court system*. Examples include

       (a) most of *subject-matter jurisdiction*, which is discussed in Chapter 4,

       (b) the *Erie doctrine*, which is the topic of Chapter 5, and

       (c) the Seventh Amendment right to a *jury trial*, which applies in federal courts only and is discussed in Chapter 10.

  b. **Limited jurisdiction:** The federal courts are courts of *limited jurisdiction*. They may hear only certain categories of cases. Determining what cases a federal court may adjudicate involves a question of *subject matter jurisdiction*, which is discussed in Chapter 4.

  c. **Three levels:** The federal court system has three levels:

    i.   **District courts:** The *district courts* serve as the trial court for most cases.

       (a) **Organization:** Every state has at least one federal district. Many have two or more districts. There are also federal district courts for the *District of Columbia*, *Puerto Rico*, and the federal territories. However, with one minor exception, see 28 U.S.C. §131, no federal district includes land in more than one state.

       (b) **District of Columbia:** The District of Columbia also has a separate local court system. Although this court is technically federal, it acts in many respects more like a state court.

    ii.   **Courts of appeal:** The *courts of appeal* review decisions of the district courts. The appellate courts are divided into *thirteen circuits*.

       (a) **First through Eleventh and D.C. Circuits:** The First through Eleventh Circuits, and the District of Columbia Circuit, review cases from district courts located within their geographic boundaries.

       (b) **Federal Circuit:** The Thirteenth Circuit is called the *Federal Circuit*. Unlike the others, its jurisdiction is defined in terms of subject matter, not geography.

    iii.   **Supreme Court:** The *U.S. Supreme Court* is the highest federal court. The Supreme Court reviews decisions of the federal courts of appeal and, in certain rare cases, hears appeals from the district courts.

       (a) **State court decisions:** Unlike any other federal court, the Supreme Court may also review certain decisions of the *state high courts*. However, the U.S. Supreme Court reviews state court decisions only when they involve questions of federal or constitutional law.

       (b) **Trial court:** In certain rare cases, such as suits between states, the Supreme Court can sit as a trial court.

3. **Jurisdiction often shared:** Although the United States has a wide array of different courts, it is generally true that *more than one court* is available in a given case. For example:

    a. In most cases, ***both state and federal courts can hear claims arising under the U.S. Constitution and federal law***.

    b. Similarly, a federal court may hear ***claims arising under state law*** if the parties are from different states and the amount in controversy is sufficiently high.

      Example: In Hawkins v. Master Farms, Inc., 2003 WL 21555767 (D. Kan. 2003), the court found that a plaintiff who had moved to another state had established a sufficient connection to become a citizen of the new state and therefore could sue someone from his original state in federal court.

    c. A state court is ***not limited*** to hearing cases arising ***under the law of that state***. A state court can hear cases arising under the law of any other state or foreign nation.

C. Law vs. equity: Historically, the legal system contained an additional division of labor: between courts of ***law*** and courts of ***equity***. Today, virtually all jurisdictions have merged the systems. Although this historical distinction is no longer significant for most purposes, it remains important in determining ***remedies***, see Chapter 6, and in determining whether a party has a right to a ***jury trial***, see Chapter 10.

III. STAGES IN A CIVIL LAWSUIT

A typical lawsuit goes through several stages. Different issues can arise at each of these stages. To understand the many issues you study in Procedure, always attempt to determine the stage of the suit at which the question arises. As the case progresses, each side usually learns more about both the underlying facts and their opponent's claims.

A. Determining what claims to bring: The first step is for the potential plaintiff and her attorneys to decide what claim or claims to bring in the action. This issue is largely determined by the substantive law, not the law of Civil Procedure.

B. Determining where to sue: The next stage is to determine *where* to sue. Although the plaintiff might prefer to sue in her home state, if the defendant resides elsewhere, her home state courts might not be able to hear the case because they lack ***personal jurisdiction***. Similarly, the plaintiff must make sure that the chosen court is a proper ***venue***. Finally, regardless of which state the case ends up in, the plaintiff must make a choice between the state and federal courts in that state, a choice that turns on the issue of ***subject matter jurisdiction***.

    1. Personal jurisdiction (Chapter 2): The chosen court must have the authority to subject ***every defendant*** to its sovereignty. This authority is called ***personal jurisdiction***. A court's authority to exercise personal jurisdiction is constrained both by the ***U.S. Constitution*** and the ***service statutes or rules*** of the jurisdiction in question.

      a. Purposeful connections: In general, the Constitution allows a court in a given state to exercise jurisdiction over a defendant only if that defendant resides in a state or has established other ***purposeful connections*** with that state.

      b. Notice: In addition, every defendant must be afforded ***notice*** of the lawsuit.

    2. Venue (Chapter 3): Like personal jurisdiction, ***venue*** narrows the universe of courts that are available to hear a case. Venue, however, is not a constitutional consideration. Instead, it results from statutes that attempt to place the litigation in a ***convenient*** forum.

3. **Subject matter jurisdiction (Chapter 4):** Although every state has both state and federal trial courts, a given court is an option only if it has *subject matter jurisdiction* to hear the case.

   a. **Federal courts:** Most of the discussion of subject matter jurisdiction in Civil Procedure concerns the federal courts. Federal courts can hear only certain categories of cases.

      i. **Three main categories:** Federal courts may hear cases in three main categories: *cases arising under federal law*, *state law cases between citizens of different states where the amount in controversy exceeds $75,000*, and *state law claims that arise out of the same basic facts* as those federal claims (so-called supplemental jurisdiction).

      ii. **Exceptions:** However, this is merely a rough guideline. There are cases in all three categories that fall outside federal jurisdiction.

   b. **State courts:** Subject matter jurisdiction is also an issue in state court. Federal courts have exclusive jurisdiction over a few types of claims.

C. **Pleading the case (Chapter 7):** The plaintiff commences the case by filing a complaint with the court and serving it on the defendant. The defendant can respond in several different ways.

   1. **The complaint:** The complaint contains the statement of plaintiff's claims. The form and contents of the complaint vary from court to court. In federal court and in many states, the plaintiff must merely provide general *notice* of the claims. In some states, and on certain issues, the plaintiff must go into greater detail.

   2. **Responding to the complaint:** The defendant may respond to the complaint by filing one or more motions or by filing an answer.

      a. **Motion:** A motion is a request for a ruling on a specific subject. If the defendant feels that the plaintiff's action is deficient in one or more respects, she may file a motion to *dismiss* the case. A defendant uses that sort of motion if, for example, she feels that the claims are not recognized at law or if the court lacks jurisdiction over the case or over the defendant.

      b. **Answer:** Unlike a motion, which focuses on one or a few narrow issues, the answer is the defendant's response to *all of the assertions in the complaint*.

         i. **Types of responses:** Defendant may *admit* some matters, *deny* others, and offer *affirmative defenses* that shield defendant from liability. However, a defendant who filed a pre-answer motion may be precluded from raising certain defenses in the answer.

         ii. **Counterclaim:** Moreover, if the defendant has any claims against the plaintiff, she may file a *counterclaim*.

   3. **Amending the pleadings:** The parties may be able to amend their pleadings to cure any defects. Depending on the timing of the proposed amendment, court permission or the consent of the other party may be required to amend a pleading.

D. **Determining who will sue and be sued (Chapters 14 and 15):** Once the claims and court are established, the parties then determine who will be litigants in the case. This stage requires consideration both of the substantive law (which determines who can be liable on a given claim) and Procedure.

   1. **Plaintiffs and defendants:** It is fairly common for *two or more plaintiffs* to join together. Similarly, it is possible to sue *multiple defendants* on the same claim or even on different claims.

    a. Compulsory joinder: Although joinder of parties is usually optional, in certain rare situations a party must join another party to the case or risk dismissal of the action.

    b. Intervention: If a person who is not made a party to the case has a significant interest in the outcome of the case, that party may be able to intervene in the case.

2. Additional parties: Additional parties may also be brought into the case. The most common situation is *impleader*, where a defendant adds a third person to the suit by claiming that the person must reimburse the defendant for all or part of any judgment rendered against the defendant.

3. Additional claims between parties: The rules of Procedure typically give a party considerable leeway to bring additional claims against the other parties. For example, one defendant may *cross-claim* against another defendant.

4. Class actions (Chapter 15): If a significant number of people are injured in roughly the same way, those people may be joined into a class. In a class action, a representative adjudicates the rights of the class members.

E. Discovery (Chapter 8): Once the claims and parties are joined, the case is under way. The parties then prepare for trial by amassing information concerning the claims and defenses. In complex cases, discovery may take several years.

1. Mandatory disclosures: In the federal courts, parties are required to turn over certain information to the other parties immediately after commencement of the case, and other information before the trial begins.

2. Party-initiated discovery: Parties may also seek information that they feel would be helpful to the case. Information may be obtained both from parties to the case and from nonparties such as witnesses. A number of different discovery devices are available; the most common of these are *depositions* and *interrogatories*.

3. Limits on discovery: Not all information that a party desires can be discovered. The rule protects certain information from disclosure through the *privilege, work product,* and *expert information* rules. There are also limits on abuse of discovery.

★   **Example:** In Butler v. Rigby, 1998 U.S. Dist. LEXIS 4618 (E.D. La. 1998), the court held that a health provider's list of patients was protected by the doctor-patient privilege and, accordingly, could not be discovered by another party, even though it was relevant to the party's case.

F. Resolving the case before trial (Chapter 9): Most civil actions never reach trial. Parties may negotiate a mutually acceptable settlement. In other cases, one side's position proves untenable, allowing the other side to obtain a judgment in its favor before trial ever begins.

1. Voluntary dismissal: If the parties settle the case, the plaintiff typically dismisses the action voluntarily.

2. Involuntary dismissal: A case can also be dismissed involuntarily if a party does not comply with the rules. Such dismissals are also used if the court lacks jurisdiction or if the plaintiff's complaint does not state a legally recognized claim.

3. Summary judgment: After the parties have had a chance to engage in discovery, it may turn out that the facts are not really in dispute. If there is no genuine issue of fact, the court may enter a summary judgment, which resolves the case as a matter of law.

★   **Example:** Houchens v. American Home Assurance Co., 927 F.2d 163 (4th Cir. 1991), is a good example of how the summary judgment standard is applied. In that case, neither party had any direct evidence on the crucial issue of whether a person's death was accidental. Because the plaintiff had the burden of proving that the death was accidental, the court held that summary judgment for defendant was appropriate.

G. The trial (Chapters 10 and 11): For those few cases that reach trial, the parties must deal with a whole host of issues.

    1. Jury trial issues (Chapter 10): Many of these issues relate to the jury, the body of laypeople who decide the case. A party may or may not be entitled to a jury, depending on the jurisdiction and the claims in the case.

        a. Jury selection: If a jury is to be impaneled, issues can arise concerning how the jury is selected.

        b. Not allowed to decide: In addition, if the evidence presented at trial overwhelmingly favors one side, the jury may not be allowed to decide the case. Instead, the court will issue a ***judgment as a matter of law***.

    2. Other trial issues (Chapter 11): The main issue at trial concerns what ***evidence*** is admissible. Fortunately for you, the vast majority of evidence issues are not covered in Procedure, but are instead taught in a separate Evidence course. Other issues that may come up at trial concern improper influences on the jury and the form of jury instructions.

H. Appeals (Chapter 12): An unfavorable judgment may be appealed to a higher court. There are issues concerning the timing of an appeal, as well as an appellate tribunal's authority to overturn certain findings of the trial court. Generally speaking, an appellate court has only a very limited ability to overturn a trial court's findings of fact.

I. Effect of a judgment (Chapter 13): Finally, a judgment has effects beyond the actual case.

    1. *Stare decisis:* As you will learn in all your courses, one of the crucial features of the common law is that courts defer to the decisions of other courts on the same issue of law. The course in Procedure usually does not focus much on this general principle.

    2. Preclusion: The main issues in Procedure, by contrast, are ***claim and issue preclusion***. These are a form of "super *stare decisis*," for unlike *stare decisis*, a court does not have the option to ignore a prior ruling.

★   **a. Claim preclusion:** This prevents a party from asserting claims that either were or should have been asserted in a prior case involving the ***same parties***. For example, in Rush v. City of Maple Heights, 147 N.E.2d 599, cert. denied, 358 U.S. 814 (1958), the court held that claim preclusion prevented a plaintiff from bringing separate suits to recover for personal injury and proper damage stemming from the same accident.

        b. Issue preclusion: This bars not claims but individual issues of fact. Unlike claim preclusion, issue preclusion applies only if the issue was ***actually litigated*** and if it is possible to determine what the prior court ***actually decided***. On the other hand, in some jurisdictions it is possible for people who were not parties in the first action to use issue preclusion against someone who was a party.

3. Full faith and credit: Claim and issue preclusion may apply across state lines. Both state and federal courts must give *full faith and credit* to each other's judgments.

CHAPTER 2

PERSONAL JURISDICTION

ChapterScope ━━

This chapter deals with the rules that determine whether a court has jurisdiction over the parties to an action. A court must have personal jurisdiction over a party to enter a judgment that binds that party.

- In most cases, a court needs to worry only about personal jurisdiction over the *defendant*. A plaintiff consents to the court's jurisdiction by filing suit in that court.

- There are two basic types of personal jurisdiction: *in personam* and *in rem*.

- There are two basic requirements for personal jurisdiction: *nexus* and *notice*. The Due Process Clause of the U.S. Constitution prevents a court from hearing a case unless a sufficient connection exists between the forum and the defendant. In addition, the defendant must receive adequate notice of the action.

- The *minimum contacts test* is used to determine if an adequate nexus exists. This analysis measures the number of contacts between the defendant and the forum, as well as the fairness of forcing the defendant to litigate in the forum.

    - A contact counts only if it is *voluntary*, that is, if the defendant purposefully engaged in some act by which she affiliated herself with the forum.

    - The number of contacts required to meet the constitutional test depends on whether the claim in the case *arises out of* those contacts. If the claim arises out of the contacts, even a single contact may suffice.

    - *Fairness* is a second and separate part of the minimum contacts test. It considers the burden on the defendant in litigating in the forum as well as other factors.

- Notice is ordinarily accomplished by *service of process*. Service of process must be authorized by statute or rule.

    - A state statute that allows service on an out-of-state defendant is often referred to as a *long-arm statute*.

- In most cases, a *federal court* may exercise personal jurisdiction over a defendant only if the courts of the state in which that federal court sits could exercise jurisdiction.

- *Challenges* to personal jurisdiction must be raised early in the case, or they are deemed waived. A party can waive jurisdiction explicitly or by taking action in the case inconsistent with the defense of lack of jurisdiction.

I. OVERVIEW

A. Definition of personal jurisdiction: Personal jurisdiction is a court's power over the parties to the case. If a court does not have personal jurisdiction over a party, any order or judgment that the court may render will not be binding on that party.

B. Subject matter jurisdiction distinguished: Personal jurisdiction is separate and distinct from subject matter jurisdiction, the focus of Chapter 4. A court must have both personal and subject matter jurisdiction in order to hear a case.

C. Constitutional requirement: Personal jurisdiction is a constitutional requirement for both state and federal courts. A judgment rendered against a person over whom the court has no personal jurisdiction violates that person's right to **due process.**

D. Two categories of personal jurisdiction: Courts have traditionally distinguished between two distinct categories of jurisdiction, *in personam* and *in rem*.

   1. *In personam:* Jurisdiction *in personam* is jurisdiction over the defendant herself.

   2. *In rem:* Technically, jurisdiction *in rem* is not jurisdiction over a person but over a particular item of property owned by a person. Practically speaking, however, it allows the court to adjudicate the rights of one person or many people in the property.

      a. True *in rem:* A "true" *in rem* action is one in which the main purpose is to adjudicate competing legal interests in the property in question. The ***quiet title*** action and ***mortgage foreclosure*** are forms of true *in rem* actions.

      b. *Quasi in rem:* Actions brought for purposes other than determining competing rights to property are deemed ***quasi in rem***. *Quasi in rem* actions are sometimes divided into two subcategories.

         i.   Type 1: If the claim before the court arises out of or is otherwise related to the property, the action is sometimes referred to as *quasi in rem type 1*.

         ii. Type 2: If the claim before the court is unrelated to the property, the action is sometimes referred to as *quasi in rem type 2*. In these cases, the property mainly serves as an asset to satisfy any judgment that the court may enter against the owner. This type of jurisdiction was extremely limited by *Shaffer*, discussed below.

   3. Differences: There are several significant differences between *in personam* and *in rem* jurisdiction.

      a. How jurisdiction obtained: *In personam* jurisdiction is obtained by serving the defendant personally with process. Jurisdiction *in rem* is obtained by seizing the property. Although notice to the defendant was not historically required in *in rem* actions, more recent decisions require the plaintiff to notify the defendant directly if the defendant can be found.

      b. Effect of judgment

         i.   *In personam:* If *in personam* jurisdiction exists, the judgment binds the defendant personally. The judgment winner can have certain assets owned by the defendant seized and sold in order to satisfy the judgment.

         ii. *In rem:* A judgment in an *in rem* case affects only the property and, accordingly, is ***limited to the value of the property***. The plaintiff **cannot** use the judgment to seize other property owned by the defendant. Moreover, although the judgment victor can sue the defendant personally to recover any deficiency, the prior judgment is not binding on the defendant in the second suit.

E. Service of process: Proper service of process is also necessary before a court may exercise personal jurisdiction over a defendant. Any judgment rendered without reasonable notice violates the defendant's *due process* rights and therefore is invalid. Statutes and rules provide various means of serving process.

II. DEVELOPMENT OF THE MODERN CONSTITUTIONAL TEST

The modern personal jurisdiction analysis is the product of a long and sometimes tortured genesis. The current *minimum contacts test* evolved through a series of significant Supreme Court decisions.

★ **A. Pennoyer v. Neff (1877):** Pennoyer v. Neff, 95 U.S. 714 (1877), was the first decision to treat personal jurisdiction as a *constitutional issue*. It set out a clear, albeit somewhat restricted, test for when a court might constitutionally exercise jurisdiction over a person or that person's property. Although this restrictive approach has been greatly relaxed in many respects, some aspects of *Pennoyer* remain valid.

   1. Synopsis: *Pennoyer* involved a dispute over title to certain land. Neff originally owned the land. After Mitchell obtained a judgment against Neff, the land was sold at a sheriff's sale to Pennoyer. Neff then sued Pennoyer in a separate action to recover possession of the land. This second action eventually made it to the Supreme Court.

      a. Judgment valid? If the judgment in the first action was valid, the second court would have been required to treat it as binding, which would mean that Pennoyer should prevail.

      b. No: However, the Supreme Court held that the earlier *judgment was invalid* because the court *lacked jurisdiction* over either Neff or the land.

   2. Analysis: Although recognizing that the U.S. Constitution created some interdependence among the states, the Court reasoned that the states still had many of the attributes of independent nations. The Court turned to basic principles of public international law to determine when a state could govern a particular situation.

      a. Two territorial principles: The Court held that two basic principles of international law applied to the case at hand. The first was that "every State possesses exclusive jurisdiction and sovereignty over persons and property within its territory." The second, which was the converse of the first, was that "no State can exercise direct jurisdiction and authority over persons and property without its territory."

      b. Limits on jurisdiction: From these two principles, the Court distilled the limits on personal jurisdiction.

         i. Person or property in state: A court could exercise *in personam* jurisdiction over any *person*, and *in rem* jurisdiction over any *property*, found within its borders at the time the suit was commenced.

            (a) Presence sufficient: It was irrelevant how long the person or property was in the state. Therefore, a state had jurisdiction over a person merely passing through the state provided the person was served while within the borders. In addition, a court could hear any claim, regardless of whether it related to the reason the person or her property was present in that state.

  (b) Notice: However, the court also had to provide adequate notice in order to exercise jurisdiction.

   1. *In personam:* In the case of *in personam* jurisdiction, the person had to be served *while in the state*.

   2. *In rem:* In the case of *in rem* jurisdiction, the court had to seize or otherwise exercise dominion over the property *at the outset of the action*.

 ii. Person or property without state: Because a state's authority ended at its borders, a person who was not in the state ordinarily could not be served *in personam*. Similarly, if that person had no property within the state, *in rem* jurisdiction was impossible.

 iii. Exceptions: However, the Court identified several exceptions to the basic rule that a court could not exercise *in personam* jurisdiction over a person who was not in the state.

  (a) Status: A court had the authority to determine the *status* of one of its citizens in relation to a nonresident. Jurisdiction over the citizen gave the court jurisdiction over the status too. For example, a court could grant a *divorce* even though only one spouse was a resident.

  (b) Consent: If a person appointed an in-state agent for service of process, service on the agent was effective to create jurisdiction over the person.

c. Constitutional concerns: The Court held that these basic principles of international law were incorporated into the U.S. Constitution. The opinion discusses two separate constitutional provisions, which have different ramifications.

 i. Full faith and credit: Article IV of the Constitution requires states to enforce the judgments of sister states. *Pennoyer* held that this provision was not meant to apply to judgments that would be invalid under international law. Therefore, a court *need not enforce a judgment* entered without personal jurisdiction.

 ii. Due process: *Pennoyer* also stated that the Fourteenth Amendment requirement of due process guarantees an individual that his rights can be adjudicated only by a court that has personal jurisdiction over him. Therefore, a court *cannot enforce a judgment* rendered without personal jurisdiction even it it wants to.

  Note: The discussion of due process in *Pennoyer* is *technically dictum*. The Due Process Clause was not yet effective when the judgment in the first case was rendered, so that judgment could not violate Neff's due process rights. Nevertheless, the courts have treated the due process discussion as good law.

★ **B. *International Shoe* (1945):** International Shoe Co. v. Washington, 326 U.S. 310 (1945), greatly extended the reach of jurisdiction by allowing a state to exercise jurisdiction over defendants who are not present in the state. The court replaced *Pennoyer*'s strictly territorial analysis with one that focused on a person's connections with a state. *International Shoe*'s basic *minimum contacts test* remains the test used to this day.

 1. Synopsis: The state of Washington attempted to levy an unemployment tax on defendant, a corporation. When the corporation did not pay, the state sued it in a Washington court.

a. Connection sufficient? The corporation's only connection with Washington was that it employed salesmen in the state. These salesmen did not enter into contracts with buyers, but merely sent orders to the corporation's Missouri headquarters for acceptance.

b. Yes: The Court held that Washington ***had personal jurisdiction***. Although the corporation was not physically present in the state, jurisdiction was constitutional because the corporation had sufficient contacts with that state, and the claim arose out of those contacts.

2. Analysis: *International Shoe* rejected *Pennoyer*'s territorial approach in lieu of an approach that looked to the ***connections between the defendant and the forum***.

    a. Minimum contacts test: The Court indicated that jurisdiction was proper over a defendant who had "certain ***minimum contacts*** with [the state] such that the maintenance of the suit does not offend 'traditional notions of ***fair play and substantial justice***.' "

    b. Specific and general jurisdiction: The Court then noted that the number of contacts necessary for jurisdiction turned on whether the claim arose out of those contacts.

        i. Arose out of: If the claim arose from the contacts, even single or occasional acts might suffice. Today, this is referred to as ***specific jurisdiction***.

        ii. Did not arise out of: Conversely, if the claim was unrelated to the contacts, jurisdiction would be not be allowed even if there were a significant number of contacts.

        iii. Overwhelming contacts: However, the Court also suggested that there might be cases where the contacts were so "continuous and systematic" that jurisdiction over the corporation might be allowed even if the claim was completely unrelated to those contacts. Today, this is referred to as ***general jurisdiction***.

        Example: *D*, a Florida corporation, produces parts in its Florida factory. It sells all of its parts to a buyer in Tennessee. Once a month, *D* sends a truck filled with parts to this plant. On the way, the truck passes through Alabama. *P*, a citizen of Florida, works at *D*'s plant. When *P* is injured on the job, she sues in an Alabama state court. The court cannot exercise personal jurisdiction over *D* in Alabama based on these facts. Although *D* has significant contacts with Alabama, they do not rise to the level necessary to meet the minimum contacts test because they are not related to *P*'s claim.

    c. Fairness: The opinion provides little guidance into what the Court means by "fair play and substantial justice," other than to indicate that the "inconvenience" of litigating in a distant forum is relevant.

3. Analysis still used: Although the Court in *International Shoe* provided few details, the Court's basic two-part minimum contacts/fairness test remains in use. Later Supreme Court opinions have filled in many of the details.

★ **C.** ***Shaffer* (1977):** *International Shoe* dealt only with *in personam* jurisdiction. Shaffer v. Heitner, 433 U.S. 186 (1977), held that the ***minimum contacts test*** also applied to ***in rem*** jurisdiction. *Shaffer*, for all intents and purposes, eviscerated the use of *in rem* jurisdiction in cases where the claim did not arise out of the property.

    1. ***In rem* as a fiction:** The Court held that the notion of an *in rem* suit as one against property was a legal fiction. The suit really affected a person's *interest* in that property. Because due process protects a person's interest in property, *in rem* cases should be analyzed according to the same due process standard used in *in personam* cases.

2. **Application of minimum contacts test to *in rem*:** The Court then applied the minimum contacts test to the situation at hand.

     a. The property involved in *Shaffer* was stock owned by the defendant.

     b. The case did not arise out of the stock. Defendants were being sued because of acts they committed as corporate officers, not because of their status as shareholders.

     c. Based on these facts, the Court found that although the stock was a contact, it was not by itself enough to satisfy the minimum contacts test.

     d. The only other connection between the defendants and the forum was the defendants' status as officers or directors in a corporation that had been incorporated in Delaware. However, because the Delaware jurisdiction statutes did not base jurisdiction on this particular connection, the Court held that the status did not count as a contact for purposes of the minimum contacts analysis.

3. **Limits of holding in *Shaffer*:** Notwithstanding some careless assertions to the contrary, there are a number of important limits to the holding in *Shaffer*.

     a. ***Shaffer* does not destroy *in rem* jurisdiction:** *Shaffer* merely prevents the use of *quasi in rem* jurisdiction when the ***property is the only contact*** and the ***action has nothing to do with the property***. The practical effect of *Shaffer* is to make *quasi in rem* jurisdiction much less appealing to a plaintiff. If minimum contacts exist, the party ordinarily will forgo *in rem* jurisdiction and use *in personam*.

     b. **Property is a contact:** Property should be considered along with any other contacts in determining whether there are minimum contacts.

     c. **Property alone may be enough:** If the case directly involves ownership of the property — that is, if the case is a true *in rem* action — the property is enough of a contact to satisfy the minimum contacts test. Although the case is not clear on this point, property alone may also be a sufficient contact in a *quasi in rem type 1* action, where the claim arises out of the property.

     d. **Other limits on *in rem* remain:** Although *Shaffer* extends the test used in *in personam* cases to *in rem*, the historic limitations on *in rem* continue to exist. For example, any judgment in an *in rem* action is limited to the value of the property, and the factual findings in the action do not bind the owner in later cases.

★ **D.** ***World-Wide Volkswagen* (1980):** World-Wide Volkswagen Corp. v. Woodson, 444 U.S. 286 (1980), fleshes out both the contacts and fairness portions of the minimum contacts test.

     1. **Synopsis:** A New York resident purchased an automobile in New York. The purchaser then decided to move to Arizona, but was involved in an automobile accident in Oklahoma while in route. The purchaser sued the New York dealer, the regional distributor, and other parties in an Oklahoma state court, alleging a design defect.

     2. **Holding:** The Court held that Oklahoma ***could not exercise jurisdiction*** over the dealer or distributor because the minimum contacts test was not satisfied.

3. **Analysis:** The Court found there were *no contacts* between the dealer and distributor and Oklahoma.

   a. **Purposeful availment test:** Although the automobile was a connection between the defendants and the state, it did not count as a contact. The Court held that a connection counts as a contact only if it results from an act that the defendant *purposefully directed* at the forum state. Because defendants did not know that the automobile was going to Oklahoma, the automobile did not qualify as a purposeful contact.

   b. **Fairness:** The Court also discussed the fairness portion of the minimum contacts analysis. Fairness, the Court indicated, comprised five factors:

      i.   the *burden on the defendant*, which the Court indicated was the *"primary concern"*;

      ii. the interest of the *forum* in adjudicating the case;

      iii. the *plaintiff's interest* in obtaining "convenient and effective relief";

      iv. the interest of the interstate judicial system in *efficient resolution* of controversies; and

      v.   the "shared interest of the several States in *furthering fundamental substantive social policies.*"

   c. **Fairness irrelevant absent contacts:** However, the Court held that these fairness factors were not to be considered unless there were purposeful contacts between the defendant and the forum. Because there were no contacts in the case itself, the Court spent little time analyzing the fairness factors.

III. APPLICATION OF THE MODERN CONSTITUTIONAL TEST

The cases discussed above, together with several more recent Supreme Court rulings, provide a template for analyzing personal jurisdiction cases. However, on certain issues, the Court has not been able to reach a consensus.

A. **Basic approach:** The *minimum contacts test* is used to analyze most questions of jurisdiction.

   1. **Two-step test:** The minimum contacts test involves two discrete steps.

      a. **Contacts:** First, the court determines if there are *any "contacts"* at all between the defendant and the forum. If there are no contacts, *the analysis stops*, and there is no personal jurisdiction. If there are contacts, the court determines whether the claim arises out of those contacts.

      b. **Fairness:** If there are *any significant contacts*, the court then considers fairness, incorporating the five factors set out in *World-Wide Volkswagen*.

   2. **Contacts:** As discussed in *World-Wide Volkswagen*, a contact is considered only if it is the result of *purposeful activity*. In more recent decisions, the Court has restated this notion as *purposeful availment of the benefits and protections of forum law*.

   3. **Fairness:** The factors each deal with unique concerns.

a. **Burden on the defendant:** This factor considers not only the distance that the defendant must travel, but also any other circumstances that make defending in the forum burdensome on the defendant.

b. **Interest of the state:** A state is interested in hearing a case if any of the parties are from that state or if the dispute directly affects that state.

c. **Interest of the plaintiff:** This factor is satisfied if the plaintiff is from the forum or if the forum is a convenient place to try the case because of the availability of witnesses or other evidence.

d. **Efficient resolution:** It is inefficient when a case involving multiple parties must be split up and litigated in several different places. If the chosen forum is the only place that all claims can be heard, this factor supports jurisdiction.

e. **Furthering social policies:** If the alternate forum does not recognize plaintiff's claim, refusing to exercise jurisdiction frustrates the policy underlying the substantive law. This is most likely to be an issue when the plaintiff is forced to refile in a foreign court.

4. **Lack of fairness rarely defeats jurisdiction:** If there are purposeful contacts, it requires a *very strong showing* of unfairness to defeat jurisdiction.

★   a. *Asahi:* Asahi Metal Industry Co. v. Superior Court, 480 U.S. 102 (1987), is the only case in which the Court has refused to allow jurisdiction even though there were contacts. *Asahi* involved a somewhat unique situation. A plaintiff had sued a Taiwanese defendant, who in turn impleaded a Japanese third-party defendant. All claims other than the claim by the Taiwanese defendant against the Japanese third-party defendant were settled. These facts directly affected the fairness analysis:

   i. The burden on the defendant was tremendous, not only in terms of distance but also because of differences in language and legal systems.

   ii. The forum had no great interest. Although the underlying accident had occurred in the forum, the forum had no real interest in whether a Japanese parts manufacturer had to indemnify a Taiwanese parts manufacturer.

   iii. The ''plaintiff'' (in this case, the Taiwanese defendant) was brought into California and had no real interest in having the claim litigated there.

   iv. Because the case could be litigated just as easily in Taiwan or Japan, there were no real efficiency concerns.

   v. The underlying ''substantive policies'' were those of Taiwan and Japan. Therefore, the Court held that forcing the claim to be brought there would better protect those policies.

B. **Application to particular circumstances:** Certain situations have proved troublesome to courts charged with applying the minimum contacts test.

1. **Contract cases:** Three Supreme Court cases demonstrate how the courts apply the test to contract cases.

★   a. *McGee:* McGee v. International Life Insurance Co., 355 U.S. 220 (1957), dealt with an *insurance policy*. A California resident purchased a life insurance policy. The policy was then assigned to a Texas insurance company. The purchaser paid premiums from California to Texas until his death. The Court held that maintaining an insurance policy on a Californian was sufficient to establish minimum contacts between the insurer and California. The policy established a "substantial connection" with California. Therefore, the California courts had personal jurisdiction over the insurance company in an action under the policy.

★   **b.** *Hanson:* In Hanson v. Denckla, 357 U.S. 235 (1958), a person had established a trust with a Delaware trustee. The person later moved to Florida. After the person died, an action was brought in the Florida courts to gain the assets in the trust, which required personal jurisdiction over the Delaware trustee.

    i. The Court held that the person's unilateral move to Florida did not establish contacts between the Delaware trustee and Florida. The trustee did not play a role in the person's move.

    ii. Although the trustee continued to perform under the trust agreement, the trustee had no choice in the matter. The trustee could not cancel the trust based on the move.

★   **c.** *Burger King:* Burger King Corp. v. Rudzewicz, 471 U.S. 462 (1985), is the Court's most detailed discussion of how the minimum contacts test applies to contracts. That case dealt with a ***commercial contract***. A Michigan person obtained a Burger King Franchise from Burger King, a Florida corporation. When the agreement soured, Burger King sued the franchisee in Florida. Although the defendant had never been to Florida, the Court allowed the Florida courts to exercise jurisdiction.

    i. Merely entering into a contract with a resident of the forum is not alone sufficient.

    ii. However, if the contract is ***negotiated*** and/or to be ***performed*** in the forum, that is evidence that the parties have ***purposefully availed*** themselves of the forum. In *Burger King*, the franchisee knew that he was negotiating with a Florida corporation. In addition, the contract called for him to make payments to the Florida office, meaning that performance would take place in Florida. The Court held that these activities were "purposefully directed" at a Florida resident.

    iii. Finally, the Court held that it was not unfair to make the defendant appear in Florida. The Court noted that both parties were experienced in business.

2. Stream of commerce cases: The stream of commerce problem has plagued the courts since shortly after *International Shoe*. The Supreme Court has provided no clear answer to the question.

    a. "Stream of commerce" defined: The stream of commerce problem arises when a defendant distributes its goods nationally through a third party. Although the defendant knows that some of its goods go to a particular state, it does not know exactly which products go where. Moreover, it may not particularly care if any of its product is sold in a certain state.

    b. Stream of commerce as a contact: The issue in personal jurisdiction is whether ***purposefully injecting goods into the stream*** of commerce constitutes purposeful availment with a state in which one of those goods causes injury.

★   **c.** *Asahi:* The Supreme Court dealt with the stream of commerce problem in Asahi Metal Industry Co. v. Superior Court, 480 U.S. 102 (1987). Unfortunately, the Court issued a ***plurality opinion*** with no clear guidance as to whether injecting goods into the stream of commerce counts as a contact.

    i. **O'Connor's view:** Justice O'Connor, joined by three others, argued that the *mere awareness* that defendant's goods would enter the forum was *insufficient*. Such awareness could constitute a contact only if it was accompanied by *other acts specifically directed* at the forum (such as advertising or designing the product for the special needs of the forum).

    ii. **White's view:** Justice White, joined by three others, argued that *mere awareness* that products entered the state *was enough* to qualify as a contact.

    iii. **Stevens's view:** Justice Stevens reasoned that the *sheer volume of defendant's goods* that entered the forum in the case *was enough* to qualify as a minimum contact, but *did not opine* whether the ''mere awareness'' or ''awareness plus'' standard should be applied to future cases.

  d. **Lower courts:** The lower courts have continued to struggle with the issue. However, if the additional factors identified by Justice O'Connor are present, note that the stream of commerce counts as a contact under either her analysis or White's.

3. **Internet cases:** The Internet presents issues that are conceptually similar to the stream of commerce problem. The Internet allows parties to interact even though neither may know where the other is located. Although the Supreme Court has not faced the question, the lower courts have developed general rules for these sorts of cases.

  a. **Basic issue:** The typical Internet case involves the issue of whether someone who views a Web site may sue the person who operates the site in the viewer's home state.

  b. **Classification of Web site:** Most courts consider the type of Web site involved. A *passive* site is one that may only be viewed; the viewer cannot submit information. An *active* site, by contrast, is one where the viewer may input information and enter into a transaction. An *interactive* site lies somewhere in between: The viewer may enter information that affects the site but not enter into a transaction.

  c. **General rules:** Classification usually affects the outcome.

    i. **Passive site:** Jurisdiction *rarely exists in the case of a passive site*. The main exception is when the site contains material clearly directed at another state, such as information that defames a specific person in another state.

    ii. **Active site:** Operation of an *active site clearly constitutes a contact* with the viewer's state, at least if the viewer does interact. Therefore, a seller who contracts to sell goods to a buyer has established contacts with the buyer's state.

    iii. **Interactive site:** In the case of an *interactive site, courts look to all of the circumstances*, including the level of activity and whether the site is commercial in nature.

    ★   **Example:** In Pavlovich v. Superior Court, 29 Cal. 4th 262, 58 P.3d 2 (2002), the court determined that because defendant's Web site was passive, there were not sufficient purposeful contacts between the defendant and the state to allow the court to exercise personal jurisdiction.

4. **General jurisdiction:** *International Shoe* indicated in *dictum* that if a party had a substantial and continuing relationship with a state, the courts of that state could hear any claim arising against the defendant, even those *unrelated to the contacts*. This form of jurisdiction is called *general jurisdiction.* Although the Supreme Court has never actually found general jurisdiction to exist in a case, the lower courts occasionally have relied on the theory of general jurisdiction to uphold jurisdiction over defendants with long-term, regular, and substantial contacts with a state.

C. **Cases outside the minimum contacts test:** Although *Shaffer* declared that the minimum contacts test applied to all attempts to assert jurisdiction, in some situations courts eschew the test and automatically find jurisdiction based on concepts left over from *Pennoyer.*

1. **Domicile:** In Milliken v. Meyer, 311 U.S. 457 (1940), the Supreme Court upheld jurisdiction over a domiciliary of the state even though the person was not in the state at the time. Although this case predates the *International Shoe* minimum contacts test, its continued validity remains largely unquestioned.

2. **State of incorporation:** *Pennoyer* also suggested a state could exercise jurisdiction over a corporation in its state of incorporation, even though the defendant had no assets, employees, or operations in that state. This rule is still universally accepted, although the Supreme Court has never formally approved it.

3. **Presence:** The most important part of *Pennoyer* was its rule allowing a state to exercise jurisdiction over anyone who was *served while present* in the state. Although the validity of jurisdiction on this basis was questionable after *Shaffer*, the Supreme Court specifically approved it in 1990.

★ a. *Burnham:* In Burnham v. Superior Court, 495 U.S. 604 (1990), the Supreme Court upheld California's exercise of *in personam* jurisdiction over a defendant who was served while present in the state. Defendant was a nonresident who was visiting California for three days on a matter unrelated to plaintiff's claim. However, the Court was divided, with no majority opinion.

   i. **Scalia's view:** Justice Scalia, joined by three others, held that the long tradition of exercising jurisdiction over people who were present was enough to show that the practice complied with traditional notions of due process. Therefore, it was *unnecessary to apply the minimum contacts test.* That test developed as a way to allow courts to exercise jurisdiction over people who were *not present.*

   ii. **Brennan's view:** Justice Brennan, joined by three others, argued that the minimum contacts test applied. However, the defendant's voluntary presence, coupled with service while he was there, gave California *general jurisdiction* over the defendant.

   iii. **Stevens's view:** Justice Stevens refused to join either camp, simply indicating that the dispute was "a very easy case."

   b. **Presence as a basis for jurisdiction after *Burnham:*** In most cases it does not matter if the court applies Justice Scalia's or Justice Brennan's view: Jurisdiction based on in-state service is acceptable. The only situation where the different approaches might affect the outcome is when the defendant's *presence is not voluntary.* Although jurisdiction would still be acceptable under Scalia's view, the presence would no longer count as a contact, and therefore general jurisdiction under Brennan's view might not be available.

4. **Consent:** Because personal jurisdiction is a personal defense, a party may waive it either expressly or by taking actions inconsistent with the defense.

a. **Minimum contacts irrelevant:** If a party consents to a court's jurisdiction, it is ***unnecessary to evaluate minimum contacts***. Consent alone is sufficient to establish jurisdiction.

b. **Express consent:** A party may expressly consent to the jurisdiction of a particular court. The most common example of this form of consent is a ***contract*** that specifies that disputes arising under the contract may be heard in a specific court.

   i. **Enforceability:** As long as the agreement is enforceable under the ordinary rules of contract law, it creates court personal jurisdiction over the parties. That the consent to jurisdiction was nonnegotiable rarely renders the consent ineffective.

   ii. **Forum selection clause:** A twist on the contractual consent is the forum selection clause, where the parties specify that disputes can be heard ***only*** in a particular court. If a party sues elsewhere, the other side may move for dismissal. In most jurisdictions, forum selection clauses are enforceable provided they are ***fundamentally fair***. Fairness is measured at the time the agreement is made, not when the case is filed.

   ★   **Note:** The Supreme Court's decision in Carnival Cruise Lines, Inc. v. Shute, 499 U.S. 585 (1991), held that a nonnegotiable forum selection clause on a cruise ship ticket was enforceable. However, this Supreme Court decision applies only to contracts involving ships. As a general matter, the enforceability of forum selection clauses is ***governed by state law***, not federal. Not all states enforce such clauses.

c. **Implied consent:** A party may also consent to personal jurisdiction by taking actions inconsistent with his argument that the court lacks power over him.

   i. **Plaintiffs:** A plaintiff who files suit in a forum consents to personal jurisdiction for all matters arising in that lawsuit, including counterclaims and cross-claims. Adam v. Saenger, 303 U.S. 59 (1938).

   ii. **Failure to assert defense:** A defendant may waive any defense to personal jurisdiction by filing other claims or defenses in the proceeding. Therefore, if a defendant files a counterclaim against the plaintiff before taking any other action, she will be deemed to have consented to the court's jurisdiction. The Federal Rules of Civil Procedure have special rules governing the timing of the personal jurisdiction defense. These rules are discussed in Part V of this chapter.

★ d. **Jurisdiction to determine jurisdiction:** Finally, Insurance Corp. of Ireland v. Compagnie des Bauxites de Guinée, 456 U.S. 694 (1982), establishes that when a party challenges jurisdiction, she agrees to cooperate with the court in determining whether jurisdiction exists. Therefore, if a party challenges jurisdiction but then refuses to answer discovery questions dealing with the facts necessary to establish jurisdiction, the trial court could enter a sanction finding that jurisdiction exists.

Quiz Yourself on
APPLICATION OF THE MODERN CONSTITUTIONAL TEST

1. While driving to Florida, Ashley, a citizen of New York, is involved in a wreck with John, a citizen of Georgia. After Ashley returns to New York, John sues Ashley in a Georgia state court. May the Georgia courts constitutionally exercise personal jurisdiction over Ashley? _____

2. Ivan invents a high-powered heater to warm the inside of his Alaska home. Ed Entrepreneur signs an agreement with Ivan under which Ed will distribute the heater nationally. Ed arranges to have an infomercial broadcast in Canada and the northernmost states in the United States. Although Ivan is aware of Ed's activities, he has no control over where Ed advertises and ships the product.

    Frieda sees Ed's infomercial while visiting a friend in North Dakota. When she returns home to Tennessee, Frieda calls the toll-free number and orders a heater from Ed. Frieda uses the heater to heat her lake cabin in Tennessee. The heater is too powerful for the temperate climate and vaporizes the varnish on Frieda's furniture, causing Frieda to become very ill. Frieda wants to sue Ivan in a Tennessee state court. Can she satisfy the minimum contacts test? _____

3. Rachel is a student at a university in Oregon. Every summer, she returns home to Virginia to live with her parents. While at home during the summer between her third and fourth years of school, Rachel gets into a fight with Steve, who lives in Oregon but is visiting Rachel in Virginia. During this fight Rachel pours a container of caustic fluid all over the brand-new paint job on Steve's car.

    Although Rachel is still spending the summer with her parents, Steve wants to sue her in Oregon. Can he? _____

4. Tasty Taters, Inc. (TT) is a corporation chartered under the law of Delaware, but with its sole place of business located in Idaho. TT manufactures a variety of frozen potato products. TT packages its products in plastic bags. For two years now, TT has obtained its plastic bags from Herman's Hermetics, a Vermont company. The parties have a ten-year contract, which was negotiated over the phone between representatives of TT in Idaho and Herman's in Vermont. The contract requires Herman's to deliver the bags to TT in Idaho. After delivery, TT wires payment to Herman's in Vermont.

    TT has now found a cheaper source for its bags. Therefore, although eight years remain on the contract, TT refuses to accept delivery of any more bags from Herman's. Herman's sues TT for breach of contract in a Delaware state court. May the Delaware court constitutionally exercise jurisdiction over TT? _____

5. Same facts as Problem 4, except that Herman's sues in a Vermont state court. May the Vermont state court constitutionally exercise jurisdiction over TT? _____

6. Roger, a citizen of Indiana, books an Alaskan cruise with Sea Tours, which is located in Alaska. The tickets contain a forum selection clause that states that all disputes arising from the cruise can be heard only in an Alaska court. Roger slips on a wet spot in the ship's hallway, tumbles down a flight of stairs, and breaks both his legs. Roger files a negligence claim against Sea Tours in a federal court in his home state of Indiana. Will the case be dismissed? _____

Answers

1. A two-step minimum contacts test is used to establish personal jurisdiction — contacts and fairness.

    To establish contacts, the defendant must have taken actions that were purposefully directed toward the forum state and from which defendant derived the benefits and protections of the state's laws. Ashley's contact was driving through the state of Georgia. This is purposeful activity. While driving in Georgia, Ashley was protected by Georgia police and traffic laws.

    However, even if there are minimum contacts with the forum state, the state may not exercise jurisdiction if considerations of "fair play and substantial justice" make defending the action in the forum state highly unreasonable. The burden on the defendant is minimal. The distance from New York to Georgia is not that great, and Ashley has already demonstrated that she is able to travel to that state. The interest of the state of Georgia is high because John, the plaintiff, is from Georgia, and the accident occurred there. The interest of the plaintiff is also high both because he would like to sue in his own state and because the witnesses and other evidence are likely to be in Georgia. The interest in efficient resolution of controversies does not apply in this case. Nor does the interest in furthering fundamental policies, as the tort laws of New York and Georgia are likely to be generally the same. Therefore, the Georgia state courts may constitutionally exercise personal jurisdiction over Ashley in this matter.

2. At first glance, this appears to be a stream of commerce case. However, it is different in one respect from *Asahi*. In *Asahi*, the defendant's product was a component that was incorporated into a product. Here, by contrast, the defendant produces the complete product. Nevertheless, the stream of commerce analysis is the most appropriate for dealing with jurisdiction here. Like the component manufacturer in *Asahi*, Ivan turns the product over to Ed and has no control over where it ends up. He is aware, however, of where his products end up.

    The *Asahi* plurality opinion does not provide a clear test for contacts in these cases. The Court split between a "mere awareness" test and an "awareness plus" test. However, under both tests, it is crucial that the defendant be aware that the product ends up in the forum state. From the facts of the problem, not even this much is clear. If Ivan does not know that any of his product ends up in Tennessee, he cannot be subject to jurisdiction in that state.

    If Ivan is aware, he is not subject to jurisdiction if the "awareness plus" test applies. "Awareness plus" is awareness that the product will end up in the forum state, coupled with activities aimed at the forum state such as advertising, soliciting, marketing, and designing the product especially for the forum state. None of the plus factors are present in this problem.

    Under the mere awareness test, by contrast, Ivan is subject to jurisdiction in Tennessee as long as he realizes that some of his product goes to that state. Ivan's fate depends on which test the courts use.

3. Steve can sue Rachel in Oregon, although he might have to wait until Rachel returns to school in the fall.

    There are three potential ways a suit in Oregon could comply with the minimum contacts test. First, it could be argued that by intentionally causing an injury to an Oregonian, Rachel established minimum contacts with that state. This theory is not likely to succeed. Although Rachel did injure someone she knew was an Oregonian, the harm happened in Virginia. Rachel did nothing in connection with this suit to obtain the benefits and protections of Oregon law. Even though Oregon and the plaintiff have an interest, the fairness factors cannot override a complete lack of contacts.

    Second, if Rachel is domiciled in Oregon, Oregon could exercise personal jurisdiction over her in this or any other suit. However, it is unlikely that Rachel is an Oregon domiciliary. She attends school in Oregon, but nothing in the problem suggests that she intends to remain.

Third, Steve could wait until Rachel returns to school in Oregon and serve her personally while she is present in the state. Under *Burnham*, personal service on someone in the state gives the state jurisdiction over that person, even for claims that have nothing to do with the person's presence in the state. This is Steve's best option.

4. Delaware may exercise personal jurisdiction over TT because the corporation was incorporated in that state. This is a holdover from *Pennoyer* and is not subject to the minimum contacts test.

5. Vermont probably can exercise personal jurisdiction over TT. This case is closest to *Burger King*. Like in that case, TT entered into a long-term contract with someone from another state (in this case, Vermont). That contract requires TT to submit payments to the Vermont seller. It is easily foreseeable that failure to make payments — which is the breach here — will have an immediate impact on Herman's in Vermont.

The fairness factors are also relevant here. There is no great burden on TT to defend in Vermont. Vermont and plaintiff Herman's also have a strong interest in Vermont. The fourth and fifth fairness factors are indeterminate because efficiency and underlying policy will be furthered regardless of whether suit takes place in Vermont, Idaho, or Delaware.

6. Forum selection clauses on ships are enforced provided that they are "fundamentally fair." Fairness is measured at the time the agreement is made. A cruise is a luxury good, not a necessity, so Roger easily could have rejected the term had he found it unacceptable. The clause was on his ticket, which he should have read to find out when to board the ship. Although Roger does not live in Alaska, Sea Tours does all its business in Alaska. It is inefficient for Sea Tours to have to defend in every passenger's home state court. Because the clause is fair, the Indiana court will dismiss the case.

IV. NOTICE

Notice is the ***other primary requirement*** for exercising personal jurisdiction.

A. Constitutional requirement: The ***Due Process Clause*** of the Fourteenth Amendment to the U.S. Constitution requires that the defendant receive adequate notice of the litigation. A judgment without notice is constitutionally deficient and therefore invalid.

B. Both contacts and notice required: Contacts and notice are not substitutes. Due process requires both.

C. Definition of notice: A plaintiff gives notice of a pending action when she ***serves*** the ***summons*** and a ***copy of the complaint*** on the defendant. The summons commands the defendant to answer the plaintiff's complaint within a fixed period of time. An example of a summons is set out in ***Federal Form 1***.

★ **D. Adequacy of notice:** Due process requires that service of process be "***reasonably calculated***, under all the circumstances, to apprise interested parties of the pendency of the action and afford them an opportunity to present their objections." Mullane v. Central Hanover Bank & Trust Co., 339 U.S. 306 (1950).

   1. Receipt of notice unnecessary: As long as the method of service meets this reasonableness standard, defendant is subject to jurisdiction even if the defendant never actually receives the summons. However, if defendant never receives notice, almost every court system has a procedure whereby defendant may have the judgment set aside. See Chapter 13, Part V.A.

2. **Acceptable means:** In addition to the traditional means of serving the defendant in hand, various forms of ''substituted service'' meet the reasonableness standard. Examples of substituted service include service by first-class or certified mail, service on the secretary of state with instructions to deliver it to the defendant, or service to an adult at the defendant's usual place of residence. Courts have begun to experiment with the idea of service by email or other electronic means.

3. **Service by publication:** In some cases, notice of the pendency of a lawsuit is published in the newspaper, typically in fine print.

   a. *In rem* **cases:** Several early cases, including *Pennoyer*, held that service by publication alone was sufficient in *in rem* actions. ***Mullane rejects this old rule*** and holds that when the addresses of the property owners can be ascertained, some other method of service that is more likely to reach the defendants is required.

   b. **When publication alone is sufficient:** However, if the wherabouts of the defendant is not known and cannot be ascertained with reasonable effort, service by publication is the only viable option. In these cases, service by publication is acceptable in both *in rem* and *in personam* actions.

E. **How notice provided:** State and federal courts allow for various methods of service.

   1. **Who serves:** The court itself does not serve process. In addition, service need not be effected by the sheriff or other official except in certain rare cases. Court rules typically allow service by a private process server or the party's attorney. However, the party itself usually cannot serve.

   2. **Methods of service — state court:** States typically have two sets of service rules: those pertaining to defendants who can be found within the borders of the state, and a long-arm statute that allows service on an out-of-state defendant.

      a. **Defendant in state:** States allow for a variety of service methods. Most allow for service in hand and on an agent of the defendant designated to receive service.

      b. **Defendant out of state:** Service on an out-of-state defendant is accomplished by means of the state's ***long-arm statute***. These statutes are a response to the Supreme Court's decisions in *International Shoe* and later cases, which made it clear that a defendant can be sued in a state as long as contacts exist. Generally speaking, these statutes are divided into two classes.

         i. **Specific cases:** Most statutes allow for service on an out-of-state defendant only in situations specifically enumerated in the statute itself. The listed situations usually represent an attempt to codify those situations where the Supreme Court has held that an out-of-state defendant can be sued.

         ★   **Example:** In Gibbons v. Brown, 716 So. 2d 868 (Fla. Dist. Ct. App. 1998), the court analyzed the Florida long-arm statute, which enumerates specific instances in which service on an out-of-state defendant is allowed. The court held that the defendant was not ''engaged'' in activity in the state within the meaning of that statute.

    ii.   **To limits of Constitution:** A few statutes forgo the difficulties of specifying when service will be constitutional and simply state that service is allowed ***whenever the state can exercise personal jurisdiction*** over the defendant consistent with the Due Process Clause. Some states have specific statutes but interpret those to extend to the full limits of the Constitution.

3. Service in federal court: The Federal Rules of Civil Procedure specify the means that can be used to serve process. In addition, another provision of these rules narrows the reach of a federal court's personal jurisdiction in most cases so that it mirrors the personal jurisdiction of the state in which the court sits.

   a. Methods: ***Fed. R. Civ. P. 4(e)-(j)*** specify the acceptable means of service in federal court.

      i.   **Defendants within United States:** For ***defendants within the United States***, service can be made by serving ***in hand***, leaving process at the defendant's ***usual place of abode*** with someone of ***suitable age and discretion*** who also resides there, serving on an ***agent*** authorized by contractual arrangement or law to receive service of process, or serving according to any method authorized by either the ***state in which the district court sits*** or the ***state where service takes place.*** Fed. R. Civ. P. 4(e).

      ii.   **Corporations within the United States:** For ***corporations and associations within the United States***, service can also be made by delivering process to a ***managing or general agent***.

      iii.   **Special defendants:** The Federal Rules of Civil Procedure contain special service rules for ***infants and incompetents***, ***defendants in foreign nations***, and suits against the ***government or government agencies or officials***.

      iv.   ***In rem* actions:** A federal court may exercise jurisdiction based on seizure of property only when a federal statute provides for such jurisdiction or when plaintiff cannot obtain *in personam* jurisdiction over the defendant by reasonable means in that district. Fed. R. Civ. P. 4(n). Because *Shaffer* (discussed above) allows *in rem* only when there are enough contacts to exercise *in personam*, Fed. R. Civ. P. 4(n) greatly limits the use of *in rem* jurisdiction in federal courts.

   b. Territorial limits: The Supreme Court's minimum contacts analysis was developed for ***state courts***, not federal. Arguably, a federal court could exercise personal jurisdiction over a defendant whenever there are minimum contacts with the United States as a whole. However, in most cases, the Federal Rules of Civil Procedure significantly limit this potential jurisdiction and require a federal court to act like a court of the state in which the federal court sits.

      i.   **General rule:** ***Fed. R. Civ. P. 4(k)(1)(A)*** provides that service of process using any of the methods described in a.i to a.iii above is effective to establish jurisdiction over a defendant only if the defendant "could be subjected to the jurisdiction of a court of general jurisdiction in the state in which the district court is located."

         (a)   To apply this test, it is necessary to consider both whether there are ***minimum contacts*** with the state and whether state law provides a means of ***serving the defendant***.

(b) However, although it is necessary to consider state service laws in determining whether a federal court may exercise personal jurisdiction, the plaintiff in federal court does not necessarily use the state law methods to effect service. Plaintiff instead *uses the methods set out in the Federal Rules of Civil Procedure*. Of course, the Federal Rules of Civil Procedure also allow the plaintiff to "borrow" state law service rules.

> **Example:** *P* sues *D* in a federal district court in Oklahoma. *P* serves *D* at *D*'s home in South Dakota by leaving the process with *D*'s spouse. Because there are minimum contacts between *D* and Oklahoma, an Oklahoma state court could exercise personal jurisdiction over the defendant. To obtain such jurisdiction, however, a plaintiff would have to use the Oklahoma long-arm statute, which requires the plaintiff to send process to the defendant by certified mail. The federal court has personal jurisdiction over the defendant. Even though an Oklahoma state court could use only the state service methods, a federal court can use the "abode" service provided for in Rule 4(e).

ii.   Exceptions: In some cases, a federal court is not confined by the territorial limits on jurisdiction that apply to the states.

(a) Impleader and involuntary plaintiffs: Service on *third-party defendants* joined under Rule 14 and *involuntary plaintiffs* joined under Rule 19 is proper either if it meets the state territorial rule set out above or if the party is served anywhere in the United States within 100 miles of the *court issuing the summons*. Fed. R. Civ. P. 4(k)(1)(B).

(b) Statutory interpleader: A party joined to a statutory interpleader action may be served *anywhere in the United States* under 28 U.S.C. §1335. Fed. R. Civ. P. 4(k)(1)(C).

(c) Federal statute: Service is effective to create jurisdiction whenever authorized by a specific federal statute. Fed. R. Civ. P. 4(k)(1)(D).

(d) No state court has personal jurisdiction: If no state court could exercise jurisdiction over the defendant, service is effective if the claim *arises under federal law* and if the exercise of jurisdiction would comply with any limits imposed by the U.S. Constitution. Fed. R. Civ. P. 4(k)(2). In this case, a federal court may exercise jurisdiction as long as the minimum contacts/fairness test is met with regards to the United States as a whole, not merely with respect to the state where the federal court sits.

c. Waiver of service: *Fed. R. Civ. P. 4(d)* also allows a plaintiff to ask the defendant to waive service. Waiver is an *alternative* to actual service.

i.   Request for waiver: A plaintiff may ask a defendant to waive by *mailing* a *written request for waiver*, coupled with a copy of the *complaint* and a *prepaid means of return*.

(a) Invalid request: A request for waiver may not be used when the defendant is an *infant, incompetent, or governmental unit or officer*.

(b) Date requirement: The request must specify a date by which it must be returned, which cannot be less than 30 days from the date it was sent for defendants within the United States or less than 60 days for defendants outside the United States.

ii. **How waiver effected:** The defendant waives service by returning the request by the specified deadline. Failure to return the request does not constitute a waiver.

iii. **Effect of waiver:** A party who returns the request waives only the requirement of formal service. The party does ***not waive*** any defenses based on lack of ***personal jurisdiction*** or ***venue***. Therefore, a defendant may argue lack of minimum contacts even if it waives service.

iv. **Failure to waive:** A defendant is ***not required*** to waive. However, the rule provides both a carrot and a stick to encourage waiver.

   (a) **Carrot:** A defendant who waives service receives an automatic extension of the time to answer. Rather than the usual 20 days, the defendant has 60 days following the day the request was ***sent*** in order to answer. If the request was sent to an address outside the United States, the time for answering is extended to 90 days. Fed. R. Civ. P. 4(d)(3).

   (b) **Stick:** The Rule also provides that a defendant is under a ''duty'' to avoid unnecessary service costs. If defendant is located within the United States, failure to return the request results in an order requiring the defendant to ***reimburse plaintiff for the costs of actual service***, unless there was good cause for the failure. It is not clear whether lack of personal jurisdiction constitutes good cause.

Quiz Yourself on *NOTICE*

7. Pamela sues Don in a Dakota state court. Dakota law explicitly provides for service of process by first-class mail. Pamela mails the summons and complaint to Don in full compliance with this Dakota law. However, unbeknownst to Pamela, the Postal Service loses the letter, and Don does not receive it. When Don fails to answer, Pamela obtains a default judgment against Don. Is the default judgment valid? _____

8. Same facts as Problem 7, except that Pamela brings her case in a federal court situated in the state of Dakota. _____

9. Nine-year-old Jeremy is a latchkey kid who goes home after school and stays by himself until his parents get home from work. One afternoon, the doorbell rings. When Jeremy answers, a man gives Jeremy a package and tells him to give it to his dad because his dad needs to come to court. Jeremy is scared and hides the package; he does not want his dad to go to court because that is where they put people in jail. A judgment is entered against Jeremy's dad because he never showed. Is Jeremy's dad bound by the judgment? _____

10. Robert receives a request for waiver and a copy of the complaint with a prepaid envelope for return service. Robert, a citizen of the United States, is unsure whether to waive service. He has 30 days to

decide. What are Robert's options? If Robert waives, is he consenting to the court's jurisdiction over him? _____

Answers

7. Don is bound by the judgment because the notice was reasonably calculated to reach him. First-class mail generally makes it to the recipient. That he did not actually receive notice, through no fault of Pamela, does not mean that the service was not designed to reach him.

    Note, however, that Don will almost certainly be able to reopen the judgment based on the lack of notice. But until he reopens, the judgment is valid and enforceable.

8. The judgment is valid. Unlike Dakota state rules, the Federal Rules of Civil Procedure do not explicitly authorize service by first-class mail (the Rules allow a request for waiver of service to be sent by first-class mail, but that is different than actual service of the summons and complaint). However, Fed. R. Civ. P. 4(e) also allows a federal court to serve an individual using any method authorized by the law of the state in which the federal court sits. Because Dakota law allows for service by first-class mail, the federal court may also use that method.

9. Again, service need not actually reach a defendant to be valid. However, in this case the method of service does not comply with the Federal Rules of Civil Procedure. Fed. R. Civ. P. 4(e) specifies that service is proper when the process is left at the defendant's home with someone of suitable age and discretion who also resides there. Jeremy is not of suitable age. Therefore, service is improper, and Jeremy's dad is not bound by the judgment.

10. It is definitely to Robert's advantage to waive, even though technically he is not required to waive. If Robert waives service of process, he gains an extra 40 days to answer the complaint (60 days versus 20 days — see Fed. R. Civ. P. 4(d)(3)). Unless there is a good cause for failure to waive, Robert would be ordered to reimburse the plaintiff for the costs of actual service.

    If Robert returns the waiver request, he is not consenting to the court's jurisdiction but merely to the formal service requirement. He is not waiving any defenses based on lack of jurisdiction.

V. CHALLENGES TO PERSONAL JURISDICTION

Personal jurisdiction is a ***personal defense*** that can be waived by inaction or by taking acts inconsistent with the defense. Courts traditionally were very strict concerning how the defense could be raised. The approach set out in the Federal Rules of Civil Procedure relaxes the rules somewhat.

   A. **Traditional approach:** Under the traditional approach, defending yourself in any fashion waived any personal jurisdiction defense, as it was deemed tantamount to an admission that the court had jurisdiction to decide the matter.

       1. **Default and collateral attack:** Therefore, defendant's only option was simply to ***do nothing*** in the action. If defendant never appears in an action, the court will enter a ***default judgment*** against the defendant. Defendant could challenge jurisdiction if plaintiff attempted to enforce that default judgment elsewhere, arguing that the default judgment was invalid because the

court that issued it lacked personal jurisdiction. This method is called a ***collateral attack*** and was the method of attack used by Neff in Pennoyer v. Neff.

2. **Dangers:** This method of challenge is risky. First, if the defendant appeared in any way in the initial action, she was deemed to have waived personal jurisdiction, thereby making collateral attack impossible. Second, the only issue that the defendant could raise in the second action was ***the first court's lack of personal jurisdiction***. If the defendant lost on the jurisdictional question, she could not litigate the merits of the case but would instead be bound by the default judgment.

B. **Special appearance:** Many states ameliorated the harshness of the collateral attack approach by allowing the defendant to make a ***special appearance***. A special appearance is one where the defendant is allowed to appear and ***argue only lack of personal jurisdiction***. Some states still use this method to deal with challenges.

1. **Limit:** The defendant making a special appearance is limited to arguing the question of jurisdiction. A defendant who raises any other defenses or issues is deemed to have made a ***general appearance*** and thereby waives the jurisdictional defense.

2. **Options after jurisdiction challenge fails:** A defendant who ***loses*** on the jurisdictional question has two options. He can proceed to defend the case on the merits, which means that he has conceded the jurisdictional question. Or, he can take no further action in the case, allow the court to enter judgment against him, and ***appeal*** the ruling on the jurisdictional question. Under this second avenue, however, the defendant runs the same risk as under the strict traditional rule. If the defendant loses on the jurisdictional question on appeal, he cannot reopen the merits of the case.

C. **Federal approach:** Most jurisdictions today follow the approach of ***Fed. R. Civ. P. 12(g) and (h)***, or something close to it, when dealing with jurisdictional challenges.

1. **Time limits:** Fed. R. Civ. P. 12 sets strict time limits on objecting to personal jurisdiction. A party must raise the objection no later than the answer, and even earlier in some cases.

   a. **If pre-answer motion filed:** The Federal Rules allow a party to raise certain defenses in a pre-answer motion. If a party files a pre-answer motion ***raising any Fed. R. Civ. P. 12 defense or objection***, he must also include any objections to personal jurisdiction in that motion. If he does not, the objection is lost. Fed. R. Civ. P. 12(g).

      i. **Rule 12 objections:** Note that a pre-answer motion can result in a waiver under Fed. R. Civ. P. 12(g) if it raises a defense or objection listed in ***any subsection of Fed. R. Civ. P. 12***, not only the items listed in Fed. R. Civ. P. 12(b). Therefore, for example, if defendant files a pre-answer motion to strike (Fed. R. Civ. P. 12(f)), he must include any defenses based on personal jurisdiction and service, or those defenses are waived.

      ii. **Non-Rule 12 objections:** However, there are also objections that a party may make prior to the answer that do not involve Fed. R. Civ. P. 12. For example, a party need not include the personal jurisdiction objection in a motion to disqualify a judge for bias.

   b. **If no pre-answer motion:** If the defendant does not file a pre-answer motion based on Rule 12, he must object to personal jurisdiction in the ***answer*** or in an ***amendment as of right to the answer***.

Example: *P* sues *D*. *D* files a pre-answer motion claiming that *P*'s complaint fails to state a claim on which relief can be granted. That request is denied. *D* then files an answer that challenges personal jurisdiction. *D* will be deemed to have waived her personal jurisdiction challenge. Failure to include the defense in the pre-answer motion prevents defendant from raising the defense, either in the answer or by another motion. Fed. R. Civ. P. 12(g).

Example: *P* sues *D*. *D* brings no pre-answer motions. *D* files a timely answer but forgets to include the defense of lack of personal jurisdiction. The time period for amending the answer as of right (see Fed. R. Civ. P. 15(a)) has expired. *D* has waived his personal jurisdiction challenge. Fed. R. Civ. P. 12(h)(1).

2. **Special appearance compared:** Although the pre-answer motion authorized by Rule 12 bears some facial resemblance to the special appearance rule, there are some important differences.

   a. **Not limited to jurisdiction:** A defendant may include in his pre-answer motion any and all defenses listed in Rule 12. Thus, the defendant may argue both that the court lacks jurisdiction and that the plaintiff's claim is not supported by any legal theory.

   b. **Ability to litigate merits:** If defendant loses her challenge to jurisdiction, she may proceed to litigate the case on the merits and still raise the jurisdictional issue (along with any other objections) on appeal.

3. **Waiver by inconsistent action:** A party may waive personal jurisdiction even without filing a motion governed by Fed. R. Civ. P. 12(g). If the party takes any action in the case inconsistent with the court's lack of personal jurisdiction, he will lose his right to object to jurisdiction.

Quiz Yourself on
PERSONAL JURISDICTION

11. Batman, a citizen of New York, has grown tired of all the dastardly deeds that his enemies have committed against him over the years. Batman therefore sues Joker, a citizen of Ohio, and Penguin, a citizen of Kentucky, in an Ohio state court. Penguin moves to sever Batman's claim against him from the claim against Joker, arguing that it is prejudicial to try them together. The court denies the motion. Penguin then moves to dismiss the claim against him for lack of personal jurisdiction. Penguin has incontrovertible proof that he has never been to Ohio and that all his dealings with Batman and Joker took place in New York. Is Penguin likely to succeed on his motion to dismiss?

12. Same facts as Problem 11, except that Batman sues only Joker. Batman files his case in a federal district court in Cincinnati, Ohio. Joker joins Penguin to the case under Fed. R. Civ. P. 14. Joker obtains a summons from the federal courthouse in Cincinnati and hires a private process server to serve process. The process server serves the summons and a copy of the third-party complaint on Penguin at his home in Covington, Kentucky. Even though his house is considerably closer to Cincinnati (less than ten miles) than it is to the closest federal courthouse in Kentucky, Penguin files a timely motion to

dismiss the case for lack of personal jurisdiction and for improper service of process. Will the court grant the motion? _____

13. Rick, a citizen of California, is a billionaire real estate developer. Rick does most of his business on the West Coast. However, Rick also owns a rustic hunting cabin in Wyoming and decides to look into developing land in that state. Rick signs a contract to purchase a large plot of land in Wyoming. Jennifer, a citizen of Wyoming, is the real estate agent on this contract. Rick later refuses to go through with the contract.

Jennifer sues Rick for the lost real estate commission. Because a Wyoming jury would be more sympathetic to the plight of a local citizen, she brings the action in a Wyoming state court. Jennifer does not serve Rick personally but instead uses *in rem* jurisdiction by seizing Rick's hunting cabin. Rick files a timely motion to dismiss for lack of personal jurisdiction. May Wyoming exercise *in rem* jurisdiction in this case? What are the limitations on suing Rick *in rem* as compared to *in personam*? _____

14. Sarah is a graduate student at the University of Minnesota. Sarah decides to travel by bus to her home in Atlanta, Georgia, for the holiday break. The bus travels to Nashville, Tennessee, and then takes Interstate 24 to Atlanta.

Although Tennessee borders Georgia, Interstate 24 does not travel in a straight line. Instead, it actually dips down into Alabama for a mile or two. Sarah has not looked at a map and has no idea the bus enters Alabama. Moreover, although there are signs along the road advising people of this fact, Sarah's bus passes through this area at night, when the signs are not obvious to passengers on a bus.

Just after the bus enters Alabama, another passenger on the bus gets up and serves Sarah with process in an Alabama state court action. The claim arises out of an automobile accident that Sarah had with a North Dakota resident in Minnesota. Because Sarah has no other contacts with Alabama, she files a timely challenge to personal jurisdiction. Will she prevail? _____

Answers

11. **Timeliness:** Penguin's motion is timely notwithstanding his prior motion. The issue raised in the earlier pre-answer motion (severance) is not a defense listed in Fed. R. Civ. P. 12. Therefore, the waiver rules of Fed. R. Civ. P. 12(g) do not bar this motion.

    Merits: Penguin will succeed on his motion. There are insufficient contacts between Penguin and Ohio. The facts state that he has never been there, and the case involves Penguin's exploits that occurred in New York. Any other contacts that might exist would be unrelated to the claim and would therefore be insufficient to sustain personal jurisdiction.

12. The facts specify that the motion to dismiss is timely, so there is no need to discuss Fed. R. Civ. P. 12. Nevertheless, Penguin will lose the motion to dismiss.

    First, service is proper. Fed. R. Civ. P. 4(c)(2) allows a party to hire a process server to serve process. There is no indication that the process server is under 18 years of age. In addition, Fed. R. Civ. P. 4(e)(2) explicitly allows service on a defendant personally. (Although the rule also mentions leaving process with *someone else* at the person's usual place of abode, that is merely another option. Nothing prevents service on the defendant personally at the place of abode.)

    Also, no constitutional problems are evident. Admittedly, in most cases, service from a federal court is effective to create personal jurisdiction over a party only if a state court of that state could exercise jurisdiction. And as discussed in Problem 1, an Ohio state court could not exercise jurisdiction.

However, Fed. R. Civ. P. 4(k)(2)(B) provides that for a claim against a party joined under Fed. R. Civ. P. 14, service is also effective to establish jurisdiction if the service occurs anywhere within 100 miles of the federal courthouse — even if the location of service is in another state. The facts specify that Penguin was served within ten miles of the courthouse in Cincinnati.

Is it constitutional for a federal court in Ohio to exercise personal jurisdiction over a defendant if that defendant has no minimum contacts with Ohio? The answer is probably yes. When federal courts are involved, due process requires only that there be minimum contacts between the defendant and the United States as a whole. There are clearly contacts between Penguin and the United States.

13. Jennifer can use *in rem* jurisdiction here. Admittedly, Shaffer v. Heitner places significant restrictions on the use of *in rem* jurisdiction. If the property is the only contact, *in rem* is proper only if the claim arises out of the property. The claim here clearly does not arise out of the property because it involves unrelated land.

    In this situation, however, the **land is not the only contact** between Rick and Wyoming. Rick entered into a contract to buy land in Wyoming. A Wyoming citizen was the real estate agent. Therefore, the contract, which involved Wyoming land and would affect the Wyoming agent, is a purposeful contact. And the claim clearly arises out of this contact. Because the contract alone establishes minimum contacts with Wyoming, a plaintiff suing in Wyoming may use either *in personam* or *in rem* jurisdiction.

    The fairness factors do not change this result. The burden on the defendant is not great, especially given that he owns a home there. Wyoming has an interest in this case because the subject matter and plaintiff are in Wyoming. Plaintiff has an interest in suing in her home state. In terms of efficiency, it might be more efficient to try this case in Wyoming. And because there is no indication that California and Wyoming law differ to any appreciable extent, the last fairness factor does not really apply in this case.

    A judgment *in rem* is limited to the value of the property. Because the rustic hunting cabin may be worth far less than the real estate commission owed, Jennifer will not recover all she is owed (assuming she prevails). In addition, even if she should sue Rick in a later *in personam* action, the factual findings in the first case would not bind Rick in the later case. A judgment *in personam*, by contrast, binds the defendant personally, allowing the plaintiff to seize and have sold nonexempt assets owned by the defendant in the forum in order to satisfy the judgment.

14. It is impossible to state for certain whether Sarah will win or lose this case. The problem involves service on a defendant while physically present in a state. *Burnham* is therefore the closest precedent. Although all of the justices in *Burnham* agreed that the in-state service was sufficient in that case, there were two competing theories, neither of which commanded a majority. Under Justice Scalia's theory, presence automatically complies with due process. If this theory represents the rule, Sarah is subject to jurisdiction. Under Justice Brennan's theory, presence qualifies as a contact for purposes of the minimum contacts test. Unlike in *Burnham*, however, it is difficult to call Sarah's presence in Alabama voluntary. Even though she is deriving protection from Alabama law, she did not realize that she was in the state and did not arrange her bus ride with the knowledge that she would be there. If the contact was not purposeful, it does not count.

    With respect to fairness, the fairness factors are not relevant to Scalia's approach. His view is that jurisdiction over a defendant served in the state always satisfies due process and is not subject to the minimum contacts test. Under Brennan's view, the fairness factors are relevant. Application of the factors here further reinforces the conclusion that jurisdiction is not proper under Brennan's view. Because neither the plaintiff nor the accident were in Alabama, that state has no real interest in being the forum. Nor does the plaintiff have any real interest in Alabama. Although the burden on the defendant is not great, Alabama is not an efficient place to hear the dispute.

 Exam Tips on
PERSONAL JURISDICTION

☞ Be sure to remember that the personal jurisdiction question has two parts. Not only must the exercise of jurisdiction meet the requirements of due process, but a rule or statute must also authorize ***service***. Because the classroom discussion tends to emphasize the constitutional issues, students often overlook the question of service.

☞ Your casebook traces the development of the personal jurisdiction test over time. On the test, however, apply only the test as it exists today.

☞ When evaluating whether minimum contacts exist, keep certain basic notions in mind.

  ☞ First, be sure to determine whether the defendant's contacts with the forum are ***purposeful***. If not, the connection does not count as a contact.

  ☞ In addition, carefully analyze whether the claim being brought ***arises out of*** the contact. If so, then jurisdiction is quite likely. If not, then jurisdiction exists only if there is a long-term connection sufficient to give rise to ***general jurisdiction***.

   ☞ However, be careful before concluding that a forum can exercise general jurisdiction over a party. Unless the forum is the party's residence (or, in the case of a corporation, its state of incorporation or perhaps principal place of business), general jurisdiction is not common.

☞ Notwithstanding some careless statements to the contrary, *Shaffer* does not get rid of ***in rem*** jurisdiction. It merely limits the use of *in rem* when the property is the only, or the primary, contact with the forum. If the suit arises out of the property (e.g., a quiet title action), the property alone is probably a sufficient contact.

☞ In certain situations, most notably the ***stream of commerce*** and ***service while present*** cases, the Supreme Court offers no clear majority view. In these situations, save yourself some time by focusing on the test that makes it more difficult to reach the position you want to assert. If you satisfy the more difficult test, you certainly will meet the more lenient one. Therefore, after discussing the more difficult test, your answer can discuss the more lenient test quickly.

☞ Do not forget to discuss the five ***fairness factors*** in the constitutional analysis. Although those factors make a difference only in a very few cases (such as *Asahi*), you nevertheless need to mention them in your analysis.

☞ Remember that there are certain situations, including consent and possibly service on an in-state defendant, that are not governed by the minimum contacts test.

☞ Have a solid grasp on the somewhat detailed service provisions, including the waiver of service option. Because service is relatively straightforward, knowing the rules well can earn you significant credit on the examination.

☛ Remember that service in a ***federal proceeding*** requires reference to state law. A federal court either can use the methods listed in Rule 4 or can borrow state law methods. In addition, in most cases, service in a federal proceeding creates personal jurisdiction only if the state courts could exercise personal jurisdiction over that defendant.

☛ If the exam question includes a novel method of service, consider whether that method meets the constitutional requirements set out in *Mullane*.

☛ Finally, be sure to consider whether the challenge to personal jurisdiction is timely. A party must challenge personal jurisdiction very early in the proceeding and can easily waive the defense by taking other actions in the suit.

CHAPTER 3

VENUE

ChapterScope ━━

This chapter deals with venue, the second of the three main issues that arise in determining which court may hear a lawsuit.

- ■ Like personal jurisdiction, venue considers convenience to the parties. However, venue restrictions come from statutes, not from the U.S. Constitution.

- ■ While venue is also a factor in state courts, this chapter focuses on *federal* venue. The rules governing state venue often differ significantly from those that apply in federal court.

- ■ The chapter also covers the doctrine of *forum non conveniens*, pursuant to which a court will refuse to hear a case even though the court has venue.

- ■ A case filed in a proper venue may be *transferred* to another court of the same sovereign. Transfer is also possible from an improper venue to a proper one.

I. BASIC PRINCIPLES OF VENUE

Venue is the place the legislature requires a particular action to be brought.

A. Both state and federal: Venue is a consideration in both state and federal courts.

B. Statutes control: Venue is primarily a creature of statute. Although state and federal venue statutes differ significantly, all tend to focus in one way or another on locating the ***most convenient place*** for litigating the case.

C. Not constitutional: The concept of venue is ***not required by the Constitution***. Therefore, a judgment issued by a court lacking venue is valid and enforceable.

II. STATE VENUE

State venue rules require an action to be filed in one or more county, district, or parish courts. The statutes look to a variety of factors, such as where the ***cause of action arose***, where ***defendant resides***, where ***defendant conducts business***, where ***plaintiff resides***, and, in a suit involving real property, where the ***property is located***.

III. FEDERAL VENUE

The primary federal venue statute is ***28 U.S.C. §1391***. There are also other statutes that specify venue in certain specific cases, but these are not covered in this chapter.

A. Overview of §1391

1. **Venue defined by district:** Unlike personal jurisdiction, venue in the federal courts is defined by *district*, not by state. While some states have only a single federal district (e.g., Minnesota), most have two or more.

2. **Plaintiff may choose:** In many cases, §1391 makes more than one district a proper venue. In these cases, plaintiff may freely choose the district in which she will file suit. However, plaintiff may choose a district only if that district also has ***personal jurisdiction*** over all defendants in the case.

3. **Venue in diversity cases:** In cases where subject matter jurisdiction is ***based solely on diversity***, venue is proper in *any* of the following districts:

   a. any district in which a ***defendant resides, if all defendants reside in the same state*** (§1391(a)(1));

   b. any district in which a "***substantial portion*** of the events or omissions giving rise to the claim occurred" (§1391(a)(2)); and

   c. ***if there is no other option***, any district in which ***any defendant is subject to personal jurisdiction*** at the time the action is commenced (§1391(a)(3)). Note that unlike §1391(a)(1), under this "safety valve" provision only a ***single defendant*** needs to be subject to personal jurisdiction.

4. **Venue in federal question, "combined," and supplemental jurisdiction cases:** In cases where jurisdiction is ***not based solely on diversity***, venue is proper in *any* of the following districts:

   a. any district in which a ***defendant resides***, if all defendants reside in the same state (§1391(b)(1));

   b. any district in which a "***substantial portion*** of the events or omissions giving rise to the claim occurred" (§1391(b)(2)); and

   c. ***if there is no other option***, any district in which ***any defendant may be found*** (§1391(b)(3)). Like under §1391(a)(3), only a single defendant need be found in the state.

5. **Interpreting §1391(a) and (b):** Because §1391(a) and (b) are almost identical, the same interpretive rules generally apply to both.

   a. **No real difference:** The only substantive difference in the two subsections relates to the "safety valve" found in the third subsection of each provision. However, most courts have interpreted the phrase "may be found" in §1391(b)(3) to mean "is subject to personal jurisdiction," even if personal jurisdiction is pursuant to a long-arm statute. Therefore, §1391(a) and (b) are identical for all intents and purposes.

   b. **Multiple defendants:** Both §1391(a)(1) and (b)(1) allow for venue where ***any defendant resides, if all defendants reside in the same state***.

      i.   **Residence, not domicile:** The venue statute considers the defendants' residence, not domicile. Although similar, residence and domicile are distinct concepts. Residence is where a person ***actually resides***, even if that is a temporary home. A party's residence is determined at the time the action is commenced against that party.

ii. **Defendants in more than one state:** Note that §1391(a)(1) and (b)(1) apply only if *every defendant lives in the same state*. If even one defendant lives in a different state, venue cannot be determined by the defendants' residence.

iii. **All defendants in same multidistrict state:** However, if all defendants do reside in the same state, any district where at least one defendant resides is proper.

Example: *P* sues four *D*s, alleging federal questions against all four. Two of the *D*s reside in the Southern District of California. The third *D* resides in the Northern District of California, while the final *D* resides in the Eastern District of that state. *P* is free to sue the *D*s in the Northern, Eastern, or Southern Districts of California, but not in the Central.

c. **Substantial portion of events or omissions:** Section 1391(a)(2) and (b)(2) both allow venue where a substantial portion of the events or omissions occurred.

i. **Pre-1990 language:** Section 1391 was reworked in 1990. The prior version allowed venue wherever "the cause of action arose." In most cases, the cause of action was deemed to arise in a single state. The current language is significantly broader. In fact, it is often the case that several districts will meet the "substantial portion" test and therefore be proper venues.

ii. **Relevant vs. irrelevant events or omissions:** Events or omissions are "substantial" only if they are relevant to the plaintiff's claim.

Example: *P* is injured in the Southern District of Ohio when the brakes on his automobile fail to operate. *P*'s car was designed in the Eastern District of Michigan and manufactured in the Middle District of Tennessee. *P* also had the brakes serviced in the Western District of Oklahoma. *P* sues both the manufacturer and the repair shop, alleging negligence either in the manufacture of the car or in the repair. The Southern District of Ohio, Middle District of Tennessee, and Western District of Oklahoma are proper venues. The Eastern District of Michigan is not a district where a substantial portion of the events or omissions occurred because *P*'s claim does not relate to the design of the automobile.

6. **Corporate defendants:** *Section 1391(c)* provides that a corporate defendant "shall be deemed to reside in any judicial district in which it is subject to ***personal jurisdiction*** at the time the action is commenced." Section 1391(c) is not a separate venue provision for corporations, but rather a provision that defines where a corporation resides for purposes of §1391(a)(1) and (b)(1).

a. **Application in single district states:** In a state with only one federal judicial district, §1391(c) causes the personal jurisdiction and venue analyses to dovetail. If a corporation is subject to personal jurisdiction in a state, venue is also proper in the federal district for that state under §1391(a)(1) or (b)(1).

b. **Application in multidistrict states:** Personal jurisdiction does not necessarily equate to venue in a state with two or more districts. In these situations, §1391(c) *treats each district as a separate state* and provides that a corporation is deemed to reside in that district only if it has ***minimum contacts with that district***.

i. **No single district with contacts:** If no single district has sufficient contacts, but there are sufficient contacts with the state as a whole, the district with the ***most significant contacts*** is deemed to be the district where the corporation resides.

ii. **State of incorporation:** A corporation can always be sued in ***any district*** in its state of incorporation. If the state of incorporation has more than one district, the corporation has sufficient contacts with *all* of those districts, regardless of whether the corporation does any business anywhere in the state.

> **Example:** *P* plans to sue XYZ Corporation for wrongful discharge under state law. XYZ was chartered under the laws of Georgia, and the office where *P* worked was in Nashville, Tennessee (Middle District of Tennessee). Venue is proper under §1391(a)(1) and (b)(1) in the Middle District of Tennessee and in any of the three districts in Georgia.

7. **Aliens:** Section 1391(d) provides that an alien may be sued ***in any district***.

★   a. **Need personal jurisdiction:** As a practical matter, an alien cannot be sued in any district. The court must also have ***personal jurisdiction*** over the alien defendant. See Dee-K Enterprises, Inc. v. Heveafil Sdn. Bhd., 982 F. Supp. 1138 (E.D. Va. 1997) (although venue is proper over alien corporation in any district, personal jurisdiction still required).

b. **Multidistrict states:** If a multidistrict state has personal jurisdiction over an alien defendant, the ***alien can be sued in every district*** in that state.

c. **Case involving alien and citizens:** If a plaintiff sues both an alien and a citizen of the United States, courts interpret §1391(d) to mean that the ***alien is deemed to reside in every district*** in the United States. Thus, venue would be proper under §1391(a)(1) or (b)(1) where the United States citizen resides.

> **Example:** *P* sues *D1*, a U.S. citizen who resides in the District of Connecticut, and *D2*, an alien who resides in the District of New Hampshire. Venue is proper in the District of Connecticut because all *D*s are deemed to reside there. Of course, venue would also be proper where a substantial portion of the events or omissions giving rise to the cause of action occurred.

B. **Local action exception:** All of the above provisions are subject to an important exception that applies in cases involving real property. If the case is a "local action," it may ***only*** be brought in the ***district where the real property is situated***. This exception is not explicitly set out in §1391 but is the result of ***case law***.

1. *Local action* **defined:** Although all local actions involve real property, not all suits involving real property are local actions. Local actions are those that ***determine or affect the title to property*** or involve **physical harm** to real property.

2. **Overrides regular venue statute:** Note that in a local action, the district where the property is located is the ***only proper venue***. Section 1391 is ignored in these cases. The residence of the parties is irrelevant.

3. **State venue:** A number of states have abolished the local action rule by statute or judicial decision.

C. **Removal exception:** If a case is properly removed from state court to federal court, ***venue*** is ***automatically satisfied*** in that district, even if it would not otherwise satisfy §1391. See Chapter 4, Part VI.E.

Quiz Yourself on
APPLYING THE FEDERAL VENUE STATUTES

15. Lon Moher recently bought a new riding mower, the Megamower 2100, from Yolanda's Yard Supply in Rockford, Illinois. However, the first time Lon used the mower, it flipped and caused him serious injury.

    Lon is planning to file a lawsuit against Cal Culater, the engineer who designed the mower, and Yolanda, the owner of Yolanda's Yard Supply. Lon will claim that a design defect caused by Cal led to the accident and that Yolanda is liable for selling him a defective product.

    Because Lon is a citizen of Wisconsin, and Cal and Yolanda are both citizens of Illinois, Lon can sue in federal court using diversity jurisdiction. However, Lon is unsure *which* federal districts can hear the case. Yolanda lives in the Northern District of Illinois. Cal lives in the Southern District of Illinois.

    Lon obviously prefers to bring suit in his hometown of La Crosse, Wisconsin, which is located in the Western District of Wisconsin. In the alternative, because he knows an excellent attorney in Peoria, Illinois, a city in the Central District of Illinois, Lon is not averse to suing in the Central District. List all the proper venues for Lon's case. _____

16. Same facts as Problem 15. However, instead of suing Cal, Lon decides to sue Yolanda and Megamower, Inc., the company that manufactured the mower. Megamower is a corporation chartered under the laws of Illinois. Its headquarters and all of its manufacturing facilities are located in the Southern District of Illinois. However, it distributes its products in all 50 states.

    Lon still prefers to bring suit in either the Western District of Wisconsin or the Central District of Illinois. On the other hand, because Megamower is subject to personal jurisdiction everywhere in the state of Florida, and because Yolanda takes a trip to Panama City Beach, Florida, every winter, Lon is considering bringing his case in the Northern District of Florida, which encompasses Panama City. List all proper venues for Lon's suit. _____

17. Same facts as Problem 15, except that the mower did not cause any harm to Lon. Instead, the design defect caused the mower to tear up Lon's precious yard, causing $100,000 in damage. Will this change in facts affect the determination of venue? _____

Answers

15. The proper venues are the Western District of Wisconsin and the Northern and Southern Districts of Illinois.

    The problem is governed by §1391(a) because jurisdiction is founded only on diversity. Under §1391(a)(1), jurisdiction is proper in any district in Illinois in which a defendant resides because all the defendants reside in the same state. Therefore, *either* the Northern or Southern District of Illinois is proper. However, the Central District is not proper because no defendant lives there.

    Under §1391(a)(2), venue is also proper where a substantial portion of the events or omissions that gave rise to the claim occurred. This again includes the two Illinois Districts, as well as the Western District of Wisconsin where the injury occurred.

    Section 1391(a)(3) is inapplicable because there is another district where the action can be heard.

16. In addition to the three districts listed in the prior problem, Lon could sue in the Central District of Illinois. Section 1391 again governs. However, it is necessary to determine where Megamower resides. Under §1391(c), Megamower is deemed to reside in any district in which it is subject to personal jurisdiction. Because it is chartered in Illinois, it is therefore subject to personal jurisdiction in all three districts in that state. Under §1391(a)(1), then, *any* of those three districts would be a proper venue.

   The Northern District of Florida is not a proper venue. Megamower is admittedly deemed to reside there by virtue of the fact of personal jurisdiction. However, §1391(c) applies only to corporations. Yolanda resides only in Illinois.

   Under §1391(a)(2), venue is, as in the prior problem, proper in the Northern and Southern Districts of Illinois, as well as the Western District of Wisconsin where the injury occurred.

   Section 1391(a)(3) does not apply.

17. Now only the Western District of Wisconsin is a proper venue. Damage to land is a *local action*, which can be heard only where the land is situated.

IV. CHALLENGES TO VENUE

Venue, like personal jurisdiction, is a ***personal defense*** that can be waived by inaction or by taking acts inconsistent with the defense.

   A. Time limits: ***Federal Rule of Civil Procedure 12*** sets strict time limits on objecting to improper venue. The rule is the same as the rule that applies to personal jurisdiction (see Chapter 2, Part V): A party must object to venue no later than the answer, and even earlier in some cases.

   Example: *P* sues *D*. *D* files a pre-answer motion requesting a jury trial, which the court grants. *D* then files a timely answer objecting to venue. The objection is timely. Although *D* did file a pre-answer motion, that motion did not raise any defenses or objections listed in Fed. R. Civ. P. 12(b) and therefore does not invoke the rule of Fed. R. Civ. P. 12(g).

   B. Waiver by inconsistent action: A party may waive venue even without filing a motion subject to Fed. R. Civ. P. 12(g). If the party takes any actions in the case inconsistent with the venue defense, she loses her right to object to venue. For example, several courts have held that a motion to transfer the case under ***28 U.S.C. §1404*** (see Part VI of this chapter) waives venue since that motion presupposes that the court is a proper venue.

V. *FORUM NON CONVENIENS*

Forum non conveniens is a **court-created doctrine** that allows a court to dismiss an action even though ***venue is proper***.

   A. Federal courts: *Forum non conveniens* usually does not apply in federal court. If plaintiff has chosen an inconvenient federal forum, the court can usually *transfer* the case under 28 U.S.C. §1404 (discussed below), a result that is far superior to dismissal. However, if the more convenient forum is a *foreign* court, federal courts will use *forum non conveniens*.

   B. Factors considered in the analysis: In order to dismiss based on *forum non conveniens*, the court must ascertain that there is an ***alternate forum available to hear the case***. If such a forum is available, the court will then consider certain *private* and *public* factors in determining whether the chosen forum is *grossly inconvenient*.

1. **Alternate forum:** The more convenient forum must have *subject matter and personal jurisdiction*.

   a. **Differences in remedy:** Sometimes plaintiff will not be able to obtain the same relief in the alternate court as he could obtain in the chosen forum. Courts differ on whether this fact should prevent dismissal. In the federal courts, differences in remedy bar dismissal only if they effectively deny plaintiff any rights in the alternate forum. Piper Aircraft v. Reyno, 454 U.S. 235 (1981).

   b. **Conditional dismissal:** A court that is considering whether to grant a *forum non conveniens* dismissal often cannot ascertain whether the alternate forum will hear the dispute. Lack of personal jurisdiction or expiration of the statute of limitations may prevent plaintiff from bringing her claim before the new court. To deal with these problems, courts often impose *conditions* on the dismissal. For example, the court may grant defendant's motion to dismiss only if defendant agrees not to challenge lack of personal jurisdiction in the new forum.

2. **Factors:** Courts consider different factors when deciding whether to grant a *forum non conveniens* dismissal. The factors considered in federal court are fairly typical.

   a. **Private factors:** Private factors are those related to the individual litigants, such as:

      i.   where the *underlying events occurred*;

      ii. where the *witnesses* and *physical evidence* are located;

      iii. the comparative overall *costs* of litigating in the two places;

      iv. whether it would be possible to *compel witnesses to testify* in the forum chosen by plaintiff (especially an issue when witnesses are located in other nations);

      v.   *language* issues; and

      vi. whether a judgment by the chosen court would be *enforceable* in the place *where defendant's assets are located*.

   b. **Public factors:** Public factors relate to the court system and include:

      i.   *choice of law questions*, including familiarity with and ease of determining the law that will govern the case;

      ii. the *policy implications* of the case in the more convenient forum;

      iii. the *backlog* in the court chosen by plaintiff;

      iv. the *burden* on the court system and on citizens who may be called upon to sit on a jury.

★   **Example:** The Supreme Court's decision in Piper Aircraft v. Reyno, 454 U.S. 235 (1981), is a good illustration of how these factors are applied. *Piper* involved a plane crash in Scotland. Plaintiffs, all residents of Scotland, sued the American manufacturers of the plane and the propeller in a U.S. court. The Supreme Court indicated that the lower court should have granted a *forum non conveniens* dismissal. Considering the private factors, the Court noted that the wreckage and other witnesses were in Scotland, making Scotland a more convenient place. For the public factors, the Court noted that Scots law would govern and that Scotland had the predominant concern with the dispute. That Scots law would make it more difficult for plaintiff to recover was held not to prevent dismissal.

    3. Discretion: A court has considerable *discretion* as to whether to dismiss an action based on *forum non conveniens*.

  C. Timing of *forum non conveniens* motion: There are no fixed time limits for moving for a *forum non conveniens* dismissal. As a general rule, however, the longer the case remains in the original court, the less likely it is that the court will dismiss.

VI. TRANSFER OF VENUE IN THE FEDERAL COURT SYSTEM

A case filed in one federal district can sometimes be transferred to a more convenient district. The governing statutes distinguish between transfers from a court *where both personal jurisdiction and venue are proper* and from a court where one or both of these is lacking.

  A. Overview of transfer: Transfer in the federal court system is governed by three statutes: *28 U.S.C. §§1404, 1406, and 1631*. Which statute applies depends on the circumstances of the particular case.

    1. Federal courts only: The transfer provisions *apply only in federal court*. State courts cannot use the federal law. In addition, a federal court may transfer the case only to *another federal court*, not to a state or foreign court. Although many states allow transfer of venue from one court within that state to a different court in that state, *nothing allows a state court to transfer a case to a federal court, a court of a different state, or a foreign court*. If a state court determines that an action could more conveniently be litigated in a different state or nation, its only option is a *forum non conveniens* dismissal.

    2. Transferee court must be proper: Although the transfer statutes allow transfer even when the original court lacks personal jurisdiction or venue, the *transferee* court must always be a court in which the case "could have been filed," i.e., where *both personal jurisdiction and venue are proper*.

  B. Transfers from a court with venue and personal jurisdiction — §1404: Section 1404 allows a court that has venue and personal jurisdiction to transfer a case to another federal district "[f]or the convenience of parties and witnesses, in the interest of justice...."

    1. Transferor court must be proper: Section 1404 applies only if the court hearing the case has both personal jurisdiction and venue. If either is lacking, the court must turn to §1406 or 1631.

    2. Who may move: Either party may seek a §1404 transfer. In a case involving multiple plaintiffs or defendants, *any one party* may move for transfer. The party requesting transfer has the burden of showing that the alternative forum is more convenient.

    3. No time limit: There is no time limit for making a motion under §1404. Such motions can be, and often are, granted well into the process of litigation as developments make it clear that another forum would be more convenient.

    4. Discretionary: Section 1404(a) does not require transfer. Instead, the *court has considerable discretion* as to whether to transfer the case.

5. Factors: Courts hearing a §1404(a) motion consider many of the same factors that enter into a *forum non conveniens* determination. These factors can also be grouped into *private* and *public* *factors*.

  a. Private factors: The private factors measure the interests of the litigants and include:

   i. the *convenience of the witnesses*, which many courts consider the most important factor;

   ii. the *convenience of the parties*;

   iii. *where the claim arose*;

   iv. the location of *physical evidence*, such as business records or real property; and

   v. in a case involving a contract, any *forum selection clause* in the contract will be considered as evidence of what the parties thought would be a convenient forum (Stewart Organization, Inc. v. Ricoh Corp., 487 U.S. 22 (1988)).

  b. Public factors: The public factors consider the interest of the court system:

   i. the comparative ease of *enforcing the judgment* in the transferor and transferee courts;

   ii. whether the judges in each district are likely to be *familiar with the governing law*;

   iii. any considerations of relative *judicial economy*; and

   iv. any *local interest* in deciding issues at home.

  c. Plaintiff's choice strongly considered: Courts emphasize that plaintiff's initial choice of forum is to be given considerable weight in the §1404 decision. Therefore, if the balance of factors is even relatively close, the court may well choose not to transfer.

6. Governing law: In a *diversity case*, a §1404 transfer *does not change the substantive law* that will be used to decide the dispute. Therefore, the transferee court will apply the same law that would have been applied by the transferor court. This rule applies regardless of which party moves for transfer. Thus, a plaintiff may select an inconvenient court to gain advantage of a favorable rule such as a longer statute of limitations and then move to transfer the case to a more convenient forum. Ferens v. John Deere Co., 494 U.S. 516 (1990).

C. Transfer from improper court: If the court currently hearing the case is lacking either personal jurisdiction or venue, transfer under §1404 is impossible. However, transfer may still be possible in these cases under 28 U.S.C. *§1406(a) or 1631*.

1. Common principles: Certain basic principles apply to transfers under both of these sections.

  a. Transferee court must be proper: Even though one or both are lacking in the transferor court, the transferee court *must have both personal jurisdiction and venue*. Transfer *to* a court that lacks either is forbidden.

  b. Either party may transfer: As under §1404(a), either party may seek transfer under §1406(a) or 1631. However, as a practical matter, it is usually the plaintiff who avails himself of these provisions. The party seeking transfer has the burden of establishing that the conditions for transfer are satisfied.

   c. Governing law: Unlike §1404(a), the transferee court does not automatically apply the law that the transferor court would apply, but instead applies the law that would be applied by the courts of the state in which the transferee court sits.

2. Transfer when venue improper — §1406(a): Section 1406(a) provides that if venue is improper, the court "shall dismiss, or if it be in the interest of justice, transfer" the case.

   a. Personal jurisdiction irrelevant: By its terms, §1406(a) applies whenever the court lacks venue. Whether the court has personal jurisdiction is irrelevant. A party can use §1406(a) even when the court lacks *both* personal jurisdiction and venue.

   b. Justice, not convenience: Section 1406(a) is not designed to make litigation more convenient. Rather, it gives the court that lacks venue an alternative to outright dismissal. Section 1406(a) allows for a transfer only if, under the circumstances of the case, transfer is more just than dismissal for lack of venue. The main situation in which a court will deem transfer "just" is when the *statute of limitations expired* after plaintiff filed in the transferor court.

3. Transfer when personal jurisdiction lacking — §1631: Section 1631 serves as a counterpart to §1406(a). It provides that a court lacking personal jurisdiction "shall, if it is in the interest of justice, transfer such action" to any federal district in which personal jurisdiction and venue requirements are met. Because §1406(a) is available even when a court lacks both personal jurisdiction and venue, §1631 applies mainly when a court lacks personal jurisdiction but not venue.

Quiz Yourself on
VENUE

18. Pan World Airlines is a new airline that specializes in "long haul" international flights. Pan World's main offices are in Pittsburgh, Pennsylvania (Western District of Pennsylvania). However, it operates most of its flights out of the international terminal in the Cleveland, Ohio (Northern District of Ohio) airport.

    Because Pan World's routes involve great distances, standard airplanes are not really suitable for its needs. Pan World therefore negotiates a deal to have planes custom built for its special needs. Pan World enters into a four-way contract with Boeing, Inc., a Washington corporation with its main facilities in Seattle, Washington (Western District of Washington); Rolls-Royce, Ltd., an English corporation with its main facilities in England; and Joan Jett, an aviation engineer who resides in Seattle. This contract was negotiated and signed entirely in Chicago, Illinois (Northern District of Illinois).

    Under this contract, Rolls-Royce, a leading jet engine manufacturer, agrees to produce a special engine in its factory in England. Rolls will then ship those engines to Boeing's Seattle plant. Once the engines arrive, Jett will undertake the delicate task of mounting the engines to the planes. Boeing will then fly the completed plane to Cleveland.

    Rolls never ships the engines to Boeing. Frustrated, Pan World decides its only course is to sue. Because Rolls-Royce is having serious financial difficulties, Pan World opts not to sue it. Instead, Pan World sues both Boeing and Jett in a federal district court in the Western District of Pennsylvania.

Subject matter jurisdiction is based solely on diversity. Personal jurisdiction proves not to be a problem either because Boeing is subject to jurisdiction throughout Pennsylvania, and Pan World is able to serve Jett while she is passing through the state.

Jett and Boeing immediately file a joint motion to dismiss the case based on Fed. R. Civ. P. 19, arguing that Rolls-Royce is a necessary party in the action. The district judge denies the motion. Boeing and Jett then file answers in which they argue that the district court does not have venue over the action.

How should the judge rule on the venue objection? _____

19. Same facts as Problem 18, except that Pan World also sued Rolls-Royce in the same action. Subject matter jurisdiction is based solely on diversity. Because Rolls is a party, Jett and Boeing do not move to dismiss for failure to join Rolls. All three defendants instead file a timely motion to dismiss for lack of venue. Rolls-Royce is not subject to personal jurisdiction anywhere in the United States except for the Southern District of New York. How should the court rule? _____

20. Same facts as Problems 18 and 19, except that Pan World sues the three defendants in a Pennsylvania state court. Because there is diversity, the defendants properly remove the case to the Western District of Pennsylvania. After removal, the defendants file a timely motion to dismiss for lack of venue. How should the court rule? _____

21. Brigid, a first-year law student in Ohio, purchased a new notebook computer to help her in her studies. Two hours into her Civil Procedure exam, however, Brigid's computer suddenly crashes. Brigid cannot recover any of her work and, as a result, fails the exam.

The ill-fated notebook was purchased in the neighboring state of Kentucky from Chip Douglas, a resident of Kentucky. The notebook was manufactured by Pathway Computers, Inc., a South Dakota corporation. Pathway's engineers designed the computer in South Dakota. However, the unit was manufactured at one of Pathway's factories in the Eastern District of Louisiana.

Brigid decides to sue both Pathway and Chip Douglas. Her complaint alleges that the computer was negligently assembled by someone on the assembly line, leading it to malfunction at the crucial moment. With some creative pleading, Brigid manages to work up a claim in excess of $75,000. Therefore, because diversity is present, she files her suit in the federal district court for the District of South Dakota. Pathway immediately files a timely motion to dismiss the action for lack of venue. How should the court rule on the motion? _____

22. Same facts as Problem 21, except that Brigid sues in a federal court in the Southern District of Ohio, where venue is clearly satisfied. After two months, Brigid moves under 28 U.S.C. §1404 to transfer the case to the Eastern District of Louisiana. Her reason for requesting the transfer is that she wants to inspect the manufacturing facility. Moving the case would present only a slight hardship for Pathway and Chip. The defendants nevertheless contest Brigid's motion, arguing in the alternative that it was filed too late and that it should be denied on the merits.

How is the court likely to rule on the motion to transfer? _____

23. Edna is enjoying her "golden years." Immediately after retiring, Edna left her home in chilly Vermont and moved to southern Florida. Although Florida weather agrees with her most of the time, Edna does miss the fall foliage. Therefore, Edna signs up for an October bus tour of New Hampshire. The bus company is located in Florida and maintains its fleet of buses there. All 50 passengers on the bus reside in Florida.

During the trip, the bus inexplicably goes off the road and runs into a tree. Other than the passengers, no witnesses were present. The bus driver is killed, and a number of the passengers, including

Edna, are seriously injured. All of the injured passengers are taken to Florida to recover. When Edna recovers, she sues the bus company in a New Hampshire state court, alleging negligence.

You are the attorney for the bus company. Although there is personal jurisdiction and venue in New Hampshire, your client does not want to litigate in that state. First, it prefers to litigate closer to home. More importantly, while New Hampshire would allow punitive damages in this case, Florida not only would disallow punitive damages, but would cap each victim's pain and suffering to a modest $10,000. Under their respective choice of law rules, Florida and New Hampshire courts would each apply its own law to decide this case.

What is the best way for your client to proceed in getting the case out of the New Hampshire court? Is it likely to succeed? _____

Answers

18. The judge should deny the objection because it is not timely. The parties' motion to dismiss was a motion raising a Fed. R. Civ. P. 12 defense (Fed. R. Civ. P. 12(b)(7)). Therefore, by failing to include the venue objection in that motion, the objection is waived pursuant to Fed. R. Civ. P. 12(g).

19. Now the court should grant the motion to dismiss. The case is governed by §1391(a) because jurisdiction is based solely on diversity. Under §1391(a)(1) (where all defendants reside), venue is proper only in the Western District of Washington. Jett clearly resides only in the Western District of Washington. Boeing also "resides" in that district because of §1391(c), which deems that a corporation resides wherever it is subject to personal jurisdiction. Boeing is clearly subject to personal jurisdiction where its plant is situated.

Note that Rolls-Royce will also be deemed to reside in the Western District of Washington. True, it is not subject to jurisdiction in that district. However, it is both a corporation and an alien. Although the statute does not make this perfectly clear, the alien corporation should be treated like all other aliens. As an alien, then, Rolls is deemed to reside in every district.

Under §1391(a)(2), venue is also proper wherever a substantial portion of the events or omissions giving rise to the claim occurred. However, no acts or omissions relevant to this case occurred in Western District of Pennsylvania, so that district is not a proper venue under (a)(2).

Section 1391(a)(3) does not apply because there are proper venues under (a)(1) and (a)(2). Therefore, the Western District of Pennsylvania is not a proper venue.

20. The court will deny the motion to dismiss. If a case is properly removed under §1441, venue is automatically proper in the federal court.

21. The court should grant the motion. Venue in South Dakota is improper under §1391(a)(1) because the defendants do not reside in the same state. Under §1391(a)(2), venue is proper wherever a substantial portion of the events or omissions giving rise to the cause of action occurred. Note, however, that Brigid is claiming a manufacturing defect, one caused by the negligent acts of a worker. Therefore, the design of the product, which admittedly occurred in South Dakota, is not an event or omission that counts.

Because there is a proper venue under §1391(a)(2), §1391(a)(3) is not applicable.

Note that it does not matter that the challenge in this case was filed by Pathway, the party who does reside in the chosen forum. Venue is still improper.

22. This problem actually has several subissues. First, is the motion timely? Section 1404 has no fixed deadline. However, it allows transfer only if it is in the "interest of justice." If Brigid has waited too

long, the court may deny the motion. However, it is unlikely that either defendant has suffered any real harm from the two-month delay here.

Second, a court may transfer under §1404 only to a district where the case could be brought. The Eastern District of Louisiana is a proper venue. Under §1391(a)(2), a substantial portion of the events and omissions — the assembly of the computer — took place there.

Even though the Eastern District of Louisiana is a proper venue, the court would likely deny the request for transfer. The transfer is proper only if it is for the convenience of the parties and the witnesses. Brigid does not need to move the entire case to Louisiana in order to inspect the factory; she can just take a trip to that state. And the problem states that there is no real advantage to either defendant in moving.

23. The best way to proceed is to move for a *forum non conveniens* dismissal. Note that transfer under §1404 will not work because this is a state court.

In evaluating the *forum non conveniens* request, the court will consider both private and public factors. Here, the private factors strongly favor dismissal. It is more convenient to the parties to litigate in Florida. Witnesses and business records, such as any maintenance records on the bus, are also likely to be located in Florida. The overall cost of litigation is probably less in Florida too. The only factor pointing toward New Hampshire is that the "event" (the accident) occurred there. But since there are no witnesses in that state, that factor is of little importance. It would be slightly more difficult to enforce a New Hampshire judgment in Florida than it would a Florida judgment, but that difference is insignificant.

The public factors do not weigh strongly here. There are no choice of law issues, as each court would apply its own law. For the same reason, the New Hampshire court will have no difficulty applying its own law. The only potential issue is the difference in recovery. However, if New Hampshire follows the federal approach, it will not consider that factor. Florida law does allow recovery, merely not as much.

Taken together, then, the public and private factors suggest that a *forum non conveniens* motion is likely to succeed.

 Exam Tips on
VENUE

Venue is not particularly difficult. But precisely because it is fairly straightforward, venue issues are often overlooked by students in Civil Procedure exams.

☛ **How to spot venue issues:** Venue issues can be presented in a fairly subtle fashion. You may encounter, for example, a party who does not like the location of the case or one who simply wants to obtain dismissal of the case.

☛ Unless you studied state venue rules, venue issues typically arise on an examination mainly when a case is in a federal court.

☛ In applying the venue statutes, remember that §1391(a)(1) and (b)(1) apply only if all defendants reside in the same state. Even if all defendants do reside in the same state, venue is not proper in all districts in the state, but only in a district where at least one defendant resides.

☛ Do not forget that special rules apply to ***corporate*** and ***alien defendants***.

   ☞ Recall that a corporation is deemed to reside in every district in its ***state of incorporation***, regardless of whether it has any physical presence in that state.

☛ Always be on the lookout for ***local actions***, cases that directly affect real property. The local action rule trumps ordinary venue provisions.

☛ If a question involves a motion to dismiss for lack of venue, you should always consider whether the motion was ***timely***.

☛ If a question deals with ***forum non conveniens***, be sure to consider the availability of ***transfer of venue***. If the case is in a federal court, and the more convenient forum is somewhere in the United States, the court will never use *forum non conveniens*, but will instead transfer under §1404. Therefore, *forum non conveniens* is likely to be a factor only when the better forum is a foreign court or when the forum is a state court.

   ☞ Also recall that the ***grant of a forum non conveniens*** motion results in ***dismissal*** of the case, not transfer.

☛ **Transfers:** Recall that there are actually *three* transfer statutes, which apply in different situations. Transfer, however, is an issue only in federal court.

CHAPTER 4

SUBJECT MATTER JURISDICTION

ChapterScope

This chapter deals with the subject matter jurisdiction of the *federal courts* in civil cases. The federal courts may adjudicate only certain categories of disputes. The limits on federal subject matter jurisdiction come from the U.S. Constitution, federal statutes, and the courts.

- **Two main categories:** There are two main categories of federal subject matter jurisdiction: *federal question* and *diversity of citizenship*. Although there are other federal question and diversity statutes, most cases arise under either the general federal question statute (28 U.S.C. §1331) or the general diversity statute (28 U.S.C. §1332).

- **Independent of personal jurisdiction:** Subject matter and personal jurisdiction are *separate requirements* that must be satisfied for a court to hear a case. Moreover, they are almost completely independent. Merely because a court has subject matter jurisdiction in no way implies that it has jurisdiction over the parties.

- **Exclusive and nonexclusive jurisdiction:** A case that qualifies for diversity jurisdiction almost always can be filed in either state or federal court. A case that qualifies for federal question jurisdiction usually can be filed in either court; however, some federal claims can be heard only by the federal courts.

- **Supplemental jurisdiction:** If a court has subject matter jurisdiction over some claims in a case, it may be possible for it to obtain subject matter jurisdiction over other claims that do not independently qualify for jurisdiction by using the doctrine of supplemental jurisdiction. Whether supplemental jurisdiction exists turns on the factual relationship between the various claims as well as other factors.

- **Removal jurisdiction:** If a case that qualifies for federal jurisdiction is filed in state court, it may be possible for the defendant to remove it to federal court.

I. BASIC PRINCIPLES

A. **Meaning of *subject matter jurisdiction:*** *Subject matter jurisdiction* is the authority to adjudicate and decide a case. If the court lacks subject matter jurisdiction, any party may move to have the action dismissed.

B. **Jurisdiction needed for every claim:** Most lawsuits involve multiple claims. A federal court must have jurisdiction over *every claim* in the case.

C. **Independent of personal jurisdiction:** Subject matter jurisdiction and personal jurisdiction are separate and independent requirements. Even if the court has jurisdiction over the parties, it cannot enter a binding judgment if it lacks jurisdiction over the subject matter.

D. **State courts:** Although this chapter deals almost exclusively with the federal courts, subject matter jurisdiction is also an issue in the state courts. For example, it is common for divorces and child custody cases to be heard by specialized state courts. However, every state has one court that can hear every case not specifically delegated to some other court.

E. **Sources of federal subject matter jurisdiction:** Federal jurisdiction is limited by the U.S. Constitution, federal statutes, and, in some cases, court-created doctrines. Most actual disputes, however, involve the wording of the statutes.

1. **Constitutional limits:** Federal courts are courts of *limited jurisdiction*. Article III, §2 of the U.S. Constitution lists nine categories of federal jurisdiction. Unless a case falls into one of these categories, it is unconstitutional for a federal court to hear it.

2. **Statutes:** Article III itself does not grant jurisdiction to the lower federal courts. Instead, it is up to Congress to allocate jurisdiction to the district courts. Although many federal statutes allocate jurisdiction, a basic Civil Procedure course focuses primarily on the general statutes, 28 U.S.C. §§1331 and 1332.

II. CHALLENGING SUBJECT MATTER JURISDICTION

Because subject matter jurisdiction is such an important limit on the authority of the federal courts, it may be challenged in a number of ways. Many of these modes of challenge are unique to subject matter jurisdiction.

A. **Any party may challenge:** Because subject matter jurisdiction is so fundamental, it can be raised by *any party* to the action. Fed. R. Civ. P. 12(h). Challenges to personal jurisdiction and venue, by contrast, can be raised only by the defendants.

B. **Court may raise *sua sponte*:** In addition, a court can raise *sua sponte* its own lack of subject matter jurisdiction. The parties cannot vest a court with jurisdiction by consent.

C. **No time limits:** Unlike virtually every other defense or objection, there are no time limits on challenging subject matter jurisdiction. The court or the parties can raise the issue at any time during the lawsuit. Moreover, the parties or the appellate court can raise lack of subject matter jurisdiction on appeal, even though it was not raised before.

Example: *P* sues *D* in federal court. The trial court enters judgment for *D*, and *P* appeals. On appeal, *P* argues for the first time that the trial court had no subject matter jurisdiction. If *P* is correct, the judgment of the trial court will be vacated.

III. FEDERAL QUESTION JURISDICTION

Federal question jurisdiction allows the federal district courts to hear cases involving federal and constitutional claims.

A. **Constitutional authorization:** Article III, §2, of the U.S. Constitution gives federal courts the authority to hear "all Cases, in Law and Equity, arising under this Constitution, the Laws of the United States, and Treaties. . . ." Two basic policies underlie this provision.

1. **State courts' hostility:** The framers feared that state courts might prove hostile to enforcing federally created rights.

2. **Uniform interpretation:** Allowing litigation to take place in the unitary federal court system would help ensure that laws of national scope were interpreted uniformly.

B. **Statutory enablement:** Congress gave the federal courts jurisdiction over federal questions in several different statutes, including:

   1. **28 U.S.C. §1331:** Section 1331 is the "general" federal question statute. Most of the discussion in this part relates to §1331.

   2. **Other statutes:** Although they are usually not discussed in a basic Procedure course, there are several other more specialized federal question statutes, including:

      a. **28 U.S.C. §1334:** This statute gives the federal district courts jurisdiction over matters connected with a ***bankruptcy***.

      b. **28 U.S.C. §1338:** Section 1338 gives the district courts ***exclusive*** jurisdiction over ***patent, plant variety protection***, and ***copyright infringement*** claims, and ***concurrent jurisdiction*** over ***trademark*** claims.

      c. **28 U.S.C. 1343:** This is a special provision that relates to cases arising under various federal ***civil rights*** laws.

C. **Overview of §1331:** The language of §1331 closely parallels Article III, §2: "The district courts shall have original jurisdiction of all civil actions arising under the Constitution, laws, or treaties of the United States."

   1. **No amount in controversy requirement:** There is no minimum amount in controversy in §1331. Federal jurisdiction exists regardless of how small a claim is involved.

      Note: Until 1980, §1331 did contain an amount in controversy requirement. Therefore, many older cases discussing §1331 do discuss the issue.

   2. **Not exclusive:** Federal jurisdiction under §1331 is concurrent, not exclusive. In most cases, a federal question may be litigated in either state or federal court.

      a. **Exceptions:** In certain situations, a federal statute creating a cause of action also specifies that only federal courts may hear the case. In other situations, such as actions under the antitrust laws, the courts imply that federal jurisdiction is exclusive from the nature of the federal statutory scheme.

      b. **Exclusivity under other jurisdictional statutes:** Some of the "special" jurisdictional statutes that apply to certain types of federal claims provide for exclusive federal jurisdiction.

      c. **Most cases litigated in federal court:** Although state courts retain the power to hear most federal questions, most litigants elect to bring their claims in federal court because of shorter dockets, greater federal sympathy to the claim, or other reasons.

   3. **Burden:** A plaintiff who wishes to invoke §1331 must include a statement in her federal complaint alleging that the requirements of the statute are satisfied.

D. **Sources of "federal" questions:** Section 1331 enumerates three separate categories of "federal questions": cases arising under the national Constitution, cases arising under federal law, and cases arising under treaties.

1. **Constitution:** A party whose constitutional rights are violated may in some cases bring an action directly under the U.S. Constitution. If the Constitution itself is the source of the plaintiff's claim, federal courts have subject matter jurisdiction to hear the case.

2. **Federal law:** Most federal question cases involve actions brought under federal law.

   a. **Statute:** The overwhelming majority of cases arise under statutes enacted by Congress. A cause of action can be set forth *expressly* in the statute, or in some cases may be *implied* by a court from the language and context of the statute. Either is sufficient for federal jurisdiction.

   b. **Federal common law:** In addition to claims created by Congress, a limited body of federal judge-made substantive law exists. Any claims arising under this federal common law may be heard in a federal district court under §1331.

3. **Treaties:** Treaties with other nations are negotiated at the federal level. If a treaty provides legally enforceable rights to the plaintiff, the federal courts may hear the claim under §1331. Most treaties, however, do not create rights themselves but are instead implemented by statute.

E. **"Arising under":** Section 1331 requires that the claim "arise under" one of the above sources of federal law.

   1. **Federal law creates right:** In the simple case, plaintiff seeks recovery based on a right specifically granted by federal law. For example, if a federal statute creates a cause of action and plaintiff's complaint invokes that federal cause of action as the basis for recovery, the case satisfies §1331.

      a. **Invoking federal jurisdiction:** In order to invoke federal jurisdiction, the plaintiff need only allege a claim based on a federal statute, the Constitution, or a treaty. Whether plaintiff ultimately prevails on that claim is irrelevant. The court does not lose jurisdiction merely because it decides that the federal law does not apply to plaintiff's situation.

      b. **Claim must be substantial:** However, the *federal claim must be substantial*. If plaintiff's federal claim is frivolous, there is no federal question jurisdiction.

   2. **State law with necessary federal element:** Sometimes a plaintiff seeks recovery under a state law that includes a federal law as one of its elements. In such a case, the court *must interpret federal law* to decide who prevails on the claim. Although that federal element may make the case look like a federal question, the Supreme Court held in Merrell Dow Pharmaceuticals v. Thompson, 478 U.S. 804 (1986), that a state law claim with a necessary federal law element presents a federal question *only if the federal law also affords a private right of action* for parties injured by violation of the statute.

      Example: Federal law requires the crew on every passenger flight to provide safety instructions. The statute is enforced solely by the Federal Aviation Administration, which can fine airlines that do not comply. *P* is seriously injured in a plane crash. *P* sues the airline in federal court for her injuries. *P*'s complaint argues that the airline was negligent per se for failing to provide the required warnings. The federal court does not have federal question jurisdiction over the claim because the federal law that forms a necessary element of the claim does not create a private right of action.

F. Well-pleaded complaint rule: The "arising under" language in §1331 has been interpreted to require the plaintiff to present the federal question *on the face of the plaintiff's complaint*. However, merely including a federal issue in the complaint does not suffice. Instead, the well-pleaded complaint rule asks whether the federal element is *necessary to plaintiff's case*.

1. **Anticipating a defense:** The most common situation in which a plaintiff fails to meet the well-pleaded complaint rule is when the complaint both asserts a state law claim and mentions a federal defense to that claim.

   ★   **Example:** The Supreme Court's decision in Louisville & Nashville R.R. v. Mottley, 211 U.S. 149 (1908), set out the well-pleaded complaint rule. In that case, two people sued to enforce a lifetime pass that a railroad had granted to them. The complaint sought an order of specific performance for the pass. The plaintiffs also alleged in their complaint that the railroad's reasons for refusing to enforce the pass violated both federal law and the Constitution. The Supreme Court held that the complaint failed to present a federal question. All plaintiff needed to allege in order to recover was the existence of a contract (the pass) and breach, which were purely state law issues. *Why* the defendant breached the contract was not an essential element of the plaintiff's claim.

2. **Declaratory judgments:** In some cases, a party does not seek damages or other affirmative relief but merely a declaration of the relative rights of the parties. This form of relief, called a *declaratory judgment*, is often intended to preempt a later lawsuit.

   a. A federal statute creates the right to seek a declaratory judgment. 22 U.S.C. §2201. However, because a declaratory judgment is a form of *remedy* rather than a substantive claim, a suit seeking a declaratory judgment does not necessarily arise under federal law.

   b. To determine if a declaratory judgment case is a federal question, a court *looks behind the declaratory judgment* claim to the essential nature of the lawsuit. The case is a federal question only if the lawsuit that is being preempted would itself qualify for federal question jurisdiction.

      Example: *P* supplies turnips to *D* pursuant to a long-term contract. Because of a major drought, *P* is unable to supply turnips to *D* this season. *P* sues *D* in a federal court, seeking a declaratory judgment under §2201 that "acts of God" like the drought excuse *P*'s performance under the contract. The federal court does not have federal question jurisdiction over this case. The dispute between *P* and *D* is merely an acceleration of the breach of contract claim that *D* would bring against *P* should *P* not deliver the turnips. Because this contract claim is governed by state law, it is not a federal question.

3. **Not constitutional:** The well-pleaded complaint requirement is not a constitutional requirement but is instead merely an interpretation of what Congress meant in §1331. Congress may give the federal courts jurisdiction over any case in which the court actually interprets a right or duty created by federal law. In fact, other federal jurisdictional statutes do not require that the federal question appear in the complaint.

Quiz Yourself on
FEDERAL QUESTION JURISDICTION

24. A federal statute limits the interest rate that lenders can charge on consumer loans to 18 percent. If a consumer loan exceeds this limit, the statute relieves the borrower of its obligation to repay the loan. Lender loans $10,000 to Borrower, which Borrower agrees to repay together with 25 percent interest. When Borrower fails to pay, Lender sues Borrower in a federal court. Lender alleges in his complaint that the loan agreement is valid notwithstanding the federal statute. Lender argues that the loan was not a consumer loan because Borrower borrowed the money to establish a home business. Borrower moves to dismiss the case for lack of subject matter jurisdiction. How should the court rule?

25. Doug Dreeler was recently convicted for trafficking in illegal narcotics in violation of federal law. In addition to levying a hefty fine on Doug, the federal government invokes a federal criminal forfeiture statute to seize Doug's house. The government conducts a forfeiture sale and sells the house to Parker.

    When Parker visits his newly purchased home, he discovers that Doug is still living there. Parker sues to evict Doug from the house. Parker brings this case in a federal district court, relying on federal question jurisdiction. In his complaint, Parker does not claim that the federal forfeiture laws give him a right to sue Doug for eviction. Nevertheless, Parker alleges that federal law is crucial to his case, for it is only because of the federal forfeiture law that Parker is now the owner of the home.

    Doug moves to dismiss for want of a federal question. How should the court rule?

Answers

24. The court should dismiss for lack of subject matter jurisdiction. In order to qualify for federal question jurisdiction, a federal question must appear on the face of Lender's well-pleaded complaint. Here, all Lender needs to allege to recover is the loan and Buyer's default. He does not need to tell the court why Borrower defaulted. Lender's anticipated federal defense does not operate to create federal question jurisdiction.

25. The court should grant the motion. Although Parker's complaint does contain a federal element (federal law provides that he is now the owner of the house), his cause of action still arises under state law. It is state law, not federal, that allows the rightful owner of property to evict someone trespassing on the property. And because the law forming the federal element does not create a private cause of action for Parker, his state claim containing the federal element is not a federal question.

IV. DIVERSITY JURISDICTION

Diversity jurisdiction allows federal courts to hear certain actions between people who live in different places.

A. Constitutional authorization: Article III, §2, of the U.S. Constitution allows the federal courts to exercise jurisdiction over "Controversies . . . between Citizens of different states . . . and between a State, or the Citizens thereof, and foreign States, Citizens, or Subjects."

B. Statutory enablement: Congress implemented this constitutional authorization in 28 U.S.C. §1332, the general diversity statute.

    1. Not exclusive statute: Section 1332 is not the only diversity statute. For example, 28 U.S.C. §1335 (discussed in Chapter 14) allows a court to hear an interpleader case when the parties are from different states.

    2. Rationale for diversity: One purpose of diversity jurisdiction is to protect out-of-state parties from discrimination by state courts. Because federal judges are appointed by the President and confirmed by the Senate, and hold life tenure, they are in theory less susceptible to local pressures than are state judges.

    3. Abolishing diversity: Regardless of the original justification, there is a real question as to whether diversity jurisdiction serves any purpose today. There remains the real possibility that diversity jurisdiction may not exist for much longer.

C. Overview of §1332

    1. Basic statutory requirements: Section 1332 contains *two basic requirements*. Unless both are satisfied, the federal court cannot hear the case.

        a. Diversity: First, the suit must involve plaintiffs and defendants who are "citizens of different states" or "citizens or subjects of a foreign state."

        b. Amount in controversy: In addition, the case must involve an "amount in controversy" in excess of $75,000.

    2. Not exclusive: Cases that meet the requirements of §1332 *may be litigated in either state or federal court*. Federal jurisdiction in diversity cases is concurrent, never exclusive. Plaintiff has discretion to decide whether to file his case in state or federal court. However, as discussed in Part VI of this chapter, if the plaintiff files a case satisfying the requirements of §1332 in state court, the defendant may be able to remove the case to federal court.

    3. When diversity determined: Diversity *must exist at the commencement* of the action. Post-commencement events, such as a move by one of the parties, do not affect the existence of diversity. Similarly, should the court determine during the course of the proceedings that plaintiff will recover less than $75,000, the court does not lose jurisdiction over the action.

    4. Burden of establishing: A plaintiff must include a statement in her federal complaint alleging that the requirements of diversity are satisfied. Fed. R. Civ. P. 8(a)(1). If jurisdiction is challenged, plaintiff also bears the burden of proving that diversity exists.

    5. Exceptions to diversity: In certain cases, a court will refuse to exercise jurisdiction even though the dispute seems to fit directly within §1332.

a. **Domestic relations and probate:** Cases involving purely family matters such as divorce, child custody, and the probate of wills are considered within the exclusive purview of the state courts. A federal court will not hear these cases even if the statutory requirements of §1332 are met. However, the "domestic relations" exception is limited to cases directly involving *divorce, alimony, and child custody*. Therefore, a tort suit by one spouse against another does not fall within the exception and may be heard in federal court if the requirements of §1332 are satisfied. Ankenbrandt v. Richards, 504 U.S. 689 (1992).

b. **Abstention:** In certain cases involving important and/or unclear issues of state law, a federal court may abstain from hearing the action in order to give the state court the chance to resolve the issue. The complex subject of abstention is beyond the scope of this work.

c. **Collusive joinder:** If parties are improperly or collusively joined to create diversity jurisdiction, 28 U.S.C. §1359 directs the court not to exercise jurisdiction. See Subpart I of this section.

D. **Complete diversity requirement:** Section 1332 has been interpreted to require "complete diversity" between plaintiffs and defendants in every case. To meet this requirement, it must be true that no plaintiff is a citizen of the same state as any defendant.

Example: Five plaintiffs sue three defendants in a federal court, bringing purely state law claims. Four of the plaintiffs are from Maine, while one is from Florida. Two of the three defendants are from Oregon, and one is from Florida. Regardless of the amount in controversy, the suit cannot proceed as structured in federal court because the complete diversity requirement is not satisfied.

1. **Source of rule:** The complete diversity requirement stems from the old case of Strawbridge v. Curtiss, 7 U.S. (3 Cranch) 267 (1806). Nevertheless, as Congress has never acted to override that interpretation, the interpretation remains in force.

2. **Application in multiparty case:** A case may involve multiple plaintiffs and multiple defendants. In some situations, a plaintiff may not have filed claims against one or more defendants.

★   a. **"Complete diversity":** *Even if no claim* has been filed by a particular plaintiff against a particular defendant, those two parties *must still be of diverse citizenship* for the case to satisfy the "complete diversity" rule. Caterpillar, Inc. v. Lewis, 519 U.S. 61 (1996).

   Example: *P1* and *P2* sue *D1* and *D2* in a federal district court. Both plaintiffs state a claim against *D1*, but only *P1* sues *D2*. *P1* is a citizen of Alpha, *D1* is a citizen of Beta, and *P2* and *D2* are citizens of Gamma. The federal court cannot hear the case, even though *P2* has filed no claim against *D2*.

   b. **§1332(a)(3) exception in case involving aliens:** This exception is discussed in Part G.4 of this section.

3. **Not a constitutional requirement:** The complete diversity rule is *not* mandated by the Constitution. In fact, Article III, §2, requires only "minimal diversity," i.e., where only one plaintiff is diverse from any defendant. In addition, the complete diversity rule applies only to §1332, not to other subject matter jurisdiction statutes.

4. **Realignment of parties.** If the plaintiff has placed a party on the wrong side of the suit — for example, listing someone as a defendant even though that person's interests are more closely aligned with those of the plaintiff — the court may realign the parties. If such realignment destroys complete diversity, the court will dismiss the case.

E. **"Citizenship" of individuals and domicile:** Section 1332 speaks in terms of "citizens" of different states. In the United States, however, citizenship is usually measured on the national rather than the state level. Courts therefore look to the ***domicile*** of a party in determining whether that person is a citizen of a state.

1. **Basic test:** In order to be a "citizen of a state" under §1332, a person must be ***both*** a ***citizen of the United States*** and be ***domiciled in a state***.

   a. **District of Columbia, Puerto Rico, and federal territories:** Section 1332 treats the District of Columbia, Puerto Rico, and federal territories as states for purposes of diversity jurisdiction.

   b. **Permanent resident aliens:** A foreign citizen who receives a grant of permanent resident alien status by the U.S. government is treated as a citizen of the state in which she is domiciled. In other words, the statute treats permanent resident alien status as the equivalent of U.S. citizenship.

      Example: Two plaintiffs, both of whom are domiciled in Wisconsin, want to sue in federal court, relying on diversity jurisdiction. Plaintiff One, a citizen of Canada, has been granted permanent resident alien status by the federal government. Plaintiff Two, a citizen of Ireland, is in the United States on a work permit. Only Plaintiff One will be treated as a citizen of Wisconsin for purposes of §1332.

      Note: In the foregoing situation, Plaintiff Two (the Irish citizen) may well be able to sue a citizen of the United States in federal court based on the language in §1332(a)(2) allowing suit between citizens of the United States and "citizens or subjects of a foreign state."

   c. **U.S. citizens domiciled abroad:** A U.S. citizen who is domiciled in another country ***cannot sue or be sued in federal court under diversity jurisdiction***, for that person will never qualify as a citizen of a state under §1332. Nor is that person a citizen or subject of a foreign state since they are U.S. citizens. In essence, the U.S. citizen domiciled abroad cannot make use of diversity jurisdiction.

      ★ **Example:** In Redner v. Sanders, 2000 WL 1161080 (S.D.N.Y. 2000), the court determined that plaintiff, a U.S. citizen, had established a domicile in France. Because plaintiff was neither a citizen of a state nor a citizen of France, he could not sue defendant in federal court based on diversity jurisdiction.

2. **Domicile:** Although similar, ***domicile and residence are not the same***. Domicile is a more permanent connection than residence.

   a. **Test:** The test for domicile is ***actual residence plus the intent to remain***. Courts often look for the place where the person keeps "his or her true, fixed, home and principal establishment, and to which he or she has the intention of returning whenever absent."

   b. **Single domicile:** Every person has one and only one domicile.

      i. **Birth:** A person acquires a domicile at birth. This is typically the domicile of her parents, not the location of her birth.

      ii. **Change of domicile:** A person retains his current domicile until it is changed. A minor keeps the domicile of his parents as they move. Once a person attains the age of majority, she can change domicile voluntarily. Most courts, however, recognize a change in domicile only when a person both **acquires a new residence** and **has the intent to remain at that place**.

> **Example:** Paulette, a domiciliary of Michigan, moves to West Virginia. While living in West Virginia, she does not intend to remain in that state. Nine months later, Paulette moves to New Mexico, where she also does not intend to remain. While residing in New Mexico, Paulette thinks fondly back to her days in West Virginia and decides that she will move back to that state as quickly as she can and make the state her permanent home. Paulette is still a Michigan domiciliary. Although her present intent is to make West Virginia her home, she did not hold the intent and the actual residence at the same time. However, as soon as she moves back to West Virginia, she will change her domicile (assuming that her intent does not change again in the meanwhile).

   c. Intent relevant to domicile: A person need only intend to make a state his current home in order to acquire a domicile there. He need not intend to live there for the remainder of his life.

      i. Proving intent: The intent to make a place a home is usually measured by objective criteria. Thus, if a person registers to vote, obtains a new driver's license and automobile tags, opens a new bank account, and sells her residence in the prior state, courts are more likely to find a bona fide change in residence.

      ii. Students: Courts are hesitant to conclude that someone who moves to a state to attend school has acquired a new domicile, even if the other objective criteria are met.

       Note concerning state law residency requirements: Domicile is used to determine whether a party meets the diversity requirements of 28 U.S.C. §1332, a federal statute. The federal law is completely independent of state laws governing residency requirements for in-state tuition or welfare benefits. Thus, although many of the factors may be the same, whether a student qualifies for in-state tuition is irrelevant in determining whether that same student is a domiciliary of that state for purposes of diversity jurisdiction.

      iii. Spouses and children: Historically, spouses were considered automatically to have the same domicile. This old rule has been almost completely rejected. Children, however, are still considered to have the domicile of their parents. In cases where the parents live in different states, the children have the domicile of the spouse with primary custody.

   d. Presuit move: On occasion, a person who is domiciled in the same state as a prospective defendant will move to another state prior to filing suit. He will then file the action in federal court, alleging diversity. Because diversity is measured as of the time the action is filed, a good faith move is sufficient to create diversity.

F. Citizenship of corporations and other special parties: The concept of domicile is obviously of little use in determining the citizenship of a ''legal person'' such as a corporation. For these entities, different tests apply.

   1. Corporations: Section 1332(c) defines the citizenship of a corporation. A corporation is a citizen of **both** the state that **incorporated it** and the state in which it has its **principal place of business**.

a. **Dual citizenship:** Note that under this section, a corporation that has its principal place of business in a state other than its state of incorporation has two citizenships. If any adverse party is a citizen of *either* of these states, diversity jurisdiction is unavailable.

   Example: *P*, a citizen of Missouri, sues *D*, a corporation chartered (incorporated) under the laws of Utah with its principal place of business in Missouri. Diversity jurisdiction is unavailable because *P* and *D* are both citizens of Missouri.

b. **State of incorporation:** *Incorporation* is the legal act by which the corporation is created. This almost always happens under the law of a particular state. Therefore, a corporation usually has only one state of incorporation.

c. **Principal place of business:** No matter how widely diversified its operations are, a corporation has only one principal place of business. Courts use two different approaches to determine the principal place of business.

   i. **Muscle test:** A slight majority of courts look to where most of the corporation's actual physical activities, such as manufacturing or sales, take place.

   ii. **Nerve center:** Many courts look to where corporate management and operations decisions are made: the corporate "headquarters."

   iii. **Combining the approaches:** Sometimes these two tests are combined. Some courts, for example, use the muscle test for the many corporations that have their physical activities located mainly in a single state, but turn to the nerve test for corporations with significant physical activities in several states.

2. **Partnerships and other unincorporated associations:** Section 1332(c) does not apply to partnerships, limited liability companies, and other noncorporate associations such as labor unions and clubs. These entities do not have their own citizenship. In an action by or against one of these entities, one must consider the citizenship of ***all of the partners or members of the organization***. If any of these partners or members are from the same state as an adversary party, diversity jurisdiction is unavailable.

3. **Insurance companies:** In a direct action suit against an insurance company, §1332(c)(1) provides that the insurance company is deemed a citizen of (a) the state in which the insured is a citizen, (b) the insurance company's state of incorporation, and (c) the state where the insurance company has its principal place of business. Note that this rule applies only when the corporation is ***sued in a direct action***, not when the insurance company is a plaintiff.

4. **Representatives:** When a person dies and leaves an estate, the representative of the estate may sue or be sued to help wrap up the affairs of the deceased. In these cases, §1332(c)(2) specifies that the actual citizenship of the representative is to be ignored, and the representative is deemed to have the same citizenship as the deceased. Similarly, §1332(c)(2) provides that the guardian or other legal representative of an infant or incompetent is deemed to have the same citizenship as the infant or incompetent. This provision prevents a party from obtaining federal jurisdiction over a dispute that is for all practical purposes between parties from the same state by the simple expediency of appointing a representative or administrator from another state.

5. **Trusts:** A trust is a legal entity with the power to sue and be sued. In most cases, the ***citizenship of the trustee*** is used to measure diversity. However, if the trustee has no real powers, the citizenship of the beneficiaries is used.

G. Alienage jurisdiction: In addition to suits between people from different U.S. states, §1332 allows a federal court to hear suits between a U.S. citizen and ''Citizens or Subjects'' of foreign states. This alienage jurisdiction is generally subject to the same rules as ordinary diversity, but has a few of its own quirks.

   1. ''Citizen or subject'' of a foreign state: These terms are somewhat antiquated, and can prove somewhat confusing. A foreign *state* refers to a foreign *nation*. A *subject* signifies a citizen of a nation ruled by a monarch.

   2. Domicile usually irrelevant: In the case of alienage jurisdiction, a person need only be a citizen or subject of the foreign nation. Where the person is *domiciled* is not relevant, even if the person is domiciled in the United States. Recall, however, that a foreigner who receives a grant of permanent resident alien status by the U.S. government is treated as a citizen of the U.S. state in which she is domiciled, not as a citizen of a foreign state.

   3. Dual citizens: When a person is a citizen of both the United States and a foreign nation, only the U.S. citizenship is counted. Thus, dual U.S.-foreign citizens cannot qualify for alienage jurisdiction. Coury v. Prot, 85 F.3d 244, 247-248 (5th Cir. 1996). However, if a dual citizen is a citizen of a state different from that of all adverse parties, he can use ordinary diversity jurisdiction.

   4. Mixing U.S. citizens and foreign citizens: 28 U.S.C. §1332(a)(3) creates a special rule for cases involving both citizens of states and citizens of foreign states. Although the complete diversity requirement still applies among the U.S. claimants, as long as every plaintiff is diverse — either through ordinary diversity or alienage — from every U.S. defendant, diversity jurisdiction is possible.

   Example: *P1* and *P2* sue *D1* and *D2* in a federal court. *P1* is a citizen of Kentucky. *D1* is a citizen of Ohio. *P2* and *D2* are citizens of Indonesia. Assuming the amount in controversy is satisfied, diversity exists.

   5. Pure alienage not covered: Neither Article III, §2, nor §1332 allow federal courts to hear a suit that involves only foreign citizens, even if they are from different nations.

   Example: *P*, an Iranian citizen, sues *D*, a subject of Denmark. Although *P* and *D* are from different countries, diversity jurisdiction is unavailable because both *P* and *D* are citizens of a foreign state and therefore outside §1332.

★   **Note:** In the prior example, most courts would not allow jurisdiction even if *P* or *D* had been granted permanent resident alien status. In such a case, §1332 suggests that the permanent resident alien is treated as a citizen of her state of domicile. However, because the diversity language in the U.S. Constitution does not extend to claims by one alien against another, courts are hesitant to interpret the permanent resident alien language of §1332 to create jurisdiction over such a suit. Instead, the permanent resident alien language tends to *defeat* jurisdiction, applying when a permanent resident alien who lives in a state sues a citizen of that state or vice versa. See Saadeh v. Farouki, 107 F.3d 52 (D.C. Cir. 1997).

H. Amount in controversy: The second main requirement of §1332 is that the suit involve an amount in controversy of more than $75,000.

   1. Increases: Congress periodically increases the amount in controversy requirement, in an effort to limit the workload of the federal courts and to mollify those who argue that diversity jurisdiction should be abolished.

2. **Sums included:** All forms of damages are included in calculating the amount in controversy. However, *interest* and *court costs* are *not included*.

   a. **Some interest allowed:** The statute excludes only interest imposed by law, *not interest required by contract*. If *P* has loaned money to *D* at 12 percent interest, any accumulated interest on the loan *would be included* in the amount in controversy.

   b. **Attorneys' fees:** If plaintiff is permitted to recover fees by contract or statute, they are included in the amount in controversy.

3. **Measured by complaint:** The amount in controversy is measured by the sum sought in the *plaintiff's complaint*. Additional amounts sought by the defendant in, for example, a counterclaim ordinarily do not count in determining whether the requirement is met. On the other hand, a minority of courts hold that the amount of a *compulsory counterclaim* (see Chapter 14, Part I.B.2) can be aggregated with the plaintiff's complaint to satisfy the amount in controversy.

   a. **Legal certainty rule:** The amount alleged in the complaint controls unless it appears to a *legal certainty* that plaintiff will recover less than $75,000. St. Paul Mercury Indemnity Co. v. Red Cab Co., 303 U.S. 283 (1938). Thus, although the party invoking federal jurisdiction has the burden of demonstrating that the amount in controversy requirement is met, the legal certainty rule makes this burden fairly easy to meet in practice.

   b. **Actual recovery irrelevant:** As long as the original claim is made in good faith, it does not matter that the court eventually awards less than $75,000. However, if plaintiff recovers less than $75,000, the court has the discretion to deny costs to the plaintiff and award costs to the defendant. 28 U.S.C. §1332(b). This discretion is rarely exercised.

4. **Nonmonetary relief:** The amount in controversy requirement can be satisfied even if plaintiff seeks only an injunction or other nonmonetary relief. In these cases, the court must place a value on the relief sought. Courts vary in the approaches used, considering the *value to the plaintiff*, the *cost to the defendant of complying with the order*, or the *cost or value to the party invoking federal jurisdiction*. Some courts consider the requirement satisfied if *any of the tests* are met.

5. **Aggregation:** If a plaintiff brings one or more claims of less than $75,000, issues of aggregation arise.

   a. **Single claim greater than $75,000:** As long as plaintiff has one claim that itself seeks an amount in excess of $75,000, the requirement is satisfied for all of that plaintiff's claims. Aggregation is unnecessary in such a case.

   b. **Single plaintiff, single defendant, multiple claims that are each less than $75,000:** A single plaintiff may aggregate all her claims against a single defendant, regardless of whether the claims are related in any way. The amount in controversy is satisfied if the total value of the claims exceeds $75,000.

   c. **Multiple plaintiffs:** Multiple plaintiffs *ordinarily may not aggregate* their claims. However, if the plaintiffs present a joint claim, aggregation is possible.

   Example: *P1* and *P2* are passengers on a bus that is involved in a collision. Because both are diverse from the bus company, *P1* and *P2* would like to join and sue in federal court. *P1* and *P2* each have damages of $50,000. *P1* and *P2* cannot aggregate their claims to meet the amount in controversy requirement because their claims are separate and distinct.

Example: In the prior example, suppose that the bus hits and completely destroys a large yacht worth $100,000. The yacht is owned jointly by *P3* and *P4*, each of whom owns an undivided 50 percent interest. *P3* and *P4* meet the amount in controversy.

d. Multiple plaintiffs, one claim greater than $75,000: If one of the plaintiffs has a claim in excess of $75,000, and the claims of the other plaintiffs are factually related to that claim, a few courts allow the parties to make use of *supplemental jurisdiction* to bring the entire case into federal court. However, this result is clearly incorrect. Supplemental jurisdiction is discussed in Part V of this chapter.

e. Multiple defendants: A plaintiff suing multiple defendants meets the amount in controversy if each defendant is potentially liable for an amount in excess of $75,000, even if that liability is joint and several.

f. Class actions: The amount in controversy presents a special problem in class actions, which is explored in Chapter 15.

I. Attempts to skirt the requirements of §1332: On occasion, a party may attempt to get a case into, or keep a case out of, federal court by manipulating the diversity requirement. Whether these attempts work turns in large part on whether the party is trying to *create* or to *destroy* diversity. Congress and the courts are considerably less solicitous of attempts to bring to federal court a case that should not be there.

1. Manufacturing diversity: *28 U.S.C. §1359* denies a federal court jurisdiction over ''a civil action in which any party, by assignment or otherwise, has been *improperly or collusively . . . joined* to invoke the jurisdiction of such court.''

a. Assignments: A party with a claim against a nondiverse party might try to manufacture diversity by transferring that claim to someone from another state. Although a good faith assignment is respected, a sham assignment defeats diversity.

Example: *D* owes $100,000 to *C* based on a contract between the parties. *C* wants to sue *D* on this claim in federal court. However, *C* cannot do so because she and *D* are both citizens of Georgia. *C* ''assigns'' the contract to *P*, a citizen of South Carolina, for the sum of $1 plus 95 percent of whatever *P* recovers from *D*. Although *P* is diverse from *D*, a federal court will not exercise jurisdiction over this case because the assignment is merely an attempt to manufacture diversity jurisdiction.

b. Other situations: Aside from the situation of assignments, §1359 is not invoked all that frequently.

c. Omitting parties: If a defendant is obligated to several plaintiffs on the same basic claim, it is ordinarily perfectly acceptable for only those plaintiffs who are diverse from the defendant to sue. In certain rare cases, however, a missing plaintiff is deemed a *necessary party* under Fed. R. Civ. P. 19. If joinder of the party would destroy diversity, the court may decide that the case must be dismissed. The necessary party rule is covered in Chapter 14, Part II.D.

2. Destroying diversity: A party who desires to keep his case out of federal court may take steps either before or during litigation to keep the case in state court. Note that situations involving attempts to destroy diversity usually arise when a defendant attempts to *remove* a case from state court to federal court, which is discussed in Part VI of this chapter.

a. **Assignments:** Because §1359 covers only attempts to *invoke* federal jurisdiction, it does not apply when a party who is diverse from the defendant assigns a claim to a nondiverse party in anticipation of litigation.

b. **Adding nominal defendants:** If a plaintiff sues multiple defendants, the complete diversity rule defeats diversity if any one of the defendants is from the same state as the plaintiff. However, if the court finds that the plaintiff has no real claim against a certain defendant, the court ignores that defendant in determining whether diversity exists.

Example: After he was banned from baseball, Pete Rose brought an action against the Commissioner of Baseball, the Cincinnati Reds, and Major League Baseball. Rose, a citizen of Ohio, sued in state court. The defendants tried to remove the action to federal court, even though both the Reds and Major League Baseball were also citizens of Ohio. The court allowed the removal, reasoning that because Rose had no real claim against either the Reds or Major League Baseball, those parties were merely nominal or formal defendants whose citizenship could be ignored for purposes of diversity. Rose v. Giamatti, 721 F. Supp. 906 (S.D. Ohio 1989).

c. **Artificially low amount in controversy:** If a plaintiff explicitly asks for less than $75,000, the case cannot be removed based on diversity.

Quiz Yourself on
DIVERSITY JURISDICTION

26. Jessica and Bob, both citizens of Kentucky, enter into a contract in which Bob agrees to sell Jessica a painting for $1,000. Bob later discovers that the painting is actually worth $100,000. Bob feels he has been taken and refuses to deliver the painting to Jessica.

    Two days after Bob's breach, Jessica suddenly sells her house in Kentucky and buys a new house in Indiana. She moves all of her possessions to the new home and establishes a new bank account with an Indiana bank. However, because her automobile license has not yet expired, Jessica decides to take a chance and continue driving on her Kentucky plates. Jessica does not bother to register to vote in Indiana because it is not an election year.

    After moving, Jessica sues Bob in a federal district court for $99,000 for breach of contract, based on diversity jurisdiction. Bob moves to dismiss for lack of subject matter jurisdiction. At the hearing on Bob's motion, Jessica frankly admits that her sole motive for moving was to allow her to sue in federal court. How will the court rule on Bob's motion to dismiss? _____

27. Same facts as Problem 26, except that Jessica does not move to Indiana. Instead, she establishes a new corporation called Jessi Corp. in Indiana. The corporation's principal place of business is also in Indiana. Jessica is the corporation's sole shareholder and its chief executive officer. In return, Jessica assigns her rights under the contract with Bob to Jessi Corp.

    Jessi Corp. sues Bob in a federal district court for $99,000 for breach of contract. The complaint alleges diversity jurisdiction. Bob immediately moves to dismiss the case for lack of subject matter jurisdiction. How should the court rule on Bob's motion to dismiss? _____

28. Eileen recently fulfilled her lifelong dream of skydiving. Unfortunately, the instructor who coached Eileen never mentioned that parachutes do not deploy automatically but require the user to pull a cord. Because of this little miscommunication, Eileen suffered serious injuries.

    Eileen sues Free Fall, Inc., the company that operates the skydiving operation and provided the faulty instructions. Eileen brings her case in federal district court based on diversity. She seeks $500,000 in damages. Eileen is a citizen of Ethiopia who moved to the United States two years ago. Last year, she obtained permanent residency papers from the government and applied for U.S. citizenship. However, she still must wait several years before being awarded citizenship. In the meanwhile, Eileen made a new home for herself in Pennsylvania.

    Free Fall is a Florida corporation with its headquarters in Georgia. It has skydiving schools in a number of states. However, Free Fall's operation in Pennsylvania is the largest of its skydiving schools.

    Free Fall moves to dismiss for lack of subject matter jurisdiction. How will the court rule? _____

29. Old McDonald is an experienced farmer who works a large farm in Nebraska. His cousin Seb Urban has traveled from his home in Cleveland to visit McDonald. McDonald and Seb indulge in a bit too much liquid corn squeezings and decide it would be a "grand idea" for Seb to take McDonald's huge combine out for a spin. Seb has no idea how to operate a combine. Seb loses control of the combine and drives it into the home of McDonald's neighbor Clarabelle.

    Clarabelle sues in federal court to recover for the extensive damage to her home. However, because she and McDonald are both citizens of Nebraska, Clarabelle does not name McDonald as a defendant. Instead she sues Seb and All Farm Insurance, McDonald's liability insurance carrier. Seb is a citizen of Ohio. All Farm is an Illinois corporation with its principal place of business in Illinois. Clarabelle asks for $150,000 in damages.

    Seb moves to dismiss, arguing that the requirements for diversity are not satisfied. How will the court rule? _____

30. Lender sues Borrower for default under a loan agreement. The parties are citizens of different states. Lender's complaint asserts that Borrower owes him $70,000 in outstanding principal, plus $10,000 in past-due interest under the loan agreement. In addition, Lender claims he is entitled to recover court costs. Borrower moves to dismiss, arguing that the requirements of diversity are not satisfied. How will the court rule? _____

31. While driving her husband Ward to the office one morning, June Cleaver is involved in an accident with Eddie Haskell. Both June and Ward are injured. June and Ward join as plaintiffs and sue Eddie in federal court. Eddie is diverse from both June and Ward. June seeks $50,000 in damages, while Ward seeks $40,000. Eddie moves to dismiss for lack of diversity jurisdiction. How will the court rule? _____

Answers

26. The court will probably deny Bob's motion because the case likely qualifies for diversity jurisdiction. First, the amount in controversy is met. Although the contract price is only $1,000, under contract law Jessica may recover the full benefit of bargain with Bob. The painting is worth $100,000. Therefore,

Jessica's claim for $99,000 in lost profit is clearly a colorable claim.

The more difficult issue is Jessica's domicile. Viewed objectively, it appears that Jessica has indeed changed her domicile to Indiana. She bought a house and opened a bank account in that state. Her failure to register to vote immediately is easily explainable. And although she has kept her Kentucky state auto tags, her intent in so doing is merely to save money, not to keep a connection with Kentucky. Therefore, it appears that Jessica has established an Indiana domicile.

Jessica's *motive* for changing domicile is irrelevant. Her motive does not make her move a "collusive act" for purposes of §1359.

27. In this case, the court should dismiss the action. The new corporation is a citizen of Indiana because it was chartered there and has its principal place of business in that state. However, the entire arrangement — establishing the corporation and assigning the contract rights to it — is merely a collusive attempt to manufacture diversity jurisdiction, and the federal court accordingly will disregard it under §1359.

28. The court will probably deny the motion to dismiss. The amount in controversy is not an issue since it far exceeds the $75,000 threshold. The real issue is citizenship of the parties.

Eileen is an alien because she does not have U.S. citizenship. However, because she has been granted permanent resident alien status, §1332 treats her as a citizen of the state of her domicile. Therefore, she is considered a citizen of Pennsylvania.

Free Fall is a corporation and is therefore a citizen of both its state of incorporation and its principal place of business. If *either* of these states is Pennsylvania, diversity is defeated. Free Fall's state of incorporation is clearly Florida. Its principal place of business is less clear. However, given that the corporation has a single headquarters and multiple places of operation, many courts will apply the "nerve center" test and use the corporate headquarters. Since the corporation's headquarters is in Georgia, the corporation is a citizen of both Georgia and Florida. Therefore, it is diverse from Eileen, and diversity jurisdiction is present.

29. The court will grant the motion to dismiss because the complete diversity requirement is not satisfied. Clarabelle is clearly diverse from Seb. With respect to All Farm, although the citizenship of a corporation is usually measured by the state of incorporation and principal place of business, §1332(c)(1) sets out a special rule for liability insurance companies. Because Clarabelle is suing the insurance company, the insurance company is treated as a citizen of the same state as the insured. All Farm is accordingly a citizen of Nebraska in this action. Because the complete diversity rule requires that Clarabelle be diverse from all defendants, she cannot satisfy the requirements of diversity jurisdiction in this case.

It does not matter that it is Seb, the diverse defendant, who makes the motion to dismiss. Any party may challenge subject matter jurisdiction at any time.

30. The court will deny the motion to dismiss. The parties are of diverse citizenship, so the only issue is the amount in controversy. The plaintiff must assert a right to recovery in excess of $75,000, exclusive of interest and costs. Therefore, the costs will not be included in the calculation. However, the $10,000 in interest will be included. The "interest" to which §1332 refers is postfiling interest, *not* interest that is due by agreement of the parties. Therefore the amount in controversy here is $80,000 ($70,000 in principal plus $10,000 in interest).

31. The court will grant the motion to dismiss because the amount in controversy is not met. Each of the plaintiffs here suffered an individual injury of less than $75,000. The plaintiffs could aggregate their claims only if they asserted some sort of joint claim. Neither Ward nor June has any ownership inter-

est in the injuries suffered by the other. The fact that they are husband and wife does not change this. Thus, the amount in controversy is not satisfied for either claim.

V. SUPPLEMENTAL JURISDICTION

If a district court can exercise jurisdiction over some of the claims in the case, in certain circumstances it may be able to exercise jurisdiction over other claims that do not themselves qualify for federal jurisdiction under §1331 or 1332. Jurisdiction over these other claims is called supplemental jurisdiction and is governed by 28 U.S.C. §1367.

A. Overview and terminology: Supplemental jurisdiction is possible only when at least one claim independently qualifies for federal subject matter jurisdiction. Courts often refer to this claim as the *federal claim*.

    1. Diversity or federal question: The federal claim may be either a diversity or a federal question claim.

    2. Exception: The supplemental jurisdiction statute contains an important exception that applies when the federal claim is a diversity claim. See §1367(b), which is discussed below.

B. History: For many years, supplemental jurisdiction was a court-created doctrine not explicitly authorized by statute. In 1990, Congress codified the doctrine for the district courts in 28 U.S.C. §1367.

    1. Pre-1990 law: The judge-made doctrine did not use the term *supplemental* jurisdiction. Instead, it distinguished between two separate forms of jurisdiction, *pendent* and *ancillary*.

    2. Current statute: Because of various problems in the court-created doctrines of pendent and ancillary jurisdiction, Congress enacted *28 U.S.C. §1367* in 1990.

        a. New terminology: Section 1367 eschews the old terms *pendent* and *ancillary* in favor of the single term *supplemental jurisdiction*. The several technical distinctions between ancillary and pendent jurisdiction no longer exist.

        b. District courts only: Note that §1367 applies only to the *federal district courts*. However, because the statutes governing the appellate and Supreme Court give those courts appellate jurisdiction over the entire lower court decision, that omission does not matter in most cases.

C. Applying §1367: Application of §1367 is essentially a *two-step process*. The first is to determine if the state and federal claims have a sufficient *factual relationship* to qualify. Second, even if a relationship exists, supplemental jurisdiction may still be precluded if the situation falls into one of the *exceptions* in §1367(b) or (c).

    1. Relationship test: The basic analysis for whether the state and federal claims are sufficiently related is whether the two "*form part of the same case or controversy* under Article III of the United States Constitution." 28 U.S.C. §1367(a).

        a. "Same case or controversy": Two or more claims comprise the same Article III case if they arise out of the same basic set of facts. If litigation of the claims involves many of the same witnesses or other evidence, the claims are more likely to satisfy the test. Similarly, claims that stem logically from the same core transaction or occurrence are likely to qualify under §1367(a).

★ **b. Constitutional grounding:** The logic behind supplemental jurisdiction is discussed in United Mine Workers v. Gibbs, 383 U.S. 715 (1966). In that case, the Court noted that Article III of the Constitution gives the federal courts jurisdiction not over "***claims***," but instead over "***cases***." The Court reasoned that the concept of a "case" was broader than that of an individual claim. A "case" comprised all claims that arose out of a "***common nucleus of operative fact***." Therefore, Article III allows federal jurisdiction over the entire case, not merely over the federal question or diversity claims.

c. "Common nucleus" standard: Although §1367(a) does not use the phrase "common nucleus of operative fact," the legislative history for §1367 shows that Congress intended to codify the common nucleus standard. On the other hand, some have argued that the "same Article III case" test of §1367 is not exactly equivalent to the common nucleus test.

2. **Exceptions:** Section 1367 sets out two main exceptions. First, §1367(b) greatly limits the use of supplemental jurisdiction in certain cases where the jurisdiction over the federal claim or claims is based ***solely on diversity***. Second, §1367(c) lists a number of situations where a court may, in its ***discretion***, refuse to exercise jurisdiction.

a. Diversity exception — §1367(b): In cases where jurisdiction over the federal claim is based solely on diversity, §1367(b) prevents the use of supplemental jurisdiction over ***claims brought by plaintiffs against parties joined under certain listed rules***.

i. Based solely on diversity: The exclusion applies only when §1332 is the *only* basis for federal jurisdiction over the federal claim. If any of plaintiff's claims qualify for jurisdiction under §1331 or any other jurisdictional statute, §1367(b) does not apply.

Example: *P* sues *D1* and *D2* in a federal court. *P*'s claim against *D1* qualifies for both diversity and federal question jurisdiction. There is no independent basis for jurisdiction over the claim against *D2*. If the two claims arise from a common nucleus of operative fact, the federal court will have jurisdiction over both. Because jurisdiction over the claim against *D1* is not based solely on diversity, a federal court is not prohibited from exercising supplemental jurisdiction over the parallel state law claim against *D2*.

ii. By plaintiffs: Section 1367(b) bars only claims by plaintiffs. The reference to "plaintiff" in §1367(b) applies only to those parties ***captioned as plaintiff*** in the original or amended complaint.

(a) Counter- or cross-claims: Thus, §1367(b) never bars counterclaims or cross-claims by defendants.

(b) Third-party claims: When a defendant impleads a third-party defendant, the rules refer to the defendant as the "third-party plaintiff." See Chapter 14. A third-party plaintiff, however, is ***not treated as a plaintiff*** under §1367(b).

iii. Listed rules: Section 1367 bars only state law claims made ***against*** parties who are ***made parties under Fed. R. Civ. P. 14, 19, 20, or 24***, or who seek to ***intervene as plaintiffs under Fed. R. Civ. P. 24***, as well as claims made ***by*** parties who intervene as plaintiffs under Fed. R. Civ. P. 24 or who are joined as involuntary plaintiffs under Fed. R. Civ. P. 19.

(a) **Most situations are barred:** The listed Federal Rules of Civil Procedure cover the vast majority of claims that a plaintiff can make, including claims by plaintiffs against multiple defendants (Fed. R. Civ. P. 20).

(b) **Situations possibly not covered by the exception:** There is some indication in the legislative history that Congress meant for §1367(b) to bar all claims by plaintiffs against nondiverse parties in diversity cases. If that was the goal, listing the rules was a poor decision because a couple of situations fell through the cracks. For example, class actions are covered by Fed. R. Civ. P. 23, which is not listed in §1367(b). A few cases have found that state law claims by parties in a class action are not barred even in diversity cases.

(c) **Single plaintiff/single defendant cases:** Note that it is unnecessary to consider supplemental jurisdiction in cases involving a single plaintiff and a single defendant, even if jurisdiction is based on diversity. If *P* has one claim against *D* that can make it to federal court because of diversity, all other claims can be *aggregated* with that claim. In fact, all that matters is that the total amount of the claims exceeds $75,000. Under the aggregation rules, no single claim needs to meet the amount in controversy requirement. Nor do the claims need to be related in any way. The rules governing aggregation are summarized in Part IV.H.5 of this chapter.

b. **Discretion exception:** Section 1367(c) allows a federal court to refuse to exercise supplemental jurisdiction over a state claim if the state claim raises a ***novel or complex issue of state law*** or ***substantially predominates*** over the federal claim, if the district court ***dismisses all federal claims***, or in exceptional circumstances, for any ***other compelling reason***.

★ **Example:** The court in Jin v. Ministry of State Security, 254 F. Supp. 2d 61 (2003), dealt with whether supplemental jurisdiction could extend to defamation claims brought by plaintiffs scattered across the United States. Although different state laws would apply to the individual claims, the court held that a dispute did not involve a complex issue of state law merely because resolving the state law claims would be difficult and time consuming. Instead, it indicated that standard would be met only when the state laws were themselves complex.

i. **Predominance:** Predominance is not measured only — or even primarily — in terms of dollars. Thus, if the state claim is factually complicated and will take the overwhelming majority of the court's time and attention, the predominance factor may be satisfied.

Example: *P*, a film director, sues *D* for copyright infringement. *P* also adds a claim arising under the state's new statute granting various categories of artists a right to be named as the producers of their artistic works. It is unclear whether the state law applies to film. Moreover, because so many people play a role in putting together a film, it is difficult to resolve whether the statute applies. Because *P* and *D* are not diverse, *P* seeks to use supplemental jurisdiction for the state law claim. The court could refuse to hear the state law claim under either the "novel or complex" factor or the predominance factor.

ii. **Other compelling reason:** Because the enumerated factors exhaust the situations where a federal court might desire not to hear the state claim, few courts have dismissed under the catchall provision.

c. **Procedure if exceptions apply:** If either §1367(b) or (c) applies, the court will dismiss *only the state law claim*. It will retain jurisdiction over the remaining claims in the case.

d. **Extension of limitations period:** If the court dismisses a state law claim, §1367(d) extends the limitations period for that claim. The limitations period is tolled while the case is in federal court, and for 30 days after dismissal, unless a longer period is provided in state law. This provision affords plaintiff the chance to refile the dismissed claim in state court.

Quiz Yourself on SUPPLEMENTAL JURISDICTION

32. Professor Hord has developed a bad reputation in the law school because she constantly checks books out of the library but never returns them. As a result, other library patrons are unable to complete their own research projects.

    Matters reach a head when Professor Smith receives a grant for a research project. Unable to find the books he needs, Professor Smith cannot complete the project and is forced to turn back the $50,000 in grant money. Smith complains to Professor Buch, the law librarian. A quick investigation reveals what the parties already suspected, namely, that the books in question were squirreled away in Professor Hord's office.

    Smith and Buch join as plaintiffs and sue Hord in federal court. Smith and Buch are both citizens of different states than Hord. Smith brings a claim under the state law of conversion, arguing that Hord's actions damaged him in the amount of $50,000. Buch, by contrast, brings a claim under the Federal Overdue Book Act, a federal statute that provides a cause of action for librarians against patrons who do not return books on time. Buch seeks the $1,000 statutory damages provided in the statute.

    Hord moves to dismiss Smith's claim for lack of subject matter jurisdiction. How will the court rule? _____

33. Same facts as Problem 32, except that Buch does not sue under the Federal Overdue Book Act. Instead, Buch brings his own state law conversion claim. The grant that Smith received provided not only $50,000 to Smith, but also provided a separate fund of $100,000 to the school library. The entire $150,000 had to be returned to the granting agency. Buch claims that Hord's actions damaged the library in the amount of $100,000. Hord moves to dismiss for lack of subject matter jurisdiction. How will the court rule? _____

34. Dora Sell sues Ray O'Vack in federal district court. Dora has two claims against Ray. The first is a claim for battery, for which Dora seeks $100,000 in damages. The second claim is a completely unrelated breach of contract claim, for which Dora seeks $10,000 in damages. Although Dora and Ray are diverse, Ray moves to dismiss the contract claim for lack of subject matter jurisdiction. How will the court rule? _____

35. Manufacturer and Supplier have a long-term contract under which Supplier provides a vital part to Manufacturer. Supplier announces that it has received a better offer from Competitor and will no long-

er honor its contract with Manufacturer. Manufacturer sues Competitor in a federal district court, alleging two claims. The first is a claim under the federal antitrust laws. The second is a state law claim for tortious interference with contract. Competitor immediately moves to dismiss the antitrust claim, arguing that the antitrust laws do not apply to this situation. The court agrees and dismisses the antitrust claim. Now, because Manufacturer and Competitor are both citizens of Wyoming, Competitor moves to dismiss the tortious interference claim for lack of subject matter jurisdiction. How will the court rule? _____

Answers

32. The court will deny the motion to dismiss. Buch v. Hord clearly qualifies as a federal question. Although there is no independent basis for jurisdiction over Smith v. Hord (no federal question and no diversity because of the amount in controversy), the court may exercise supplemental jurisdiction over Smith's claim. For purposes of §1367(a), the two claims arise out of a common nucleus of operative fact, namely, Hord's actions in checking out and refusing to return the books. That the parties suffered different injuries from that underlying conduct does not affect the result.

    The exception set out in §1367(b) does not apply here because jurisdiction over the "federal" claim (here, Buch v. Hord) is not based on diversity. Nor is the court likely to refuse to exercise jurisdiction under §1367(c). The state law claim is not terribly complex, nor is there anything in the facts to suggest it raises any novel issues. Even though the state claim far outweighs the federal in terms of damages, it will not substantially predominate at trial because it is relatively straightforward.

33. The court will dismiss Smith's claim (but not the entire case) for lack of subject matter jurisdiction. Buch v. Hord qualifies for diversity jurisdiction. As before, Smith v. Hord does not qualify of its own right. Nor will the Smith v. Hord claim qualify for supplemental jurisdiction under these circumstances. Although the requirements of §1367(a) are satisfied (the analysis is the same as in Problem 32), §1367(b) now poses an obstacle. Jurisdiction over the federal (Buch v. Hord) claim is based entirely on diversity. Therefore, §1367(b) prevents the court from exercising jurisdiction over the Smith v. Hord claim. If the court were to exercise jurisdiction over that claim, it would be inconsistent with the requirements of §1332. Note that something can be inconsistent with §1332 either because the parties are not diverse or because the amount in controversy is not satisfied.

    Incidentally, because the facts specify that the $100,000 is a separate fund, there is no possibility that the parties can aggregate their claims.

34. The court will deny the motion to dismiss. There is diversity jurisdiction over the battery claim. The contract claim cannot qualify for jurisdiction because the amount in controversy is not satisfied. However, Dora can aggregate the two claims. A single plaintiff may aggregate all claims she has against a single defendant, regardless of whether the claims are related. Because aggregation clearly works, there is no need to consider supplemental jurisdiction (which would not work anyway because the "same Article III case" requirement of §1367(a) is not met).

35. The court will probably dismiss the tortious interference claim. The only way that claim could be before the court is if it happens to qualify for supplemental jurisdiction. Section 1367(a) is satisfied because the federal and state claims arose from the same operative facts. Section 1367(b) is not an issue because jurisdiction over the federal (antitrust) claim was not based on diversity. However, the court may well exercise its discretion to dismiss the state claim under §1367(c)(3), which allows dismissal if

the court has dismissed all of the federal claims. Although dismissal is in the court's discretion, a court is likely to dismiss where, as here, the federal claim was dismissed so early in the lawsuit.

VI. REMOVAL OF CASES FROM STATE COURT TO FEDERAL COURT

The plaintiff's initial choice of forum is not set in stone. In some cases, a defendant may remove a case filed in state court to federal court.

A. Transfer distinguished: Removal should be distinguished from *transfers* under 28 U.S.C. §§1404 and 1406. Transfers are a discretionary change in venue from one federal court to another. ***Removal***, by contrast, is a ***matter of right*** and moves the case from ***state court to federal court***.

B. Governing law: In most cases, ***28 U.S.C. §1441*** provides the standard for removal. However, there are also specialized removal statutes, such as §§1442, 1442a, and 1443, which apply in particular cases. This discussion focuses only on §1441.

C. Nonremovable cases: *Section 1445* forbids removal in certain categories of cases, even if the requirements of §1441 are satisfied. For example, a case arising under the ***workers' compensation*** laws of a state cannot be removed.

D. Application of §1441: Section 1441 provides that the defendant in a state law case may remove a case "of which the district courts of the United States have original jurisdiction."

   1. Entire case: The case must be removed as a whole. If one of more of the claims in a multiclaim case does not fit within §1441, removal is impossible.

   2. Defendants: *Only the defendant may remove* a case.

      a. Plaintiffs: ***Plaintiffs may not remove***, even if the defendant has filed a counterclaim.

      b. Meaning of *defendant*: *Defendants* include all those who are ***actually parties*** to the suit and are ***directly adverse*** to the plaintiff. A defendant who has been named but has ***not been served*** need not join in the notice of removal.

      c. Multiple defendants: In a case involving multiple defendants, ***all defendants*** must join the notice of removal. If one defendant does not wish to remove, the case must stay in state court.

   3. District courts have original jurisdiction: The state court action must be one that could have been filed in federal court. In other words, the federal court must have ***federal question, diversity, or supplemental jurisdiction*** over all claims in the case. In addition, ***§1441(c)*** broadens a federal court's jurisdiction on removal to include certain state claims that could *not* have been heard in federal court had the action been originally filed there.

   4. Removal based on federal question: Determining whether a state court case presents a federal question generally works exactly as it would had the action been filed originally in federal court. The court applies the ***well-pleaded complaint rule*** to determine if the complaint states a federal question.

a. **Forgoing all federal claims:** A plaintiff is free not to assert her federal claims and file a complaint relying solely on state law. If plaintiff forgoes all federal claims, the case cannot be removed as a federal question.

b. **Exceptions to well-pleaded complaint rule:** Two exceptions to the well-pleaded complaint rule ordinarily come up only in the context of removal. In these situations, plaintiff has filed a complaint that appears to rely solely on state law. Nevertheless, the case can be removed. Both of these exceptions rarely arise.

   i. **Total preemption:** Under the doctrine of preemption, a federal law overrides contrary state law. A federal law usually preempts only a specific state law. However, sometimes federal policy is so strong that federal law preempts *an entire area of state law*. For example, the Federal Labor Management Relations Act preempts all state laws dealing with those same labor union issues. In these rare cases of total preemption, any cases arising under the preempted state law are treated as federal questions and may be removed to federal court.

   ii. **"Artful pleading" doctrine:** In some cases, a plaintiff may desire to keep her case out of federal court even though it involves a federal right. If the complaint is couched purely in terms of state law but in fact contains a disguised federal claim, the case can be removed as a federal question.

c. **When determined:** Whether the state court case presents a federal question is determined at the *time of removal*, not when the case is filed. Therefore, if the plaintiff amends a complaint by substituting a federal claim for the original state law claim, the case can be removed as a federal question.

5. **Removal based on diversity:** With two significant exceptions, diversity in a removal case is treated just as it is in a case originally filed in federal court. The exceptions are the *home-state removal bar of §1441(b)* and the *time* at which diversity must be met.

   a. **§1441(b):** The second sentence of §1441(b) allows removal based on diversity only "if none of the . . . defendants is a citizen of the State in which [the state] action is brought." If *any* of the defendants is a citizen of the state in which the state court action is pending, removal is impossible.

   Example: Plaintiff, a citizen of Wisconsin, brings an action in Michigan state court against *D1*, a citizen of Missouri, *D2*, a citizen of Montana, and *D3*, a citizen of Michigan. All claims are based on state law. Removal is impossible because *D3* is a citizen of Michigan.

   i. **Rationale:** Diversity jurisdiction exists to help thwart state court prejudice against outsiders. A defendant sued in a state court in his home state need not fear such prejudice. Although the plaintiff in such a case might face discrimination, plaintiff could have filed the case in federal court.

   ii. **Possibly waiveable:** A few courts treat the home-state removal bar requirement as a nonjurisdictional issue, which can be waived. Thus, if plaintiff does not file a timely objection to removal by a defendant sued in her home state, these courts will hear the case notwithstanding §1441(b).

   b. **Time for determining diversity:** In removal cases, diversity must exist in the state court case *both when the case was filed and at the time of removal*. This differs from the timing rule that applies to federal question removal.

    i. Therefore, if plaintiff adds a nondiverse party after the complaint was filed but before removal, removal is impossible. Similarly, a defendant cannot remove merely because the court dismisses the claims of all nondiverse plaintiffs.

    ii. **Exception #1:** However, the general timing rule does not apply to *postfiling acts by a plaintiff that create diversity*. For example, if plaintiff voluntarily dismisses his claims against all nondiverse defendants in the state court action, the case can be removed if it meets the other requirements for removal.

★   **iii. Exception #2:** In addition, if a case in which the parties are not diverse is *improperly removed* but the district court fails to remand, any judgment rendered by the district court is valid provided that diversity *did* exist *at the time judgment was entered*. Caterpillar, Inc. v. Lewis, 519 U.S. 61 (1996).

6. **Removal based on supplemental jurisdiction:** Many cases involve several claims for relief, such as multiple claims by plaintiff and/or counterclaims by the defendant. Unless federal question and diversity jurisdiction exist for every claim in the case, it is necessary to consider supplemental jurisdiction when the defendant attempts to remove.

    a. Analysis: Determining whether supplemental jurisdiction exists works exactly as it would had the case been filed originally in federal court.

    b. §1441(b): The home-state removal bar of §1441(b) may be a factor in supplemental jurisdiction cases where jurisdiction over the original plaintiff-defendant claim is based on diversity.

7. **Removal of separate and independent claims:** When plaintiff's case involves state law claims that are "separate and independent" from the federal claims, *§1441(c)* may allow removal of the entire case. This provision has proven controversial.

    a. Applies only in federal question cases: Section 1441(c) is explicitly limited to cases where one of the claims is a federal question.

    b. Not supplemental jurisdiction: Section 1441(c) requires that the state and federal question claims be separate and independent. This, it allows removal of state law claims that are *not covered by supplemental jurisdiction*.

    c. Constitutional issues: Because §1441(c) allows removal of state law claims that do not necessarily qualify for federal subject matter jurisdiction under Article III of the U.S. Constitution, there is some debate as to whether it is constitutional.

E. Place to which case removed: Section 1441(a) specifies that defendant removes to the federal district court "for the district and division embracing *the place where such action is pending*." Therefore, if the case is in a state court in Louisville, Kentucky, the defendant will remove to the federal district court for the Western District of Kentucky, Louisville division. Recall that *venue is automatically proper* in the designated district.

F. Procedure in removal: The procedural requirements for removal are mainly set forth in *28 U.S.C. §§1446 and 1447*. These requirements are strictly followed.

1. **Notice:** A defendant starts the removal process by filing a *notice of removal* with the appropriate district court. The notice must contain a brief statement of the grounds for removal. In addition, the defendant must attach copies of all state court pleadings.

a. **Not a petition:** Note that the party does not "request" removal from either the state or federal court. Filing the notice itself results in removal, subject to the federal court's authority to remand the case if the requirements for removal are not met.

b. **Copy to state court:** After filing the notice with the federal court, the defendant must promptly file a copy of the notice with the state court.

2. **Timing:** The notice must be filed within *30 days* after defendant receives *notice* that she is a defendant in a state court case that could have been filed in federal court.

a. **Original complaint states removable case:** If the original case filed by plaintiff is removable, the notice must be filed within 30 days of the *earlier of* (i) the date defendant receives a copy of the complaint, or (ii) if state law does not require the complaint to be served on the defendant, the date defendant is served with a summons.

b. **Case made removable by amendment or order:** If the original case was not removable, but the case becomes removable because of an amendment to the pleadings or an order dismissing one or more parties, the notice must be filed within 30 days of the date defendant receives the order or amended pleading.

c. **One-year limit:** Section 1446(b) sets out an important limit for diversity cases. A diversity case cannot be removed more than one year after it was originally commenced, even if the amendment or order making it removable does not occur until after that date.

Example: *P* sues *D1* and *D2* for $500,000 each, alleging only state law claims. *P* and *D1* are diverse, but *P* and *D2* are from the same state. Thirteen months after serving defendants with the summons, *P* dismisses the claims against *D2*. Even though the case now meets the requirements for diversity, *D1* cannot remove.

Example: *P* sues *D1* and *D2* for $500,000, alleging only state law claims. *P* and *D1* are diverse, but *P* and *D2* are from the same state. Thirteen months after serving defendants with the summons, *P* amends the complaint to add a federal question against *D2*. The federal question claim and state law claim arise from a common nucleus of operative fact. Defendants can remove if they file the notice within 30 days after receipt of the amended complaint.

d. **Multiple defendants:** In a case involving multiple defendants, the 30 days begins to run when the *first* defendant receives the item.

3. **Procedure after removal:** Section 1446 governs the procedure after removal.

a. **When removal effective:** Removal is effective *when the copy of the notice is filed with the state court*. 28 U.S.C. §1446(d).

b. **State court loses jurisdiction:** Once the state court receives its copy of the removal notice, §1441(d) directs it to proceed no further with the case. Proper removal strips the state court of its jurisdiction over the matter. Any orders it issues are of no effect.

c. **Objections to removal:** Objections to the procedure by which the case is removed must be filed within *30 days* following filing of the notice. Objections to the *subject matter jurisdiction* of the federal court, however, are not subject to this rule and can be made at any time.

d. **Remand:** If the federal court determines that removal was improper, it will remand the case to the state court.

Quiz Yourself on
SUBJECT MATTER JURISDICTION

36. Peter is employed by a partnership comprised of Donna and Doug. After he is fired, Peter sues Donna and Doug for violation of federal labor laws. Peter files his case on May 1 in a state court. He serves both defendants the same day. Donna files a timely notice of removal to the federal court in the district and serves copies on the other parties and the state court. Peter wants to object to removal. Where should Peter object? Assuming Peter objects properly, how will the court rule? _____

37. Same facts as Problem 36. On July 1, before the court rules on Peter's objection, the parties file an amended notice that both Donna and Doug sign. Peter objects to the new attempt to remove. How will the court rule? _____

38. While crossing the street at a marked intersection, Adam is struck and seriously injured by a vehicle driven by Don Gage. Don is a paramedic who was rushing to an accident scene at the time. Adam sues Don in a California state court for negligence, seeking $60,000 in damages. Don answers by citing a new federal statute that creates an immunity for fire, EMS, and police personnel who cause injuries in the line of duty. Don then files a timely notice of removal. Adam objects. Will the federal court hear the case? _____

39. Same facts as Problem 38, except that Adam's claim is $160,000. Adam is a citizen of Nevada, while Don is a citizen of California. Don files a timely notice of removal, and Adam objects. How will the court rule? _____

40. Barney and Floyd, two citizens of North Carolina, are embroiled in a bitter dispute. Barney is upset with Floyd for two reasons. First, Floyd, the town barber, recently took out an advertisement in the local paper that stated that getting a haircut from Floyd would help a person get the "woman of your dreams." Barney got a haircut but not a date.

Barney's second claim relates to the town choir. Barney, who fancies himself a budding opera singer, was crushed when Floyd beat him out for a spot in the choir.

Unable to resolve the matter amicably, Barney sues Floyd in a North Carolina state court. His complaint contains two counts. Count One, involving the haircut, is a claim for false advertising under 15 U.S.C. §1125(a). His second claim is a state law claim for intentional infliction of emotional distress, based on the choir fiasco.

Floyd files a timely notice of removal. Barney objects to removal. How will the court rule? _____

41. Da Vinci has just invented a better mousetrap. However, Da Vinci is reluctant to market the product. A few years ago, Edison obtained a patent on his own mousetrap. Da Vinci is worried that if he markets his invention, he will infringe the patent on Edison's mousetrap. To protect himself, Da Vinci sues Edison in a federal district court. Da Vinci asks the district court to issue a declaratory judgment finding that Da Vinci's trap is sufficiently dissimilar so that it does not infringe Edison's patent. Da Vinci and Edison are both citizens of Maine.

Later, Da Vinci changes his mind. Unable to get the court to agree to a voluntary dismissal, Da Vinci argues that the court should dismiss the case for lack of subject matter jurisdiction. Edison protests because he wants the question resolved once and for all in the federal court. What will be the ultimate outcome of the jurisdictional issue? _____

42. Walter is a junk food junkie. However, because he has a severe allergy to peanuts, Walter must avoid all foods that contain peanuts or peanut oil. A few weeks ago, Walter tried a new snack product made by Snakkum, Inc. Walter carefully perused the label and found no mention of peanuts. But soon after eating the product, Walter suffered a severe allergic reaction and had to be hospitalized. It turns out that the product contained a significant amount of peanut oil.

Walter sues Snakkum in a state court. His complaint contains one count, in which Walter alleges that Snakkum was negligent for not mentioning that the product had peanuts. Walter had considered suing under the federal product labeling laws, which require companies to list all the ingredients in their food products. Snakkum clearly violated the labeling law by failing to mention that its snack food contained peanut oil. However, Walter's further research shows that the federal product labeling laws are enforced by the Federal Food and Drug Administration. Private parties like Walter cannot sue to enforce the statute. Walter nevertheless decides to mention the federal labeling law in his complaint. Walter states that Snakkum was negligent per se for violating the standard set out in the federal labeling law.

Snakkum files a timely notice to remove the case. Walter contests removal. Walter correctly points out that both he and Snakkum are citizens of South Carolina. Walter also argues that his state law negligence claim does not constitute a federal question. Did Snakkum properly remove the case? _____

43. Refer to the facts of Problem 42. Wanda Ruhr is another junk food fan with a severe peanut allergy. Like Walter, Wanda purchased Snakkum's new product thinking that it was peanut-free and suffered a major reaction. Wanda brings her own action against Snakkum in a federal district court, basing jurisdiction on diversity.

At the time of her injury, Wanda was a citizen of Indiana. Before filing suit, however, she accepts a new position in the state of New Mexico. However, Wanda does not really like the climate in New Mexico and, although living there, does not intend to remain.

Two weeks before filing her suit, Wanda moves again, this time to South Carolina. Experiencing the stifling South Carolina heat and humidity makes Wanda realize that New Mexico was not all that bad. She soon decides that she wants New Mexico to be her permanent residence. Wanda therefore calls her old employer in New Mexico and convinces him to give Wanda her prior position. Wanda packs her belongings and prepares to return to New Mexico. The day before moving back, she files her suit in a South Carolina federal court against Snakkum. She serves process that same day.

After Wanda's move, Snakkum moves to dismiss for lack of subject matter jurisdiction. How will the court rule on Snakkum's motion? _____

44. Reva, a law student, is notoriously late for class. Determined to change her ways, Reva makes it a point to get to class earlier. On the very first day of her new plan, however, Reva finds herself running a little late. Therefore, rather than circle around the private property that sits between the parking lot and the law school, Reva cuts across the property. While crossing the property she steps in a bear trap and is seriously injured.

Reva sues Gary, the crotchety old man who owns the land, for negligence and battery. Because she and Gary are diverse, and because her damages far exceed $75,000, Reva brings her case in federal court relying on diversity jurisdiction.

Gary files an answer containing a counterclaim. In his counterclaim, Gary seeks damages for Reva's trespass to his property. Under governing state law, however, Gary can recover no more than $10 for this trespass.

Reva immediately moves to dismiss the counterclaim for lack of subject matter jurisdiction. How will the court rule? _____

45. ACME Foods produces the nation's most popular children's cereal, which it sells under the brand name Sugarsweet®. ACME advertises its product extensively on television. However, it does not use the Internet in its marketing efforts.

ACME is shocked to discover that one of its competitors, XYZ, Inc., registered the domain name *www.sugarsweet.com*. XYZ uses this Web site to tell consumers how its products are far superior to Sugarsweet.

ACME immediately sues XYZ in a state court. ACME has two claims. The first is a claim under the new federal ''cybersquatting'' statute, which allows someone with a famous mark such as ACME's Sugarsweet to prevent others from registering that mark as a domain name. The second is a claim under common law unfair competition.

XYZ files a timely notice of removal. Although the parties are not diverse, XYZ points out that one of the claims arises under a federal law, the cybersquatting statute. ACME contests removal, preferring to have the action heard in state court. How will the court rule? _____

46. Lender sues Borrower in a New York state court for failing to make payments on a loan. Lender is a citizen of New York, and Borrower is a citizen of Maryland. Lender seeks $120,000 in damages. Borrower files a timely notice of removal. Lender objects to removal, arguing that the only possible basis for federal jurisdiction is diversity. How will the court rule? _____

Answers

36. Peter should file his objection in the federal court to which the defendant attempted to remove. Section 1446(d) provides that once a copy of the notice of removal is filed with the state court, the state court ''shall proceed no further'' with the case. Therefore, Peter must ask the federal court to remand the case.

The federal court will remand the action to state court because it was not properly removed. In a case involving multiple defendants, all defendants must join in the notice of removal.

37. The federal court will remand the action to state court. Although all defendants removed, the amended notice was filed too late. Section 1446(b) requires that the notice be filed within 30 days following defendants' receipt of the complaint setting out the federal question. Because the complaint was filed and served on May 1, the notice would have to have been filed by May 30.

38. The federal court will remand the case. A case may be removed under §1441(a) only if it could have been filed originally in federal court. Because of the amount in controversy, this case could go to federal court only as a federal question under §1331. However, for the case to qualify as a federal question, a federal claim must appear on the face of the complaint. Adam's complaint states only a state law claim. The interposition of the federal defense does not turn the case into a federal question.

39. The federal court will remand the case. As modified, the case could have been brought in federal court only on the basis of diversity. However, §1441(b) bars removal solely on the basis of diversity by a defendant who is sued in her home state. Because Don is a California citizen sued in a California state court, he cannot remove.

40. Removal will be allowed. The false advertising claim can be removed as a federal question. The state law claim is more problematic. It cannot be removed on the basis of diversity because the parties are both citizens of North Carolina. Nor is it a federal question. Moreover, because the claims are unrelated, removal based on supplemental jurisdiction is not a possibility.

However, precisely because the claims are unrelated, removal is possible under §1441(c). Floyd's federal claim is a federal question. Section 1441(c) accordingly allows Floyd to remove a separate and independent claim along with that federal question.

41. There are two issues here: whether Da Vinci, as plaintiff, may challenge jurisdiction and whether the court actually has jurisdiction.

   Da Vinci clearly can raise the issue. Subject matter jurisdiction can never be waived and can be raised by any party, or the court itself, at any time.

   However, the court will not dismiss the case. Although there is no diversity, the case presents a federal question. When dealing with a declaratory judgment, a court analyzes the issue by determining what action would occur if the plaintiff had not filed for a declaratory judgment. Here, absent a declaratory judgment, Edison would eventually sue Da Vinci for infringement of his patent. That action could be heard in a federal court as a federal question (in fact, it would have to be because federal jurisdiction in patent infringement cases is exclusive). Therefore, Da Vinci's suit for declaratory judgment likewise presents a federal question.

42. Removal is not proper under these facts. In order to remove a case, the case must be one that could have been filed by the plaintiff in a federal court. Walter could only file his case in federal court if it would qualify for diversity or federal question jurisdiction. Diversity is clearly not met because the parties are from the same state.

   Nor does Walter's negligence claim involve a federal question. The basic claim arises under state law. Admittedly, the court may need to interpret the federal labeling law given the way Walter has stated his claim. A state law claim that incorporates federal law as an element may sometimes qualify as a federal question. In order to qualify as a federal question, however, the underlying federal law must itself create a private cause of action for violations. The facts specify that the federal food labeling law does not create a private cause of action. Therefore, the state law negligence claim is not a federal question notwithstanding the federal "ingredient."

43. The court will dismiss the case for lack of subject matter jurisdiction. The case does not involve a federal question. Nor are Wanda and Snakkum diverse. Wanda is probably still a citizen of Indiana, which is one of the states of which Snakkum is a citizen. She did not become a New Mexico citizen when she moved there, for the facts specify that while there she never intended to remain. Without the intent to remain, she did not become a New Mexico domiciliary.

   Her later change of plans also did not establish a New Mexico domicile. To become a domiciliary of a state, one must both reside there and have the intent to remain at the same instant. When Wanda changed her mind, she was living in South Carolina. Moreover, she filed her suit while still in South Carolina. Diversity is measured when the suit is commenced. Although she became a New Mexico domiciliary *after* filing the case, on the crucial date — the date of filing — she had not yet become a New Mexico domiciliary.

   Because she did not change her domicile, Wanda keeps her original domicile of Indiana. Note that she might also have become a South Carolina domiciliary if she had the intent to remain in that state while living there (the facts do not specify). But even if she is a South Carolina resident, she is not diverse from Snakkum.

44. The court will keep the counterclaim. Every claim in a federal case, including counterclaims, must qualify for federal jurisdiction. There is no independent jurisdiction over the counterclaim. Trespass is not a federal question. Although the parties are diverse, the amount in controversy is not met for the counterclaim (and defendants cannot aggregate a counterclaim with plaintiff's claim).

   However, supplemental jurisdiction will be available over the counterclaim. The counterclaim arises out of the same Article III case as Reva's claim. Her act of trespassing across the property not only gave rise to Gary's claim but also led to her own injuries. Therefore, §1367(a) is satisfied.

Section 1367(b) is not a bar. Although this is a case in which jurisdiction over the federal claim is based solely on diversity, Gary's counterclaim is not a claim by a plaintiff and is therefore not affected by §1367(b).

Nor will §1367(c) be a problem. The federal claim, not the state claim, predominates here. The state claim is relatively straightforward and will not occupy much of the court's time.

45. Removal will be allowed. A defendant may remove a case that could have been filed in federal court. The cybersquatting claim presents a federal question. Although the unfair competition claim is not a federal question and does not qualify for diversity because the parties are not diverse, it could be brought along with the cybersquatting claim under supplemental jurisdiction. (In truth, the party probably would not rely on §1367, the general supplemental jurisdiction statute, but instead invoke §1338(b), a specialized statute that applies to unfair competition claims. However, the analysis under each statute is basically the same.)

The two claims are sufficiently related to qualify as the same Article III case under §1367(a). Both claims arise out of XYZ's registration of the Web site. Section 1367(b) is not an issue because although this is a claim by a plaintiff, jurisdiction over the federal claim is based on federal question, not diversity. Nor is it likely that a court would exercise discretion to dismiss the common law claim.

Because supplemental jurisdiction would allow both claims to be filed in federal court, XYZ can remove under §1441(a). The facts specify that the notice of removal was timely.

46. The federal court will not remand the case. The case could have been brought in a federal court utilizing diversity jurisdiction. And although §1441(b) bars removal based solely on diversity in some cases, it does not apply here because Borrower was not sued in his home state.

 Exam Tips on
SUBJECT MATTER JURISDICTION

☛ Questions involving subject matter jurisdiction are likely to arise mainly in actions brought in, or that are being removed to, ***federal courts***.

   ☞ One important exception is a situation where the federal courts have ***exclusive jurisdiction***. If a claim over which the federal courts have exclusive jurisdiction is brought in state court, the state court must dismiss.

☛ **Analytical hierarchy:** When dealing with a question of federal subject matter jurisdiction, always consider diversity and federal question jurisdiction first. Only if these fail do you need to consider the considerably more difficult issue of supplemental jurisdiction.

   ☞ One common type of question where students fall into the trap of discussing supplemental jurisdiction is one involving ***aggregation*** of claims to meet the amount in controversy. Remember that a single plaintiff may aggregate all claims she has against a single diverse defendant, regardless of whether the claims are related in any way.

☛ Recall that defects in subject matter jurisdiction *cannot be waived*. Challenges to subject matter jurisdiction may be made at any time, by any party, and by the court itself.

☛ **Federal question jurisdiction:** The two most difficult issues in federal question jurisdiction are when a claim "arises under" federal or national law and when the "well-pleaded complaint rule" is used.

☞ Applying the *well-pleaded complaint rule* requires a consideration of both the substantive law and the rules governing pleading. In essence, you must consider what plaintiff needs to plead in order to state a claim under that particular theory of relief. Any unnecessary surplusage that plaintiff throws in will not be considered.

☞ *Declaratory judgment* claims present special problems in applying the well-pleaded complaint rule. If faced with such a claim, try to determine who would sue who if the declaratory judgment had not been brought. If that later claim would qualify for federal question jurisdiction, the declaratory judgment claim will too.

☛ **Diversity jurisdiction:** The most confusing issues in diversity jurisdiction are the complete diversity rule, determining the citizenship of the parties, and the amount in controversy.

☞ In a multiparty case, always be on the lookout for an issue of *complete diversity*.

☞ When dealing with individual litigants, be prepared to discuss their *domicile*. One's domicile need not be the same as one's current residence.

☞ Do not forget the special rules that apply to corporations, liability insurance carriers, representatives, and permanent resident aliens. For example, a corporation often has two citizenships. Recall that if either of these is the same as the citizenship of an opposing party, there is no diversity jurisdiction.

☞ Do not overlook the court-created *domestic relations and probate exceptions* to diversity jurisdiction.

☞ Make sure you have a handle on the many technical points that go into the *amount in controversy*, such as what types of interest may be included, how a court will ascribe a value to a specific remedy such as an injunction, and the rules governing *aggregation of claims*.

☞ If one or more parties are engaged in manipulative behavior to try to get the case into federal court, you should discuss §1359. That statute, however, deals only with attempts to manufacture, not defeat, jurisdiction.

☛ *Supplemental jurisdiction* augments federal question and diversity. As noted above, consider supplemental jurisdiction for a claim only after you rule out federal question and diversity.

☞ Supplemental jurisdiction replaced the older judge-made doctrines of ancillary and pendent jurisdiction. You should not mention the older doctrines.

☞ When applying the "same Article III case" test of §1367(a), use the "common nucleus of operative facts" approach of the Supreme Court's *Gibbs* decision. If the two claims arise from the same core event or series of events, the claims may comprise the same Article III case, even if they do not share all that many facts.

☞ The diversity exception of §1367(b) is particularly difficult for many students. The exception applies only to claims by plaintiffs, only to claims against parties joined under the listed rules, and only if jurisdiction over the federal claim is based solely on diversity.

☞ Do not forget to apply the discretionary exceptions of §1367(c). Recall, though, that a court usually refrains from dismissing a claim under §1367(c) unless it clearly falls into one of the listed categories.

☛ Removal from state court to federal is usually proper only when the case could have been brought originally in a federal court. Therefore, every removal question also requires you to consider federal question, diversity, and possibly supplemental jurisdiction.

☞ Be sure to consider the timing and procedural issues involved in removal.

CHAPTER 5

THE *ERIE* DOCTRINE

ChapterScope ━━━━━━━━━━━━━━━━━━━━━━━━━━━━━━━━━━

The *Erie* doctrine plays a major role in defining the nature and role of the federal courts in the United States. The doctrine ensures that state courts play the primary role in forming the common law rules in tort, contract, and other areas of substantive law.

■ The basic command of *Erie* is that the **federal courts must follow state law**, except when a valid federal statute or rule applies, or in certain areas of special federal prerogative.

■ *Erie* has its roots in the **Rules of Decision Act**, 28 U.S.C. §1652. However, the Supreme Court has made it clear that the doctrine is also grounded in the U.S. Constitution.

■ A federal court is not always required to defer to state law.

   ■ If a **federal statute** provides the substantive law for a case, the federal court will apply the federal law, not state law. Therefore, *Erie* applies mainly in **diversity cases**.

   ■ A federal court also has the **inherent power** to enact its own rules of **procedure**.

   ■ The **Federal Rules of Civil Procedure** are a special case. Although drafted by the Supreme Court, the rules are authorized by the **Rules Enabling Act**, 28 U.S.C. §2072. Because of the delegation from Congress, courts use a **different test** in cases involving the Federal Rules than they use in cases involving ordinary judge-made procedural rules.

   ■ Finally, there is a limited body of **substantive federal common law**, which overrides state law just as federal statutes do.

■ Whenever a federal court is required by *Erie* to apply state law, it must determine the current state of the law by evaluating state court precedent.

━━

I. OVERVIEW OF *ERIE*

The *Erie* doctrine has developed through a series of Supreme Court cases, which are discussed throughout this chapter. Before exploring the details, it may be helpful to take a brief look at the doctrine as it exists today.

A. Three categories of *Erie* issues: *Erie* cases fall into three basic categories. The analysis of each differs significantly.

   1. No federal positive law: The first category involves cases, like *Erie* itself, where there is **no federal positive law** (that is, no statute or codified rule) on the subject. In these cases, the **Rules of Decision Act** (28 U.S.C. §1652) applies. Part III of this chapter explores this category in depth.

   a. In these cases, the federal court is deciding **whether to ignore state law** and instead decide the issue based on the judge's own perception of how the issue should be resolved. The judge's perception may be guided by her own view of underlying substantive policy or may simply represent a custom or practice followed by the federal courts.

b. Cases in this category are resolved by determining whether ignoring state law and applying a contrary federal rule would be ***likely to cause forum-shopping***, i.e., affect the plaintiff's decision whether to sue in state or federal court. If forum-shopping is likely, state law must be applied.

2. *Federal rules:* The second category of *Erie* cases encompasses those that involve a ***Federal Rule of Civil Procedure*** or other federal rule created under the ***Rules Enabling Act*** (28 U.S.C. §2072). This situation is discussed in Part IV of this chapter.

a. Although the Federal Rules of Civil Procedure are judge-made law, they are different for purposes of *Erie*. Congress delegated part of its lawmaking authority to the Supreme Court in §2072.

b. Analysis of a Federal Rule of Civil Procedure or other Rules Enabling Act rule turns on whether the rule in question can rationally be characterized as a rule governing procedure, and whether the rule unduly abridges, enlarges, or modifies the underlying substantive claim in the case. If the Federal Rule of Civil Procedure ***is procedural***, and ***does not unduly abridge, enlarge, or modify*** the substantive right, it applies in lieu of state law.

3. Federal statute: The third category of *Erie* cases is those that involve a federal statute. Because *Erie* is not a limit on Congress, a federal statute will always be applied, provided it really governs the situation at hand. This situation is discussed in Part V of this chapter.

B. Conflicts: In all three categories of *Erie* cases, it is important to ensure that the federal "law" actually conflicts with state law.

II. THE *ERIE* DECISION

The Supreme Court issued *Erie* in 1938. However, the roots of the opinion date back to a much earlier time.

A. Historical background: *Erie* stems from the 1789 ***Rules of Decision Act*** and the Supreme Court's interpretation of that act in Swift v. Tyson.

1. Rules of Decision Act: The Rules of Decision Act (hereinafter RODA) provided that "the ***laws of the several states***, except where the constitution, treaties, or statutes of the United States shall otherwise require or provide, shall be regarded as the rules of decision" in the federal courts. RODA remains in effect, with slight modifications. It is codified at ***28 U.S.C. §1652***.

2. *Swift***:** The Supreme Court's most important pre-*Erie* interpretation of RODA was Swift v. Tyson, 41 U.S. 1 (1841). The basic holding of *Swift* was that federal courts were ***not bound by RODA to follow state judicial opinions*** on most legal issues. Instead, a federal court could make an independent interpretation of what the common law rule was on the particular subject.

a. Rationale: *Swift* turned on the meaning of the word *laws* in RODA.

i. To the Court, the term included only ***state statutes*** and ***local common law*** such as rules governing real property. By contrast, ***court decisions interpreting the general common law*** were not "laws" within the meaning of RODA.

ii.   *Swift*'s interpretation of RODA was based on a particular view of the nature of the common law that was to dominate legal thinking for decades. To the Court, the common law ***did not trace its origins to any individual state***. Instead, it was a body of unwritten law that applied in all common law nations. The decisions of a particular state court ***did not create*** the law, but rather merely ***interpreted*** this body of general law. That interpretation did not bind other courts interpreting the same general rule.

b.   **Creation of federal common law:** Of course, although the federal courts after *Swift* were not bound to follow state courts, they were bound to follow rulings of the federal courts of appeal and Supreme Court. As the federal courts continued to interpret the common law, there developed a body of law called ***federal common law***, which applied in the federal courts only.

★ **B. *Erie:*** The Supreme Court revisited RODA in Erie Railroad v. Tompkins, 304 U.S. 64 (1938). *Erie* not only overturned *Swift*'s interpretation of RODA, but replaced its view of a "general" common law with an entirely different paradigm.

1.   **Facts:** The plaintiff in *Erie* was hit by a train while walking along the tracks of defendant railroad. He sued the railroad in a federal district court based on diversity jurisdiction, claiming that the railroad had acted negligently by leaving the door to one of the cars open. The accident happened in Pennsylvania.

2.   **Clash of laws:** Under Pennsylvania law, plaintiff could recover only upon a showing of "wanton" negligence because he would be considered a trespasser on the railroad's right-of-way. Plaintiff, however, argued that the federal court should apply the "general" or federal common law rule, which required the railroad to act with ordinary care.

3.   **Holding:** The Supreme Court held that the lower court was obligated to apply Pennsylvania's wanton negligence standard.

4.   **Rationale:** The Court ***overturned*** its earlier holding in *Swift*, finding that the reference to *laws* in RODA included not only state statute law, but also ***state judicial opinions*** interpreting the common law.

a.   **View of common law:** The *Erie* Court rejected the idea that there was a "general" common law that applied with equal force in all common law jurisdictions. Instead, the court indicated that each sovereign state created ***its own common law***.

b.   **Federal courts and common law:** The Court also held that federal courts, unlike state courts, had ***no power to create common law***. Therefore, RODA required the federal courts to follow the common law rules set out by the state courts.

C. Constitutional underpinnings of *Erie*: The Court in theory could have reached the holding described above solely on the basis of RODA. However, the Court made it clear that the result in the case was dictated by the ***U.S. Constitution***.

1.   **Applicable provision:** The constitutional basis for the holding is not entirely clear. The best interpretation is that the holding is based on basic principles of ***federalism*** reflected in Article I, Article III, and the Tenth Amendment.

2.   **Constitutional argument:** The Court began its constitutional discussion (in Part III of the opinion) with the premise that "***there is no federal general common law***."

a. **Limits on Congress:** It then noted that although Congress clearly has the power to pass laws on specific subjects, it did not have the power to supplant the ***entire body of state common law*** with federal statutes. If it did, Article I of the Constitution, which carefully limits Congress's powers, would be rendered meaningless.

b. **Limits on federal courts:** Allowing federal courts to enact their own common law rules in any diversity case would give the federal government a back-door way to exercise legislative power in areas reserved to the states.

III. APPLYING *ERIE* IN THE ABSENCE OF FEDERAL POSITIVE LAW

Erie suggests that a federal court has no power to make law. Although the Court quickly backed off from that blanket rule, it struggled with how to define the sorts of rules that fell under *Erie*'s mandate.

★ **A.** ***Guaranty Trust* and the "procedural" exception:** Seven years after *Erie*, the Supreme Court recognized an important exception in Guaranty Trust Co. v. York, 326 U.S. 99 (1945). *Guaranty Trust* held that a federal court is obligated to apply a state statute of limitations.

1. **Statute of limitations vs. laches:** Because the federal court in *Guaranty Trust* was sitting in equity, it had applied the traditional equitable doctrine of laches when determining if the action was brought too late. However, the courts of New York (the state in which the federal district court sat) would have applied the state statute of limitations even when the action was in equity. The Supreme Court held that the federal court had to apply the state statute of limitations and dismiss the action.

2. **Procedural exception:** Although finding statutes of limitations within the scope of *Erie*, *Guaranty Trust* is better known for its discussion of what sorts of rules do *not* fall within *Erie*'s command. The Court held that *Erie* applied only to matters of **substance, not procedure**. A federal court is ***free to ignore state procedural rules*** and rely on the customs and practices used in federal court.

3. **Outcome determinative test:** The Court noted that the law at issue in the case itself — a statute of limitations — was usually considered a rule of procedure in other contexts. However, the Court held that it should be treated as a substantive rule for *Erie*. The Court ruled that any rule that could ***affect the outcome*** should be considered **substantive** under *Erie*. A state statute of limitations would clearly change the outcome.

4. **Problem with analysis:** The problem with the outcome determinative test is that virtually any procedural matter can change the outcome of a case. Therefore, the test would require federal courts to apply many state rules that are clearly procedural.

   Example: The fee for filing a case in federal district court is $100. The state filing fee is $120. Under the outcome determinative test, the federal court would have to charge $120. If a party walked into state court and tried to pay only $100, the clerk would not accept the complaint, and plaintiff would stand no chance of recovery. For a federal court to accept the complaint clearly could change the outcome.

B. **Redefining** *procedure: Guaranty Trust*'s outcome determinative test proved unworkable in practice. The Court struggled to develop a workable test for twenty years.

★ **1.** ***Byrd* and balancing:** In Byrd v. Blue Ridge Electric Cooperative, 356 U.S. 525 (1958), the Court held that a federal court did not have to follow a state law that required a certain question to be decided by the judge. Instead, the federal court could follow the federal practice of having a jury decide the question.

   a. Judge vs. jury: The Court recognized that whether a judge or jury decided the case could affect the outcome. However, it held that the likelihood of a different outcome was not great.

   b. Federal interest: Moreover, the Court noted a ***strong federal interest in using juries*** whenever possible, as evidenced by the Seventh Amendment to the U.S. Constitution. On the other hand, the state rule requiring a judge reflected no strong state interest, but was merely a historical practice.

   c. Holding: Comparing these interests, the Court held that the federal court could use a jury, even though the difference in laws was slightly outcome determinative.

   d. Current relevance: Although the Supreme Court's *Hanna* test, discussed just below, provides a more workable way to deal with most procedural issues, the *Byrd* balancing test has never been disavowed. It continues to apply to judge-jury questions and is often invoked by the lower courts on other issues.

★ **2.** ***Hanna* and forum-shopping:** In Hanna v. Plumer, 380 U.S. 460 (1965), the Court held that a federal court could apply Fed. R. Civ. P. 4 instead of state law to determine how process must be served. Although the case was decided on the basis of the Rules Enabling Act, discussed in Part IV of this chapter, *dictum* in the decision supplied a new test for determining whether ordinary judge-made rules are procedural.

   a. Rationale: The *Hanna* Court stated that *Erie* had "twin aims": discouraging ***forum-shopping*** and avoiding ***inequitable administration of the laws***. Therefore, a federal court should not be required to apply all state law whenever the outcome might differ, but only when that difference in outcome would contravene one of the aims of *Erie*.

   b. New test: Thus, a federal court must apply state law only when failure to do so would ***likely result in forum-shopping between state and federal courts*** because of the likelihood of a ***different outcome***.

   i. Forum-shopping: By restricting *Erie* to cases where forum-shopping is likely, the test allows a federal court to apply its own procedural customs even though there is a chance that the outcome would be different. A federal court must apply state law only if the likelihood of a different outcome is so great that the plaintiff will base her choice of forum on the different rules.

   ii. Irrelevant which court preferred: Under the *Hanna* test, it is irrelevant whether the litigant would prefer state or federal court. In either case, state law applies.

   iii. Different outcome: *Erie* is concerned with forum-shopping only when it is motivated by the hope for a ***different outcome*** based on a ***difference in applicable laws***. Other motivations for forum-shopping do not matter.

   Example: The filing fee in federal court is $100, while in state court it is $10,000. Although this difference is likely to cause forum-shopping, the federal court need not charge the state fee. Any forum-shopping that occurs will not be designed to procure a more favorable outcome.

c. Applying the test—an example: Today, the *Hanna* test covers most cases involving federal judge-made law. The following example illustrates how the test applies.

    i. Facts: *P* sues *D* in a federal court sitting in State *X*. *P*'s complaint alleges a state law fraud claim. *P* argues that two laws of State *X* should apply in the federal proceeding.

        (a) First, *P* argues that *X*'s law governing **burden of persuasion** should apply to the case. *X* requires the plaintiff to prove fraud merely by a **preponderance of the evidence**. All other states, by contrast, require a party suing for fraud to prove the fraud by **clear and convincing evidence**, a much more difficult standard.

        (b) Second, *P* argues that the federal court should schedule an **immediate trial**, following *X*'s procedural rule requiring fraud claims to be put before all other claims on the trial docket.

    ii. Decision: The federal court must follow the state burden rule, but not the scheduling rule.

        (a) If the burden rule is not followed, it could lead to forum-shopping for a different outcome. A plaintiff might be more inclined to sue in state court if it is easier for her to prove her case in that court. (Note that it does not matter that *this* particular plaintiff chose federal court, where the burden is higher.)

        (b) Differences in how a case is put on the trial docket might also lead to forum-shopping since a plaintiff usually wants his claim wrapped up as quickly as possible. However, this is not forum-shopping *for a different outcome*. Therefore, the federal court need *not follow the state rule*.

C. Choice of law: When a state court hears a dispute that has connections to several states, it does not necessarily apply its own law. The court instead engages in a choice of law analysis to determine which state's law applies. This analysis relies on the state's **choice of law rules**, which are typically rules established by precedent.

    1. *Erie* and choice of law: In Klaxon Co. v. Stentor Electric Manufacturing Co., 313 U.S. 487 (1941), the Supreme Court held that a state's choice of law rules are **substantive**. Therefore, a federal court will decide a case not necessarily under the law of the state in which it sits, but under the law that **would be applied** by the courts of the state in which it sits.

    Example: A federal district court in Maine is hearing a diversity case brought by a Québec plaintiff against a Maine defendant. The action arises out of a breach of contract that was to be performed in Québec. Maine state courts would apply Québec law to determine if defendant's act breached the contract. Contract law is clearly substantive because applying different rules on the issue of breach could result in forum-shopping. Therefore, the federal court must likewise apply Québec law.

    2. State jurisdiction irrelevant: The rule of *Klaxon* applies even if the state in which the federal court sits could not hear the case because of lack of personal jurisdiction over some defendants. Griffin v. McCoach, 313 U.S. 498 (1941).

D. Judge-jury determinations: Although the Supreme Court has dealt with relatively few cases falling into the first *Erie* category, it has faced one issue — whether a judge or jury decides a particular issue in a case — twice.

1. ***Byrd:*** *Byrd* is discussed above. Although one could argue that the *Byrd* balancing test has been replaced by the *Hanna* test, lower courts still sometimes invoke *Byrd*.

★   2. ***Gasperini:*** Gasperini v. Center for Humanities, Inc., 518 U.S. 415 (1996), is a post-*Hanna* decision that deals with how a jury verdict would be ***reviewed***. The state law allowed the ***court of appeals*** to overturn the verdict if it "***deviates materially*** from what would be reasonable compensation." Federal courts, by contrast, apply a much more stringent standard. The Supreme Court held that the federal court had to use the ***state law standard***. However, the ***trial court***, not the court of appeals, would apply the standard.

     a. The Court held that the difference in standards would be ***likely to cause forum-shopping***. Therefore, the federal court had to apply the state standard.

     b. However, the Court also held that because of the ***Reexamination Clause of the Seventh Amendment***, the court of appeals could not apply the state standard. On the other hand, because trial judges at common law could review the substance of verdicts, the Court held that the ***trial judge should apply*** the state law standard.

Quiz Yourself on
APPLYING ERIE *TO JUDGE-MADE LAW*

47. Texas is well known for its local patriotism. To instill even more state pride, the Texas legislature enacts a statute that requires all attorneys appearing before a court to wear a lapel pin of the Texas flag. If an attorney does not wear the pin, the court may not hear his argument.

     Sam Houston, a Texas attorney, is ready to try his first solo case in federal court. Although he has meticulously prepared his witnesses and arguments, he forgets to wear his Texas flag lapel pin to the federal court. Opposing counsel therefore objects when Sam stands up to present his case. Will the federal court let Sam proceed? _____

48. The state of Tranquility has suffered a series of fires in its courts, in which irreplaceable records were destroyed. To deal with this problem, the Tranquility High Court enacts a new rule that requires all documents filed with the court to be submitted on fireproof paper. Although this will take care of the threat of fire, fireproof paper costs $4 per sheet.

     Fran Chize is considering bringing a case under a federal statute. Because her case is very complex, she anticipates having to file at least 10,000 sheets of paper during the proceeding. Although Fran can sue in either federal or state court, she is inclined to pick federal court to minimize her litigation costs. If Fran does sue in federal court, can she use ordinary paper instead of the fireproof paper? _____

49. Wolverine, Inc., is a small corporation that manufactures snowblowers. Wolverine is a Michigan corporation that is located entirely in, and sells all of its product in, that state.

     Courtney is Wolverine's best salesperson. As a reward, Wolverine pays for Courtney to attend a major snowblower manufacturer's convention in Pristine Beach, Florida. While at the convention, Courtney has slightly *too* good a time at one of the free cocktail receptions. Courtney gets out the sample snowblower that she brought with her to the convention and uses it to cause hundreds of thousands of dollars of damage to the pristine beaches in front of one of Pristine Beach's finest hotels.

The hotel, a Florida corporation, decides to bring suit. Because Courtney is currently behind bars and unlikely to be able to pay a judgment, the hotel sues Wolverine. However, because the hotel is worried about personal jurisdiction, it sues Wolverine in Michigan. The hotel brings the suit in a federal district court in Michigan, basing subject matter jurisdiction on diversity.

Wolverine is glad it is located in Michigan rather than Florida. Unlike Florida law, Michigan law does not impose liability on an employer for a tort like that committed by Courtney. Wolverine therefore moves to dismiss the case. Will the case be dismissed? _____

Answers

47. The federal court will let Sam argue. True, the Texas rule is outcome determinative in the sense that Sam cannot prevail if he cannot address the court. Nevertheless, pure ''outcome determination'' is no longer the test. Now the test is whether the difference in rules would likely lead to forum-shopping. No reasonable attorney would base his choice of federal or state court on whether attorneys must wear a certain lapel pin.

48. There are two issues in this problem. First, note that the case is not exempt from the *Erie* doctrine merely because the action arises under federal law. Although *Erie* issues arise most commonly in diversity cases, they can also arise in federal question cases.

    Second, the federal court will not require fireproof paper. True, the difference in laws might well cause forum-shopping — indeed, it looks as if Fran is actually engaged in forum-shopping. However, because the forum-shopping would not seek a different outcome, it should not cause the court to apply state law.

49. This is an *Erie* question with a choice of law twist. First, it is clear that the federal court will have to follow state law on the basic issue of whether an employer can be liable for the intentional torts of an employee. To refuse to follow state law would generate forum-shopping.

    But which state's law? The Michigan federal court, under *Klaxon*, is required to apply the law that would be applied by the courts of the state in which it sits. Although the court sits in Michigan, the Michigan state courts might apply Florida law, given that the plaintiff is from the state, the defendant's employee acted in the state, and the harm occurred there. Without knowing Michigan's choice of law rules, it is impossible to predict the outcome.

IV. CLASHES BETWEEN THE FEDERAL RULES AND STATE LAW

The second category of *Erie* case involves situations where the Court must decide whether to apply a Federal Rule of Civil Procedure or similar codified court rule. The analysis applied in these cases is significantly different from that applied in cases involving ordinary judge-made rules.

A. **Federal rules defined:** Most of the cases involving this branch of the analysis have dealt with the *Federal Rules of Civil Procedure*. However, the same basic analysis also applies to the *Federal Rules of Appellate Procedure* and *Federal Rules of Evidence*.

1. **Common source of rules:** All of these rules share one crucial feature. They were ***promulgated by the Supreme Court*** pursuant to a ***delegation of power from Congress***.

   a. **Rules Enabling Act:** Congress clearly has the constitutional authority to enact laws controlling the procedure used in the federal courts. However, Congress delegated a large portion of this authority to the Supreme Court in the Rules Enabling Act (REA), ***28 U.S.C. §2072***.

   b. **Process:** Pursuant to 28 U.S.C. §2074, the Court must transmit proposed rules to Congress. Congress has a sort of veto power over rules created under the REA. But unless Congress takes action within the specified period, the rule takes effect.

2. **Supremacy:** When the Court creates a federal rule under this delegated power, the rule overrides state law under the Supremacy Clause, just as a federal statute would. 28 U.S.C. §2072.

B. **Overview of analysis:** Hanna v. Plumer, discussed in Part III above, sets out the analysis to use when dealing with a clash between a federal rule and state law. Because *Hanna* involved this very situation, this portion of the opinion is ***not dictum***.

   1. **"Valid" and "applicable":** At its core, the analysis of a federal rule is logically the same as the analysis that applies to a federal statute: If the rule is ***valid*** and ***applicable***, it ***automatically applies***. However, because of restrictions that Congress has placed on the federal rules, determining whether a federal rule is "valid" is more complicated.

   2. **Three-step analysis:** Basically, *Hanna* sets out a three-step analysis. First, you must determine that the rule ***actually applies***. Second, the state law and federal rule must actually ***conflict***. Finally, you must ensure that the federal rule is ***valid under the REA***.

C. **Determining the applicability of a federal rule:** The first step in an *Erie* analysis involving a federal rule is to make sure that the rule truly governs the situation before the Court. Although the federal rules are not to be read narrowly in order to avoid a conflict with state law, in some cases the Court seems to have read a rule more narrowly than the text would dictate.

   1. ***Walker:*** In Walker v. Armco Steel Corp., 446 U.S. 740 (1980), the Court faced an alleged clash between Fed. R. Civ. P. 3, which indicates that a case is "commenced" when the complaint is filed, and a state statute that provided that an action was not "commenced" for purposes of the statute of limitations until service occurred. The Court held that Rule 3 did not govern statutes of limitations, but was merely an internal timing rule for purposes of the Federal Rules of Civil Procedure. Therefore, the Court applied the state law because no Federal Rule of Civil Procedure was in conflict.

★ 2. ***Semtek:*** The Court's recent decision in Semtek International, Inc. v. Lockheed Martin Corp., 531 U.S. 497 (2001), also interprets a federal rule quite narrowly. At issue in *Semtek* was ***Fed. R. Civ. P. 41(b)***, which deals with the effect of an ***involuntary dismissal***.

   a. The trial court had dismissed the case based on the state ***statute of limitations***.

   b. Under Fed. R. Civ. P. 41(b), an involuntary dismissal on this basis would be deemed an "adjudication on the merits." This is a term of art that usually indicates that the claimant is barred from bringing its claim again.

   c. Plaintiff sued again in a state court in a different state. This second state had a longer statute of limitations.

d. The Supreme Court held that the claim was not barred. The Court questioned whether Fed. R. Civ. P. 41(b) might exceed the REA if it were to bar a substantive law claim. Instead, the Court held that the law of the state in which the original federal court sat would be used to determine if plaintiff's claim is barred.

e. The full reach of *Semtek* is unclear. It is likely, however, that the rule applies only to "substantive" dismissals such as the statute of limitations. The preclusive effect of involuntary dismissals on procedural grounds, such as for failure to state a claim or to cooperate in discovery, may still be governed by the explicit language of Fed. R. Civ. P. 41(b).

D. Does the federal rule clash with state law? The next step in the analysis is to determine whether a true conflict exists between the federal rule and state law. If there is a way the court can apply ***both federal and state law***, there is no conflict, and the court will apply both rules.

★   **Example:** In Burlington Northern R.R. v. Woods, 480 U.S. 1 (1987), the Court dealt with an alleged conflict between a Federal Rule of Appellate Procedure and state law. State law required that a defendant who lost an appeal had to pay a penalty of 10 percent of the original judgment. Fed. R. App. P. 38 gives a federal court authority to award a sanction only in the case of a "frivolous" appeal. However, under the federal rule, the sanction is not fixed, and the court has the discretion to award nothing. Plaintiff argued that the two rules did not conflict because a federal court could always award both a 10 percent penalty and additional costs if it found the appeal frivolous. The Court disagreed, found that the rules conflicted, and held that the federal rule applied under the *Hanna* test.

E. Determining the validity of a federal rule: The last, and most difficult, step in dealing with a federal rule is to determine if the rule is valid. A federal rule is valid if it ***fits within the authority delegated*** by Congress to the Supreme Court ***in the REA***.

     1. Limits established by REA: The REA does not give the Supreme Court unfettered discretion. Instead, the act places two key limits on the Court's power to create rules.

         a. Limit 1: The Court may enact only general rules of ***practice and procedure*** and ***rules of evidence***.

         b. Limit 2: The rule ***cannot abridge, enlarge, or modify any substantive right***.

     2. Presumption of validity: However, because a federal rule is promulgated by the Supreme Court itself and is approved by Congress, *Hanna* indicates that there is a presumption that the rule is valid under the REA. Therefore, unless the federal rule *clearly* is not a rule of procedure or clearly affects substantive rights, it will be found to satisfy the twin requirements of that act.

         a. Many courts cite Justice Harlan's concurrence in *Hanna*, which suggests that under the *Hanna* test a federal rule is valid as long as it is "***arguably procedural***."

         b. In fact, the Supreme Court has never actually found a rule invalid under the REA, although in *Semtek* it expressed some doubts concerning Fed. R. Civ. P. 41(b). The overwhelming majority of court of appeal cases similarly uphold the federal rules.

         c. Other bases for invalidity: On the other hand, a federal rule is not valid merely because it satisfies the REA. A rule could also be held invalid because it violates the Constitution or conflicts with a federal statute.

3. **Forum-shopping irrelevant:** Although the analysis of a federal rule and the analysis of judge-made law both speak in terms of *procedure*, that term *has a very different meaning* in the two contexts. When analyzing a federal rule, it is *irrelevant whether the difference in laws would lead to forum-shopping*. Even if the difference in laws makes the state or federal forum more appealing, the federal court can apply a federal rule as long as it arguably regulates procedure and does not significantly abridge, enlarge, or modify a substantive right.

4. **Examples:** The following examples illustrate application of the analysis for a federal rule.

Example 1: *P* sues *D* in a federal court for injuries sustained when *D*'s herd of cattle trampled *P*. Although *P* could obtain personal jurisdiction over *D* under state law, *P* prefers to use *in rem* jurisdiction by seizing the herd of cattle, because the value of the herd is more than sufficient to satisfy *P*'s claim. Under state law, *P* could use *in rem* jurisdiction in this case. However, *Fed. R. Civ. P. 4(n)* provides that *in rem* jurisdiction is available only when a plaintiff cannot obtain *in personam* jurisdiction. *P* argues that the federal court must follow the state rule and allow him to use *in rem* jurisdiction in this diversity case.

Outcome: The federal court will apply Fed. R. Civ. P. 4(n) and deny *P*'s request to use *in rem* jurisdiction. The federal rule here governs service of process, a subject that clearly falls within the realm of ''procedure'' under the REA. Nor does the rule in any way abridge *P*'s right since *P* will still be able to recover for the harm by using *in personam* jurisdiction.

Example 2: *P* sues *D* in federal court for injuries caused by a product manufactured by *D*. After the accident, *D* modified the design of the product in a way that would have significantly reduced the risk of accidents like *P*'s. *P* wants to introduce evidence of the postaccident modification to prove that the original design was defective. State law allows the use of such evidence. However, *Fed. R. Evid. 407* bars the use of such evidence. *P* has no other proof that the product is defective. *P* accordingly argues that the federal court must follow the state rule.

Outcome: The federal court will follow *Fed. R. Evid. 407* and not allow the evidence. Although this rule may not be a rule of ''procedure,'' it clearly is a *rule of evidence*, which the REA also authorizes. Nor does the rule abridge, enlarge, or modify *P*'s right to recover. Although *P* may not be able to recover in the instant case, the problem is not *P*'s legal right to recover, but instead *P*'s failure to obtain other evidence of the defect.

Example 3: *P* sues *D* in federal court, alleging a state law claim for discrimination based on gender. Although *P* has suffered $200,000 in damages, *P*'s complaint asks for damages in the amount of $600,000. *P* relies on a recent (and purely hypothetical) amendment to Fed. R. Civ. P. 54(c), which provides that, ''in a case alleging discrimination based on gender or race, the final judgment shall grant the party three times the damages to which he was otherwise entitled.'' State law allows only ordinary damages.

Outcome: The hypothetical *federal rule is invalid*, and cannot be applied in federal court. The rule clearly *enlarges* the underlying substantive right. Therefore, even if it is ''arguably procedural,'' it is invalid under the second limitation in the REA.

V. FEDERAL STATUTES

Cases involving federal statutes are the easiest category of *Erie* case. The **Supremacy Clause** of Article VI of the U.S. Constitution provides that federal law takes precedence over state law. Therefore, if a federal court is faced with a true conflict between a valid federal statute and a state statute or common law rule, *Erie* is **not an issue**. The federal law applies.

A. Is statute valid? Of course, a federal law takes precedence only if it is constitutional.

B. Does statute apply? A federal statute automatically applies only if it actually covers the issue before the court. It is important to isolate the actual issue before the court in order to determine whether the statute applies.

★   **Example:** An excellent example of this sort of analysis is the Court's opinion in Stewart Organization, Inc. v. Ricoh, 487 U.S. 22 (1988). *Ricoh* was a contract dispute. The defendant moved under 28 U.S.C. §1404 to transfer venue to New York, citing a **forum selection clause** that provided that all disputes under the contract had to be heard in New York. The plaintiff resisted transfer, relying heavily on Alabama law, which would not enforce such clauses. The Court held that the real issue in the case was whether to grant a transfer under §1404. The federal statute clearly applied to that issue. Moreover, in determining whether to grant a §1404 transfer, the lower court should consider the forum selection clause. Regardless of whether the clause was ''enforceable,'' it could be considered as evidence of whether the parties thought New York was a fair place to hear the case.

C. Does statute clash with state law? The final step in the analysis is to determine whether the statute and state law truly conflict. If there is a way the court can apply **both federal and state law**, there is no conflict, and the court will apply both rules.

Quiz Yourself on
APPLYING ERIE *WHEN THERE IS A FEDERAL RULE OR STATUTE*

50. Wendy Worker, a long-time employee of X, Y & Z, is fired one week before her sixty-fifth birthday. Wendy suspects that X, Y & Z fired her because of her age, which would violate state law. Nevertheless, although Wendy *suspects* that her age was the reason she was fired, she does not have sufficient evidence to prove that at trial. However, Hugh Mannresources, the Director of Personnel for X, Y & Z, knows the truth. Although Wendy has tried to speak about the matter with Hugh, he steadfastly refuses to answer any questions. Without Hugh's information, Wendy is certain that she cannot prevail in the case.

Wendy eventually sues X, Y & Z in a federal district court in Wyoming, basing jurisdiction on diversity of citizenship. Wendy chooses federal court over state court because of their different discovery rules. Under Wyoming law, a party cannot force a person who is not a party to the case to provide information in the discovery process, although the party can call the person as a witness at trial. Fed. R. Civ. P. 30, by contrast, allows a party to take a deposition of a third-party witness such as

Hugh. If a witness refuses to answer a proper question, the court can hold the witness in contempt.

When Wendy notices Hugh's deposition, X, Y & Z objects, arguing that the Wyoming law must apply. Who will prevail? _____

51. Same basic facts as Problem 50. Immediately after Wendy files suit, X, Y & Z moves to dismiss the action. X, Y & Z cites a Wyoming law that clearly states that a partnership is not a "person" in the eyes of the law. Therefore, unlike in the case of a corporation, Wyoming does not allow a partnership to sue or be sued. Anyone who was injured by partnership activity must instead sue one or more partners individually.

Wendy disagrees with X, Y & Z's contention. Wendy points out that Fed. R. Civ. P. 4(h) allows a person to serve process on a general partnership by serving one of the general partners. She argues that this language clearly authorizes suit against X, Y & Z in federal court, even though she acknowledges that she cannot sue in state court.

Who is correct? _____

52. Paulette Pedestrian is seriously injured when she is struck by an automobile driven by Dan Dangerous. Paulette sues Dan in a Vermont federal court based on diversity. Dan immediately tries to implead Neverpay Insurance Company, his liability insurance carrier, as a third-party defendant.

Neverpay objects to Dan's attempt to drag it into this suit. Neverpay cites a provision of Vermont law that prevents an insured from joining its insurance company as a party to a suit. The Vermont statute was passed because of the fear that if the insurance company is named as a party, the jury is more likely to be sympathetic to the plaintiff and award excessive damages. Nevertheless, Vermont will allow the insured to sue the insurance company in a separate action, provided that action is not commenced until *after* the suit against the insured is complete.

Dan maintains that he may sue Neverpay in a federal court. He points to Fed. R. Civ. P. 14, which specifically allows him to implead Neverpay because Neverpay "is or may be liable" to Dan.

Will Dan's claim against Neverpay be allowed in the case? _____

53. Couch Potato, a serious television fan, purchases a new diet drug called Faddiet from Rip Off Network (RON), a cable television shopping network. Couch has RON ship the product from its warehouse in the State of Confusion to Couch's humble abode in the State of Tranquility. When the product fails to work as promised, Couch sues RON in federal court under Tranquility's false advertising laws. Jurisdiction is based on diversity.

RON immediately moves to dismiss the action, citing a Tranquility law that provides that a retailer that sells a product manufactured by another is not liable for any defects in the product. In response, Couch cites a federal statute that provides that a retailer who sells products in interstate commerce is vicariously liable for defects in the product.

Should the federal court dismiss Couch's suit? _____

Answers

50. Wendy will prevail. This is a clash between a federal rule and a state law. Under *Hanna*, the federal rule will apply as long as it can rationally be deemed procedural and does not abridge, enlarge, or modify any substantive rights. Fed. R. Civ. P. 30 almost certainly meets that standard. It is "procedural" because it is designed to deal with what happens in the process of litigation, as opposed to dealing with the rights of the parties outside the court. Nor does the process change Wendy's legal right to recover. (One could make a colorable argument that Hugh has a sort of "substantive right" under

state law not to be forced to testify. But that argument is relatively weak because Wendy can force Hugh to testify *at trial* even under state law.)

Note the clear evidence of forum-shopping here. However, that is irrelevant under the Federal Rules of Civil Procedure analysis.

51. This time X, Y & Z will prevail. A court almost certainly would find **no conflict** between Fed. R. Civ. P. 4(h) and the Wyoming rule. Rule 4(h) merely deals with how service will occur *if* the party is able to sue a partnership. It nowhere states that a party *can* sue a partnership.

Note that if a court were to adopt Wendy's interpretation, Rule 4(h) might well be invalid. Creating liability against an entity where none existed at state law almost certainly would involve the creation of a new substantive right.

52. The federal court should hear the claim against Neverpay. Fed. R. Civ. P. 14 satisfies the test under the REA. Although it may appear at first glance that the federal rule creates a new substantive right, in truth it merely allows for the merger of what would be two separate lawsuits in state court. The legal rules that determine whether the insurance company is liable do not change in any way.

That the Vermont rule is supported by strong policy concerns does not change that result. Vermont's concerns relate to the fairness of the litigation process, not to the substantive rights themselves.

53. The court should not dismiss Couch's suit. This is a clash between a federal statute and state law. In that case, the federal statute controls as long as it is valid and can be read actually to cover the situation. The federal statute is clearly valid (Congress can regulate commerce, and the law does not violate any individual human rights), and governs Couch's case.

VI. FEDERAL SUBSTANTIVE COMMON LAW

Part III of this chapter discusses federal *procedural* judge-made law. However, a limited body of federal judge-made law exists that is *clearly substantive* in nature.

A. Where substantive federal common law exists: Although the cases defy easy characterization, the Supreme Court has found federal common law to exist in cases where there is a strong and unique federal interest, such as those in which the *federal government is a party*, *admiralty and maritime* cases, and cases involving *international relations*.

B. Characteristics of modern federal common law: The substantive federal common law that exists today differs in certain significant respects from the pre-*Erie* body of federal precedent. First, federal common law presents a *federal question* and can accordingly be heard in federal court regardless of whether the parties are diverse. Illinois v. City of Milwaukee, 406 U.S. 91 (1972). Second, federal common law applies not only in federal courts, but also in *state courts*.

Quiz Yourself on
THE ERIE *DOCTRINE*

54. Randy Risktaker is a precocious youth who lives in a small Iowa town. One day, Randy and his friends decide to engage in one of the rites of passage for young men in the country, namely, tipping cows. Tipping cows involves going up to a sleeping cow and pushing it over. In the process, the cow suffers nothing other than a slight surprise.

Randy and his friends travel to Nebraska to find their prey. Randy, however, does not choose his target wisely. Instead of a sleeping cow, Randy tips a wide-awake bull. The bull does not take kindly to Randy's advances and causes Randy serious injuries.

Randy sues Frieda Farmer, the owner of the bull, for negligence in a federal district court in Nebraska. Frieda moves to dismiss based on Nebraska's pleading rules. Under Nebraska law, a plaintiff cannot recover unless he pleads that he did *not* assume the risk. Because Randy did not include that in his pleadings, Frieda argues, the court should dismiss his case.

Randy counters by brandishing his copy of Fed. R. Civ. P. 8(c). That federal rule lists "assumption of risk" as an "affirmative defense." If something is an affirmative defense, the burden is on the *defendant* to raise the issue in the pleadings. If the defendant fails to raise the issue in the pleadings, the court cannot hear evidence on the issue.

Will the court dismiss Randy's case? _____

55. Same basic facts as Problem 54, but assume that the court lets Randy's case proceed to trial. Frieda and Randy both present evidence to the jury concerning assumption of the risk. When the evidence is complete, the judge prepares to issue jury instructions. The proposed instructions state that Randy has the burden of proving, by a preponderance of the evidence, that he did not assume the risk.

Randy objects to the proposed instruction. He notes that in virtually every other state that recognizes the defense of assumption of the risk, the *defendant* has the burden of showing, by a preponderance of the evidence, that plaintiff assumed the risk. Although there is no federal statute or rule on point, Randy argues that the federal court need not consider itself bound by the idiosyncratic state law standard on burden of proof.

Will Randy prevail on his objection? _____

56. After surgery, Patient suffers a severe infection. Patient sues Surgeon for medical malpractice in a federal district court. At trial, Patient testifies that soon after the infection was discovered, Surgeon had offered to reimburse Patient for any medical bills that Patient might incur because of the infection. Surgeon objects based on Fed. R. Evid. 409, which provides that evidence of such offers cannot be admitted at trial.

Patient, however, points out that under the law of the state, evidence of an offer by defendant to pay medical costs *can* be introduced to prove that the defendant is liable.

Should the federal court allow the evidence? _____

57. Priscilla Procrastinator recently bought a painting from Dan Dealer. Soon after the painting is delivered, Priscilla discovers it is a worthless forgery. However, Priscilla does not sue Dan until 363 days after the delivery. Priscilla files her breach of contract action in federal court, based on diversity.

Priscilla serves Dan three weeks after filing the complaint. Dan immediately moves to dismiss based on the statute of limitations. Under state law, a party suing for breach of contract must commence the action within one year of the breach. Moreover, state law is clear that an action is not "commenced" until service occurs on the defendant. Because service on Dan did not occur until after one year had expired, Dan claims that the action is barred.

Although Priscilla concedes that Dan has correctly stated state law, she points out she filed her action in *federal* court. And Fed. R. Civ. P. 3 clearly provides that an action is commenced when the complaint is filed with the court. Because filing occurred within a year of the breach, Priscilla is confident that she can proceed with her suit. Will Priscilla or Dan prevail? _____

58. After losing his shirt in a risky stock purchase, Investor sues Accountant for misrepresentation. Investor brings this action in a federal district court, basing jurisdiction on diversity. Soon after the action is

commenced, Accountant moves for an order requiring Investor to file a bond in the case. Accountant cites a recently enacted federal statute that requires anyone who sues an accountant for fraud or misrepresentation to file a bond in an amount equal to ten times the amount of the claim. If the plaintiff eventually loses the suit, the accountant receives the amount of the bond as compensation for the inevitable damage to reputation that flowed from the allegation. By its explicit terms, the statute applies to all claims, including state law claims. Must Investor file the bond in this diversity case?

Answers

54. Randy's case will not be dismissed. The issue here involves a clash between a Federal Rule of Civil Procedure and a state rule of procedure. In this situation, the federal rule will control as long as it is procedural and does not abridge, enlarge, or modify the underlying substantive right. Fed. R. Civ. P. 8(c) clearly passes this test. The rule does not change the substantive law in any material way. Assumption of the risk is clearly a defense under Nebraska law. All Rule 8(c) does is to determine *who* must initially raise the issue to make it an issue for trial.

55. Randy's objection will be denied. Because there is no federal positive law on point, this question is governed by the "likely to cause forum-shopping" test. Here, ignoring the state law would be quite likely to cause forum-shopping. The burden of proof concerns who wins in a close case. Therefore, a party might be likely to select the forum that made it easier for him to win.

56. This presents a clash between a Federal Rule of Evidence and state law. However, the Federal Rules of Evidence, like those of Civil Procedure, are enacted pursuant to the REA, and the analysis proceeds along similar lines. First, one must determine if this can rationally be considered a rule of "evidence" (the REA authorizes both rules of procedure and evidence). Here, the answer is yes: A rule that deals with whether testimony can be heard is a rule of evidence.

    The second part of the analysis is whether the federal rule would abridge, enlarge, or modify a substantive right. The answer is no. Although the federal rule may make it more difficult to recover, the basic standard is still the same. Patient can still offer other types of evidence to show malpractice.

57. There is no conflict between the federal and state rules. In fact, this is almost exactly similar to Walker v. Armco Steel, discussed in Part IV.C. The Court in that case held that there was no conflict because Fed. R. Civ. P. 3's definition of when a case was deemed commenced was not meant to apply to statutes of limitations. Because Rule 3 does not apply, the case involves a clash between state law and federal judge-made law. The court should apply state law if the difference between the state and federal laws could induce forum-shopping. It is highly likely that a plaintiff would choose federal court if that court used a rule that made it easier to fall within the statute of limitations. Therefore, the federal court must follow the state law.

58. Investor will be required to file the bond. The question involves a clash between a federal statute and state law. True, the federal law may well cause forum-shopping and could easily be deemed to create a substantive right. But Congress, unlike the courts, has the power to create substantive law. Although this statute may not be wise, it is within Congress's constitutional powers and therefore must be applied.

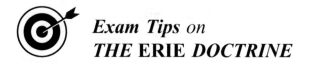

Exam Tips on
THE **ERIE** *DOCTRINE*

Erie issues can be among the most difficult issues you will face on a Civil Procedure exam. But do not let that prospect frighten you. The keys to dealing with an *Erie* problem are knowing how to spot an issue and figuring out which of the tests applies.

- ☛ **Spotting an *Erie* issue:** *Erie* issues can be among the most difficult issues to spot on a law school examination, not because your professor is trying to be sneaky (well, not *necessarily*), but instead because of the nature of the *Erie* problem itself.

  - ☞ Remember that *Erie* is an issue **only in federal court**.

  - ☞ Most of the discussion of *Erie* in a first-year course focuses on when a federal court must follow a state "procedural" rule. This means that *Erie* issues may arise in connection with virtually any topic you discuss in Civil Procedure. What may look like a relatively straightforward question of pleading or discovery may actually have an *Erie* issue lurking in the background.

  - ☞ One clue for spotting an *Erie* issue is when the question involves a suit in federal court but, for some reason, **specifies what the state law rule is on a particular matter**. After all, *Erie* only matters if state law and federal law differ.

  - ☞ Sometimes a question **gives you only a state rule of civil procedure** on a topic. However, if you studied the corresponding Federal Rule of Civil Procedure or other federal law on that topic, you should apply the federal law and determine if *Erie* applies. For example, if a question tells you that the state rules absolutely prevent a party from amending its pleadings, and you studied pleading during that particular term, you should apply the Fed. R. Civ. P. 15 rules dealing with amendments.

  - ☞ If the problem gives you a state law but there is no corresponding federal rule that you can think of, there is still an *Erie* problem. In this case, the real issue is **whether the federal court must apply the state law**. To refuse to apply the state law, as a practical matter, means that the federal court is applying a "federal" rule that is the opposite of the state law.

- ☛ **Beware of the "false conflict":** Once you have found the *Erie* issue, take a close look at the state and federal rules on the subject. **Make sure the rules actually conflict**. If application of the state and federal rules do not make a difference, then there is no conflict, and an *Erie* analysis is technically unnecessary. However, unless the case falls squarely within one of the Court's earlier decisions or the lack of any conflict is absolutely clear, **be very hesitant before basing your entire answer on a finding of "no conflict."** If you are wrong in that conclusion, you will have left out the lion's share of the analysis.

- ☛ **Do not forget precedent:** The Supreme Court has decided a number of *Erie* cases. If the case involves the same issue as one of those cases, the decision controls. There is no need to reinvent the wheel.

- ☛ **Categorizing the *Erie* issue:** Categorize any question using the three categories set out in this chapter because the analysis differs depending on the type of issue. You may find it helpful to create a flow chart, checklist, or other device to help you remember the different analyses that apply in each situation.

☛ **Federal statutes:** If the *Erie* problem involves a federal statute, the analysis is relatively simple: If the federal statute is valid and truly applies to the situation, then it applies.

    ☞ Unless you have had a course in Constitutional Law, you do not have the tools to determine whether an act of Congress is "valid." However, if the law is blatantly invalid — for example, if it impermissibly discriminates on the basis of race — then the possibility of invalidity should at least be mentioned.

☛ **Federal rule crafted under Rules Enabling Act:** If the case involves a Federal Rule of Civil Procedure or other rule enacted under the REA, then your task is to determine whether the rule fits within the powers that Congress gave to the Supreme Court under the Rules Enabling Act.

    ☞ Again, make sure the rule conflicts.

    ☞ In determining whether the rule can ***reasonably be characterized as procedural***, ask yourself whether the rule is concerned with what goes on ***during the litigation*** or what went on ***outside the litigation***.

    ☞ After that, consider the real impact of the rule. Does it change the legal parameters of the claim or defense, or make it significantly easier for one party to win? If so, the federal rule is invalid.

    ☞ ***When in doubt, conclude that an existing federal rule is valid.*** The Supreme Court has made it clear that the federal rules have a presumption of validity.

☛ If you conclude (reluctantly) that a federal statute or Federal Rule of Civil Procedure is invalid or does not apply, do not automatically conclude that state law governs. Instead, determine whether the federal court is required to follow state law even without any federal positive law to the contrary. This is governed by the "likely to cause forum-shopping" analysis.

☛ **Federal judge-made law:** If the issue is a clash between a judge-made federal rule and state law, or if the problem simply gives you a state law and the issue is whether the federal court must apply it, your task is to determine whether the ***difference*** between federal and state laws would ***likely cause forum-shopping for a different outcome***.

    ☞ ***Try to avoid using the phrases "substantive/procedural" and "outcome determinative"*** in the analysis. The "likely to cause forum-shopping" analysis is how a court determines whether a rule is substantive.

☛ **Judge-jury determinations:** Because of *Byrd* and *Gasperini*, questions involving judge and jury are not governed by the "likely to cause forum-shopping" analysis. If your question deals with those sorts of issues, apply the analysis in those cases instead.

CHAPTER 6

LITIGATION AND ITS ALTERNATIVES

ChapterScope ━━━

This chapter presents a conceptual overview of litigation. Details of the litigation process, and many of the rules that apply to that process, are reserved until later chapters.

■ Before filing a case, an attorney considers what *remedies* might be available.

■ There is a *hierarchy* of remedies in the U.S. judicial system. As a general matter, *equitable* remedies are available only if the *legal* remedies are somehow inadequate.

■ Certain remedies may be available while the case is still pending.

■ If necessary to preserve the status quo, a party may be able to obtain a *preliminary injunction* or *temporary restraining order*.

■ In addition, a party may be able to have certain assets of the defendant *seized* at the outset of a case to ensure that those assets remain available to satisfy a judgment.

■ Modern litigation is expensive. *Attorneys' fees* comprise the lion's share of litigation costs. Under the so-called *American rule*, each party pays its own attorneys' fees. However, the default American rule is increasingly being replaced by statutes authorizing fee-shifting.

■ Because of the costs of ordinary litigation, parties are increasingly making use of *alternate dispute resolution* procedures, primarily arbitration and mediation.

━━

I. REMEDIES

Generally speaking, a remedy is a statement by the court indicating one party's responsibilities toward the other. Remedies can be broadly divided into three main categories: *substitutionary*, *specific*, and *declaratory*.

A. Substitutionary remedies: A substitutionary remedy attempts to *replace* what the plaintiff lost with something that is the rough equivalent. The most common substitutionary remedy is *damages*. However, there are different types of damages.

   1. Generally: Although there are significant differences between the various forms of substitutionary remedies, all share certain basic features.

   a. Nature of money judgment: A judgment awarding damages is *not an order to pay*. Failure to pay damages does not subject the judgment debtor to contempt of court. Instead, the judgment merely states that the defendant is liable in that amount to the plaintiff.

   b. Enforcement: If the judgment debtor does not pay, the judgment victor can use a judgment to *seize assets* of the judgment debtor to satisfy the judgment.

   i. The assets are then *sold* at a sheriff's sale, and the proceeds are used to satisfy the judgment.

ii. However, the victor cannot reach all of the debtor's property with a judgment. Every state provides that certain property is *exempt* from execution, either in whole or up to a certain amount.

iii. A judgment creditor may also be able to obtain other assets of the judgment debtor. For example, it may be possible to *garnish* funds owed by a third party to the judgment debtor, such as *wages* or *bank accounts*. Garnishment of wages, however, is severely limited by federal law and many states' law.

c. **Delay in enforcement:** In federal court, a party may neither execute on a judgment nor bring another proceeding to enforce it (such as garnishment), until *10 days* after entry. Fed. R. Civ. P. 62(a). This gives the judgment loser the chance to file a motion for a new trial or to lodge an appeal. The judgment loser may also obtain an order staying enforcement during the course of an appeal. However, the party will usually be required to file a *supersedeas bond* to protect the judgment winner.

2. **Compensatory damages:** Compensatory damages are a sum of money that is meant to compensate the injured party for the harm it has suffered. Because in many cases it is impossible for a defendant to undo the injury, the court assigns a value to the injury and awards damages to the plaintiff in that amount.

a. **Caveat:** What sorts of losses are recoverable are *limited by the substantive law*. For example, tort plaintiffs are often limited in the extent to which they can recover for purely economic loss. Similarly, a plaintiff suing for breach of contract cannot recover for any emotional distress occasioned by the breach.

b. **No double recovery:** In addition, the court must be careful not to award a *double recovery*.

Example: In a case involving destruction of property, the plaintiff is entitled to the market value of the property, the transaction costs required to obtain a replacement, and any lost profit during the period between destruction and replacement. However, the plaintiff is not entitled to receive the profits it would have earned from the property after replacement because that would constitute a double recovery. Once the property is replaced, the plaintiff is able to earn those profits itself.

c. **Mitigation:** A plaintiff is generally required by the substantive law to take reasonable steps to mitigate her damages.

3. **Liquidated, statutory, and multiple damages:** In cases where it is difficult for a party to prove its injury, the party may be entitled to liquidated, statutory, or multiple damages.

a. **Liquidated damages:** Parties who enter into *contracts* often specify an amount as *liquidated damages*. As long as the amount specified is reasonable, the plaintiff need not prove actual injury but can recover the amount agreed upon by the parties.

b. **Statutory damages:** Similarly, statutes sometimes provide a *fixed amount* of *statutory damages* that a party may recover in case of a violation.

c. **Multiple damages:** Other statutes provide for *double or treble damages*.

4. **Punitive damages:** As the name implies, punitive damages are meant as a form of punishment. Thus, they are not compensatory in nature. However, the amount of actual damage may limit punitive damages.

a. **When available:** Punitive damages are usually available only in tort cases and only when the defendant acted *intentionally* or *willfully*.

b. **Calculation:** Punitive damages are designed to *deter similar conduct in the future*. How large the punitive damages award must be in order to be an effective deterrent varies depending on the defendant's wealth.

c. **Constitutional limits:** In recent years, the U.S. Supreme Court has imposed several important limits on punitive damages awards. These limits stem from the *Due Process Clause* of the Fourteenth Amendment, which prevents a state from depriving anyone of property without affording due process of law.

★   i. **Limits on amount:** The Due Process Clause prevents *grossly excessive* punitive damages awards. Whether an award is grossly excessive turns on how maliciously or reprehensibly the defendant acted, the type of harm suffered by the plaintiff (merely economic versus personal injury), and a *comparison of punitive damages with the actual damages* suffered by the victim. If the punitive damages are completely out of proportion, the award is excessive. State Farm Mutual Automobile Insurance Co. v. Campbell, 123 S. Ct. 1513 (2003).

★   ii. **Limits on procedure:** A state must also ensure that meaningful judicial review is available for a jury award of punitive damages. Honda Motor Co. v. Oberg, 512 U.S. 415 (1994).

B. **Specific remedies:** In the second major category of remedies, the court orders a party to act or refrain from acting in a certain way.

1. **Enforcement:** Unlike damages, a judgment awarding a specific remedy usually results in a *court order*. Violation of that order subjects the party to *contempt of court*.

2. **Types of specific remedies:** There is a wide array of specific remedies. The most common specific remedy is the *injunction*. Other common specific remedies include accounting, constructive trust, ejectment, mandamus, replevin, rescission of a contract, and restitution.

3. **Equity:** Most, but not all, specific remedies originated in equity and are today still considered equitable in nature.

a. **Exceptions:** However, not all specific remedies are equitable. Examples of "legal" specific remedies are ejectment, mandamus, prohibition, replevin, and *habeas corpus*.

b. **Nature of equitable remedies:** Historically, there were crucial differences between equitable and legal claims and remedies. Today, however, only two important differences remain.

i. **Defenses:** A party seeking equitable relief is subject to various equitable defenses such as *laches*, *estoppel*, and *unclean hands*. These defenses usually do not apply in cases seeking legal relief.

ii. **Hierarchy of remedies:** Historically, a party could obtain relief in equity only if she could show that her *legal relief was inadequate*. This standard *remains in force*. However, courts today are much more willing to find damages inadequate and, accordingly, to grant equitable relief.

Example: Plaintiff lives next to a factory that emits large amounts of pollution. Plaintiff sues for nuisance and asks the court to enjoin the factory from polluting. Although in theory the court could award plaintiff damages in this suit and let the plaintiff sue again for damages in the future, most courts will grant the injunction.

4. **Injunctions:** The most common specific remedy is the injunction.

   a. **Types:** Injunctions may be *mandatory* or *prohibitory* in nature. A mandatory injunction orders the defendant to undertake certain acts; a prohibitory injunction orders defendant to refrain from taking certain acts.

   b. **Factors considered:** In addition to determining whether the legal remedy is adequate, a court considers the following in determining whether to grant an injunction:

      i. a *balance of the hardship* to the defendant if the injunction were ordered and the hardship to the plaintiff if the injunction were denied, and

      ii. the *public interest*.

      ★   **Example:** Sigma Chemical Co. v. Harris, 605 F. Supp. 1253 (E.D. Mo.), illustrates how these factors are applied. The court held that an injunction was appropriate because the strong threat of injury to plaintiff from loss of its trade secrets outweighed the harm to defendant from diminished employment opportunities.

C. **Declaratory relief:** The declaratory judgment is a unique remedy. It does not obligate the loser to pay money or take specific action. Instead, it merely states the rights of the parties.

   Example: *P* is considering manufacturing a new and better mousetrap. However, *D* has a patent that covers mousetraps similar to the one that *P* plans to manufacture. *P* therefore fears that if she builds the trap, *D* will sue her for infringement. *P* may bring a suit asking for a declaration that her trap does not infringe *D*'s patent. If *P* prevails, *D* will be barred by *res judicata* from suing *P* for making that particular trap.

   1. **Statutory source:** In federal courts, declaratory judgments are authorized by 28 U.S.C. §2201.

   2. **Special problems:** Declaratory judgments present special problems with respect to federal question jurisdiction and jury trials. Those issues are discussed in Chapters 4 and 10, respectively.

II. PROVISIONAL REMEDIES

A court typically grants a remedy at the conclusion of the case. However, a party may sometimes obtain relief before the case is completely resolved. Because the merits of the case have yet to be considered, a party must make a strong case to be awarded a provisional remedy.

A. **Nature:** Provisional remedies are *always specific relief*. A plaintiff who seeks damages must wait until a final judgment, no matter how badly she needs the funds. In addition, provisional remedies are by nature *temporary*. Once the court looks into the matter more fully, the provisional remedy will be replaced by any final remedy.

B. **Primary types:** The three primary provisional remedies are the *preliminary injunction*, the *temporary restraining order*, and the *pretrial attachment* of property for security.

1. **Preliminary injunction:** A preliminary injunction is an injunction granted during the pendency of a case. Its primary purpose is to *preserve the status quo* so that any final relief granted by the court can be effective.

   a. **Standard:** The standard for a preliminary injunction is more rigorous than that for a final injunction. Courts typically require the party requesting a preliminary injunction to prove several things.

      i. **Likely to prevail:** The requesting party must prove that it is likely to prevail on the merits of the case. Ordinarily the court holds a hearing where it considers the evidence and the legal merits of plaintiff's claim.

      ii. **Irreparable injury:** The requesting party must run the risk of suffering irreparable injury if relief were delayed until the end of the case. In essence, the party must show a strong need to issue the injunction *now*, instead of after the trial.

      iii. **Balance of the hardships:** The party must show that it would be harmed more by denial of the preliminary injunction than the other party would be harmed by the injunction.

      iv. **Public interest:** The injunction must be in the public interest.

   ★ b. **Alternate analysis where threat is great:** In cases where the balance of hardships (Part iii above) is *strongly in favor of the party requesting relief*, a number of courts modify Part i's analysis to allow a preliminary injunction as long as the party demonstrates that there are *serious questions*: i.e., that the party has a ''fair'' chance of winning the case on the merits. William Inglis & Sons Baking Co. v. ITT Continental Baking Co., 526 F.2d 86 (9th Cir. 1976).

   c. **Bond:** The requesting party must usually file a bond as a condition to granting a preliminary injunction. The bond helps ensure that the enjoined party can recover any damages it may suffer as a result of a wrongfully issued preliminary injunction.

2. **Temporary restraining order:** Like a preliminary injunction, a temporary restraining order (TRO) is a form of *specific relief* granted early in the case. However, there are important differences between TROs and preliminary injunctions.

   Note on terminology: The term temporary restraining order does not always mean the same thing in different courts. Some courts use the terms TRO and preliminary injunction interchangeably. This discussion focuses on the majority definition of the term, which is the definition used in the federal courts.

   a. *Ex parte:* A TRO is typically issued *without notice to the other party*. In some cases, however, the party is given notice, but the court holds an immediate and relatively cursory hearing because of the urgency of the matter.

   b. **Showing irreparable injury:** The irreparable injury requirement is much more rigorous for a TRO than it is for a preliminary injunction. The requesting party must show that he would suffer irreparable injury *if he had to use the regular preliminary injunction process*. Thus, a TRO is available only if the situation is so urgent that even the preliminary injunction process would fail to protect the requesting party.

   c. **Limit on term:** The TRO is an emergency order that is intended to preserve the status quo until a hearing can be held on a preliminary injunction. Therefore, its term is extremely limited. In federal court, a TRO expires after **10 days** unless the court explicitly establishes a different term. Fed. R. Civ. P. 65(b).

3. Pretrial attachment: A plaintiff typically must wait until he receives a final judgment before he may reach defendant's property. In certain situations, however, a plaintiff may have the defendant's property seized at the outset of the case.

    a. When available: The purpose of pretrial seizure is to prevent the defendant from disposing of the property during the course of the case. Seizure can be very useful in a case where the plaintiff asks the court to order defendant to turn over specific property, such as *foreclosure of a security interest*. Seizure likewise may be available in a suit where plaintiff asks for damages and is worried that defendant will dispose of its nonexempt assets during the case.

    b. Limitations: Even though a pretrial seizure is for a limited time (the duration of the case), it constitutes a ''deprivation'' by the state of the defendant's property within the meaning of the Fourteenth Amendment to the U.S. Constitution. Therefore, the defendant is entitled to *due process of law*.

★

        i. *Fuentes:* The Supreme Court's landmark decision in Fuentes v. Shevin, 407 U.S. 67 (1972), held that the Due Process Clause limits pretrial seizures. In that case, the Court struck down a state law that allowed a creditor to repossess property sold on credit without prior notice to the debtor. The law allowed the creditor who had filed a suit against the debtor to file an application making only cursory allegations that he was entitled to the property. The sheriff would then seize the property. The debtor received no prior notice, either of the suit or the seizure. That the creditor was required to file a bond was not sufficient protection to satisfy the Due Process Clause.

        ii. **Factors:** However, pretrial seizure is not always unconstitutional. The Supreme Court's decision in Connecticut v. Doehr, 501 U.S. 1 (1991), held that a court must consider *three factors* in determining whether a state's pretrial attachment procedure is constitutional.

            (a) **Strength of the defendant's interest:** This factor considers how strong a right the defendant has in the property and how great an impact the deprivation would have on that interest.

            (b) **Strength of the plaintiff's interest:** The court compares the parties' interests. Other things equal, if the plaintiff has a *preexisting interest in the property* — such as a mortgage or security interest — the seizure is more likely to be upheld.

            (c) **Risk of a wrongful deprivation:** Finally, the court must consider whether the state's attachment process creates a high risk of erroneously depriving the defendant of its property.

                1. **Timing:** A key element in this factor is *when the hearing will occur*. Even if no pre-attachment hearing is available, a *prompt postseizure hearing* may save the procedure.

                2. **Strength of plaintiff's showing:** Another important factor is *how strong a showing the plaintiff must make to the court*. The procedure likely will be held invalid if plaintiff is required to make only conclusory statements.

3. **Who decides:** Similarly, *who makes the decision* is an important issue. If the decision whether to allow the attachment is made by the clerk instead of a judge, it is much more likely that the procedure will be held unconstitutional.

4. **Bond required:** Finally, it is important that the procedure require the plaintiff to file a bond to compensate the defendant for any harm that it suffers because of a wrongful deprivation.

Quiz Yourself on
REMEDIES AND PROVISIONAL REMEDIES

59. Alpha sues Beta for breach of a contract. The court enters judgment for Alpha, finding Beta liable for $30,000 in damages. After repeated requests, however, Beta refuses to pay any of the judgment. Alpha therefore petitions to have Beta held in contempt of court. Will Alpha succeed? _____

60. During a frenzied poker game, Summers and Winters suspect that Dan Dealer is dealing from the bottom of the deck. When their suspicions prove correct, Summers and Winters take Dealer "out back" and beat him up. Dealer responds by suing the two for battery. Because battery is an intentional tort, Dealer seeks both compensatory and punitive damages.

    The parties stipulate that Summers and Winters played an equal role in planning and carrying out the beating. However, the evidence also shows that Summers is five times as wealthy as Winters. The jury awards Dealer $5,000 in compensatory damages and punitive damages of $2,000 from Winters and $20,000 from Summers. Summers challenges the jury verdict, raising two arguments. First, he argues that punitive damages cannot exceed the amount of compensatory damages. Second, he contends that even if the $20,000 figure might be acceptable standing alone, it is unfair for him to be held liable for more punitive damages than Winters given that the parties played an equal role in the beating. Will the jury verdict stand? _____

61. Emma Employee is an engineer with HiTech, Inc., a company that produces cutting-edge electronics. When she took the job, Emma signed a confidentiality agreement that prevents her from disclosing certain company secrets.

    Because of her considerable talents, Emma is recruited by a number of other companies. She eventually takes a position with another firm in a different field. Worried that Emma will try to impress her new employer by revealing HiTech's secrets, HiTech asks for and receives a temporary restraining order that prevents Emma from taking her new job "until such time as the underlying issues in this dispute are resolved at a full trial."

    Emma objects to the long term of the order. She points out that it may take years for the case to get to trial, by which time her new employer will have rescinded its offer. At the very least, Emma argues, she should be entitled to appear at a hearing to challenge the need for pretrial relief. Is Emma likely to prevail on her objection? _____

Answers

59. The court will not hold Beta in contempt. Unlike a specific remedy, a money judgment is not an order to pay money. Therefore, it is not punishable by contempt.

60. The jury verdict is proper. First, although punitive damages cannot be completely out of proportion to compensatory damages, the amount of compensatories is not an absolute ceiling on punitives.

Second, that Summers is required to pay ten times more punitive damages than Winters for the same behavior is not grounds to challenge the verdict. Punitive damages are intended to have a deterrent effect. It clearly takes more to deter someone with considerable assets than it takes to deter a poorer person. Moreover, even though Summers is only five times as wealthy as Winters, the jury could conclude that a $10 penalty would have the same deterrent effect as a $1 penalty would have on the less well-to-do Winters.

61. Emma is almost certain to prevail on her objection. A temporary restraining order is an emergency order issued without notice to the affected party. Because of this lack of notice, a TRO lasts only until such time as the parties can attend a hearing to debate whether the TRO should be converted to a preliminary injunction.

III. ATTORNEYS' FEES

Litigation is expensive. The costs required to prosecute the case itself — filing fees, the costs of service, and copying charges — may prove substantial. However, ***attorneys' fees*** typically comprise the vast majority of a party's litigation expenses.

   A. American rule: The traditional rule governing attorneys' fees is the American rule, under which ***each party pays its own attorney***. Under the English rule in the United Kingdom, by contrast, the loser pays at least a portion of the victor's fees.

   B. Funding attorneys' fees: Because many litigants cannot afford an attorney at an hourly rate, the legal system allows various methods of funding the high costs of litigation.

   1. Insurance: From the defendant's perspective, insurance often helps solve the problem. A ***liability insurance policy*** requires the insurance company to pay not only for liability, but also for the ***costs of defense***. In many cases, the duty to pay for the attorney is more valuable than liability coverage.

   2. Contingent fees: The contingent fee arrangement is the most common way in which plaintiffs who could not otherwise afford an attorney obtain representation.

   a. Percentage of recovery: Under a contingent fee arrangement, the lawyer's fee is a ***percentage of any recovery***. Although the percentage varies from lawyer to lawyer and from case to case, it is usually in the range of 20 to 50 percent of the recovery. Attorneys commonly use a "sliding scale," under which the percentage is relatively low if the case is settled before filing or in the very early stages, and increases as the case goes through discovery and to trial and appeal.

   b. Ethical issues: An attorney may have an ethical obligation to advise a client of fee options, including the relative advantages and disadvantages of contingent fees.

3. **Pro bono and public interest lawyers:** Individual attorneys may provide representation on a ***pro bono*** basis. Organizations such as Legal Aid also provide representation to low income or otherwise disadvantaged litigants.

C. **Fee-shifting:** Although the American rule is the default rule in U.S. courts, in practice there are many situations where a party's fees are paid by another party.

1. **Contractual fee-shifting:** Contracts today often require the ***breaching party to pay*** the attorneys' fees of the other party. A few require the ***loser to pay*** the winner's fees, which may deter wrongful breach of contract claims.

2. **Statutory fee-shifting:** When a legislature creates a cause of action, it often provides for payment of the winner's attorneys' fee. Such provisions are especially prevalent in civil rights statutes and other statutes that allow suit against government.

   a. **Limits:** Recovery is almost always limited to a "reasonable" fee.

   ★ b. **Prevailing party:** A fee-shifting statute that awards fees to a "prevailing party" applies only when a party obtains a court judgment in its favor. Thus, a plaintiff who settles may not use the statute to recover fees from the defendant. Buckhannon Board and Care Home, Inc. v. West Virginia Department of Health and Human Resources, 532 U.S. 598 (2001).

   c. **Fed. R. Civ. P. 68 and settlements:** If a plaintiff rejects a formal settlement offer made by defendant, but at trial ultimately recovers less than the amount offered, Fed. R. Civ. P. 68 requires plaintiff to pay any costs incurred by the defendant after the offer. In most cases, these costs do *not* include attorneys' fees. However, where plaintiff sues under a statute that shifts fees, costs under Fed. R. Civ. P. 68 do include ***plaintiff's attorneys' fees***. Marek v. Chesney, 473 U.S. 1 (1985). Therefore, plaintiff will be denied fees incurred after the date of the offer (but will not be required to pay defendants' fees).

3. **Common fund and class actions:** The "common fund" theory was originally a court-created method of shifting fees. However, unlike contractual and statutory fee-shifting, it ***does not shift fees from plaintiff to defendant*** or vice versa, but instead merely spreads the fees among all those who benefit from a judgment.

   a. **Theory:** The basic theory underlying the common fund theory is that everyone who benefits from a judgment obtained by one party should have to bear their share of the costs of procuring that judgment.

   b. **Class actions:** The common fund theory underlies how attorneys' fees are allocated in class actions. See Chapter 15.

IV. JUDICIAL MANAGEMENT OF LITIGATION

Parties complain not only about the expense of litigation, but also about the time it takes to bring a case to completion. Courts have tried a number of approaches to reduce the time and cost. This discussion focuses primarily on the approaches used in federal court.

A. **Discovery conference:** The Federal Rules of Civil Procedure require the parties to meet soon after the case is commenced in order to work up a discovery plan. The discovery conference and plan are discussed in Chapter 8.

B. Dismissals and defaults: Much delay in litigation is attributable to two causes: plaintiffs who file a suit and then do nothing to bring it to completion, and defendants who engage in dilatory tactics to delay recovery. The Federal Rules of Civil Procedure contain provisions designed to combat both of these problems.

   1. Involuntary dismissal of plaintiff's case: Fed. R. Civ. P. 41(b) allows a court to dismiss plaintiff's case if the plaintiff fails to prosecute the case diligently or fails to comply with a court order. Involuntary dismissals are discussed in Chapter 9, Part III.

   2. Default judgments: When a defendant fails to defend itself, comply with a court order, or co-operate in discovery, the court may enter judgment against that defendant. As with involuntary dismissals, default judgments are fairly rare. Default judgments are explored in greater depth in Chapter 9, Part II.

C. Pretrial conference: Fed. R. Civ. P. 16 gives a federal court the discretion to order one or more pretrial conferences to discuss virtually any matter relevant to the case. A pretrial conference will result in a ***pretrial order*** that guides the remainder of the case. Although Rule 16 applies only to the federal courts, many states have also enacted a similar provision.

   1. The conference: ***Fed. R. Civ. P. 16(a)-(d)*** set forth the procedure for calling a pretrial conference. The rule leaves it to the discretion of the court whether to call a conference, but lists a number of reasons why a court might want to call a conference. However, some federal districts have enacted local rules making a pretrial conference mandatory.

   a. Types: More than one conference is possible. For example, Fed. R. Civ. P. 16(b) envisions a ***scheduling conference*** to deal with amendments to pleadings, motions, disclosures, and discovery. Similarly, Rule 16(d) specifically authorizes a ***final pretrial conference*** that is to be held as close to the commencement of trial as reasonably possible.

   b. Parties involved: The conference must be attended by the ***attorneys*** and any ***unrepresented parties***. At least one of the attorneys attending on behalf of each party must have the authority to enter into stipulations and make admissions. The court may require the parties to be available by telephone during the conference so that the case might be settled. Sanctions are available if a party fails to attend, be prepared for, or cooperate in a pretrial conference. Fed. R. Civ. P. 16(e).

   c. Matters for consideration: Virtually any issue that may arise in the pretrial or trial process is open for consideration at a pretrial conference. ***Fed. R. Civ. P. 16(c)*** contains a long list of items that may be discussed, including settlement, eliminating frivolous claims or defenses, stipulation of certain facts, discovery issues, and how to manage the trial.

   2. Order: If action is taken at the pretrial conference, the court issues an ***order***.

   a. Issuing deadlines: An order following a scheduling conference must be issued as soon as practicable, but no later than ***90 days following the appearance of the defendant*** and ***120 days following service on the defendant***. Fed. R. Civ. P. 16(b). There is no deadline for other orders.

   b. Parties affected: A pretrial order ***binds all parties*** for the remainder of the case. Fed. R. Civ. P. 16(e).

   c. Amendments: Although the scheduling order may be amended for good cause, other pretrial orders may only be amended to ***prevent manifest injustice***.

Quiz Yourself on
COSTS AND CONTROL OF LITIGATION

62. Donna operates a Burger Queen franchise in Walla Walla, Washington. When Burger Queen comes up with a new marketing campaign, Donna finds the new marketing campaign trite and demeaning and refuses to display the marketing materials in her restaurant.

    Burger Queen sues Donna for breach of the franchise contract, seeking $5,000 in damages. In addition, Burger Queen asks the court to require Donna to pay its attorneys' fees. A clause in the contract clearly requires the franchisee to pay for the franchisor's attorneys' fees in any action brought to enforce the franchise agreement. However, Burger Queen is not required to pay the franchisee's attorneys' fees if Burger Queen is sued for breach.

    Donna objects to the request for attorneys' fees, arguing that the contract provision violates the American rule that prevails in the U.S. courts. Is Burger Queen likely to recover its attorneys' fees? _____

63. Same facts as Problem 62. The court schedules a pretrial conference. The judge specifies that she called the conference to "pressure" the parties to settle. Although both sides were given notice of the scheduled hearing, only Donna and her counsel show up at the conference. The judge immediately issues an order requiring Burger Queen to pay Donna's travel expenses and attorneys' fees for attending the fruitless conference. Burger Queen objects to the order, arguing that the judge had no right to schedule a conference for the sole purpose of forcing a settlement. Will Burger Queen have to pay the sanction? _____

Answers

62. If Burger Queen wins the case, it is likely to recover its attorneys' fees. The traditional rule that each party pays its attorney can be changed by mutual agreement, such as this contract. Nothing requires that the agreement be two-sided; a term like that in the hypothetical contract, where only the franchisee has to pay the franchisor's fees, is valid.

63. Burger Queen must pay the sanction. Fed. R. Civ. P. 16 gives the court the power to call one or more pretrial conferences for a wide array of reasons, including settlement. The parties must attend the conferences. If a party fails to attend after notice, the court may impose sanctions, including the costs and attorneys' fees of any parties who do attend.

V. ALTERNATIVES TO LITIGATION

Most disputes are not resolved in court. Many are settled or otherwise resolved by the parties. Even if a case is not settled, the parties may decide to invoke the services of an arbitrator or mediator rather than incur the expense and publicity of a court trial.

    A. Settlement: A settlement is simply a contract in which the parties agree how the dispute will be resolved. Settlement prior to commencement of a civil case presents few legal issues other than those relating to whether the agreement is valid as a matter of a contract law. Settlement of a pending case presents additional issues, which are discussed in Chapter 9.

B. Mediation: Mediation is a more formalized attempt to reach a settlement. Unlike typical settlement negotiations, a third party, the mediator, works with the parties in an attempt to help them reach an agreement as to how to resolve their dispute.

   1. Mediator lacks authority: A mediator has *no power* to force the parties to do anything. Instead, the mediator talks to the parties — sometimes together, sometimes separately — in an attempt to find common ground and provide a neutral third party's perspective.

   2. Required mediation: In some situations, *mediation may be required*. For example, some states require parties going through a divorce to engage in mediation.

C. Arbitration: Arbitration also introduces a third party to the dispute. Unlike mediation, however, the arbitrator actually *renders a decision*. Thus, arbitration is more like litigation in court in several ways.

   1. Binding vs. nonbinding arbitration: In most cases, the parties are bound by the arbitrator's decision. Sometimes, however, parties submit to nonbinding arbitration. Nonbinding arbitration allows the parties to assess the strength of their respective cases.

   2. Contract: In most cases, arbitration stems from a contract in which the parties agree to submit their disputes to arbitration as an alternative to going to court. Therefore, the agreement must satisfy the general legal requirements for an enforceable contract.

★   **Examples:** Floss v. Ryan's Family Steak Houses, Inc., 211 F.3d 306 (6th Cir. 2000), and Lyster v. Ryan's Family Steak Houses, Inc., 239 F.3d 943 (8th Cir. 2001), illustrate this principle. The cases deal with an identical arbitration clause in an employment contract. In *Floss*, the court found that the contract was invalid because of lack of consideration and vagueness. In *Lyster*, by contrast, the court held that the contract would be enforceable under Missouri law.

   a. Interstate commerce: Even if the rules of contract are otherwise satisfied, some states will not honor arbitration agreements as a matter of policy. However, if the underlying contract is one involving *interstate commerce*, the *Federal Arbitration Act*, 9 U.S.C. §§2 et seq., makes the agreement to arbitrate enforceable, regardless of whether state law honors arbitration agreements. However, the contract must still meet the other state law requirements for an enforceable contract.

   b. Precondition: The contract typically makes arbitration a *precondition to suing in court*. If a party attempts to forgo the arbitration process and sue in court, the other side may move for dismissal of the court case.

   c. Limits: Not all issues may be sent to arbitration. For example, courts will not enforce an agreement between husband and wife to submit their divorce or any child custody issues to binding arbitration.

   3. Arbitration process: Arbitration can be conducted by a single arbitrator or by a panel of several (typically three) arbitrators.

   a. Flexible procedure: An arbitrator is *not bound by the rules of procedure and evidence* to the same extent a court is. Therefore, an arbitrator may hear claims even though they are not set out in the parties' briefs. An arbitrator may also accept nonadmissible evidence.

b. Inquisitorial role: An arbitrator is free to ask her own questions of the witnesses or ask to review documents not submitted by the parties in evidence.

c. Governing law: Parties to an arbitration have some ability to *specify the law* that will govern their dispute. Thus, the parties may specify that their dispute is to be governed by industry custom rather than the usual law of contract.

d. Opinion of arbitrator: The arbitrator renders a *written opinion*. Although this opinion does bind the parties in that dispute, it has little if any weight as precedent, even in later arbitrations involving the same parties.

4. Judicial review of arbitration: Although judicial review of an arbitrator's decision is available, it is extremely limited. A court *cannot review the merits* of the decision. It may only review *whether the arbitrator acted within the scope of her authority*.

Quiz Yourself on
LITIGATION AND ITS ALTERNATIVES

64. Chris and Pat live next to each other in the suburbs. When Pat announces that she is going to start raising pot-bellied pigs, a popular pet, on her property, Chris sues Pat for nuisance. Chris asks the court both to enjoin Pat from operating a pig ranch and to compensate Chris for any decrease in property value that would result from being next to a pig ranch. Assuming Chris wins on the merits, will she be entitled to the relief she requests? _____

65. Tenant leased an apartment from Landlord for two years. The apartment had a unique solar-powered water heater. Unfortunately, the water heater failed while Tenant was living in the apartment. Tenant repaired the water heater at his own expense. Because he had paid for the repairs, Tenant took the water heater with him when he moved out at the end of the lease.

  Claiming that all fixtures must remain in the apartment, Landlord demands that Tenant return the water heater. Tenant refuses. Landlord therefore sues Tenant. Because it is no longer possible to buy a solar water heater that is compatible with the apartment, Landlord asks the court to grant a mandatory injunction requiring Tenant to return the original water heater to Landlord. Is the court likely to grant an injunction? _____

66. Same facts as Problem 65, except assume that Tenant has not yet moved out of the apartment. Tenant is contemplating whether to take the water heater with him when he leaves. However, he is worried that Landlord will sue him for taking Landlord's property. Tenant wants to enlist the aid of the court system to confirm that he may take the water heater. Is there anything Tenant can do, other than taking the heater and subjecting himself to a suit by Landlord? _____

67. Lender has just sued Borrower for failure to repay a loan. Because the loan is not secured by any collateral, Lender is worried whether she will get paid if she has to wait until trial. Therefore, she asks the court to issue an order to the sheriff to seize enough of Borrower's property to repay the loan. Lender includes with the motion an affidavit in which she states she is "genuinely worried" that Borrower will not repay the loan. In addition, Lender asks that the property be seized without notice to Borrower, in case Borrower should attempt to hide the assets. Is the court likely to grant Lender's request? _____

68. Digimage, Inc., makes high-end digital cameras. Digimage obtains the lenses for these cameras from Schott Glass, Ltd. One of Schott's shipments contains a number of lenses that Digimage believes do not meet the required specifications. Because the contract between Digimage and Schott provides that all disputes arising under the contract be submitted to binding arbitration, the parties hold a three-day arbitration. The arbitrator finds that the lenses do not meet specifications and issues a ruling that Schott should immediately send along a complete new shipment.

   Schott refuses to comply with this order. It claims that notwithstanding the language in the contract that suggests that the arbitration was ''binding,'' only a court has the power truly to adjudicate the rights of the parties. Is Schott correct? _____

Answers

64. Chris will be awarded either damages or an injunction, but not both. If Chris obtains an injunction, her property will not decrease in value. Therefore, for a court to award her both the injunction and damages would constitute a double recovery.

65. Even if Landlord wins, she will not receive an injunction. An injunction is a form of equitable relief. To obtain equitable relief, Landlord must demonstrate that the available legal remedies are insufficient. The legal remedy of damages may not be sufficient here because it is impossible to buy a new water heater. However, the legal remedy of replevin, which would require Tenant to return the property, provides exactly the relief Landlord seeks.

66. Tenant may be able to sue for a declaratory judgment. Tenant has a demonstrable fear of being sued in the future and needs a court's decision in order to determine how to act.

67. Lender's request will almost certainly be denied. For prejudgment attachment of a defendant's assets to satisfy due process, Lender must demonstrate a significant interest in the property and take steps to minimize the risk of a wrongful deprivation. Lender has no security interest or other preexisting interest in the property that will be seized. Although this sort of preexisting interest is not absolutely necessary, without such an interest Lender must make a very strong showing that Borrower will dispose of the property before final judgment. Lender's affidavit comes nowhere close to meeting this rigorous standard, because it does not assert any facts that lead the court to conclude that the Borrower is planning to dispose of the property.

   Moreover, Lender's request to have the attachment occur without notice to Borrower compounds the problem. Due process usually requires a hearing prior to the deprivation. Only if the party seeking seizure makes a very strong showing of potential harm will seizure without notice be upheld. Again, Lender has not come close to making such a showing.

68. Schott is not correct. Parties may agree to binding arbitration, which adjudicates their rights fully. Because the contract clearly specified that the arbitration was binding, the decision binds Schott. Of course, Digimage may need to go to court for an order enforcing the ruling, but the court will not review the arbitrator's findings in a case like this.

Exam Tips on
LITIGATION AND ITS ALTERNATIVES

☞ There are important differences between *legal* and *equitable* remedies. Because of the remedial hierarchy that courts recognize, equitable relief is not available unless the legal remedy is inadequate. Thus, if an exam question involves a party who seeks equitable relief, you should discuss whether damages or some other legal remedy would solve the problem.

  ☞ Unfortunately, the only way to know which remedies are legal and which are equitable is to learn them by rote.

☞ When calculating *damages*, you need to draw on the knowledge acquired in your other substantive law courses. For example, although a party can recover expectation damages for breach of contract, she cannot recover punitive damages or damages for emotional distress.

  ☞ In addition, when calculating damages, always make sure that a party is not getting compensated twice for essentially the same harm.

☞ *Punitive damages* are only available in exceptional cases, such as intentional torts.

☞ Recall that a court considering whether to grant an *injunction* considers not only the private interests of the parties but also the *public interest*.

☞ When dealing with provisional remedies, be sure that you understand the difference between a *preliminary injunction* and the more drastic *temporary restraining order*.

☞ If a question involves *pretrial attachment* of a defendant's assets, make sure you address the due process limits on such attachment.

☞ **Attorneys' fees:** Do not forget that although the American rule is the default rule, it can be — and often is — changed by statute or by agreement of the parties.

☞ Be sure to have a solid grasp on the difference — both legal and practical — between *mediation* and *arbitration*.

CHAPTER 7

PLEADING

ChapterScope

Pleading is the means by which the parties advise the court and each other of the claims and defenses that they plan to assert at trial. This chapter focuses on the pleading system that applies in the *federal courts*. Although the Federal Rules of Civil Procedure pleading rules have been adopted by a number of states, other states have systems that are significantly different.

- The two main pleadings in a case are the *complaint* and the *answer*.

  - The *complaint* is the paper filed by the plaintiff that describes the underlying event and sets out the claim or claims for which plaintiff seeks to recover.

  - The *answer* contains defendant's responses to plaintiff's allegations. In addition to setting forth defenses, the defendant may also *counterclaim* against the plaintiff.

- In certain situations, a plaintiff may be required to respond to the answer with a *reply*.

- The Federal Rules of Civil Procedure also allow the parties to bring various *motions*. A motion differs from a pleading in that it focuses narrowly on one or a few issues.

- **Stating a claim:** Under the Federal Rules of Civil Procedure, a complaint need not satisfy any magical litany in order to state a claim. For most claims, the Federal Rules of Civil Procedure simply require a *short and plain statement of the claim*. This is a very low threshold.

  - However, more detail is required for certain issues, such as *fraud*.

  - The plaintiff must also set out a *demand for relief*.

- **Federal forms:** The Federal Rules of Civil Procedure also include a set of forms, which illustrate how a party can allege various matters. Although most attorneys provide far more detail than the forms suggest, a party who uses the form can be assured that the pleading is sufficient.

- **The answer:** The rules governing answers are somewhat more complicated than those governing complaints. Basically, a defendant can respond to a complaint by *admitting* all or part of what the plaintiff says, *denying* what the plaintiff says, and/or alleging an *affirmative defense*.

  - A *denial* must directly respond to the allegations in the complaint. Failing to deny an allegation in the complaint or filing an ineffective denial is treated as an admission.

  - Logically, an *affirmative defense* concedes that the facts as presented by plaintiff are correct, but alleges additional facts that relieve defendant from liability.

- Fed. R. Civ. P. 11 attempts to ensure truthful and good faith pleadings. Under this provision, the party or the party's attorney must *sign* all pleadings and motions.

- Pleadings may be *amended*. Depending on the circumstances, the party wanting to amend may have to obtain *court permission*.

I. HISTORICAL DEVELOPMENT OF PLEADING

The law of pleading has changed significantly over the years. The history of pleading involves *three distinct stages*.

A. Common law pleading: The common law pleading system evolved in England over several centuries.

1. Purpose of pleading: In the historic system, pleading served two main roles.

a. Appropriateness: First, it was meant to demonstrate that the case was an appropriate case for the King's court to hear, as opposed to the local courts. One of the main categories of cases that the King's courts would hear were those involving a *breach of the peace*. If the court decided the case was appropriate, it would issue one of a limited number of *writs*.

b. Single issue: Second, the pleadings were meant to *narrow the case down to single issue for trial*.

2. Highly formalistic: These historical factors led to a pleading system that was highly formalistic, fairly arcane, and contained traps for the unwary.

a. Pro forma allegations: Because of the need to make the facts fit the particular writ, pleadings sometimes made allegations that simply were not true. For example, a plaintiff who was injured by a falling object in defendant's home would allege that his injury was caused by ''force of arms'' — a necessary allegation for the writ.

b. Law, not facts: The common law pleading system focused on pleading legal theories, not the underlying facts. With the various pro forma allegations, the pleadings provided very little factual information about the underlying dispute.

3. Historical significance: Although common law pleading has been abandoned by all U.S. jurisdictions, it still has an important, albeit indirect, impact. First, it created the basic paradigm where a suit is commenced by a plaintiff filing a pleading, followed by a pleading from defendant responding to the plaintiff's allegations. Second, the common law writs evolved into the modern common law causes of action. The nature of many tort, contract, and property claims was defined by the writs.

B. Code pleading: Code pleading, which is still in force in several states, represented a *fundamental change* from the basic notions underlying common law pleading.

1. Purpose: Code pleading was built on the premise that the purpose of pleadings was to *give notice* to the other side of what the party was alleging.

2. Facts, not law: Code pleading required the pleader to make ''a statement of the *facts* constituting the cause of action, in *ordinary and concise language*.'' In fact, a complaint can be held insufficient in a Code pleading state if it states *legal conclusions* instead of simply setting out the facts leading to that conclusion.

C. Pleading under the Federal Rules of Civil Procedure: The remainder of this chapter discusses the third main category of pleading, which is the system provided in the Federal Rules of Civil Procedure. This system is often called *notice pleading*.

1. **Purpose:** As with Code pleading, the purpose of pleading under the Federal Rules of Civil Procedure is to give other parties notice of what claims and defenses are being raised.

2. **Both facts and law:** Unlike Code pleading, however, the Federal Rules of Civil Procedure do allow a party to make legal conclusions. The pleading need only provide general notice of the underlying event and the claims or defenses arising from it.

II. FEDERAL RULES OF CIVIL PROCEDURE PLEADING — OVERVIEW

Under the common law pleading system, pleadings could continue through many stages. The Federal Rules of Civil Procedure reject this approach and allow only a limited number of pleadings. All other issues are raised by motion.

A. Pleadings allowed: *Fed. R. Civ. P. 7(a)* is quite specific concerning what pleadings are allowed.

1. **Pleadings between plaintiff and defendant:** In a lawsuit involving only a single plaintiff and a single defendant, *Fed. R. Civ. P. 7(a)* allows only a *complaint*, an *answer*, and, in some situations, a *reply*.

   a. **Complaint:** The complaint is the paper filed by plaintiff that specifies all claims he has against the defendant.

   b. **Answer:** The answer is the paper filed by defendant in which she responds to all of plaintiff's claims and files any counterclaims. Note, however, that defendant may raise certain defenses prior to the answer by filing a motion.

   c. **Reply:** A reply is plaintiff's response to defendant's answer. However, a reply results only when defendant's answer contains a *counterclaim* that is explicitly designated as a counterclaim or when the court orders a reply.

2. **Pleadings in cases involving additional parties:** As Chapter 14 discusses, many cases involve additional parties. In these cases, *Fed. R. Civ. P. 7(a)* allows the parties to allege their claims and defenses in additional pleadings.

B. Forms of pleadings: All pleadings must fit a basic format.

1. **Case information:** Every pleading must contain a *caption* indicating the *name of the court*, the *title* of the action (which in the case of the complaint must include the names of all parties, but in subsequent pleadings need only state the first plaintiff and the first defendant), the *file number* assigned to the case, and a designation of the *type of pleading* involved.

   Note: The caption typically takes the following form (see following page).

**United States District Court for the
Southern District of Iowa**

Civil Action, File No. 2004-1234

John Doe and Jane Doe, Plaintiffs   )
)

v.   )   COMPLAINT
)

Richard Roe, Defendant   )

---

2. **Separating allegations:** *Fed. R. Civ. P. 10(b)* requires parties to divide their claims and defenses into separate statements. However, Rule 10(b) is *rarely enforced* in actual practice. It is extremely unusual for a complaint or answer to be held defective because of a party's failure to divide material into separate paragraphs, counts, or defenses.

   a. **Separate claims:** Averments must be made in *numbered paragraphs*. The contents of each paragraph must be limited to a single set of circumstances.

   b. **Separate transactions:** If a party includes multiple claims based on separate transactions or occurrences, or separate defenses, each such claim or defense must be *stated separately*. Separate claims are usually referred to as Count I, Count II, and so on.

   c. **Adoption by reference:** Parties making multiple claims may avoid repeating the same facts for each claim by adopting allegations of a prior paragraph by reference.

3. **Exhibits:** *Fed. R. Civ. P. 10(c)* allows a party to attach written documents, such as contracts, as exhibits to the pleadings.

C. **Motions:** All requests to the court other than a pleading are made by motion.

   1. **Requirements:** *Fed. R. Civ. P. 7(b)* sets out certain requirements concerning motions.

      a. The motion must be *in writing*; however, the writing requirement can be satisfied by the written notice of hearing on the motion.

      b. The motion must *state with particularity* the grounds on which the motion is based.

      c. The motion must *state the relief sought*.

      d. All motions must be *signed* in accordance with Rule 11.

   2. **Hearing:** The court typically will hold a *hearing* on the motion as soon as it is feasible.

III. MODERN PLEADING — CLAIMS FOR RELIEF

In federal court, filing the complaint commences the action. *Fed. R. Civ. P. 3*. In addition, parties other than the plaintiff may seek relief by way of a counterclaim, cross-claim, or third-party claim. Although the rules significantly relax the technical requirements for stating claims, *Fed. R. Civ. P. 8 and 9* nevertheless establish certain standards for all these claims.

A. Applies to all claims: The rules discussed in this section apply not only to the plaintiff's complaint, but also to *counterclaims, cross-claims, and third-party claims*. However, to simplify matters, the following discussion is phrased only in terms of the plaintiff's complaint. All references to the *plaintiff* and to the *complaint* should be read to apply equally to these other parties and claims for relief.

B. Contents of complaint: A complaint contains three basic components (Fed. R. Civ. P. 8(a)):

  1. a short and plain statement of the *basis for subject matter jurisdiction*,

  2. a short and plain statement of the plaintiff's *claim*, and

  3. a demand for judgment setting out the *relief* plaintiff seeks.

C. Jurisdiction: The plaintiff must allege the basis for the court's jurisdiction over all claims.

  1. Federal question: If jurisdiction is based on a federal question, the complaint typically cites the federal statute or constitutional provision involved. See Federal Form 2(b) and (c).

  2. Diversity of citizenship: If jurisdiction is based on diversity of citizenship, the complaint will state the citizenship of the parties and specify that the amount in controversy exceeds $75,000. See Federal Form 2(a).

  3. Supplemental jurisdiction: If jurisdiction is based on supplemental jurisdiction, the complaint should indicate the claim in the suit to which the claim in question is supplemental and specify that the claim in question forms part of the same Article III case as that other claim.

D. Statement of the claim: The "short and plain statement" standard of Fed. R. Civ. P. 8(a) sets a fairly low threshold.

  1. Basic standard: A claim is sufficient as long as it provides the defendant *adequate notice* of the plaintiff's claims and of the basic situation or situations from which those claims arise.

  2. Pleadings construed to do justice: *Fed. R. Civ. P. 8(e) and (f)* reinforce this principle. Rule 8(e) provides that all averments shall be "simple, concise, and direct." Rule 8(f) provides that all pleadings are to be construed "as to do *substantial justice*."

  Example: *Federal Form 9*, the sample complaint for negligence, provides an example of how much detail Rule 8 requires. The short and plain statement of the claim constitutes two brief paragraphs:

   2. On June 1, 1936, in a public highway called Boylston Street in Boston, Massachusetts, defendant negligently drove a motor vehicle against plaintiff who was then crossing said highway.

   3. As a result plaintiff was thrown down and had his leg broken and was otherwise injured, was prevented from transacting his business, suffered great pain of body and mind, and incurred expenses for medical attention and hospitalization in the sum of one thousand dollars.

3. **Legal conclusions:** Note that Form 9 merely pleads that defendant was "negligent." The plaintiff ***need not allege*** exactly ***how*** defendant was negligent.

4. **Legal theories:** Although the Form 9 complaint does state that the defendant was negligent, a plaintiff need not explicitly state the legal theory on which she relies. As long as the plaintiff states sufficient facts, she can rely on any legal theory that provides a cause of action under those facts. On the other hand, plaintiff must provide enough of the basic facts to allow defendant to form a response.

5. **Interplay between pleading and discovery:** One key feature of the Federal Rules of Civil Procedure is the interplay between pleading and discovery. Information missing from the complaint — such as how the defendant was negligent or the full injuries suffered by plaintiff — can be fleshed out in the process of ***discovery***.

6. **Inconsistency:** A party may assert alternative, or even inconsistent, grounds for relief. ***Fed. R. Civ. P. 8(e)(2)***.

E. **Elevated pleading standards:** Although the short and plain statement standard applies to the vast majority of claims, the Federal Rules of Civil Procedure impose a higher standard of specificity for certain issues.

1. **Fraud and mistake:** A party who brings a claim based on fraud or mistake must state the ***circumstances*** constituting fraud or mistake ***with particularity***. Fed. R. Civ. P. 9(b).

★   a. **General allegation insufficient:** Therefore, a general allegation that defendant "fraudulently" caused plaintiff to sign the contract is not sufficient. Plaintiff needs to describe in detail the representations made by the defendant and how they were incorrect. See, e.g., Olsen v. Pratt & Whitney Aircraft, 136 F.3d 273 (2d Cir. 1998).

     b. **Exception:** Other issues in a fraud or mistake case, namely ***malice, intent, knowledge***, and any ***other condition of mind***, are ***not subject to the higher standard***, but may be alleged generally like other matters under Fed. R. Civ. P. 8(a).

2. **Special damages:** A party who claims any items of special damage must state those items with particularity. Fed. R. Civ. P. 9(g). The concept of special damages is more accurately thought of as special ***injury***. It refers to any injury suffered by the plaintiff that would not be reasonably expected. If a plaintiff seeks to introduce evidence on any such special injuries at trial, it needs to allege the injuries specifically in the complaint.

Example: In the Form 9 negligence complaint set forth above, if the plaintiff had suffered a heart attack as a result of the accident (an injury that normally does not occur in auto wreck cases), any damages due to the heart attack would have to be alleged with specificity.

★   3. **Other issues:** Although courts sometimes apply heightened pleading standards for other issues, the Supreme Court in Leatherman v. Tarrant County Narcotics Intelligence & Coordination Unit, 507 U.S. 163 (1993), held that courts may not apply a heightened standard to a civil rights claim against a municipality. Given that Fed. R. Civ. P. 9 mentions only fraud and mistake, the lower court erred in applying the same heightened pleading standard in civil rights cases.

F. **Pleading special matters:** While Fed. R. Civ. P. 9(b) and (g) raise the bar on fraud, mistake, and special damages, other provisions of Rule 9 simplify pleading of other matters.

1. **Capacity:** A claimant does not need to allege that it has the capacity to sue or that the defendant has the capacity to be sued. Fed. R. Civ. P. 9(a). Note, however, if the party is suing in a *representative* capacity or suing the representative of another, it may need to allege the capacity to the extent necessary to prove *jurisdiction*.

2. **Conditions precedent:** When a claim turns on the satisfaction of one or more conditions precedent, plaintiff may allege generally that all conditions have been met. Fed. R. Civ. P. 9(c).

3. **Official documents and acts:** If plaintiff's claim turns on an official document or act, she need only allege that the document was issued or the act performed "in compliance with law." Fed. R. Civ. P. 9(d).

4. **Judgment of other court:** If plaintiff is suing to recover on a judgment rendered by another court, he need not allege that the rendering court had jurisdiction. Fed. R. Civ. P. 9(e).

G. **Prayer for relief:** The third requirement imposed by Fed. R. Civ. P. 8(a) is that the plaintiff include "a demand for judgment for the relief the pleader seeks." Thus, the *plaintiff must specify the remedy* that he would like the court to grant.

1. **Different types allowed:** A plaintiff may seek several different types of relief, even on a single claim. The rule even allows plaintiff to seek *alternate forms of relief.* For example, a plaintiff who claims that a defendant fraudulently induced her to enter a contract could ask the court to rescind the contract or, in the alternative, to reform it to correspond to the parties' true agreement.

2. **Prayer nonbinding:** Even though the Federal Rules of Civil Procedure require a prayer for relief, the *court is not limited to the prayer* when it determines the actual relief to which plaintiff is entitled. Fed. R. Civ. P. 54(c). A court may even grant damages in excess of that sought by a plaintiff. The only exception is a default judgment, where the prayer for relief does bind the court. Fed. R. Civ. P. 54(c).

Quiz Yourself on
THE COMPLAINT

69. Captain's prize possession is his luxurious 60-foot yacht. One day, Captain arrives at his marina just in time to see Tennile sailing away in the yacht. Captain wants to sue Tennile for conversion in a federal district court, relying on diversity jurisdiction. However, Captain is unsure whether diversity jurisdiction exists. May Captain file a complaint that says nothing about diversity, thereby putting the burden on Tennile to raise lack of jurisdiction in her answer? _____

70. Same facts as Problem 69. Captain files a complaint in the federal district court. His complaint alleges that diversity jurisdiction exists. The remainder of his complaint is short and to the point, stating merely:

   2. On August 9, 2003, defendant Tennile converted to her own use a 2002 model year Nautilus 60-foot yacht of the value of 100,000 dollars, which was the property of plaintiff.

Wherefore, plaintiff demands judgment against defendant in the sum of 200,000 dollars, interest, and costs.

Tennile brings the proper motion to challenge the complaint. Tennile accurately points out that conversion is an intentional tort. Tennile accordingly alleges that Captain's complaint is insufficient because it says nothing about Tennile's intent. Is the complaint sufficient? _____

71. Same facts as Problems 69 and 70, except assume that the complaint set out in Problem 70 is sufficient to state a claim for conversion. At trial, Captain plans to introduce evidence not only concerning the value of the yacht, but also including that Captain lost his job as a nightclub singer at a club on a nearby island because he had no means of transport. As the complaint is currently worded, will Captain face any difficulties introducing that evidence? _____

72. Same facts as Problems 69 and 70, except that Captain also includes the following paragraph in his complaint:

> 3. In the alternative, defendant Tennile breached an oral lease between plaintiff and defendant, dated on or about January 1, 2002, in which defendant agreed to pay plaintiff 20,000 dollars within three weeks following every occasion on which she used the yacht.

Tennile files the proper motion to contest paragraph 3. She correctly points out that the paragraph sets out a new and different cause of action, which should be labeled as a second count. Tennile argues that the complaint is defective for failure to distinguish the separate counts. Is she likely to prevail on this argument? _____

73. Same as Problems 69, 70, and 72, except instead of challenging the complaint for failure to divide the allegations into counts, Tennile argues that the complaint is deficient because of a fatal inconsistency. Tennile correctly points out that the second and third paragraphs are logically inconsistent: If she could take the boat provided she paid for it later, she could not have committed conversion. Is the complaint deficient because of this inconsistency? _____

74. Borrower sues Lender in federal court for breach of a commitment to make a real estate loan. Borrower attaches a copy of the commitment contract to the complaint. This contract explicitly states that Lender's obligation to make the loan was dependent on the satisfaction of several specific conditions: Borrower had to obtain an opinion letter from an attorney demonstrating that the property was free of any liens, to submit a satisfactory credit report, and to obtain consent letters from the current tenants living on the property. In his complaint, however, Borrower alleges only that "all conditions precedent set out in the contract have been satisfied." Lender challenges the complaint, arguing that Borrower needs to describe each condition and to state how each was met. Is Lender correct? _____

Answers

69. No. A complaint in a federal action must specify the basis for subject matter jurisdiction. Fed. R. Civ. P. 8(a).

70. Although cursory, the complaint is sufficient. In fact, the complaint mirrors the language of Federal Form 11, which makes it per se sufficient.

71. Tennile could successfully object to the evidence about the lost gig. This harm is an example of special damages, which Fed. R. Civ. P. 9(g) requires Captain to plead with particularity. By failing to plead such damages specifically, Captain may be barred from proving them at trial.

72. Tennile is not likely to prevail. Although the rules do specify that separate legal claims should be set out as separate counts, courts rarely grant motions to force parties to comply.

73. The inconsistency does not make the complaint improper. Fed. R. Civ. P. 8(e)(2) explicitly allows a party to allege inconsistent theories.

74. Lender is not correct. Fed. R. Civ. P. 9(c) provides that it is sufficient for a complaint to state simply that all conditions precedent are satisfied.

IV. MODERN PLEADING — DEFENDANT'S RESPONSE TO THE COMPLAINT

Defendant responds to the complaint in two basic ways. The ***answer*** is the defendant's required response, in which defendant deals with all of plaintiff's allegations. However, before filing the answer, defendant may make one or more ***motions*** challenging specific issues.

A. Pre-answer motions: Defendant may raise certain procedural issues by motion.

    1. General considerations concerning pre-answer motions: ***Fed. R. Civ. P. 7*** provides that a party seeking any form of relief from a court will usually ask for that relief by way of a motion.

        a. Examples: Thus, if the defendant wishes to ***challenge the judge*** because of bias or to have the case ***transferred to a different venue*** under 28 U.S.C. §1404, she would make the request by motion, which might occur either before or after the answer.

        b. Other pre-answer motions: In addition, however, ***Fed. R. Civ. P. 12*** allows a defendant to raise certain ***defenses and objections*** — matters usually raised in the answer — in a pre-answer motion. Rule 12(b) allows defendant to move for ***dismissal*** of the case, while Rules 12(e) and (f) ask plaintiff to ***correct*** parts of the complaint.

    2. Rule 12(b) defenses: Fed. R. Civ. P. 12(b) allows the defendant to make certain listed defenses by motion. These motions are often referred to by their Rule 12 notation; e.g., a motion to dismiss a complaint for failure to state a claim is often called simply a Rule 12(b)(6) motion. The defenses that Rule 12(b) allows to be raised by motion include:

        a. lack of ***subject matter jurisdiction*** (Fed. R. Civ. P. 12(b)(1)),

        b. lack of ***personal jurisdiction*** (Fed. R. Civ. P. 12(b)(2)),

        c. improper ***venue*** (Fed. R. Civ. P. 12(b)(3)),

        d. insufficiency of ***process*** (Fed. R. Civ. P. 12(b)(4)),

        e. insufficiency of ***service*** of process (Fed. R. Civ. P. 12(b)(5)),

        f. ***failure to state a claim*** upon which relief can be granted (Fed. R. Civ. P. 12(b)(6)), and

        g. ***failure to join a party*** as required by Rule 19 (Fed. R. Civ. P. 12(b)(7)).

3. **The Rule 12(b)(6) defense:** The substance of all the other defenses is covered elsewhere. Only the Fed. R. Civ. P. 12(b)(6) motion presents considerations unique to this chapter.

   a. **Standard:** When considering a Fed. R. Civ. P. 12(b)(6) motion, the court *applies the "notice pleading" standards* discussed above. Thus, a court dismisses only if there is no reasonable way to construe a complaint to allege a recognized cause of action.

   b. **How complaint defective:** A complaint can be defective in two basic ways.

      i. **Facts:** First, the plaintiff may have left out allegations concerning one crucial element of a given claim. Given the "notice pleading" approach of Fed. R. Civ. P. 8(a), however, these cases are relatively rare.

   ★ ii. **Law:** In the alternative, plaintiff may have fully set out the facts, but those facts do not allow plaintiff to recover under any legal theory. For example, in Haddle v. Garrison, unpublished, Docket No. 96-00029-CV-1 (S.D. Ga. 1996), the trial court granted defendant's Fed. R. Civ. P. 12(b)(6) motion because under the facts alleged in the complaint, the law would not allow plaintiff to recover. When the case was appealed to the U.S. Supreme Court, however, the Court held that a cause of action would exist under federal civil rights laws. As a result, the Court reversed and held that the complaint was sufficient to state a claim. Haddle v. Garrison, 525 U.S. 121 (1998).

   c. **Conversion to summary judgment:** If a Fed. R. Civ. P. 12(b)(6) motion includes facts not set forth in the pleadings, the court treats the motion as one for *summary judgment*. See Chapter 9, Part V.

   d. **Effect of grant of Rule 12(b)(6) motion:** Before dismissing, a court will almost always grant plaintiff *leave to amend* the complaint to allow it to cure the defect. However, in federal court, a Rule 12(b)(6) dismissal for failure to state a claim is a dismissal *on the merits* unless the court specifies otherwise. Fed. R. Civ. P. 41(b); Federated Department Stores v. Moitie, 452 U.S. 394, 399 n. 3 (1981).

      i. A dismissal on the merits prevents plaintiff from bringing any claim against the same defendant based on the same underlying set of facts.

      ii. Some states do not treat a dismissal for failure to state a claim as a dismissal on the merits, even if the state rules otherwise mirror the federal rules.

4. **Other challenges to ambiguous or objectionable complaints:** Fed. R. Civ. P. 12 also allows defendant to challenge a complaint because it is ambiguous or includes objectionable material.

   a. **Rule 12(e) motion for a more definite statement:** If a party is served with a *pleading to which a responsive pleading is required*, but that pleading is so *vague or ambiguous* that the party cannot reasonably frame her response, the party may move for an order requiring the pleader to clear up the ambiguity.

      i. **Must be specific:** The motion must specify the ambiguous portions of the pleading.

      ii. **Rarely used:** In practice, *parties rarely use Fed. R. Civ. P. 12(e)*. If a claim is truly too ambiguous to allow the party to frame an answer, the party usually simply moves to dismiss under Rule 12(b)(6) for *failure to state a claim*.

   b. **Rule 12(f) motion to strike:** Fed. R. Civ. P. 12(f) allows a party to move to strike portions of a pleading that are *redundant, immaterial, impertinent*, or *scandalous*.

i. **Timing:** The motion must be made ***before a responsive pleading is served*** or, if no responsive pleading must be served, within ***20 days*** of service of the pleading.

ii. **Redundant or superfluos material:** Courts ***rarely grant*** these motions merely because a pleading contains some redundant or superfluous material. However, if the party served with the pleading faces a ***considerable burden*** responding to the immaterial information, the court may order the extra material to be stricken.

iii. **Dismissing portions of complaint:** Fed. R. Civ. P. 12(f) may also be used to dismiss some, but not all, of the counts in a complaint. Some courts do not allow a Rule 12(b)(6) motion to be used in these situations. In these courts, the Rule 12(f) motion can be used to strike the improper counts.

Example: *P* sues *D* for intentional and negligent infliction of emotional distress. Although governing law recognizes intentional infliction of emotional distress, it does not recognize negligent infliction. Depending on the court's practice, *D* may obtain dismissal of the negligent infliction claim either by a Rule 12(b)(6) or Rule 12(f) motion.

iv. **Scandalous allegations:** With respect to scandalous allegations, courts strike only when the scandalous allegation is of ***marginal or no relevance*** or when the allegations are worded in a particularly ***inflammatory way***.

5. **Timing of pre-answer motions and waiver of defenses:** ***Fed. R. Civ. P. 12(g)*** and ***12(h)*** set out strict time deadlines governing when defenses must be raised. If a party fails to raise certain defenses in time, he is deemed to have ***waived*** the defenses.

   a. **Joinder of defenses:** ***Fed. R. Civ. P. 12(g)*** allows a party who raises a Rule 12 defense by pre-answer motion to ***join all Rule 12 defenses*** available to that party.

   b. **Waiver of omitted defenses:** However, if a party raises any Rule 12 defense or objection by pre-answer motion but ***omits*** a defense of ***lack of personal jurisdiction, improper venue, insufficiency of process***, or ***insufficiency of service of process***, the party ***waives*** the omitted defense for the remainder of the action. ***Fed. R. Civ. P. 12(h)(1)***.

      i. Note that the second sentence of ***Fed. R. Civ. P. 12(g)*** precludes the party from avoiding waiver by filing a ***second pre-answer motion***.

      ii. This strict waiver rule ***does not apply to lack of subject matter jurisdiction, failure to state a claim***, and ***failure to join a party under Rule 19***.

         (a) Even if a party raises a pre-answer motion asserting a different Rule 12 defense, the party preserves these three defenses.

         (b) However, the party may not raise these defenses in a second pre-answer motion. Instead, in the case of failure to state a claim or failure to join a Rule 19 party, the defense may be raised only in a ***pleading***, a ***motion for judgment on the pleadings***, or at ***trial***. As discussed in Chapter 4, any party can raise the question of subject matter jurisdiction at any time.

         Example: Defendant files and serves a pre-answer motion asking the court to dismiss the case for lack of subject matter jurisdiction. The court denies the motion. Defendant now wants to raise ***insufficiency of service*** and ***failure to state a claim upon which relief can be granted*** in his answer. Defendant has lost the service defense by failing to include it in the pre-answer motion. However, he can still raise the failure to state a claim defense in his answer. Fed. R. Civ. P. 12(h)(2).

> **Example:** Defendant files and serves a pre-answer motion to transfer venue under 28 U.S.C. §1404. The court denies the motion. Defendant now wants to raise the defenses of *insufficiency of service* and *failure to state a claim upon which relief can be granted*. Defendant can still raise both defenses, either by pre-answer motion or in the answer. Although she did file a pre-answer motion, that motion *did not raise any Rule 12 defenses* and therefore is not a "motion under this rule" within the meaning of the first sentence of Fed. R. Civ. P. 12(g).

B. The answer: Regardless of whether the defendant files a pre-answer motion, the defendant must also respond to the complaint by filing an answer. Unlike a motion, the answer must deal with all of plaintiff's allegations. The answer may include claims against the plaintiff or other defendants.

1. Rules not limited to the defendant: The rules discussed in this section apply not only to the defendant's answer to the complaint but also to the *reply* (plaintiff's responsive pleading to defendant's counterclaim), an *answer to a cross-claim*, and an *answer to a third-party claim*. However, to simplify matters, the following discussion is phrased only in terms of the defendant's answer. All references to the *defendant* and to the *answer* should be read to apply equally to these other parties and pleadings.

2. Time for filing the answer: *Fed. R. Civ. P. 12(a)* requires defendant to file an answer within a certain time period. The period varies depending on the defendant and whether plaintiff asked defendant to waive service.

> **a. Default rule—20 days:** In most cases, the defendant must *serve* its answer within *20 days* of the date she was served with the summons and complaint. Fed. R. Civ. P. 12(a)(1)(A).

> **b. Effect of waiver of service:** However, if defendant agrees to the plaintiff's request to *waive service*, these time periods are automatically extended. A *domestic* defendant who waives service has *60 days* following the date the request was sent to answer. Fed. R. Civ. P. 12(a)(1)(B). A defendant situated *outside the United States* has *90 days* following the date the request was sent to answer. Fed. R. Civ. P. 12(a)(1)(B).

> **c. United States as defendant:** The United States, a federal agency, or a federal officer, has *60 days* to answer. Fed. R. Civ. P. 12(a)(3)(A). The 60-day rule also applies to federal officers sued in an *individual capacity* in connection with duties performed on behalf of the federal government. Fed. R. Civ. P. 12(a)(3)(B). The waiver of service rules do not apply to the United States, so there is no extension of this time period as there is in the case of other defendants.

> **d. Effect of motions:** If a party files a pre-answer motion, the time to answer is extended.

>> **i.** In most cases, the defendant is required to answer within *10 days* of the *court's ruling* on the motion. Fed. R. Civ. P. 12(a)(4)(A). Of course, if the court grants a motion to *dismiss* the action, defendant is not required to file an answer.

>> **ii.** If the court grants a motion for a more definite statement, the answer must be filed within *10 days* of the date the *more definite statement is filed*. Fed. R. Civ. P. 12(a)(4)(B).

3. Denials and admissions: The basic rule dealing with how defendant responds to the allegations of plaintiff's complaint is ***Fed. R. Civ. P. 8(b)***. This rule requires defendant to "***admit or deny*** the averments upon which the adverse party relies."

    a. Effect of failure to deny: The consequences of failing to deny something in the complaint can be quite severe. Pursuant to Fed. R. Civ. P. 8(d), ***failure to deny an allegation*** made in a pleading constitutes an ***admission*** of the matter in question.

        i. Exception: Defendant is not required to deny averments relating to ***damages***. Thus, a defendant can litigate the amount of damages at trial even if it did not deny the prayer for relief in its answer.

        ii. Responsive pleading required: Failure to deny operates as an admission only when ***a responsive pleading is required***. If no responsive pleading is required to a particular pleading, all averments in that pleading are automatically ***deemed to be denied***. Fed. R. Civ. P. 8(d). For example, all allegations in a reply are deemed denied.

    b. Lack of knowledge: All averments in a pleading must be made in good faith and be grounded in fact. Thus, Fed. R. Civ. P. 8(b) could pose a problem for a defendant who does not have enough information to deny in good faith something alleged in the complaint. However, ***Rule 8(b)*** allows a defendant to plead that it is "***without knowledge or information sufficient to form a belief as to the truth of an averment***."

        i. Effect: A response alleging lack of information is ***treated as a denial***. Thus, the issue remains in controversy for purposes of discovery and trial.

        ii. Information and belief: A variation on this theme is a ***denial based on information and belief***. In this situation, the defendant strongly suspects something but does not have first-hand knowledge. Like the denial based on lack of information, it works as a denial.

            (a) The denial based on information and belief is ***not explicitly authorized*** by the Federal Rules of Civil Procedure. Instead, it is a vestige of prior practice that still lingers on today.

            (b) In truth, there is no longer any need for a denial based on information and belief. If a party has a good faith belief that an averment is false, it may deny the matter outright consistent with the requirements of Rule 11 (discussed below in Part VII). If it does not have enough information to make a good faith denial, it can simply plead lack of information.

    c. Denials must meet substance of complaint: All denials must "fairly meet the substance of the averments denied." Fed. R. Civ. P. 8(b). A denial that fails to meet this standard is called an ***ineffective denial***. An ineffective denial may constitute an ***admission*** of the matter in question.

        i. Partial denials: If defendant in good faith intends to deny only part of an averment, it must specify which portions it denies.

        ★   **Example:** Paragraph 4 of plaintiff's complaint states simply that defendant "hit and kicked me." Defendant denies paragraph 4. In truth, defendant did kick plaintiff but did not hit plaintiff. Because the denial does not specify which portion of plaintiff's allegations are actually being denied, the ***denial is ineffective***. See Zielinski v. Philadelphia

Piers, Inc., 139 F. Supp. 408 (E.D. Pa. 1956) (it is an ineffective denial for defendant simply to deny plaintiff's allegations that defendant ''owned, operated, and controlled'' a forklift when defendant owned the forklift, but did not operate and control it).

ii. **Objection permitted:** Although no specific rule covers these motions, the rules allow a party to *object* to the form of a denial. Cf. Fed. R. Civ. P. 12(h)(2).

iii. **Caveat:** Fed. R. Civ. P. 8(f), which provides that pleadings should be *construed to do substantial justice*, applies to the answer as well as the complaint. Therefore, courts are not likely to treat an ineffective denial as an admission unless the defendant intended to mislead the plaintiff or unless the plaintiff has irreversibly relied to its detriment on the misleading denial. In the prior example, most courts would allow the defendant to amend the response.

d. **General denials:** A general denial is when defendant denies *every allegation of the entire complaint*.

i. **Rarely appropriate:** Although the general denial was a significant feature of *common law pleading*, it is rarely proper in modern practice. For example, if the complaint correctly states plaintiff's residence, defendant cannot in good faith use a general denial. Nevertheless, the last sentence of Fed. R. Civ. P. 8(b) explicitly allows a defendant to make use of a general denial when she in good faith wants to controvert everything in the complaint, including plaintiff's allegations of jurisdiction.

ii. **General denial with exceptions:** Although a true general denial is rare, parties sometimes file an answer in which they deny everything in the complaint *except* for certain items that they explicitly admit.

iii. **''Backup'' general denial:** In addition, defendants often include a general denial as a backup to their individual admissions or denials. Thus, after admitting certain matters and denying others, an answer typically closes with a statement such as ''every other averment in Plaintiff's complaint not specifically admitted or denied above is hereby denied.''

e. **Alternative and inconsistent denials:** Just as a plaintiff may make inconsistent claims, a defendant may make alternative and inconsistent denials.

Example: *P* sues defendant for breach of contract. In its answer, *D* first denies that a contract between the parties exists. *D* then alleges that even if there is a contract, *D* did not breach. Although logically inconsistent, these alternative denials are acceptable.

4. **Defenses:** A defendant may also respond to the complaint by setting forth one or more defenses. A *defense* is a reason, put forth by defendant, as to why plaintiff is not entitled to the relief it requests. Logically, the defendant argues that even if the facts alleged by plaintiff are true, plaintiff cannot recover.

a. **Defenses and denials can be mixed:** Defendants often include both denials and defenses. Therefore, in a breach of contract case, a defendant could both deny that the parties ever entered into an agreement and, in the alternative, argue that the agreement was not enforceable because of the statute of frauds.

b. **Types of defenses:** Conceptually, there are two basic categories of defenses.

i. **Ordinary defenses:** An ordinary defense considers only the complaint and argues that plaintiff may not recover because of a procedural, legal, or pleading defect. All of the *Fed. R. Civ. P. 12(b) defenses* fall in this category.

ii. **Affirmative defenses:** An affirmative defense usually involves the introduction of *new facts* that, when coupled with the facts alleged by plaintiff, prevent plaintiff from recovering.

   (a) **Types of affirmative defenses:** *Fed. R. Civ. P. 8(c)* defines the following as affirmative defenses: accord and satisfaction, arbitration and award, assumption of the risk, contributory negligence, discharge in bankruptcy, duress, estoppel, failure of consideration, fraud, illegality, injury by fellow servant, laches, license, payment, release, *res judicata*, statute of frauds, statute of limitations, and waiver.

   (b) **Additional affirmative defenses:** The list in Rule 8(c) is *not exclusive*. The rule also includes as an affirmative defense "any other matter constituting an avoidance or affirmative defense." Thus, while *comparative negligence* is not listed in Fed. R. Civ. P. 8(c), it is treated as an affirmative defense. Similarly, if defendant wants to defend a trespass claim by arguing that it had an *easement* across the land, it has the burden of pleading the easement. It cannot simply deny the trespass claim. Layman v. Southwestern Bell Telephone Co., 554 S.W.2d 477 (Mo. Ct. App. 1977).

   (c) **Plaintiff can supply facts for affirmative defense:** Although a defendant usually alleges new facts when pleading an affirmative defense, in some situations the plaintiff itself will provide the necessary facts. Suppose, for example, that plaintiff is suing defendant for a contract for the sale of goods with a purchase price of $800. Because the sales price exceeds $500, that contract falls within the statute of frauds. If plaintiff's complaint specifies that the contract was *oral*, plaintiff in essence has supplied all of the facts necessary to prove defendant's affirmative defense.

c. **Rules do not "create" defenses:** Merely because a defense is listed in Fed. R. Civ. P. 8(c) does not mean that it exists as a matter of substantive law. Many states, for example, have abandoned the defense of assumption of the risk. In an action in federal court governed by the law of one of these states, a defendant cannot use that defense.

d. **Burden of pleading:** If neither plaintiff nor defendant raises a particular issue in their pleadings, that issue usually cannot be litigated at trial (the main exceptions are subject matter jurisdiction and an issue raised at trial by one party without objection by the other). In that case, the party who does *not have the "burden of pleading"* on that issue automatically prevails on the issue.

i. **Who has burden of pleading:** Determining which party has the burden of pleading an issue is sometimes fairly difficult. After all, a defense is the logical inverse of the elements of plaintiff's claim.

ii. **Rules 8(c) and 12(b):** Fed. R. Civ. P. 8(c) and 12(b) help resolve the burden of pleading issue for many common issues. By providing that certain issues are defenses, those rules clearly put the burden of pleading the issue on the defendant. Thus, unless the defendant pleads the affirmative defense of contributory negligence in the answer, defendant cannot argue the question at trial.

  iii. **Court decides:** For other issues, the court must determine who bears the burden of pleading. Although there is no mechanical test used in these cases, courts consider the following factors:

    (a) whether the *facts necessary to establish the defense* are more likely to be known by one party than the other;

    (b) if the underlying claim arises under a statute, whether the *language of the statute* treats the issue as part of the claim or as an exception; and

    (c) whether *analogous issues* are usually treated as elements or defenses.

★

    Example: Gomez v. Toledo, 446 U.S. 635 (1980), illustrates how this analysis is applied. In that case, the Court dealt with the good faith immunity under 42 U.S.C. §1983, under which a state officer is not liable if she acted in good faith. The Court held that the defendant had the burden of pleading good faith, rejecting the claim that the plaintiff had to plead *bad* faith. The Court supported its ruling by noting the inherently subjective nature of the immunity, which meant that plaintiff would not be likely to have the necessary information.

  iv. **Burden of production distinguished:** The burden of pleading must be distinguished from the burden of production. The burden of production determines who must introduce evidence on that issue at trial. It is an issue in summary judgment and judgment as a matter of law. See Chapters 9 and 11.

C. **Heightened pleading standards, special matters:** The heightened pleading standards discussed in Part III.E and the special rules discussed in Part III.F apply equally to defenses and denials. For example, a defendant who wants to defend a breach of contract claim based on fraud or mistake must allege the *circumstances* constituting the fraud or mistake with particularity. Fed. R. Civ. P. 9(b). With respect to capacity, Rule 9(a) specifies that the party *challenging* capacity must raise the issue by a *specific negative averment*.

★ **Example:** In Stratford v. Zurich Insurance Co., 2002 WL 31027517 (S.D.N.Y. 2002), the court held that defendant's counterclaim for fraud was insufficient because it failed to identify the false statements allegedly made by plaintiff.

D. **Counterclaims, cross-claims, and third-party claims:** In addition to denials and defenses, the defendant may also file claims against the plaintiff or codefendants. A claim against the plaintiff is called a *counterclaim*, while a claim against a codefendant is called a *cross-claim*. In addition, the defendant may be able to *implead* additional parties to the action. The rules governing when counterclaims, cross-claims, and third-party claims are allowed are discussed in Chapter 14. The standards governing how a party states a claim in a counterclaim, cross-claim, and third-party claim are identical to the standards that apply to plaintiff's complaint.

Quiz Yourself on
RESPONDING TO THE COMPLAINT

75. Alpha sues Beta in federal court for breach of contract. Beta does not file a pre-answer motion. Beta's answer alleges that the chosen court did not have personal jurisdiction over her. Alpha argues that Beta waived the jurisdiction defense by failing to raise it in a pre-answer motion. Did Beta waive the defense of lack of personal jurisdiction? _____

76. Same facts as Problem 75, except that Beta does file a pre-answer motion to strike one paragraph in Alpha's complaint, alleging that the paragraph is scandalous. The court denies the motion. Beta raises personal jurisdiction for the first time in her answer. Has Beta waived the defense of lack of personal jurisdiction? _____

77. Pedro sues Dante in federal court, alleging two separate claims. Pedro's first claim is for negligent infliction of emotional distress, based on Dante's breach of a contract between the two. Pedro's second claim is for fraud, based on certain other financial dealings between the two.

Dante is sure that Pedro cannot recover on either claim. Under applicable law, breach of a contract cannot give rise to a claim for negligent infliction of emotional distress. Although the law of the jurisdiction does recognize fraud as a viable grounds for recovery, Pedro fails to plead the circumstances surrounding the fraud with sufficient specificity, as Fed. R. Civ. P. 9(b) requires. What motion or motions should Dante bring to challenge the complaint? _____

78. Client sues Attorney for malpractice. Client has the summons and complaint served on Attorney on Monday, March 3, 2003. Attorney files no pre-answer motions. When is Attorney's answer due? If, on the other hand, Attorney files a pre-answer motion before the answer is due, does the due date for the answer change? _____

79. Professor Jones sues Student Smith for defamation, based on an article in the school newspaper that denigrated Jones's classroom teaching. This article was signed with Smith's name. In paragraph three of his complaint, Jones alleges, "An article written by defendant Smith appeared in the February 2002 version of *The Docket*, the law school's newspaper. This article defamed plaintiff by falsely alleging that he was 'boring' and 'pompous.' These false allegations greatly harmed plaintiff's reputation."

In truth, it was another student, not Smith, who wrote the article. Smith rather enjoys Jones's classes. Smith also has no idea whether the statements harmed Jones's reputation. Nevertheless, because paragraph three is false when read as a whole, Smith's answer states simply, "Defendant denies paragraph three of the complaint." Is this a proper way for Smith to deal with paragraph three? _____

80. Same facts as Problem 79, except that Smith deals with paragraph three of the complaint as follows: "Defendant denies that she wrote the article referenced in paragraph three. In the alternative, if defendant did write the article, defendant denies that the statements in the article were false."

Jones argues that because the statements in Smith's answer are inconsistent, Smith's denial is ineffective. Will Jones prevail? _____

81. Lender sues Guarantor in federal court for breach of a contract in which Guarantor agreed to guaranty a loan from Lender to Borrower. Guarantor moves to dismiss for failure to state a claim. Guarantor correctly notes that under governing law, a guaranty contract must be in writing. Guarantor further notes that the complaint nowhere states that the contract was in writing, nor did Lender attach a copy of the contract to the complaint. Will the court grant Guarantor's motion?   _____

Answers

75. Beta did not waive the defense. Nothing requires Beta to bring a pre-answer motion. Because Beta did not file a pre-answer motion, she can raise personal jurisdiction for the first time in her answer. Fed. R. Civ. P. 12(h)(1).

76. Now Beta has waived the defense. Note that Fed. R. Civ. P. 12(g) applies whenever a party files a pre-answer motion ''under this rule'' (Rule 12). A motion to strike, although not listed in Fed. R. Civ. P. 12(b), is a motion under Rule 12. By failing to join the personal jurisdiction defense in this motion, Beta has waived it. Fed. R. Civ. P. 12(g).

77. A single Fed. R. Civ. P. 12(b)(6) motion will take care of both claims. The defense of ''failure to state a claim'' applies both when a party states a claim that is not recognized at law (the negligent infliction of emotional distress claim) and when the party's allegations do not meet the requirements of the pleading rules (the fraud claim). Note, however, that the court is likely to give Pedro leave to amend the fraud claim, assuming that Pedro can allege facts sufficient to meet the heightened pleading standard.

78. Because the facts specify that Attorney was ''served'' (as opposed to a request for waiver of service), Attorney has 20 days to answer. Fed. R. Civ. P. 12(a)(1)(A). Under Fed. R. Civ. P. 6, because the time period is greater than 10 days, it includes intervening weekends and holidays. Therefore, the answer is due on Sunday, March 23, 2003. However, because this date occurs on a Sunday, the due date is delayed until Monday, March 24, 2003.

If Attorney files a pre-answer motion, the due date for the answer may be changed. If the court dismisses, the case is over and no answer is required. If the court requires a more definite statement, the answer is due 10 days after the more definite statement is served.

79. Smith's denial is ineffective because it fails to meet the substance of what was alleged. Smith should deny only the statement about authorship.

In theory, an ineffective denial constitutes an admission. In a case like this, however, the court is very likely to allow her to amend her answer. If she did not write the article, she should not be forced to act as if she did for purposes of trial.

80. The answer is fine. Just as a plaintiff may plead in the alternative, a defendant may defend in the alternative.

81. The court will deny the motion. Guarantor is in essence arguing the statute of frauds. Fed. R. Civ. P. 8(c) explicitly indicates that statute of frauds is an affirmative defense. Therefore, the burden of pleading falls on Guarantor. Guarantor has the burden of pleading that the contract was *not* in writing; Lender need not specify that it was in writing.

V. AMENDMENTS TO THE PLEADINGS

Flexibility is the hallmark of pleading under the Federal Rules of Civil Procedure. That flexibility is also apparent in the rules allowing amendment of the pleadings. A pleading can be changed to cure a defect in the original, to reflect new information acquired since the original, or to incorporate events that occurred after the pleading was filed. In some situations, however, the party must obtain permission to amend.

A. When permission of the court is required: ***Fed. R. Civ. P. 15(a)*** allows a party to amend its pleading *once* without obtaining court permission (which the rule calls ''as a matter of course''), provided that the amendment is made within certain time limits.

1. **Before responsive pleading served:** If the pleading is a *complaint, an answer with a counter-claim, a cross-claim*, or *a third-party complaint*, the party must amend *before the responsive pleading is served*. Note that this time limit is based on *actual service* of the responsive pleading, not the deadline for service. Thus, even though the defendant is allowed 20 days to answer a complaint, the time to amend as a matter of course expires when the answer is served, which can be significantly less or more than 20 days.

2. **Twenty days after pleading served:** For all other pleadings, the party must amend within *20 days after the pleading is served*. The reason for the fixed deadline is that no responsive pleading is required for these pleadings.

3. **Obtaining court permission:** If a party desires to amend after these deadlines or to amend a second time within the period, she must obtain the permission of the court. However, Fed. R. Civ. P. 15(a) indicates that leave to amend ''shall be freely given when justice so requires.'' In practice, courts are extremely accommodating. Leave to amend is denied only if the other party can show *prejudice* by the amendment or the defect in the original pleading was the result of *inexcusable neglect or carelessness* on the part of the pleader.

★   **Example:** In Beeck v. Aquaslide 'N' Dive Corp., 562 F.2d 537 (8th Cir. 1977), defendant discovered several months into the case that it had not produced the slide in question. It therefore asked to amend its answer to deny that it made the slide. Even though the mistake was not due to any carelessness on the part of the defendant, the court denied the request because of prejudice. It noted that because the statute of limitations had run, plaintiff would be left without a claim if the amendment were allowed. Note that this result is very harsh and may well be attributable to the fact that the same insurance company insured both the defendant and the actual manufacturer.

4. **Amending during or after trial:** A party can amend its pleadings during, or even after, trial, with the court's permission. ***Fed. R. Civ. P. 15(b)***.

B. Relation back of amendments: ***Fed. R. Civ. P. 15(c)*** allows some amendments to relate back to the date of the original pleading.

1. **Affects statute of limitations:** Relation back is important when a party wants to add new claims after the statute of limitations has expired. If the original pleading was timely, and the amended pleading adding the new claims relates back, the new claims will not be barred by the statute of limitations.

2. Relation back unrelated to need for court permission: Whether an amendment relates back has nothing to do with whether the party needs to obtain the court's permission to amend. Fed. R. Civ. P. 15(a) and 15(c) are entirely separate questions.

3. When amendments adding claims relate back: An amendment relates back when:

a. the particular statute of limitations allows the amendment to relate back; or

b. the claim or defense set out in the amended pleading arose from the ***same conduct, transaction, or occurrence*** as that set out in the original pleading.

4. When amendments changing parties relate back: A more difficult standard applies if the amendment changes the party against whom a claim is asserted or renames that party. An amendment changing or renaming the party relates back only if:

a. the amended complaint meets the standard discussed just above for relation back of claims, and

b. the party being brought in by amendment acquires ***sufficient notice*** about the existence of the lawsuit within the ***specified time***.

    i. **Formal notice of the lawsuit is not required:** ''Notice'' in this context is not the same as service. It is sufficient if the party learns of the action by word of mouth or other informal means.

    ii. **Sufficiency of notice:** In order to qualify as sufficient, the notice must ***be received early enough to prevent any prejudice*** to the party in preparing its defense and ***contain enough information*** that the party is aware or should be aware that he would have been named a defendant in the original action if a mistake had not been made as to the identity of the parties.

    iii. **Timeliness:** The notice must be acquired by the Fed. R. Civ. P. 4(m) deadline for serving the summons and complaint. This deadline is typically ***120 days after the complaint is filed***, but may be extended by the court. Note that the time period turns on the ***deadline for service***, not when service is actually effected.

        Example: *P* and *D* are neighbors who share a common driveway between their houses. Late one evening, a large rental truck runs into *P*'s house while backing out of the driveway, causing extensive damage. *P* thinks he saw *D* driving the truck. *P* therefore sues *D* in a federal court. The complaint is filed and served 10 days before the statute of limitations expires on the claim.

        Two months later, *D*'s twin sister calls *P*. In this conversation, the sister admits that it was she, not *D*, who was driving the truck. The sister had just learned of the lawsuit from *D* and felt obligated to confess to *P*. The sister also admits that she did not have a license to drive a truck of this size but that the rental company rented to her anyway.

        Because *D* did not know her sister was driving the truck, *D* is not liable to *P* under governing law. Therefore, *P* immediately files and serves an amended complaint that substitutes *D*'s sister for *D* as defendant. Moreover, the complaint adds the truck rental company as an additional defendant, claiming that the rental company is also liable for renting a truck to a person without the proper license. The rental company admits that it knew of the accident on the day it happened and of *P*'s lawsuit on the day it was filed.

The sister and the rental company both move for summary judgment, claiming that the limitations period has expired.

   P's claim against the sister does relate back, but the claim against the rental company is barred by the statute of limitations. The sister received notice within 120 days following service, and it is clear that she knew that she should have been a defendant. Note that *P* need not show that the sister was "hiding" her guilt; the amendment relates back even though the sister came forward. With respect to the rental company, however, the requirements of Fed. R. Civ. P. 15(c) are not satisfied. Even though the company knew of the lawsuit, there was no "mistake concerning the identity of the proper party." *P* knew, or could have determined, the name of the rental company prior to filing suit.

C. Other changes to the pleadings: Rule 15 also authorizes amendments to conform the pleadings to the evidence and supplemental pleadings.

   1. **Amendments to conform to the evidence:** During trial, if a party attempts to introduce evidence on matters outside the pleadings, the other parties may object. However, if a party fails to object, he is deemed to have ***impliedly consented*** to litigation of the issues raised in the evidence. In addition, a party may ***expressly consent*** to litigation of matters outside the pleadings.

      a. If a party consents, Fed. R. Civ. P. 15(b) provides that any issues raised "shall be treated in all respects" as if they were raised in the pleadings and allows a party to amend its pleadings to make them conform to the newly raised issues.

      b. Even if a party objects to the introduction of the evidence, the issue may end up forming part of the trial. Fed. R. Civ. P. 15(b) provides that a court ***should freely allow amendments*** to the pleadings at trial if it will help resolve the merits of the action, unless the late amendment would cause the other parties ***undue prejudice***.

   2. **Supplemental pleadings:** A party may also be allowed to supplement its original pleadings to set forth new matters. Fed. R. Civ. P. 15(d).

      a. **Amendments distinguished:** Supplemental pleadings set forth facts that ***arise after the original pleading was filed***. Amended pleadings, in contrast, deal with facts that existed at the time of the legal pleading, but change the way those facts are alleged or the claims or defenses arising out of those facts.

      b. **Court permission:** Supplemental pleadings ***always require court permission***. However, leave to amend is freely given.

Quiz Yourself on
AMENDMENTS TO THE PLEADINGS

82. Reva, a stellar law student, is upset to learn that Jeff, the class entrepreneur, secretly copied her detailed Civil Procedure outline. After months of negotiating with Jeff prove fruitless, Reva sues Jeff in federal court for copyright infringement, asking for $5,000 in damages.

Three months after serving the complaint, Reva discovers that on the same day Jeff copied her Procedure outline, he also copied her Contracts outline. She wants to amend her complaint to add a second claim for copyright infringement. However, given that Jeff has not yet filed or served an answer, she is unsure how to amend. In addition, she is unsure whether the amendment will be effective. The statute of limitations on the infringement claims expired three weeks after the original complaint was filed.

How may Reva amend her complaint? Given that the statute of limitations has expired, will the amendment do her any good?   _____

83. Same facts as Problem 82, except that at the same time Reva learns about the Contracts outline, she also discovers that Jeff had set up a kiosk in the law school lobby two weeks after Reva filed her suit. From this kiosk Jeff sold copies of Reva's Civil Procedure outline to other students. Because these acts cause further harm to Reva, she wants to modify her complaint to ask for additional damages. How can she modify her complaint?   _____

Answers

82. This problem raises two questions: how to amend and whether the amendment relates back. These are separate questions, governed by different standards.

   Fed. R. Civ. P. 15(a) allows Reva to amend her complaint once as a matter of course before Jeff answers. Because the problem indicates that Jeff has not yet answered, Reva may amend without obtaining either the court's or Jeff's permission.

   Of course, if the claim is barred by the statute of limitations, amending does Reva little good. However, Fed. R. Civ. P. 15(c) provides that, in certain circumstances, an amendment of a pleading may relate back to the date of the original pleading. If the amendment relates back to the date of her original complaint, the claim for the copying of the Contracts outline is not time-barred.

   There is no indication that the applicable statute of limitations allows the claim to relate back. Under Fed. R. Civ. P. 15(c)(2), however, the claim relates back as long as it arises out of the same transaction as the claim set out in the original pleading. Technically, there are two basic occurrences here: Jeff's copying of the Civil Procedure outline and his copying of the Contracts outline. Nevertheless, because these happened on the same day and were probably caused by the same basic motivation, the two claims probably arise from the same occurrence. Reva accordingly should be able both to amend and to survive any statute of limitations challenge.

83. The events in question occurred *after* the complaint was filed. Therefore, Reva needs to file a supplemental complaint pursuant to Fed. R. Civ. P. 15(d). Note that the court must approve the supplemental pleading, although approval is almost certain here.

VI. MOTION FOR JUDGMENT ON THE PLEADINGS

Once pleading is complete, ***Fed. R. Civ. P. 12(c)*** allows any party to move for judgment on the pleadings.

    A. Timing: A motion for judgment on the pleadings may be filed only ***after all pleading is complete***, but early enough so as not to ***delay the trial***.

B. Standard: The court considering the motion accepts all facts alleged in all the pleadings as true. If the court nevertheless concludes that one party is entitled to judgment as a matter of law, it will grant the motion and render judgment.

C. When used: The motion for judgment on the pleadings is most commonly used by a ***claimant*** against a party who has ***failed to defend*** against that person's claim. In a way, it is the logical counterpart to the Fed. R. Civ. P. 12(b)(6) motion for failure to state a claim.

    1. ***Fed. R. Civ. P. 12(h)(2)*** allows a party to raise ''failure to state a legal defense to a claim'' at any stage of the proceedings and lists the motion for judgment on the pleadings as one of the means by which the objection can be raised.

    Example: *P* sues *D* for both battery and negligence. *D*'s answer denies all allegations of negligence but says nothing about the battery claim. Because failure to deny constitutes an admission, *P* can move for a judgment on the pleadings since *D* in effect has admitted the battery. (Of course, the court may allow *D* to amend her answer if the failure to defend was an oversight.)

    2. If a party moving for judgment on the pleadings introduces matters outside the pleadings, the court treats the motion as one for ***summary judgment***.

VII. ETHICAL LIMITATIONS ON PLEADINGS, MOTIONS, AND OTHER ARGUMENTS

Fed. R. Civ. P. 11 sets out strict standards designed to ensure honesty and accuracy in pleadings and motions. The same rule also attempts to ensure that parties and attorneys are honest in their oral representations to the court.

A. Signing requirement: Fed. R. Civ. P. 11(a) requires that certain documents be ***signed***.

    1. Documents governed: The requirement applies to ***most documents*** that the parties file with the court, including ***pleadings and motions***.

        a. Unfiled documents: Although Fed. R. Civ. P. 11(a) does not explicitly limit the signing requirement to papers filed with the court, other language in the rule makes it clear that only filed papers are covered. Therefore, the rule does not apply to correspondence between the parties and the like.

        b. Discovery not included: The provisions of Fed. R. Civ. P. 11 do not apply to discovery, including motions filed with the court to compel or object to discovery requests. Note, however, that ***Fed. R. Civ. P. 26(g)*** establishes a separate signing requirement for discovery.

    2. Who must sign: Each paper must be signed by at least one ***attorney*** of record for the party. If the party is not represented, the party himself must sign the paper.

    3. Required information: In addition to the signature, the signer must provide her address and telephone number, if any.

    4. Effect of failure to sign: If a paper subject to the signing requirement is presented to the court without the required signature, it is stricken.

B. Representations made to court: The crux of Fed. R. Civ. P. 11 is its ***implied certifications***. Whenever an attorney or unrepresented party presents a matter to the court, he is deemed to have certified things concerning that matter. If these certifications are not accurate, the party is subject to sanctions.

1. **Acts constituting certification:** In many states, Rule 11 applies only when a signed paper is submitted. In the federal system, however, Rule 11 is *not limited to signed papers*. Instead, the certifications are deemed made whenever a pleading, motion, or other paper is *presented to the court*. A matter may be "presented" by:

   a. *signing* the paper,

   b. *filing or otherwise submitting* the paper, regardless of whether it is signed, or

   c. *advocating* the contents of the paper to the court.

   Note: Fed. R. Civ. P. 11 requires the *existence* of a paper of some sort. Merely advocating a matter not set out in a pleading, motion, or other paper does not expose a party to Rule 11 sanctions.

2. **Certifications made:** By doing any of the above, the attorney or unrepresented party certifies that:

   a. she has conducted an *inquiry* into the matter that is *reasonable under the circumstances*, and

   b. that the following are *true to the best of the person's knowledge, information, and belief*:

      i. the pleading, motion, or other paper is not being presented for any *improper purpose* (*improper* explicitly includes harassment and delay);

      ii. all legal arguments in the paper are supported either by *existing law* or by a *nonfrivolous argument* to extend, modify, or reverse existing law;

      iii. all *factual contentions* are either currently *supported by evidence*, or are *likely to be supported by evidence after further investigation or discovery* (provided the currently unsupported contentions are *specifically identified*); and

      iv. all *denials of factual contentions* are either currently *supported by evidence*, or are reasonably based on *belief or lack of information* (provided the currently unsupported denials are specifically identified).

      Example: *P* sues *D* in federal court for trademark infringement. After *D* wins the case, he brings a motion for Rule 11 sanctions against *P* based on two items in *P*'s complaint. First, *P* alleged that *D* earned $250,000 in profits from infringing *P*'s mark. Although this allegation turned out to be correct, *P* merely made up this number without any background investigation. Second, *P*'s legal argument as to why *D*'s acts constituted infringement had previously been explicitly rejected by the court of appeals for that circuit, even though they had been accepted in seven other federal circuits. *P* is subject to sanctions for the factual allegation, but not the legal one. With respect to the facts, *P* wrongfully certified that she had conducted a reasonable background investigation. That her allegation turned out to be true does not matter. The legal allegation, by contrast, could be supported by a good faith argument for reversing existing law in the circuit, based upon the views of the other circuits.

★   **Example:** The Eighth Circuit's decision in Walker v. Norwest Corp., 108 F.3d 158 (8th Cir. 1996), involves an example of a pleading that makes claims not supported by the law. Plaintiffs sued several defendants in federal court, relying on diversity jurisdiction. The complaint alleged that plaintiffs were citizens of South Dakota and that one of the defendants was a citizen of Minnesota. The complaint did not specifically state the citizenship of the other defendants. However, the plaintiffs did allege that some of the other defendants "resided" in South Dakota. The court imposed sanctions because plaintiff's allegations of diversity jurisdiction were not supported by the law. (Recall that the complete diversity rule used in diversity cases requires that no defendant can be from the same state as any plaintiff.)

★   **Example:** Christian v. Mattell, Inc., 286 F.3d 1118 (9th Cir. 2003), by contrast, deals with the factual inquiry required by Rule 11. Plaintiff sued defendant, claiming that defendant's Barbie doll infringed the copyright in plaintiff's doll. The facts, however, showed that defendant had copyrighted its Barbie doll before plaintiff obtained its copyright. As a result, plaintiff was not entitled to recover. The court held that sanctions on plaintiff would be appropriate, especially because plaintiff could easily have discovered defendant's copyright date by examining the back of the Barbie doll's head.

C. Sanctions: If any of the certifications prove untrue, Fed. R. Civ. P. 11(c) allows a party to move for the imposition of ***sanctions***. However, the rule contains a ***safe-harbor provision*** giving the offender the opportunity to cure her error in certain situations. ***Sanctions are never required.*** Moreover, the rule limits a court's discretion concerning the type of sanction.

     1. Process: Sanctions may be imposed either following motion by the party or on the court's own initiative. In all cases, however, the person to be sanctioned must be afforded ***notice*** and an ***opportunity to be heard***.

         a. By motion: *Fed. R. Civ. P. 11(c)(1)(A)* allows a party to move for sanctions.

             i. Service: The party first ***serves*** the motion on the offending party.

             ii. Safe harbor: However, a motion for Rule 11 sanctions is ***not immediately filed***.

                 (a) Timing: The motion may be filed only if the offending party does not withdraw or correct the challenged paper within ***21 days*** following service of the motion or other period established by the court.

                 (b) Use with complaints: The safe-harbor provision may not apply to false allegations made in a ***complaint***. Religious Technology Center v. Gerbode, 1994 U.S. Dist. LEXIS 6432 (C.D. Cal.). The court in *Gerbode* reasoned that it was impractical to apply the rule to the complaint given that the defendant was required to answer before the safe harbor expired.

             iii. Costs and fees: The court may award costs and reasonable attorneys' fees to the party who prevails on a motion for sanctions.

         b. Court's initiative: The court may also impose sanctions on its own initiative. ***Fed. R. Civ. P. 11(c)(1)(B)***.

             i. Before imposing sanctions, the court must issue an ***order to show cause*** why sanctions should not be imposed.

ii. The ***safe-harbor provision does not apply*** to sanctions imposed on the court's own initiative.

c. Order: An order imposing sanctions must specifically describe the offending conduct and justify the sanctions imposed. ***Fed. R. Civ. P. 11(c)(3)***.

2. **Persons subject to sanctions:** The court may impose sanctions on the ***individual attorneys*** who violated the rule, their ***law firm***, and a ***party***. However, there are limits on a court's power to sanction a party.

   a. A court may sanction a party only if she either violated the rule herself or was responsible for the violation. ***Fed. R. Civ. P. 11(c)***.

   b. Monetary sanctions cannot be imposed against a ***represented party*** for violating the provision dealing with wrongful ***legal*** contentions. ***Fed. R. Civ. P. 11(c)(2)(A)***.

3. **Sanctions allowed:** The rule limits sanctions to whatever is "***sufficient to deter repetition***" of such conduct in the future. Thus, a sanction may be ***punitive***. Fed. R. Civ. P. 11(c)(2) allows for the following sanctions:

   a. ***nonmonetary*** sanctions, which the Advisory Committee notes suggest may include an order striking pleadings or issuance of a reprimand;

   b. a ***penalty***, which must be paid to the ***court*** instead of the other party; and/or

   c. in a case where a ***party moved*** for sanctions, an order requiring the offending party to reimburse the movant for any or all costs and attorneys' fees ***caused by the violation***. However, costs and fees are available only when needed for ***effective deterrence***.

   Note: It is important to distinguish an order for fees imposed as a sanction from an order for reimbursement of fees under Fed. R. Civ. P. 11(c)(1)(A). Rule 11(c)(1)(A) allows only those fees incurred in prosecuting or defending the ***motion***. The fees granted as a sanction are those incurred as a result of the ***violation itself*** and may therefore include amounts expended on unnecessary discovery or legal research.

4. **Determining appropriate sanction:** The ***Advisory Committee notes*** indicate that a court has ***considerable discretion*** in determining an appropriate sanction. However, they also suggest certain factors to consider in determining an appropriate sanction:

   a. whether the violation was ***willful*** or merely negligent;

   b. whether the offending party ***intended to injure*** the other party;

   c. whether the offending person has had ***legal training***;

   d. whether there was a ***pattern*** of offending conduct, in this case or in others;

   e. whether the wrongful activity ***pervades*** an entire pleading or motion or only a particular claim or defense; and

   f. the effect the violation had on the process of litigation, including a consideration of any ***added time or expense***.

Quiz Yourself on *PLEADING*

84. While attending a fireworks show, Spencer Spectator is seriously injured when a shell detonates too close to the ground. Spencer sues Charlie Cherrybomb, who both organized and oversaw the pyrotechnics display. Spencer brings his case in federal court.

    Spencer's complaint reads (other than the caption and signature) as follows:

    1. Jurisdiction in this case is based on 28 U.S.C. §1332.
    2. On or about August 2, 2003, at a fireworks show at the Woodford County Fairgrounds in Eureka, Illinois, Plaintiff was seriously injured by an explosion caused by fireworks.
    3. Defendant Cherrybomb owed a duty to Plaintiff by virtue of the fact that Defendant both organized and operated the fireworks show in question.
    4. Defendant Cherrybomb breached that duty by failing to act as a reasonable person would under the circumstances.
    5. Defendant's negligent acts caused Plaintiff's extensive injuries.
    6. As a result of Defendant's negligence, Plaintiff suffered serious burns, causing him great pain, and requiring him to incur over twenty thousand dollars in medical expenses.

    Wherefore, Plaintiff demands judgment against Defendant in the sum of one hundred thousand dollars together with costs.

    Charlie feels that both the jurisdictional and substantive allegations in Spencer's complaint are worded too vaguely. What motion or motions should Charlie bring to challenge the allegations? _____

85. Same facts as Problem 84. Suppose that Charlie first objects to subject matter jurisdiction by filing a pre-answer motion to dismiss for want of jurisdiction. The court denies the motion. In his answer, Charlie raises the defense of failure to state a claim, based on the allegations concerning negligence. Will the court hear Charlie's defense of failure to state a claim? _____

86. Same facts as Problems 84 and 85, except assume that the court finds that Charlie raised both defenses in timely fashion. Is Charlie likely to prevail on either his challenge to the jurisdictional allegations or his argument that Spencer has not stated a claim? _____

87. Karen shows cairn terriers at dog shows. When she learns that a champion cairn is expecting puppies, Karen contacts the owner, Breeden, to see if Breeden might be interested in selling. Karen and Breeden enter into a contract in which Karen agrees to pay $2,000 for her choice of one puppy from the litter.

    Shortly after the birth, Karen goes to visit the new litter. In one glance, she realizes that the mother had been fooling around, probably with the local English bulldog. The puppies clearly are not purebred cairn terriers.

    Karen sues Breeden for rescission of the contract. She wants to argue that the contract is voidable because of a mutual mistake of fact as to whether the puppies would be purebred cairns. The relevant portions of Karen's complaint read as follows:

    2. On or about March 5, 2003, Plaintiff and Defendant entered into a contract. This contract provided that Plaintiff would pay $2,000 to Defendant. In return, Defendant promised Plaintiff that Plaintiff could have her choice of one puppy from a litter to be delivered by Toto2, a dog belonging to Defendant.

3. Said contract is invalid because of a mutual mistake of fact concerning the pedigree of the puppies.

Wherefore, plaintiff demands that the aforementioned contract between Plaintiff and Defendant be rescinded, and the parties restored to their position before the agreement.

Breeden moves to dismiss for failure to state a claim. Although she acknowledges that mutual mistake is a basis for rescission, she claims that Karen's complaint is too vague. How will the court rule? _____

88. Same facts as Problem 87, except that rather than suing to rescind the contract, Karen simply refuses to pay or accept possession. Breeden sues Karen in federal district court for breach of contract. Karen files an answer that denies both that there was a contract and that she breached.

Several weeks after the pleadings are closed, Karen files a motion for judgment on the pleadings. In this motion, Karen points out that Breeden's complaint did not specify that the contract was in writing. The statute of frauds requires that contracts for the sale of goods for a price in excess of $500 be in writing. Will Karen prevail? _____

89. Snidely Whiplash was seriously injured in an automobile collision at an intersection. After talking to the other driver, Snidely strongly suspects that the traffic light at the intersection was malfunctioning. Snidely therefore sues the City in a federal district court. Snidely claims that (a) the light did not work properly, (b) the City was negligent in failing to make sure that the light worked properly, and (c) as a result, Snidely was involved in an accident and suffered $100,000 in damages.

The City is now preparing its answer. It is prepared to admit that Snidely was involved in an accident but to deny that it was in any way negligent. However, the City really has no idea whether the light was malfunctioning on the date in question. City engineers have inspected the light since the accident, and although it is working fine now, this brand of light has a history of malfunctioning. In addition, the City has no idea whether Snidely really suffered damages of $100,000. Therefore, the City is thinking about simply not responding to Snidely's allegations concerning the light and his damages. Does the City run any risk if it fails to respond? _____

90. Hatfield and McCoy are neighbors who have never really gotten along. One day McCoy comes home to find his house burned to the ground. McCoy is sure that Hatfield intentionally set the blaze. McCoy's suspicions are confirmed when he sees footprints leading from Hatfield's house to McCoy's and back again. McCoy therefore sues Hatfield for $200,000 in damages. McCoy's complaint specifically alleges that Hatfield intentionally set the fire.

Furious at these allegations, Hatfield refuses to speak to McCoy. Instead he immediately files a motion for sanctions under Fed. R. Civ. P. 11. Will the court impose sanctions on McCoy? _____

Answers

84. Charlie should bring two motions to dismiss: a motion to dismiss for lack of subject matter jurisdiction based on the jurisdictional allegation, and a motion to dismiss for failure to state a claim for the remainder of the complaint.

85. The court will consider the motion to dismiss for failure to state a claim. Fed. R. Civ. P. 12(g) does provide that if a party brings a pre-answer motion based on any grounds listed in Rule 12, he must include those defenses listed in Rule 12(h)(1) or they are waived. Failure to state a claim is not listed

in Rule 12(h)(1) and therefore is not waived. Fed. R. Civ. P. 12(h)(2) explicitly provides that a party can raise the defense of failure to state a claim in a pleading.

86. Charlie is correct when he argues that the allegations concerning jurisdiction and the cause of action are insufficient. However, he is not likely to prevail on either motion.

   The jurisdictional allegation is not sufficient. Although Spencer has alleged the basis for jurisdiction, he has supplied the court with no facts that would allow it to determine whether jurisdiction is met. Federal Form 2(a), the "barebones" form that applies to diversity, suggests at the very least that Spencer should have told the court of the parties' citizenships.

   Although it is a closer case, the allegations of negligence are also insufficient. The federal rules use "notice" pleading, under which the plaintiff need only give the defendant a general idea of the claims. Spencer has not done this. Given that Charlie both organized and oversaw the show, he could have been negligent in a number of different ways — in choosing the location, in hiring help, or through his own acts in shooting off the fireworks. Spencer has not given Charlie enough information to enable him even to guess what it is he did wrong. Compare Form 9, where the plaintiff at least alleges that the defendant was careless in driving the automobile.

   Nevertheless, it is unlikely that the court will dismiss on either ground. Instead, it will probably give Spencer leave to amend.

87. The court should grant Breeden's motion to dismiss. Karen's complaint is sufficiently detailed to survive the general "notice pleading" standard of Fed. R. Civ. P. 8(a). However, Rule 9(b) requires that a party alleging fraud or mistake must set out the circumstances surrounding the fraud or mistake with particularity. Karen needs to provide more details concerning what the parties assumed when entering into the contract.

88. Karen will not prevail. Statute of frauds is an affirmative defense. Fed. R. Civ. P. 8(c). Karen therefore has the burden of pleading that the contract was not in writing.

89. Under Fed. R. Civ. P. 8(d), failure to deny an averment constitutes an admission, except for averments as to the amount of damage. Therefore, if the City does not respond, it may be deemed to have admitted that the light was not working properly. However, it will not have admitted Snidely's damages.

   The City does have another option. Because it truly has no way to determine with certainty whether the light was working, it can plead that it is without knowledge or information sufficient to form a belief. That plea of lack of knowledge is treated as a denial. Fed. R. Civ. P. 8(b).

90. The court will not impose sanctions. It is probably true that McCoy violated Fed. R. Civ. P. 11. He really has no factual support leading him to conclude that Hatfield intentionally set the blaze. Fed. R. Civ. P. 11(b)(3). The footprints do not show that Hatfield set the fire since any number of alternate explanations are possible. Although McCoy may find evidence supporting his claim, he should have specified that the particular allegation was not currently supported by evidence.

   Whether sanctions will be imposed depends on how the court interprets the safe-harbor provision of Fed. R. Civ. P. 11(c)(1)(A). Some courts do not apply that provision to the complaint. If the court follows this interpretation, it may impose sanctions immediately. However, if the court concludes that the safe-harbor provision applies to complaints, it will not impose sanctions because Hatfield did not meet the rule's requirements. Hatfield should have served on McCoy his motion pointing out the problem. Only if McCoy refused to withdraw the allegation within the 21-day period would Hatfield be entitled to file the motion and obtain an order for sanctions.

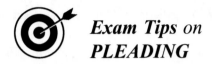

Exam Tips on
PLEADING

☛ Most pleading questions involve the Federal Rules of Civil Procedure. Questions concerning common law or Code pleading are relatively rare, unless you are in a Code pleading state.

☛ Be sure to keep the difference between *pleadings* and *motions* distinct in your mind.

   ☞ Pleadings are the general documents that set out all of the parties' claims and most of their defenses.

   ☞ Motions, by contrast, are more specific requests to the court. They typically deal with procedural requests. However, certain defenses such as lack of jurisdiction or venue may also be raised by motion.

☛ **The complaint:** The basic "short and plain statement" standard of the federal rules is very easy to satisfy. As long as the complaint gives the defendant notice of the claims and the basic events giving rise to those claims, it is sufficient.

   ☞ The notice pleading standard applies not only to the complaint but also to all other affirmative claims for relief, such as counterclaims and cross-claims.

   ☞ Be sure to remember the *Federal Forms*. A complaint that complies with the simple language set out in these forms automatically is sufficient.

   ☞ Look out for questions involving the *heightened pleading standards* set out in Fed. R. Civ. P. 9, such as claims for fraud, mistake, and special damages.

☛ **Motions by defendant:** Defendant may raise certain objections to the complaint by motion.

   ☞ Students dealing with motions often overlook the issue of *timing*. You must thoroughly understand the Fed. R. Civ. P. 12(g) and (h) rules governing when certain defenses can be raised.

      ☞ Recall that Fed. R. Civ. P. 12(g) comes into play whenever a party raises a defense or objection mentioned *anywhere in Rule 12*. Its use is not restricted to those items listed in Fed. R. Civ. P. 12(b). A motion to strike, for example, triggers Rule 12(g).

   ☞ When dealing with a *Rule 12(b)(6)* motion, ask yourself two questions.

      ☞ Is the claim stated in sufficient detail under the standards of Fed. R. Civ. P. 8 and 9? Courts usually give leave to amend if the problem is one of insufficient detail.

      ☞ Is claimant trying to recover under a legal theory recognized by the substantive law? Even if the complaint is incredibly detailed, if the law does not recognize the claim a Rule 12(b)(6) motion is appropriate.

☛ **The answer:** The rules governing the answer are much more detailed, and in some ways less forgiving, than those governing the complaint. The *same rules* also *apply to the reply*.

   ☞ If a question mentions dates, be sure to consider whether the answer is filed on time.

☞ The most important criterion to recall in framing an answer is that failure to answer — which includes an ineffective denial — can be deemed an admission.

☞ Recall that if a party does not know whether a particular allegation is true, she can always plead *lack of information*, which is treated as a denial.

☞ Make sure you know which issues are ***affirmative defenses***. If something is an affirmative defense, the defendant has the burden of initially pleading it. Fed. R. Civ. P. 8(c) contains a partial list of affirmative defenses.

☞ **Amendments:** There are two key issues in amendments, which must be kept separate. The first is whether a party needs court permission for amending. The second is whether an amendment adding claims or changing parties relates back. Merely because the court gives permission does not mean the amendment relates back.

☞ **Ethical limitations:** Recall that under Fed. R. Civ. P. 11, an attorney (or in some cases a party) who presents a motion or pleading to a court makes a number of certifications concerning the factual and legal matters alleged in that motion or pleading.

☞ When dealing with Rule 11 sanctions, do not forget the ***21-day safe-harbor provision***, during which the party may withdraw the offending presentation.

☞ Recall that any monetary ***penalties*** for Rule 11 violations are paid to the court, not to the other party.

CHAPTER 8

DISCOVERY

ChapterScope ━━━━━━━━━━━━━━━━━━━━━━━━━━━━━━━━

This chapter deals with discovery, the process by which a party gathers information from other parties and nonparties to help her prepare for trial. It discusses discovery only under the *federal rules*. Although many states pattern their discovery rules after the Federal Rules of Civil Procedure, others use significantly different methods.

▪ The federal rules recognize *six primary methods* of discovery.

- ▪ *Mandatory disclosures*, under which each party may be required to disclose certain background information to the other, such as the names of eyewitness and copies of contracts and other key documents;

- ▪ *Depositions*, where a witness is questioned under oath by one or more of the parties;

- ▪ *Interrogatories*, which are written questions that the other party must answer in writing;

- ▪ *Inspection* of tangible property or documents;

- ▪ *Requests for admission* of facts or the application of law to fact; and

- ▪ *Physical and mental examinations* of parties.

▪ *Most of these methods* apply only as *between the parties*. A deposition is the only one of the main discovery devices that can be used to obtain information from nonparties.

▪ Parties can obtain discovery of facts even though those facts *could not be introduced as evidence* at trial. As long as the information sought might lead to facts that could be introduced, it can be discovered.

▪ Certain types of information, including *work product*, information protected by a *privilege*, and *trade secrets*, may either be not discoverable at all or discoverable only on terms set by the court.

▪ A party may be required to *supplement* prior discovery to correct errors.

▪ Discovery usually proceeds without oversight by the court. Other than physical and mental examinations, a party *need not obtain the court's permission* before seeking discovery.

- ▪ However, when obtaining information from a nonparty, the party usually needs to obtain a *subpoena* from the court.

▪ Federal courts, and many state courts, must hold a *pretrial conference*, which narrows down the case by weeding out uncontested issues.

I. OVERVIEW OF DISCOVERY

A. Increased emphasis on discovery: Pleading and discovery work in concert. Modern pleading usually requires the parties to disclose only minimal information in the pleadings. Discovery allows the parties to refine their cases as they prepare for trial.

B. Mandatory disclosures: Traditionally, discovery reflected the adversarial nature of litigation. A party had to ask for information before it was provided. Recently, the Federal Rules of Civil Procedure, and the rules of some states, have been amended to require parties to **disclose** certain basic information **without a request** from the other side. Parties must disclose information at the beginning of the case and again on the eve of trial.

C. Discovery methods: Once mandatory disclosure is complete, parties may obtain information through a wide array of discovery methods. Each method has its advantages and disadvantages.

D. Broad scope: To help discovery achieve its aims, the rules place very few limits on what can be discovered. Fed. R. Civ. P. 26(b) allows for the discovery of most information that is **relevant** and **not privileged**.

E. Certification of discovery: The party or the party's attorney must sign all mandatory disclosures and discovery requests and responses. By signing the document, the party or attorney certifies that the disclosure, request, or response is both proper and not unduly burdensome.

II. STANDARD FOR DISCOVERY

Fed. R. Civ. P. 26(b)(1) sets out the general standard for determining whether information can be discovered. A party can discover information relating to "any matter, **not privileged**, that is relevant to the claim or defense of any party. . . ."

A. Applies to ordinary discovery: This standard applies to all situations in which **a party seeks information** from someone else. It technically does **not apply to mandatory disclosures**. However, most information that must be disclosed also meets the standard.

B. Relevance: The first step in determining whether information is discoverable is to determine whether it is relevant. Relevance is a low threshold.

1. **Relevance defined:** Information is relevant as long as it may help a party prepare his case. It need not necessarily be evidence that the party uses at trial.

   Example: In Davis v. Precoat Metals, 2002 WL 1759828 (N.D. Ill. 2002), plaintiffs sued defendant for discrimination based on race and national origin. Plaintiffs asked defendant to disclose all complaints that nonclerical employees had brought against defendant for race and national origin discrimination. The court held that the information sought was relevant because it could be used to demonstrate that defendant's alleged basis for taking action against plaintiffs was a mere pretext.

★ **Example:** By contrast, in Steffan v. Cheney, 920 F.2d 74 (D.C.C. 1990), the court held that the requested information was irrelevant. The plaintiff had been discharged from the navy based on his *statements* that he was a homosexual. The navy sought information about whether he had actually engaged in homosexual *acts*. The court found the information irrelevant, given that the navy's stated reason for discharge was the statement, not any alleged acts. That the acts might themselves constitute a reason for discharge did not matter, given that the navy had not relied on any acts in making its decision.

2. **Relevance to party's claim:** The Fed. R. Civ. P. 26(b)(1) standard was ***significantly narrowed*** by an amendment in 2000. The prior provision allowed discovery of any information relevant to the subject matter of the action. Under the new standard, it must be relevant to a claim or defense of a party.

   a. **Any party:** Note that under the new standard the information can be relevant to the claim or defense of any party, not merely the one requesting it.

   b. **Good cause:** Information that is relevant to the subject matter of the action but not to a party's claim or defense can be discovered, but only if the party obtains a ***court order*** upon a showing of ***good cause***.

3. **Need not be admissible at trial:** Fed. R. Civ. P. 26(b)(1) further provides: ''Relevant information need not be admissible at trial if the discovery appears ***reasonably calculated*** to lead to the discovery of admissible evidence.'' Therefore, a party must disclose information even though that information could not be used at trial.

   a. **Background information:** The rule allows a party to discover background information that plays no role at trial, such as a witness's telephone number.

   b. **Information precluded as evidence:** More significantly, however, the rule allows a party to discover information, such as hearsay evidence, that the Federal Rules of Evidence specifically prevent from being admitted at trial.

      Example: *P* is injured when his toaster bursts into flame. *P* sues the manufacturer of the toaster. *P* serves interrogatories on the manufacturer, asking the manufacturer to disclose any ''changes in the design of the toaster'' that were made after the accident. *D* had redesigned the toaster after the accident to use a more heavy-duty power cord. However, evidence of the design change could not be introduced at trial. *D* must nevertheless disclose the design change. Even though the information itself is not admissible, it may help *P* determine what was wrong with the toaster. *P* can use other evidence at trial to prove that the original power cord was dangerous.

4. **Financial information:** A plaintiff may want information concerning defendant's assets in order to decide whether it is economically worthwhile to seek a money judgment against that defendant. Such information is generally ***not discoverable*** because it is irrelevant to whether plaintiff is entitled to a judgment. However, there are exceptions.

   a. **Punitive damages:** Punitive damages consider a party's net worth since the amount necessary to ''punish'' a defendant varies depending on the defendant's wealth. Therefore, a plaintiff who seeks punitive damages can discover the defendant's assets.

   b. **Insurance:** In the ***initial mandatory disclosures***, a party must disclose to the other side any ***liability insurance coverage*** that may cover the claim being litigated.

C. **Privileges:** Even if it is relevant, information cannot be discovered if it is protected by a privilege. A privilege protects information from being disclosed ***by a particular source***. The party may still obtain the information from other sources.

Example: *P* sues *D* for injuries sustained in an automobile accident. *P* deposes *D*'s attorney, asking the attorney what *D* told the attorney about the accident. *P* cannot discover the information because it is protected by the attorney-client privilege. However, *P* can discover what *D* knows by asking *D* directly. The information is not immune from discovery merely because it was relayed to the attorney.

1. **Common privileges:** The law of privileges varies from state to state. However, certain privileges are recognized in many states.

   a. **Self-incrimination:** The privilege against self-incrimination allows a person to refuse to provide information that constitutes admission of a criminal act by that person. The privilege is guaranteed by the U.S. Constitution, and therefore applies equally in all courts.

   b. **Attorney-client:** The attorney-client privilege gives a past or present client the right to prevent an attorney from disclosing information pertaining to the legal representation that the client relayed to the attorney.

   c. **Doctor-patient:** The doctor-patient privilege gives a past or present patient the right to prevent a doctor, and in some states other medical practitioners, from disclosing information relating to the treatment that the patient relayed to that person.

   d. **Priest-penitent:** The priest-penitent privilege gives a person the right to prevent a religious leader from disclosing information relayed in confidence.

   e. **Spousal:** The spousal privilege gives a person the right to prevent a spouse from disclosing information relayed in confidence.

2. **Governing law in federal court:** Federal Rule of Evidence 501 provides that when a federal court hears a case that will be governed by state law, the federal court uses that same state law to determine the existence and scope of any privileges.

3. **Privileges absolute:** Unlike the work product and expert ''privileges'' discussed in Part V of this chapter, a true privilege is an ***absolute bar*** to discovery of the information. No matter how badly the other side needs to obtain the information from the protected source, the privilege prevents disclosure.

4. **Claiming privilege:** A party cannot withhold information based on a claim of privilege unless the party makes the claim ***expressly*** and provides enough of a ***description*** of what is being withheld to allow the requesting party to determine if the privilege applies. Fed. R. Civ. P. 26(b)(5).

III. SEQUENCE OF DISCOVERY

Discovery typically begins shortly after the pleadings are filed and may continue until shortly before the trial. Discovery usually proceeds in a particular order.

A. **Discovery conference:** *Fed. R. Civ. P. 26(f)* requires the parties to meet ''as soon as practicable'' to discuss the claims and defenses that have been filed and whether there is any possibility of settlement. If no settlement is reached, the parties are required to prepare a ''discovery plan'' for the case.

   1. **Discovery plan:** This discovery plan covers the ***subjects*** on which discovery is to be had, the ***timing and form*** of mandatory disclosures and discovery, any agreement that the parties may

reach that either *limits* discovery or *relaxes limits* prescribed by the rules, and any orders that the court should issue to facilitate the discovery process.

2. **Prerequisite to discovery:** A party may not engage in formal discovery until after the discovery conference.

B. **Initial disclosures:** Shortly after the discovery conference, the parties make the initial mandatory disclosures required by Fed. R. Civ. P. 26(a).

C. **Party-initiated discovery:** Once the initial disclosures are complete, the parties may serve discovery requests on each other and on third-party witnesses. This phase may take months or even years in a complex case.

D. **Pretrial disclosures:** As the case nears trial, the parties again make certain mandatory disclosures of expert witness information and other evidence to be offered at trial.

Quiz Yourself on SCOPE AND SEQUENCE OF DISCOVERY

91. Graffiti, Inc., manufactures a line of spray paints. During the past two years, several consumers have been seriously injured when cans of Graffiti paint exploded during use. Two of these consumers, Albert and Betty, join as plaintiffs and sue Graffiti in federal court. Before the answer, Albert serves a set of interrogatories on Graffiti. Graffiti refuses to answer. Is Graffiti justified in refusing to respond to the interrogatories? _____

92. Same facts as Problem 91. Albert's claim against Graffiti alleges a design defect, arguing that the company designed a defective spray mechanism. Betty, by contrast, relies on a theory of manufacturing defect, claiming that one of the employees was careless in assembling the can. Graffiti denies liability to either plaintiff.

   Several months into the case, Albert serves two timely discovery requests. First, he sends interrogatories to Betty, asking her to reveal any information that she has that might indicate a problem in the manufacture of the can. Betty objects to the relevance of these questions. Second, Albert notices the deposition of Caleb. Caleb is another victim of an exploding Graffiti spray paint can. Caleb has sued Semi Conscious Co., a trucking company, in state court. Caleb claims that the problem with the can arose because Semi transported the cans in trucks that were too hot, causing stress to the delicate components of the spray paint can. At the deposition, Albert asks Caleb to disclose any information he has about problems in the transport of the spray paint cans. Caleb also objects to the relevance of the questions. Is Albert entitled to receive the information he wants from Betty and Caleb? _____

93. Same facts as Problem 91. Several months into the case, Graffiti serves a timely set of interrogatories on Albert. One of the interrogatories asks Albert to describe in detail the circumstances under which he was using the spray paint can. Albert is reluctant to answer the question, for in truth Albert was

using the can to paint graffiti on the outside walls of the local law school. Vandalism is a felony in that state. Must Albert answer the question? _____

Answers

91. Graffiti's refusal to respond is justified. Fed. R. Civ. P. 26(d) provides that parties may not use interrogatories or other methods of discovery until after the parties meet in the discovery conference. Because Graffiti has not yet answered, the conference has not been held.

92. Albert may receive the information he wants from Betty, but probably not from Caleb. Neither of the requests is relevant to Albert's claim or any defense to his claim. Because he claims only a design defect, information about the manufacture or transport of the product is not relevant. However, Fed. R. Civ. P. 26(b)(1) allows a party to obtain any information that is relevant to the claim or defense of *any party*, not merely the claims and defenses that affect the requesting party. Therefore, because the information is clearly relevant to Betty's claim and Betty is a party, Albert can discover it.

Because Caleb is not a party, Albert is not automatically entitled to information that relates only to Caleb's claim. However, the information is relevant to the subject matter of the case. Therefore, Albert could petition the court to allow him to discover that information. However, it is unlikely that Albert can show good cause. Given that he is relying only on the design defect theory and that Graffiti is not asserting that the defect arose in transport, Albert really has no need for information about transport.

93. Albert need not answer the question. Although the information is clearly relevant, it is privileged. The U.S. Constitution provides a privilege against self-incrimination, under which a party cannot be required to admit a crime.

IV. DISCOVERY METHODS

The Federal Rules of Civil Procedure require parties to disclose certain information to other parties. In addition to these mandatory disclosures, the rules allow parties to obtain information from other parties, and in some cases nonparties, through a variety of means.

A. Mandatory disclosures: The mandatory disclosure rules require parties to turn over information that is typically sought as a matter of course in formal discovery. There are *two main stages* of mandatory disclosures.

    1. Background and overview: The mandatory disclosure provisions of *Fed. R. Civ. P. 26(a)* are a relatively recent addition to the rules (originally adopted in 1993). Because the notion of mandatory disclosure runs counter to the tradition of litigation as an adversarial process, only a few states include mandatory disclosure requirements in their rules.

        a. 2000 amendments: The mandatory disclosure rules were amended in 2000 in response to certain recurring criticisms. The most significant change was to limit the information that must be disclosed.

        b. No opt-out: Rule 26(a) originally allowed individual federal districts to "opt out" of the mandatory disclosure rules. The 2000 amendments removed that option.

2. **Initial disclosures:** *Rule 26(a)(1)* requires each party to turn over certain listed items of information.

   a. **Timing:** The initial disclosures must be made within *14 days* following the discovery conference unless the parties agree otherwise or the court extends the time.

   b. **What must be disclosed:** The following items of information must be disclosed:

      i. the name and, if known, the contact information of any *person with discoverable information* (such as an eyewitness) that the party *may use to support its claim or defense in any way other than impeachment*;

      ii. a copy or description of all *documents, data compilations, and tangible things* (for example, a written contract) that the party *may use to support its claim or defense in any way other than impeachment*;

      iii. a computation of *damages*, together with supporting documentation; and

      iv. any *liability insurance policy* that may apply to the claim or claims.

   c. **"May use to support":** This language comes from the 2000 amendments. Today, a party must disclose only items she *may use to support her claim or defense, unless* these items will be used *solely for impeachment*.

      Example: *P* sues *D* for injuries sustained in an automobile collision at an intersection. *P* claims *D* ran a red light. Before filing suit, *P* tracked down and interviewed an eyewitness to the collision. This eyewitness told *P* in the interview that *P*, not *D*, ran a red light. *P* need not disclose this witness to *D* because *P* will not call the witness at trial. Under the rules prior to 2000, by contrast, the witness would have to be disclosed.

      Example: impeachment: *P* sues *D* for breach of an oral contract. *D* denies that the parties ever entered into a contract. *P* is in possession of a letter that *D* wrote to a friend, in which *D* admits that she in fact did enter into an oral contract with *P*. *P* plans to use this letter at trial only if *D* takes the witness stand and denies a contract. *P* need not disclose the letter to *D*. Because using the letter to contradict *D*'s testimony constitutes use for purposes of impeachment, the rule does not require *P* to disclose the letter.

   d. **Exempted proceedings:** *Fed. R. Civ. P. 26(a)(1)(E)* exempts certain proceedings from the initial disclosure requirement.

3. **Pretrial disclosures:** Rules 26(a)(2) and (a)(3) require the parties to disclose additional information to other parties as the date for trial draws near.

   a. **Expert testimony:** The party must disclose the *identity* of any person who will testify as an **expert**. If the person is retained or employed specifically to provide expert testimony, the party must also include a *report* signed by the expert witness describing the person's qualifications as an expert, the opinions that the expert will give and the grounds for those opinions, all information considered by the witness in forming the opinion, the amount of compensation the person will receive for testifying, and a list of all other cases during the past four years in which the person has testified as an expert. Fed. R. Civ. P. 26(a)(2).

   b. **Lay witnesses:** The party must disclose the name and, unless already provided, the contact information, for all witnesses the party may call at trial. The disclosure must differentiate between witnesses a person plans to call and those he may call depending on the circumstances. If the party will present a witness's testimony by means of a deposition, the party must so indicate and provide transcripts of the portions of the deposition that apply.

   c. Tangible evidence: The party must identify documents and other tangible evidence that may be used at trial. The disclosure must differentiate between evidence the person plans to use and that which he may use depending on the circumstances.

   d. Timing: These disclosures must be made at least *30 days before trial* in the case of lay witnesses and tangible evidence, and *90 days* in the case of experts, unless the court otherwise specifies.

B. Overview of methods of obtaining information from others: Other than the mandatory disclosures, all formal discovery in a lawsuit in a case proceeds by a party requesting the information from others. The Federal Rules of Civil Procedure provide various means of obtaining this information.

   1. When discovery may commence: *Rule 26(d)* provides that discovery cannot commence until *after the discovery conference*. (The only exception is the Rule 27(a) pretrial deposition, discussed below.) This limit can be waived by stipulation of the parties or by order of the court.

   2. Choice of methods: A party may usually obtain discovery using whatever method he deems most effective. The Federal Rules of Civil Procedure generally do not mandate the use of one type or another. The most important exception is the *physical or mental exam*, which is available only if the information cannot be obtained by alternate means. See Part G.

   3. Informal information gathering not barred: Nothing in the discovery rules limits a party's ability to gather information by informal means, such as voluntary exchanges of information between parties or witness interviews. Informal information gathering may occur before the case is filed and can continue while the case proceeds. In many cases, most ''discovery'' is of this informal type.

C. Depositions: Taking a deposition resembles questioning a witness at trial. The witness is placed *under oath*. One or more of the parties poses questions to the witness, which the witness answers. The entire proceeding is *transcribed*.

   1. Who may be deposed: A deposition is the only formal discovery device that may be used against *nonparties*. The person who answers the questions is called the *deponent*.

   2. Limit on availability: A party usually does not need the court's permission to conduct a deposition. However, certain exceptions exist. First, leave of court is required if the deponent is *in prison*. Second, a party needs either leave of the court or a stipulation signed by all parties if the deponent has *already been deposed* or, if as a result of the proposed deposition, there would be *more than 10 depositions* by the party and those aligned with the party. Fed. R. Civ. P. 30(a)(2).

   3. How initiated: A party initiates a deposition simply by giving *reasonable notice* to all other parties. The notice specifies the time and location of the deposition, as well as the name of the deponent.

      a. Party deponent: If the person to be deposed is a party, the notice places a duty upon the party to appear at the deposition and submit to questioning. A party may be required to travel to a distant location, including other states, for purposes of providing deposition testimony. However, if the location or timing is too burdensome, the party deponent may petition the court for a *protective order*.

b. Nonparty deponent: If the person to be deposed is not a party, the notice alone does not obligate the person to appear. In these cases, the party may also obtain a *subpoena* requiring the witness to appear at the time and place specified in the notice of deposition. *Fed. R. Civ. P. 45* sets forth detailed rules governing subpoenas.

   i. Location of deposition: The nonparty witness may move to quash the subpoena if it requires him to travel to a place *more than 100 miles* from the place where that person resides, is employed, or regularly conducts business in person.

   ii. Issuing court: The subpoena must be issued by the district court in the *district where the deposition* is to be conducted. Fed. R. Civ. P. 45(a)(2).

   iii. Service: The subpoena may only be served:

   (a) anywhere in the *district where the subpoena was issued*;

   (b) anywhere *within 100 miles* of the place *where the deposition is to be conducted* (which may lie outside the district where the issuing court sits); or

   (c) if state law so allows, *anywhere within the state* in which the *deposition is to be conducted*.

   iv. Consequences of failure to obtain subpoena: If the party fails to obtain a subpoena and the witness does not appear for the deposition, the witness cannot be sanctioned in any way. However, the party who noticed the deposition may be required to pay the expenses and attorneys' fees of all other parties who attended the deposition. Fed. R. Civ. P. 30(g)(2).

c. Production of documents: The deposing party may also request the deponent to bring documents or tangible things to the deposition. In the case of a nonparty deponent, the subpoena may specify that the person should bring along the document or tangible thing. Such a subpoena is commonly called a *subpoena duces tecum*.

d. Deposing corporations and other associations: Often, a party suspects that someone within a corporation has the desired information, but is not sure *who*. In this situation, *Fed. R. Civ. P. 30(b)(6)* allows the party simply to notice the deposition of the corporation itself, describing in detail the type of information being sought.

   i. Designated person: The corporation or association must then *designate one or more persons* either within the organization or who agree to testify on behalf of the organization, and *inform the requesting party* about what each person will testify. The designated person then appears at the deposition and testifies as to any specified matters either known or readily available to the organization.

   ii. Particular person: If the party requesting information knows of a particular corporate official or employee who is likely to have information, the party *may forgo the above process* and simply depose that particular person.

4. Deposition procedure: A deposition may be *held anywhere*, although it is usually conducted in the offices of an attorney representing a party. However, Fed. R. Civ. P. 30(b)(7) also allows the deposition to be conducted by *telephone*.

a. Court officer: Unless the parties stipulate otherwise (which they usually do), the deposition is conducted before an officer of the court.

b. Oath: The deponent is placed under oath.

c. Questioning and cross-examining: The party requesting the deposition then asks questions of the deponent. Other parties may cross-examine the deponent.

d. Inspection: If documents or tangible things have been produced, inspection of those items will occur.

e. Recording deposition: The questions and answers are *transcribed* by a court reporter or by *electronic means*. The party noticing the deposition may select the means of preserving the testimony and bears the cost. Any other party, with prior notice to the deponent and other parties, may specify *additional means* of preserving the testimony.

f. Objections: The deponent or any party may object to the content or form of a question. Objections must be made *concisely* and in a nonargumentative and *nonsuggestive* manner. Fed. R. Civ. P. 30(d)(1). This prevents an attorney from "coaching" the witness to provide a certain answer or to frame the answer in a particular way.

   i. However, because no judge is at the deposition to resolve the objection, the objection is *noted on the transcript*, and the *deponent usually must then answer the question* notwithstanding the objection.

   ii. An attorney may instruct a party not to answer a question only when necessary to protect a *privilege*, pursuant to a limit on discovery already imposed by the court, or if the party plans immediately to seek a *protective order* under Rule 30(d)(4).

g. Protective orders: Fed. R. Civ. P. 30(d)(4) allows a party to seek a protective order when a deposition is conducted in *bad faith* or in a way that unreasonably *annoys, embarrasses, or oppresses* the deponent or a party. For example, continually asking about irrelevant matters may lead to a protective order.

   i. The order must be obtained from a district judge in the district *where the deposition is being taken*.

   ii. Because protective orders disturb the judge in the midst of a deposition, most attorneys seek them sparingly and only in egregious cases.

h. Time limit: Rule 30(d)(2) limits a deposition to a *single day of 7 hours*, unless the parties stipulate or the court orders a longer time.

i. Review of transcript: *If the deponent or a party requests*, the deponent may review the transcript. If the deponent would like any changes, she may sign a statement indicating the requested changes and the reasons for them.

5. Special depositions: The discussion above deals with the standard oral deposition, the type most commonly used in federal litigation. However, the rules also allow for two other types of depositions.

   a. Deposition before commencement of action: In certain situations, *Fed. R. Civ. P. 27* allows a person to depose another person even before a lawsuit is commenced.

   i. When used: A person might want to take such a deposition to *preserve the testimony* of an important witness who is in poor health or about to leave the country for an extended period of time.

    ii. **Petition:** A pre-action deposition requires ***court approval***. The person seeking the deposition must file a petition describing the underlying dispute, the likely parties to that dispute, the information that the person thinks the deponent has, and the reasons why the information needs to be obtained now rather than during the case. ***Notice*** must be provided to all expected adverse parties.

    iii. **Depositions pending appeal:** *Fed. R. Civ. P. 27(b)* also allows for depositions to be taken while a case is on appeal.

  b. **Deposition on written questions:** *Fed. R. Civ. P. 31* allows a party to conduct a deposition without showing up in person. The party instead submits ***written questions***, which the person presiding at the deposition will then ask the deponent. The presiding official also records the answers.

    i. **When used:** The deposition on written questions is typically used only to obtain background information from ***nonparty witnesses***: If the witness is a party, the information can be obtained more expeditiously by use of interrogatories.

    ii. **Cross-examination:** Copies of the written questions are provided to all parties. Those parties may then submit ***written cross-examination questions*** to the presiding officer and other parties. The party noticing the deposition can then serve ***redirect*** questions.

D. **Interrogatories:** Interrogatories are ***written questions*** that the recipient answers ***under oath***. *Fed. R. Civ. P. 33* governs interrogatories.

  1. **Availability:** Interrogatories may only be against ***parties***. Court approval is not necessary.

  Note: Nothing prevents a party from sending written questions to a nonparty. Although the nonparty is under no obligation to answer, if the nonparty voluntarily answers, the party is free to use the information.

  2. **Limit on number:** *Fed. R. Civ. P. 33(a)* prevents a party from serving more than ***25 questions*** on any other party, unless the court approves or the parties agree to more. If a given question has subparts, each ***subpart*** counts as a ***separate question***.

  3. **Answers:** The recipient must answer the questions ***under oath***. The answers must also be ***signed***. Typically, the party will work with an attorney in framing the answers.

    a. **Time to answer:** The questions must be answered within ***30 days*** unless the court orders or the parties agree otherwise.

    b. **Duty to investigate:** Unlike depositions, where the witness answers from personal knowledge, a party answering interrogatories has a ***duty to investigate***. Therefore, if the answer is not personally known to the party but can be obtained from the party's records or other sources, the party must investigate and provide the information.

    c. **Exception: Option to produce business records:** The duty to investigate can prove cumbersome, especially if the party's records are not organized in a way that makes the information easy to recover. ***Rule 33(d)*** therefore provides that if the answer to an interrogatory can be obtained from the party's business records, and the burden of ascertaining the information is substantially the same for both parties, the party served may ***specify the records*** in which the answer may be found and allow the asking party to ***conduct its own search*** of those records.

d. Objections: Unlike in a deposition, if a party objects to a question, it may refuse to answer that question and instead state with specificity why the question is objectionable. Fed. R. Civ. P. 33(b)(5). The asking party's only recourse is to obtain an order compelling the served party to answer under Fed. R. Civ. P. 37.

    i. A question will be objectionable if, for example, it is overly burdensome or calls for privileged information.

    ii. However, Rule 33(c) makes it clear that a question is not objectionable merely because it asks the answering party to apply law to fact. For example, a plaintiff can ask the defendant if the defendant was ''negligent'' because that involves the application of law to fact.

E. Inspection of documents and things: *Fed. R. Civ. P. 34* allows one party to inspect *documents and tangible things* in the possession of another party.

  1. When available: Rule 34 can be used only against *parties*. Even if the party is not in actual possession of the item, he must make it available for inspection if it is in the possession of someone *under that party's control*.

  Note: obtaining documents and tangible things from nonparties: Although Rule 34 is available only against parties, the rules provide two ways for a party to inspect physical evidence controlled by a nonparty. First, as discussed above in Part C dealing with depositions, a party may inspect movable things in the possession of nonparties by *noticing the deposition* of that person and obtaining a *subpoena duces tecum* requiring the person to bring along certain described items. Second, if the nonparty's testimony is not necessary, the party may simply obtain a subpoena under *Fed. R. Civ. P. 45(a)(1)(C)* requiring the nonparty to produce and permit inspection of tangible items or to permit inspection of premises.

  2. Procedure: A party seeking inspection of tangible items under Rule 34 serves a *request* upon the party in possession or control of the item. The request must describe the items to be inspected and specify a reasonable time and place for the inspection to occur. The other party then files a *response* within 30 days, indicating whether the inspection will be allowed or, if applicable, any grounds for objection.

  3. Other parties: Rule 34 does not require that the request for inspection be served on parties other than the one possessing or controlling the item in question.

F. Requests for admission: *Fed. R. Civ. P. 36* allows a party to ask another party to admit certain matters. If the other party does not either object to or effectively deny the matter, the matter may be *deemed admitted* for purposes of trial.

  1. When available: Requests for admission may only be used against *parties*. A party will typically use the device near the end of discovery to weed out matters in the pleadings that have been resolved by discovery and thereby to pare down the case for trial.

  Note: Although technically a discovery device, requests for admission are conceptually closer to *pleadings*. They are like a second round of pleadings on the eve of trial, helping the parties determine what issues remain in dispute.

  2. What may be requested: A party may request anything within the scope of discovery, including *opinions of fact or the application of law to fact*. A party may also ask another party to confirm that a particular document is genuine, for example, that a particular item is indeed a deceased party's last will. A party may not object to a request to admit merely because it involves an issue that constitutes the crux of the case or because the matter is something that "should be proved at trial."

3. **Process:** A party seeks an admission by serving a *request* on the other party. Unlike depositions and interrogatories, there is no limit on the number of requests that may be served.

    a. **Response:** The party served with the request may

        i.   *admit* that the matter is true;

        ii.   *deny* the truth of the matter, if the party can deny it in good faith;

        iii.   state in detail reasons why the party *cannot admit or deny* the request; or

        iv.   *object* to the request.

    b. **Form of denial:** A denial must "fairly meet the substance of the requested admission." Fed. R. Civ. P. 36(a). Moreover, if a party intends to deny only part of a statement, he must specify in detail which parts are admitted and which are denied. This is the same standard that applies to the answer to a complaint.

    c. **Effect of failure to deny:** A party who does not deny a request to admit, or who sets forth an ineffective denial, is deemed to have *admitted* the matter requested. Any admission *applies only in the particular case* and has no effect in other cases.

G. **Physical and mental examinations:** *Fed. R. Civ. P. 35* makes it possible to force a *party* to submit to a *physical or mental examination*. Unlike all other discovery devices, a party seeking a physical and mental exam must obtain a *court order*.

    1. **When available:** A physical or mental exam may be ordered only for a *party* or person in *custody or under the legal control of a party*.

        a. **Custody or control:** The reference to a person under the custody or control refers to a ward, such as an infant or incompetent. The rights of infants and incompetents are usually litigated by *guardians*.

        b. **Need not be adverse:** The party to be subjected to the examination need not be adverse to the movant. However, it is rarely possible to show good cause for examining a coparty since the requesting party will usually have no need for the information at trial.

    2. **Court order required:** Unless the party to be examined consents, a party seeking a physical exam must obtain an order from the court *in which the action is pending*. The order is granted only if the party demonstrates that the physical or mental condition is *in controversy* and if *good cause* exists for the examination.

        a. **In controversy:** The physical or mental condition of a party is *in controversy* if the condition is *relevant* to one or more claims or defenses before the court and if there is a *genuine dispute* concerning the condition.

            i. **Relevancy:** For example, if a defendant in a breach of contract case argues that the contract was invalid because the defendant was insane when the alleged agreement was reached, the mental condition of the defendant is in controversy.

★

    ii. **Placing condition in controversy:** Because of the highly intrusive nature of exams, the Supreme Court in Schlagenhauf v. Holder, 379 U.S. 104 (1964), limited the ways in which a person's physical or mental condition could be placed in controversy.

        (a) A party may *place her own condition* in controversy *in the pleadings* by alleging a claim or defense that turns on that condition.

        (b) However, a party *may not place the condition of another party* in controversy *in the pleadings*. Instead, the party needs to offer an *affidavit* or other affirmative evidence tending to show that the person's condition is in controversy.

            Example: *P* and *D* are injured in an automobile collision. *P* sues *D*, alleging that *D* was negligent for failing to wear eyeglasses while driving on the day in question. *D* denies negligence. *D*'s vision is not yet in controversy. However, if *P* finds a person with personal knowledge that *D* has bad eyesight, *P* could use an affidavit by that person to put *D*'s vision into controversy.

  b. **Good cause:** To demonstrate good cause, the movant must show that the *information cannot be obtained by other means*. For example, if the party to be examined is willing to turn over his medical records, the movant may not be able to demonstrate good cause.

    Example: Consider the prior example. The state in question has no doctor-patient privilege for optometrists. Because *P* can obtain all the information she needs from the optometrist, there is no good cause for an exam.

  c. **Violation of order:** A party who disobeys a court order to submit to an exam is subject to sanctions under *Fed. R. Civ. P. 37(b)*. However, unlike other discovery orders, the court *cannot hold the party in contempt*. Fed. R. Civ. P. 37(b)(2)(D) and (E).

3. **Particulars concerning the exam:** The exam must be conducted by a *licensed or certified* examiner. The *movant* may select *where* the examination is held and must *pay all costs* associated with the examination.

4. **Examiner's report:** After the examination is conducted, the examiner prepares a *written report* and delivers it to the party requesting the examination. The party who was examined may obtain a copy of the report by request. However, such a request comes at a significant cost. If the examined party requests a copy of the report, the party requesting the examination may obtain copies of *all other examinations of the examined party* involving the same condition. By requesting the report, the examined party *waives any doctor-patient or similar privilege* protecting all other reports.

Quiz Yourself on
DISCOVERY METHODS

94. Roxanne hires CoverUp Roofing Co. to re-roof her house. Several days later, Roxanne comes home to find the president of CoverUp waiting at her door. The president declares that the job was completed that very day. Roxanne gladly pays the president the agreed-upon fee. Later, however, Roxanne talks to I. M. Nozy, a retired gentleman who lives across the street. Nozy tells Roxanne that he saw the president go up to Roxanne's house early that morning and ring the doorbell. When no one answered, he drove away. Suspicious, Nozy watched the house all day. Nozy is certain that no roofers ever worked on Roxanne's house.

 Infuriated, Roxanne sues CoverUp for fraud. The case reaches the mandatory initial disclosure stage. Roxanne wonders whether she needs to disclose I. M. Nozy to CoverUp. She prefers to keep him a secret and surprise CoverUp with the damning proof of fraud at trial. Must Roxanne disclose Nozy? _____

95. Same facts as Problem 94. Assume that Roxanne discloses Nozy in the initial disclosures. CoverUp deposes Nozy. The deposition turns out to be quite lengthy. After six full hours, Nozy declares, "If this isn't over in another hour, I'm going home — and don't even think of trying to depose me again!" Is Nozy entitled to make good on this threat? _____

96. Same facts as Problem 94, except that Roxanne sues both CoverUp and the president as separate defendants. Roxanne serves interrogatories on each defendant. The set she serves on CoverUp contains 19 questions. The set she serves on the president contains 22 questions. Although three of the questions are the same, the rest are significantly different. CoverUp and the president object to the interrogatories, claiming that Roxanne has exceeded the maximum allowed by the rule. How should the court rule on the objections? _____

97. Alpha runs a red light at a congested intersection, colliding with Beta and Gamma. Beta and Gamma each sue Alpha for their injuries, but in separate actions. In his case, Beta asks Alpha to admit that he ran a red light. Alpha responds by admitting that he ran the red light. Now, Gamma attempts to use Alpha's admission in Beta v. Alpha in her case. Can Gamma use the admission? _____

98. Bill Billionaire is 95 years old. After Bill has a brief but scintillating conversation with his postman, he asks his attorney to change his will to name the postman as sole beneficiary of his vast estate. Upon hearing of Bill's plans, Bill's children bring an action to have a guardian appointed to handle Bill's affairs. The children allege that Bill has "become insane." Later, the children ask Bill submit to a mental examination. Bill refuses. Is there any way the children can force Bill to undergo an exam? _____

99. Rosie is seriously injured when a bone in a can of baked beans breaks her tooth. Rosie sues Barbara's Baked Beans Company, the manufacturer, for her injuries. Rosie needs to find out how the bone got in the can. She wants to depose a company employee but does not know who has this information. How can Rosie find out what she wants to know? _____

Answers

94. Roxanne is required to disclose Nozy's name, address, and telephone number, as well as a summary of the information he knows. Fed. R. Civ. P. 26(a)(1)(A) requires a party to disclose this information about any individual who has discoverable evidence that the party will use at trial for purposes other than impeachment. Roxanne probably will use Nozy's testimony to prove her claims.

95. Fed. R. Civ. P. 30(d)(2) specifies that no deposition may exceed a single day of seven hours. No person may be deposed a second time without the court's or the other party's permission. Nozy therefore

is justified in refusing to continue the deposition past seven hours or to come back a second day. However, CoverUp may petition the court for more time.

96. The objection will fail. Fed. R. Civ. P. 33(a) allows a party to "serve upon any other party written interrogatories, not exceeding 25. . . ." Therefore, Roxanne is entitled to serve up to 25 questions on *each defendant*. It does not matter whether the questions are the same or different.

97. No. Under Fed. R. Civ. P. 36(b), an admission applies only in that particular case.

98. Fed. R. Civ. P. 35 allows a party to force another party to submit to a mental (or physical) examination. However, the party must obtain a court order. To obtain the order, the party must demonstrate that the mental condition of the other party is in controversy and that good cause exists for the exam. The latter requirement is met, for absent a mental exam, there is no way the children can prove Bill's lack of capacity. However, on the facts, Bill's condition is not yet in controversy. A party cannot put another party's condition in controversy by the pleadings alone. Instead, the children need more proof, such as an affidavit of someone who has observed Bill's eccentric behavior.

99. Fed. R. Civ. P. 30(b)(6) allows Rosie to notice the deposition of the company and describe the information sought. The company must designate one or more people who have knowledge of the subject matter to testify and then tell Rosie what their testimony will cover.

V. POLICY-BASED LIMITATIONS ON DISCOVERY

In some situations, a court may limit discovery even of relevant nonprivileged information.

    A. Protective orders: *Fed. R. Civ. P. 26(c)* allows a court to enter a protective order limiting discovery when needed to protect a person or party from "***annoyance, embarrassment, oppression, or undue burden or expense.***" A protective order can forbid discovery altogether or limit the timing or scope of discovery, including barring discovery into certain subjects.

        1. Proper court: The party seeks the order from the district court where the action is pending. In the case of a deposition, the party may also obtain an order from the court in the district where the deposition is taking place.

        2. Informal discussion as prerequisite: The movant must certify that she *conferred or attempted to confer* with the other affected parties in an attempt to resolve the discovery dispute without court intervention. Fed. R. Civ. P. 26(c).

        3. Reasonableness standard: Discovery by its very nature can be annoying and burdensome. A court will grant a protective order only if the annoyance, embarrassment, oppression, burden, or expense is "unreasonable" under the circumstances of the case.

    B. Privacy: Unnecessary intrusions into private matters are common reasons for a protective order. Parties sometimes make such inquiries to pressure another party into settlement.

        1. Highly personal matters: Information about a person's private life, such as past or present sexual relationships or drug use, may prove highly embarrassing to a party.

            a. Relevance: One factor a court considers is how important the information is to the party seeking discovery. The less relevant the information, the more likely a protective order will issue.

b. Disclosure: Even if the private information is highly relevant, the court may limit disclosure of the information *to third parties*. Disclosure outside the context of the trial rarely serves an important function.

★
> **Example:** In Stalnaker v. Kmart Corp., 71 Fair Empl. Prac. Cas. (BNA) 705 (D. Kan. 1996), the court was faced with a sexual harassment claim. Plaintiff sought to depose certain other employees about any romantic or sexual conduct with the defendant and others, both voluntary and coerced. The court allowed discovery about conduct with the defendant, but not with others. Although acknowledging that the information was highly personal, the court also concluded that it was very relevant to plaintiff's case.

2. Trade secrets: A trade secret is secret information, such as a chemical formula, list of ingredients, industrial process, or customer list, that affords the party that possesses it an advantage over competitors.

a. Relevance and harm: A trade secret can be *highly relevant*, especially in a products liability case. For example, a party who becomes ill after consuming a manufacturer's food product would very much like to know the ingredients in that product. However, if the information falls into the hands of a competitor, any commercial advantage to the manufacturer would be lost.

b. Ways to protect: Courts often exercise considerable creativity in dealing with trade secrets. For example, the court may conduct an *in camera inspection* of the secret, where the information is provided to the court but not to the requesting party. The court then distills the information and provides the requesting party only what it needs.

C. Limits designed to protect the adversarial process — overview: The discovery rules also impose limits on the discovery of information prepared in anticipation of trial, including work product (covered in Part D) and information concerning experts (covered in Part E).

1. Privilege distinguished: These limits are sometimes referred to as "privileges." Unlike a true privilege, however, the limits on work product and expert information can usually be overcome by a showing of need.

2. Claiming protection: A party cannot withhold information based on the work product or expert testimony rules unless the party makes the claim *expressly* and provides enough of a *description* of what is being withheld to allow the requesting party to determine if the protection applies. Fed. R. Civ. P. 26(b)(5).

D. Work product: The work product exception, set out in *Fed. R. Civ. P. 26(b)(3)*, covers documents and tangible things prepared *in anticipation of litigation*. These items may only be obtained upon a showing of *need*.

1. History: Although now codified into the Federal Rules of Civil Procedure, the work product doctrine was originally a court-created exception to discovery. The Supreme Court first explicitly recognized the doctrine in Hickman v. Taylor, 329 U.S. 495 (1947). Although *Hickman* applied only to items prepared by *attorneys*, the rule has been extended to things prepared by other representatives.

★ **2. Purposes of work product rule:** *Hickman* established that the limited exception for work product serves two purposes.

a. First, it prevents one side from *piggybacking* on the work of another side. By encouraging each side to prepare its own case, the rule helps to ensure that the adversary system works as intended.

b. Second, in the case of work prepared by attorneys, the rule helps to minimize the number of situations in which the *attorney will be called as a witness*. Testimony by a party's attorney is a particularly problematic issue in litigation.

3. **Overview of Rule 26(b)(3):** To understand the current work product rule, it is crucial to understand that Rule 26(b)(3) is written against the backdrop of *Hickman*.

   a. It proceeds from the unstated premise that work product as a general rule is *not discoverable*, *except as specifically allowed* in the rule.

   b. As a result, information that meets the general characteristics of work product but is not listed in Rule 26(b)(3) *cannot be discovered even on a showing of need*. Most significantly, the rule mentions only documents and tangible things. Information that is *nontangible* — such as what an attorney heard when interviewing a witness or what an insurance agent recalls seeing when investigating the scene of an accident — does not fall within the exception and *cannot be discovered* at all.

4. **Work product:** Fed. R. Civ. P. 26(b)(3) allows discovery of documents and tangible things that are otherwise discoverable under Rule 26(b)(1) that were *prepared in anticipation of litigation or trial* by the *party or the party's representative*.

   a. **Documents and tangible things:** The rule does not define ''document or tangible thing.'' Courts generally have interpreted the term loosely and have protected letters, notes taken during an interview, photographs, and tapes.

   b. **Otherwise discoverable:** The material must be *relevant* and *not privileged*, as required by Fed. R. Civ. P. 26(b)(1).

   c. **In anticipation:** The material must have been prepared in anticipation of a litigated dispute.

      i. It is not necessary that the case actually have been filed when the item is prepared. Once the underlying event giving rise to the litigation has occurred, materials prepared in anticipation of a later case are protected.

      ii. The protection does not extend to documents prepared in the *ordinary course of business*, such as the personnel records of a business or the medical records of a hospital, which would have been prepared regardless of whether litigation occurs.

   d. **Representatives:** The rule explicitly includes as representatives a party's ''attorney, consultant, surety, indemnitor, insurer, or agent.'' Other representatives may also fall under the rule.

5. **When work product can be discovered:** A party may discover work product only by demonstrating that it has *substantial need* for the information and that the same basic information cannot be acquired *from another source* without undue hardship.

   a. **How request made:** A party may seek work product either by serving interrogatories on the party or by deposing the representative.

b. Demonstrating need: Need considers both the importance of the information and whether the equivalent can be obtained by other means.

    i. First, the information should be important to the party seeking it. Information that merely verifies evidence the party already has cannot be discovered, unless the evidence in the party's possession is weak or ambiguous.

    ii. In addition, if the party with the information obtained it from another source, and that source is likewise accessible to the party seeking the information, the party seeking the information must similarly go to the primary source. However, if the party cannot obtain the information from the other source because of **substantial cost** or because the primary source is a witness who is **hostile** to the party, then he may be able to obtain it from the other party.

    Example: *P* is injured while hiking with his friend *W* on *D*'s land. Shortly after the injury, *D* interviews *W*. *P* sues *D* and files a Rule 34 request for production of *D*'s notes of the interview. Assuming *W* is still available, *D* should not be required to turn over the notes. Because *P* can interview or depose his friend and obtain the information directly, he has no need for *D*'s notes.

    iii. Exception: Rule 26(b)(3) makes an exception for a **party's own statement** concerning the action. A party may obtain a copy of its own statement from the other side's representative **without showing need**.

c. Mental impressions: When ordering discovery of work product, a court is obligated to protect against disclosure of the **mental impressions, conclusions, opinions, or legal theories** of the attorney or other representative. To the extent that work product information reveals these matters, the court will order it to be turned over only if there is no other way for the requesting party to obtain the information.

Example: In the prior example, suppose that *D* taped the interview with *W*. In addition, *W* signed a written statement setting forth what *W* saw. Because *W* is now unavailable, *P* seeks both the tape and the statement. *D* refuses. The court should order disclosure of the statement but not of the tape. The tape may reveal *D*'s legal strategies in the selection and order of the questions. And once *P* has the statement, it does not need the tape to discover what *W* saw.

E. Expert information: *Fed. R. Civ. P. 26(b)(4)* governs discovery of information and opinions held by experts. The rule draws a clear distinction between experts who **may testify at trial** and those who were **retained, but will not testify**.

1. *Expert* defined: An expert is someone with **specialized knowledge** in a particular subject area who **gives an opinion** based on facts presented to her or which she obtains by investigation. Only experts are allowed to give opinions.

Example: *X* is a police investigator who specializes in arson. *X* wakes up one night to find his neighbor's house on fire. *X* watches the house burn down. After her insurance company refuses to pay, the neighbor sues. The insurance company calls *X* as a witness. Even though *X*'s perception of the fire will be affected by his expertise in arson, *X* is not testifying as an expert if he simply describes what he saw that night. However, *X* would be testifying as an expert if asked to give his opinion as to how the fire started.

2. **Testifying expert:** The ***mandatory disclosure*** rules require a party to provide detailed information about experts who may testify at trial. Fed. R. Civ. P. 26(a)(2). ***Rule 26(b)(4)(A)*** allows a party freely to ***depose*** anyone identified as a testifying expert.

3. **Nontestifying expert:** If the expert will not testify, the facts he knows and the opinions he has formed are usually ***not discoverable***. Other parties may discover that information only upon a showing of need. ***Fed. R. Civ. P. 26(b)(4)(B)***. When discovery is allowed, it must be by ***deposition*** or ***interrogatories***.

   a. Given that other experts in the field are usually available, this standard is usually very difficult to meet. However, in cases where the underlying facts are no longer available for other experts to examine, a party can show need.

   ★ **Example:** Thompson v. The Haskell Co., 65 Fair Empl. Prac. Cas. (BNA) 1088 (M.D. Fla. 1994), is one case where the requesting party could show need. A crucial issue in that case was a party's mental state at a particular time. Because the mental state could well have changed over time, the other party was allowed to discover the opinions of a nontestifying psychologist who examined the party during the crucial period.

   b. **Exception:** Although a physician or other medical professional is technically an expert, the report prepared following a ***Rule 35 physical or mental examination*** can be obtained without a showing of need under the circumstances set out in that rule.

4. **Costs:** A party who seeks discovery from an expert is usually required to pay a reasonable fee to the expert providing the information, as well as the expert's costs.

Quiz Yourself on
POLICY LIMITS ON DISCOVERY

100. After years of experimentation, Sarah finally discovers a cure for the common cold. Sarah's remedy is a complex mixture of herbs and other natural ingredients. Only Sarah knows the ingredients in her product. Because it is herbal, Sarah was not required to obtain FDA approval for the product. Nor does the law require her to list the ingredients. Sneezy, who suffers from frequent colds, brings a product liability suit against Sarah after suffering a severe allergic reaction to her product. Sneezy is allergic to several different herbs and asks Sarah to disclose the ingredients in her product. If Sarah objects, is it likely that Sarah will be required to disclose all the ingredients? _____

101. Ali and Frazier are involved in a serious fight, in which both suffer significant injuries. Ali hires Ann Attorney to sue Frazier. Before filing the case, Ann interviews Ali, Frazier, and Leonard, a third party who happened to be watching as the two pugilists fought. She obtains written statements from all three. After the case is commenced, Frazier serves timely interrogatories on Ali, asking Ali to turn over copies of any statements made by Frazier, Ali, and Leonard. Will Ali be required to turn over the statements taken by Ann? _____

102. Author sues Publisher for copyright infringement based upon Publisher's unauthorized publication of a book that is somewhat similar to Author's manuscript. In preparation for trial, Author retains two experts, Fitzgerald and Hemingway. Author concludes that Fitzgerald will make a much better witness and therefore decides to have only Fitzgerald testify at trial. Publisher wants to depose both Fitzgerald and Hemingway to find out their conclusions. Will Publisher succeed? _____

Answers

100. If Sarah seeks a protective order, it is likely that the court will not order full disclosure. The information sought is clearly both relevant to Sneezy's claim and not privileged. However, that information qualifies as a trade secret because it affords Sarah a competitive advantage.

Trade secrets are not completely protected from disclosure. Here, the facts indicate that Sneezy knows that he has allergies to certain herbs. Therefore, the court might allow him to discover only whether those herbs are present. Second, the court might have Sarah submit the information to the court, not to Sneezy, to control the amount of unnecessary information that Sneezy can learn.

101. Frazier may obtain his own statement, but not those of Ali or Leonard. This problem raises issues of work product and privilege. The written statements collected by Ann are clearly documents prepared in anticipation of litigation. Frazier may obtain Leonard's statement only upon a showing of need. Frazier does not seem to be able to show need. He clearly already knows Leonard's name and, accordingly, can conduct his own interview. Frazier can obtain a copy of the statement taken by Ann only if Leonard is not available or refuses to cooperate. Although Frazier's statement is also work product, Fed. R. Civ. P. 26(b)(3) explicitly provides that a party can always obtain a copy of his own statement without showing need. Ali's statement goes beyond work product — it is protected by the attorney-client privilege. Therefore, Frazier cannot obtain it under any circumstances. However, Frazier can depose Ali and obtain the information directly.

102. Publisher can clearly depose Fitzgerald but probably cannot depose Hemingway. Because Fitzgerald is an expert who will be testifying at trial, Fed. R. Civ. P. 26(b)(4)(A) allows Publisher to depose him. However, because Hemingway is not testifying, Publisher can obtain information from him only upon a showing of need. Since Publisher already has access to Fitzgerald, it really does not need to talk to Hemingway.

VI. SUPPLEMENTING DISCLOSURES AND RESPONSES

In some situations, Fed. R. Civ. P. 26(e) requires a ***party*** to ***supplement or correct*** disclosures and responses made earlier.

A. Only parties: Nonparties are never under a duty to supplement.

B. Court-ordered supplementation: A party must supplement a response when ordered to do so by the court.

C. Supplementing disclosures: Even without a court order, a party must supplement its mandatory disclosures if it learns that the earlier disclosure was ***incomplete or incorrect*** in some ***material*** way and the additional or correct information has ***not been acquired*** by the other parties through discovery or in writing.

D. Supplementing other discovery: A party may also be required to supplement its responses to other forms of discovery.

  1. Types of discovery that must be supplemented: A party must supplement its ***answers to interrogatories***, ***response to a request for production of documents***, and ***answer to requests for admission***. Note that answers to a deposition need not be supplemented.

  2. When supplementation required: A party must supplement a response if it learns that the earlier answer or response was ***incomplete or incorrect*** in some ***material*** way, and the additional or correct information has ***not been acquired*** by the other parties through discovery or in writing.

  Example: *P* and *D* are embroiled in a lawsuit in which *P* claims that *D* failed to pay her for painting *D*'s house. The contract required *P* to paint *D*'s house on or before May 10. *P* has recently learned that three pieces of information she gave to *D* are incorrect. First, in her initial disclosures, *P* failed to mention the name of a witness who saw her perform the work. *P* knows, however, that *D* also found this witness in an informal conversation with the neighbors. Second, in her deposition, *P* told *D* that she painted the house on May 3, when in truth she did it on May 20. Third, when *D* filed a request to admit that the house was not painted by May 10, *P* refused to admit, still thinking at the time that she had performed the work on May 3. *P* must supplement her disclosures and her answer to the request to admit. Even though *D* has learned of the witness, *D* did not acquire that information by way of discovery or in writing. *P* need not supplement her answer in the deposition because depositions are not subject to the supplementation requirement.

VII. PREVENTING DISCOVERY ABUSE

Although discovery is designed to proceed with little or no supervision by the court, disputes invariably arise. The discovery rules provide the court with a number of different tools to police abuse.

A. Signing of discovery: ***Fed. R. Civ. P. 26(g)*** attempts to prevent abuse from occurring by requiring all discovery documents to be ***signed***. Rule 26(g) is discovery's counterpart to Fed. R. Civ. P. 11.

  1. What must be signed: The rule requires that all ***mandatory disclosures and discovery requests, responses, and objections*** be signed.

  2. Who signs: At least one attorney of record must sign. If a party has no attorney, the party signs.

  3. Effect of signing: Signing the discovery constitutes a certification that the signer has ***conducted a reasonable inquiry*** and that, to the best of the signer's knowledge, information, and belief:

   a. In the case of ***mandatory disclosures***, that the disclosure is ***complete*** and ***correct*** when made.

   b. In the case of ***other discovery requests, responses, and objections***, that the item is:

    i.   consistent with the ***rules***;

    ii. warranted by existing ***law*** or a good faith argument for changing existing law;

    iii. not made for any *improper purpose*, including harassment or delay; and

    iv. not unreasonably or unduly *burdensome*, considering the needs of the case, the amount in controversy, the importance of the issues, and the discovery already conducted.

4. Violation of rule: If a party signs discovery in violation of the above standards, the court may impose an appropriate sanction on the signer and/or the represented party. No motion is necessary, although sanctions on the court's own volition are very rare. Although the judge has considerable discretion in determining an appropriate sanction, the rule specifically authorizes an award of the expenses and *attorneys' fees*.

5. Rule 11 not applicable: Fed. R. Civ. P. 11 does not apply to discovery. Fed. R. Civ. P. 11(d). Therefore, Rule 26(g) is the only certification provision applicable in discovery.

B. Compelling discovery: A party facing what it considers to be an improper or overly burdensome discovery request will sometimes simply refuse to turn over the information. In these situations, the requesting party may obtain an *order compelling discovery*. *Fed. R. Civ. P. 37(a)*. The order itself may impose sanctions on the disobedient party. Failure to comply with the order may lead to additional sanctions.

1. Proper court: If the person who refuses to provide information is another *party*, the motion is filed in the court in which the *case is pending*. If the person who refuses to provide information is a *nonparty* who is being deposed, the motion is filed in the court where the *deposition is pending*.

2. Must attempt to negotiate: A motion to compel discovery must include a certification that the movant has previously conferred in good faith or attempted to confer with the person refusing to provide information in order to resolve the matter without court intervention. Fed. R. Civ. P. 37(a)(2)(A) (disclosures); 37(a)(2)(B) (other discovery).

3. Compelling disclosure or discovery: An order compelling discovery is available for all discovery *except requests for admission* and *physical and mental examinations*. Of course, in the case of a physical or mental exam, the party seeking the exam was already required to obtain an order under Fed. R. Civ. P. 35.

4. Sanctions for unsuccessful motion: If a party's motion to compel discovery is *unsuccessful*, and the court finds that the motion was *not substantially justified*, the court may order that party and/or the party's attorney to pay the expenses, including attorneys' fees, of the party defending the motion. However, the court must give the movant notice and opportunity to be heard before imposing such a sanction. *Fed. R. Civ. P. 37(a)(4)(B)*.

5. Order, additional sanctions: If the moving party *prevails*, the court will order the other side to cooperate in discovery and may impose *sanctions* in some situations.

    a. Costs and attorneys' fees on successful motion: The court may require the party or person against whom the order compelling discovery was issued to reimburse the movant for costs and attorneys' fees, unless the failure to provide information was *substantially justified*.

    b. Additional sanctions: *Fed. R. Civ. P. 37(d)* allows a court to impose additional sanctions on a *party* who refuses to provide information in certain situations.

        i. When available: Additional sanctions are available against a party who *refuses* to *answer an interrogatory*, or *refuses* to serve a written response to a *request for inspection* of documents or tangible things.

ii. These additional sanctions usually accompany an order to compel discovery. However, they may also be imposed absent such an order. Therefore, if a party obtains the information from another source, it may seek sanctions against the noncooperative party even without an order compelling discovery.

iii. **Sanctions available:** Fed. R. Civ. P. 37(d) allows a court to order that:

(a) certain *matters* in the discovery request are *deemed established*;

(b) the *noncooperating party be barred from making certain claims or defenses* or from introducing evidence on certain matters;

(c) parts of the noncooperating party's *pleadings be struck*;

(d) the *action be stayed* until the party complies; or

(e) the *action be dismissed*, or that a *default judgment* be entered.

iv. **Proportionality requirement:** Notwithstanding the broad array of listed sanctions, there is a proportionality requirement in the application of Rule 37, which prohibits use of the most severe sanctions in cases of minor transgressions.

(a) When considering how severe a sanction to impose, courts focus on whether the sanctioned party acted in *good faith or willfully*, if the rule was *clear* or open to interpretation, and the degree to which the failure *affected the underlying case*.

(b) Within the above restrictions, the trial judge has wide discretion in selecting which sanctions to impose. An appellate court will overturn that decision only upon a showing of *abuse of discretion*.

6. **Sanctions for disobeying order:** An order compelling discovery is a *court order*. Violation of that order exposes the violator to *additional sanctions*, even if the party was already sanctioned when the order was issued.

a. **When available:** The sanctions are available whenever a *party* violates a court's discovery order. The rule applies not only to an *order compelling discovery*, but also an *order to take part in a discovery conference* (Fed. R. Civ. P. 26(f)) and an *order to submit to a physical or mental examination* (Fed. R. Civ. P. 35).

b. **Sanctions available:** The sanctions available for violation of an order are generally the same as those set out in 5.b.iii. However, there is one crucial difference. Because the order to compel is issued by a court, the violating party may also be held in *contempt of court*.

i. **Contempt:** Contempt is a severe sanction. Typically, the party will be required to pay a monetary fine to the court. The fine may be *levied on a daily basis*, until the party "removes the contempt" by complying with the order. In cases of especially willful disobedience, the party may be *jailed* until she is willing to obey the order.

ii. **Exception:** Note, however, that the sanction of contempt is *not available* for refusing to submit to a *physical or mental examination*. Fed. R. Civ. P. 37(b)(2)(D).

iii. **Proportionality requirement:** The proportionality requirement also applies to sanctions imposed for violating a court order. However, because the party has been specifically directed to respond, a court is much more likely to determine that a party acted *willfully*, thus allowing for the imposition of *more severe sanctions*.

★   **Example:** Thompson v. Department of Housing & Urban Development, 199 F.R.D. 168 (D. Md. 2001), deals with abuse by the party seeking discovery. In that case, plaintiffs brought a class action alleging that defendants had engaged in discrimination in public housing from 1933 to the time of the suit. Plaintiffs sought broad discovery dealing with virtually all aspects of public housing in Baltimore. The court held that the request was too broad. Instead, the plaintiffs and defendants were required to meet in a discovery conference, in which plaintiffs would be required to show how the particular information sought might relate to their actual claims and how the benefit of the information would outweigh the burden imposed on defendant.

★   **Example:** Poole v. Textron, Inc., 192 F.R.D. 494 (D. Md. 2000), deals with abuse by the party from whom discovery is sought. The court held that sanctions should be imposed on the defendant for failing to respond adequately to plaintiff's discovery request. It explicitly found that defendant was not justified in objecting to plaintiff's request, refusing to search its records, and failing to turn over documents and information to plaintiff.

C. Specific sanctions: In addition to the general provisions discussed above, the discovery rules contain several sanctions that apply to specific discovery problems.

    1. Failure to attend depositions: If a party who is supposed to attend a deposition fails to attend or fails to ensure that a nonparty attends, that party may be subject to sanctions.

        a. Party requesting deposition: If a party who gives notice of a deposition fails to attend at the scheduled time, that party may be required to pay the expenses and attorneys' fees of any parties who do attend. Fed. R. Civ. P. 26(g)(1). A party may also be required to pay costs and attorneys' fees of other parties if he notices the deposition of a nonparty witness but neglects to serve a subpoena on that witness, and the witness accordingly fails to attend the deposition. Fed. R. Civ. P. 30(g)(2).

        b. Party deponent: If a party who is scheduled to testify at a deposition fails to attend, Fed. R. Civ. P. 37(d) allows the imposition of an "appropriate sanction," which may include costs and attorneys' fees. The rule also applies to the situation where a party notices the deposition of an organization on certain matters, leaving it to the organization to determine which officers or agents will testify. If the people designated by the organization fail to attend, the organization is subject to sanctions.

    2. Failure to answer question at deposition: A *party* or *nonparty* deponent who refuses to be sworn in at a deposition or to answer a question after being sworn in may be held in *contempt of court. Fed. R. Civ. P. 37(b)(1).*

    3. Failure to disclose or supplement: A party who fails to provide information that must be disclosed under the mandatory disclosure rules (see Part IV.A) or to supplement a response as required by Rule 26(e) is subject to sanctions unless the party demonstrates that the failure was *substantially justified* or that the failure to disclose was *harmless.*

        a. Sanction: A party who fails to disclose or supplement is *barred from introducing evidence* on that matter at trial or at any hearing on a motion. As an additional or alternate sanction, the court may order the party to pay the expenses and attorneys' fees that any other parties incurred in obtaining the information from other sources.

b. When failure is "harmless": A failure to disclose or supplement is deemed harmless when the information is of *little significance* to the other party in proving or defending his case or when the other party *already had obtained the information* from another source when the disclosure or supplementation should have occurred.

4. **Failure to admit:** If a party unreasonably fails to admit a matter covered by a request to admit, the requesting party may recover all reasonable expenses, including attorneys' fees, that it incurs in proving that matter at trial. *Fed. R. Civ. P. 37(c)(2).*

5. **Discovery plan:** A party who refuses to participate in the framing of the discovery plan may be required to reimburse other parties for any reasonable expenses, including attorneys' fees, that they may incur because of the failure to participate. *Fed. R. Civ. P. 26(f).*

Quiz Yourself on *DISCOVERY*

103. A newspaper prints an article that claims Lieutenant Smith, an officer in the local police force, is "on the take." The story quotes an "anonymous source." Smith sues the newspaper. The newspaper answers by claiming that the story is true. Smith learns that the anonymous source is a senior citizen who supposedly witnessed him at an alleged payoff. However, Smith has also learned from several friends of this witness that the senior citizen suffers from extremely poor eyesight. Smith asks the court for an order requiring the senior citizen to submit to an optical exam. Will the court grant the order? _____

104. Same facts as Problem 103, except that rather than ask for an optical exam, Smith serves the senior citizen with a set of interrogatories to glean what the senior citizen really saw. The senior citizen gladly obliges, sending back a complete set of answers. The newspaper moves for a protective order preventing Smith from using the answers in any way. The newspaper argues that interrogatories may be used only against parties to the action. Will the court grant the protective order? _____

105. During a hotly contested volleyball game, Spike purposefully shoves Danny, causing serious injuries. Danny's girlfriend, Dawn, witnesses the event. Danny sues Spike for battery. Spike sends notice to Danny and Dawn that he wants to take their depositions. Neither Danny nor Dawn shows up on the appointed date. What can Spike do? _____

106. Same facts as Problem 105, except suppose that Dawn attends her deposition. After being sworn in and answering a few questions, Dawn suddenly becomes defensive and refuses to answer any more. What can Spike do? _____

107. Horace Mann is a claims adjuster for an insurance company. While driving down a busy highway, Horace sees a truck change lanes and collide with three cars. All three car drivers are seriously injured. Horace stops and tries to comfort the three victims. As a trained claims adjuster, Horace also instinctively takes photographs of the crash scene. Horace, however, is not the only person who pho-

tographs the scene. A police forensics unit, which shows up fairly quickly, also takes detailed photographs of the accident scene.

The next day, Horace discovers that his company has issued a liability insurance policy on the truck driver. Horace therefore visits all three drivers in the hospital to try to get a clearer picture of what happened. All three drivers give Horace written statements.

One of the car drivers soon sues the truck driver for her injuries. Horace is assigned to collect more background information concerning the case. Horace discovers the names of two bystanders who happened to see the collision. He interviews these bystanders and obtains written statements from them too.

You are representing the truck driver in this case. The driver asks you the following four questions:

a. Must he reveal Horace's name, or the names of the bystanders, in the list of witnesses disclosed in the initial disclosures? _____

b. If the plaintiff learns Horace's name by any means, can the plaintiff depose Horace about what Horace saw on the day of the wreck? _____

c. Can the plaintiff obtain Horace's photographs of the crash scene? _____

d. Must your client turn over the statements that Horace took from the three car drivers and two bystanders? _____

108. Attorney Albert has brought an action against Megacorp, Inc., alleging a violation of the Americans with Disabilities Act. Albert's client, who is 6′ 3″ tall, alleges that she was fired because of her height. Albert serves interrogatories on Megacorp. One of the interrogatories asks for the names and employment histories of all employees, present and past, who were taller than 6′. Although Megacorp does have this information in its personnel files, the files are organized on the basis of the employees' names, not their height. Therefore, to provide this information, Megacorp would need to search every one of its many thousands of employee files. Is there anything that Megacorp can do to spare itself this trouble? _____

109. Dean Deponent is testifying at a deposition. When the line of questioning turns to certain intimate aspects of Dean's life — aspects that Dean feels are completely irrelevant to the case — he refuses to answer the questions. Flustered, the attorney immediately goes to the court and seeks an order compelling discovery. Will the court issue the order? _____

Answers

103. The court will refuse the request. Under Fed. R. Civ. P. 35, physical and mental exams may be used only against parties.

104. The court will not grant the protective order. The Federal Rules of Civil Procedure merely provide that nonparties are not required to respond to interrogatories. If they choose to respond, the party can still use the answers. In essence, the interrogatories are a form of informal discovery.

105. Fed. R. Civ. P. 26(g) requires a party who fails to attend his deposition to pay the expenses and attorneys' fees of any party who did attend. Therefore, Danny must reimburse Spike for these expenses.

Dawn, however, is not a party. Because Spike did not obtain a subpoena requiring her to attend (the problem says only that he sent her notice), she cannot be sanctioned.

106. Fed. R. Civ. P. 37(b)(1) says that, as a nonparty deponent, Dawn can be held in contempt by the court for refusing to answer questions after taking the oath.

107. This problem presents issues of work product. Horace is a representative of the truck driver. Therefore, documents prepared by Horace may qualify for work product protection, but only to the extent that they were prepared in anticipation of litigation.

    a. What Horace observed at the accident scene was not information prepared in anticipation of litigation. Horace is an ordinary witness, just like any other bystander. Therefore, his name, as well as the names of the other witnesses, must be disclosed to the plaintiff.

    b. For the same reason, the plaintiff is free to depose Horace.

    c. The photographs of the accident scene were not prepared in anticipation of litigation either. Therefore, they can be discovered. (Note that the discussion in the problem about the police photographs is therefore irrelevant — the plaintiff can obtain the photographs of Horace even without a showing of need.)

    d. The statements that Horace took from the drivers and the bystanders, by contrast, were all prepared in anticipation of litigation. Therefore, the work product rule applies. However, the statement that Horace took from the plaintiff must be turned over. Fed. R. Civ. P. 26(b)(3) provides that a party can always obtain a copy of her own statement without showing need. With respect to the other statements, it is unlikely that the plaintiff can demonstrate need. As long as she has the names of the witnesses, she can interview those witnesses himself.

108. The information is relevant because it may show how Megacorp has treated tall employees in the past. However, Megacorp does not need to amass the data itself. Instead, Fed. R. Civ. P. 33(d) allows it to open up its records to Albert, and let Albert seek the information. The burden on Albert of poring through the records is the same as the burden would be on Megacorp.

109. The court will not issue the order. Dean's refusal to answer is wrongful. If he felt that the questions were improper because irrelevant, Fed. R. Civ. P. 30(c) requires the witness to object, but then to go ahead and answer the questions, with the objection noted on the transcript. Dean cannot simply refuse to answer.

    However, the attorney did not follow the proper procedure for an order compelling discovery. Under Fed. R. Civ. P. 37(a)(2), the party seeking the order must certify that she made a good faith attempt to confer with the deponent to work out an amicable solution to the problem. The attorney made no such effort here.

 Exam Tips on
DISCOVERY

☞ With the recently added mandatory disclosures and the discovery conference, discovery now follows a fairly regimented schedule. You may find it helpful to set out a timeline for the entire discovery process, which details the point at which certain events will occur.

☛ Be sure that you understand the practical differences between the different types of discovery. For example, most of the discovery methods apply only to parties to the case.

   ☞ It is especially important to draw a clear distinction between ***mandatory disclosures*** and other forms of discovery.

☛ The concept of ***relevance*** often proves difficult. It may help to think of relevance as a two-part question: ***whether*** the information is relevant, and ***to what*** it is relevant.

   ☞ Whether information is relevant is a very loose standard. In order to be relevant, information need only make a given proposition more or less likely to be true.

      ☞ Recall that information can be relevant for discovery even though it cannot be used as evidence at trial.

   ☞ On the other hand, in order to be discoverable, information must be relevant to ***a claim or defense in the case***. Information that tends to prove or disprove other issues in the case cannot be discovered.

☛ ***Privileged*** information cannot be discovered even if it is relevant.

   ☞ Privileges protect the ***source*** of information, not the information itself.

   ☞ Privileges are also an issue in ***work product***. If a question deals with an attempt to obtain information from an attorney, think both of privilege and of work product. If the attorney learned the information from the client, then a privilege is likely to apply.

☛ **Depositions:** A deposition is the only one of the main discovery devices that can be used against nonparties. Recall that a party needs a subpoena to ensure the witness's attendance.

   ☞ In most cases, someone being deposed must answer even objectionable questions. The objection is noted on the transcript.

☛ **Interrogatories:** Unlike in the case of a deposition, a party answering interrogatories has a ***duty to investigate*** to find the information.

☛ **Examining documents and tangible things:** Recall that although Fed. R. Civ. P. 34 can be used only against parties, a party who seeks discovery of documents or tangible things from someone not a party can obtain a subpoena allowing access to and inspection of the items.

☛ **Physical and mental examinations:** Because a physical and mental examination is the only form of discovery against another party that requires court permission, make sure you discuss the ''in controversy'' and ''good cause'' issues in your answer.

   ☞ Recall that a party usually cannot put the other party's condition into controversy by the pleadings alone. Instead, the party must obtain an affidavit.

   ☞ If there is some other way to obtain the information, the party cannot show good cause.

☛ **Work product:** Law school examinations often contain questions concerning work product, so be comfortable with the rule.

   ☞ Work product no longer applies only to documents prepared by an attorney. Under the Federal Rules of Civil Procedure, it also applies to things prepared by any other representative of the party.

☞ Recall that something can be "prepared in anticipation of litigation" even if it was prepared before the lawsuit was even filed.

☞ The work product protection is only a qualified privilege that can be overcome on a showing of need. Thus, when discussing work product, be sure to discuss whether the requesting party can acquire the same information from other sources.

☞ The rule governing *nontestifying experts* is very similar to the work product rule. However, it is much more difficult to show need in the case of an expert.

☛ When dealing with *sanctions*, remember that a party must attempt to negotiate with the offending party before running off to court for sanctions.

☞ A court will rarely impose the most severe sanctions without providing some sort of warning first. However, once the party violates an order compelling discovery, more severe sanctions are possible, at least if the violation is willful.

CHAPTER 9

RESOLUTION BEFORE TRIAL

ChapterScope ━━

This chapter deals with how a pending case can be resolved before trial. The focus is on disputes that have already found their way into the court system. For a discussion of how parties can resolve a dispute without resort to litigation, see Chapter 6. Because state rules dealing with pretrial resolution sometimes differ markedly, this chapter focuses on the *federal courts*.

■ The parties may settle their dispute by themselves. If so, they typically enter into a settlement agreement, which may result in a *voluntary dismissal* or a *consent judgment*.

■ A *plaintiff* may also *voluntarily dismiss* his case even without a settlement. Depending on what has happened in the case, the plaintiff may need the consent of the other side or a court order to dismiss.

■ If a defendant fails to participate in a case after being served with process, the court may declare the defendant *in default* and issue a *default judgment*.

■ Conversely, if the plaintiff fails to prosecute the case diligently to completion, to abide by governing rules, or to cooperate with court orders, the court may *dismiss* the case against plaintiff's will.

■ Either party may ask the court to issue a *summary judgment* on one or more claims in the case. If the court determines that there is no genuine dispute concerning the facts, it will issue a judgment on that claim.

I. SETTLEMENT

Statistics show that *most pending cases* are resolved by *settlement*.

A. Judicial approval usually unnecessary: The parties usually do not need to notify the court or obtain court approval before settling the case. However, there are certain *exceptions*. For example, court approval of a settlement may be required in a case involving *minors*. Moreover, *Fed. R. Civ. P. 23(e)* requires court approval before a *class action* may be dismissed or settled.

B. Termination of case: Once the parties settle the case, they arrange to have the case terminated. In most cases, dismissal is accomplished by a *voluntary dismissal* (typically by stipulation), which is discussed below. However, the parties may arrange to have the court enter a *consent decree*. Consent decrees have been widely used in civil rights cases.

★ **C. Postjudgment settlement:** Special issues arise when the parties settle a case after the trial judge renders judgment but while the case is still on appeal. The judgment loser in such a case often wants to *expunge the trial court's judgment*, in order to prevent other parties from relying on that judgment as precedent or collaterally estopping the judgment loser in later litigation. However, courts are split as to whether they will honor the parties' agreement to expunge a judgment. Compare U.S. Bancorp Mortgage Co. v. Bonner Mall, 513 U.S. 18 (1994) (federal courts should not expunge judgments), with Neary v. University of California, 844 P.2d 119 (Cal. 1992) (California courts will honor agreement and expunge judgment).

D. Barring later actions: Whether the settlement bars later actions depends on the form of dismissal.

1. **Settlement agreement:** The settlement agreement itself typically forbids either party from suing on the claim again. Because the agreement is a contract, it binds the parties (assuming the agreement is valid under contract law). However, although the parties are contractually obligated not to sue, the agreement ***does not affect a court's jurisdiction***. If a party sues in violation of a settlement agreement, the other side must assert the substantive defense of ***accord and satisfaction***.

2. **Voluntary dismissal:** The *res judicata* effect of a voluntary dismissal is discussed in Part IV.

3. **Consent decree:** A consent decree or order approving a class action settlement is a judgment and accordingly is entitled to full *res judicata* effect.

★ 4. **No subject matter jurisdiction:** Parties may by settlement prevent a claim from being asserted in later litigation even if the court in which the action was filed would not have had subject matter jurisdiction over that claim. Matsushita Electric Industrial Co. v. Epstein, 516 U.S. 367 (1996) (settlement evidenced by consent decree).

★ 5. **Confidentiality provision:** A settlement agreement often contains a confidentiality provision that bars the parties from speaking about the underlying dispute or the terms of the settlement. Although these agreements are generally enforceable, they do not necessarily protect a party who is later subpoenaed to testify in litigation involving the same basic subject but involving a different plaintiff or defendant. Kalinauskas v. Wong, 151 F.R.D. 363 (D. Bev. 1993).

II. DEFAULT

A party who fails to respond to a claim can be declared in default and may have judgment rendered against it. Defaults and default judgments are governed by ***Fed. R. Civ. P. 55***.

A. Two stages: There are two distinct stages in issuing a default judgment. The first is the ***entry of default*** against the party. Following that, the court enters a ***default judgment***.

B. Entry of default: ***Fed. R. Civ. P. 55(a)*** allows for an entry of default whenever a party ***fails to plead or otherwise defend*** against a claim.

1. **Not only defendants:** Although it is normally the defendant who defaults, the rule applies to all parties against whom a claim is filed. Thus, a plaintiff who fails to defend against a counterclaim can have a default entered against her on the counterclaim.

2. **Who enters:** The ***clerk*** enters the default. Fed. R. Civ. P. 55(a). However, because the clerk does not know whether the defendant has served an answer, the clerk usually acts only following a request by the plaintiff.

3. **"Plead or otherwise defend":** Entry of default occurs after a party fails to plead or otherwise defend. A party pleads by filing an ***answer*** or ***reply***. The phrase "otherwise defend," however, is more ambiguous.

   a. Filing a ***pre-answer motion*** raising a FRCP 12(b) defense or a ***summary judgment motion*** clearly constitutes "defending" the action, and precludes the entry of default.

b. Whether other actions qualify as "defending" is less clear. For example, a ***motion to transfer venue*** does not qualify as "otherwise defending" because the defendant is not challenging either the merits of the case or the court's power to hear it.

c. A party must plead or otherwise defend within the time period allowed for an answer (which is usually 20 days but which can be extended, as discussed in Chapter 7). However, a court typically refuses a request for default judgment filed immediately after the time for filing an answer has expired.

4. Exception — sanction defaults: The Federal Rules of Civil Procedure also allow for default judgment as a ***sanction*** against a defendant who refuses to cooperate in discovery or to obey a court order. Although sanction defaults are governed in most respects by Rule 55, there are certain differences. First, the ***court***, not the clerk, ***enters the default***. Second, the "plead or otherwise defend" language of Rule 55(a) obviously does not apply.

5. Notice: The defendant ***does not receive notice*** of the ***entry*** of default. Of course, the defendant was already served with process and should realize there is an action pending.

6. Effect of entry of default: Entry of default against a party has several significant consequences.

a. Most ***facts*** alleged in the pleadings are ***deemed admitted***. However, the defaulting party may contest the amount of damages, unless damages are liquidated. Note that the party admits facts but does not concede the claimant's conclusions of law.

b. The party is ***not entitled to notice*** of future proceedings in the case.

C. Default judgment: After default is entered against a party, the claimant may move for entry of the default judgment. However, the defaulting party may be entitled to notice and a hearing at which it can present evidence on certain issues.

1. Who enters judgment: The default judgment may be entered by the clerk or the court.

a. Clerk: The clerk may enter the default judgment if all of the following conditions are satisfied (Fed. R. Civ. P. 55(b)(1)):

i. the claim is for a ***sum certain***, or a sum that can be made certain by calculation (Fed. R. Civ. P. 55(b)(1));

Example: *P* sues *D* to recover on a promissory note. The outstanding principal balance is a sum certain. If interest accrues on that principal at a defined rate, the claim is for a sum that can be made certain by calculation.

ii. the entry of default was based on the party's ***failure to appear*** (which means that the clerk cannot enter the default judgment when default is imposed as a sanction) (Fed. R. Civ. P. 55(b)(1));

iii. the defaulting party is ***not an infant or an incompetent person*** (Fed. R. Civ. P. 55(b)(1)); and

iv. the defaulting party is ***not the United States or a federal officer or agency*** (Fed. R. Civ. P. 55(e)).

b. By court: In all other cases, the court enters the default judgment. Fed. R. Civ. P. 55(b)(2).

2. **Motion required:** The claimant must *apply* to the clerk or court to have judgment entered. Typically this application takes the form of a motion. Again, a court rarely grants a motion that is made soon after the time for answering has expired.

3. **Hearing:** If damages are not a sum certain, or if the court desires evidence to substantiate any of the allegations in the claim, the court schedules a hearing prior to entering the default judgment. In other cases, no hearing is necessary.

   a. At the hearing, the claimant *proves up the damages* by offering evidence. The defaulting party, if he attends, may counter that evidence.

   b. However, unless the court specifically asks for such evidence, the claimant *need not prove the other elements* of her claim. Nor may the defaulting party, if he appears, offer evidence on the merits.

4. **Notice of hearing:** If the defaulting party has *appeared* in the action, Fed. R. Civ. P. 55(b)(2) requires that he be *served with written notice* of the application for judgment at least *3 days* before the hearing.

   a. **Defaulting party who "appears":** A party can be declared in default for failing to plead or otherwise defend. Thus, the notice requirement applies only to a party who *appears* in the action, *but does not defend* by serving an answer or other defensive motion. A party may appear by filing a motion to extend the time for an answer, by moving for a change in venue, or, in some courts, even by sending a letter to the opposing party discussing settlement options.

   b. **When notice not required:** A *party who does not appear* does not receive notice. In addition, most courts do not require notice when the default judgment is imposed as a *sanction*.

5. **Limit on default judgment:** A judgment by default cannot award damages in excess of that set out in the complaint, nor can it grant relief that is different in kind than the complaint requests. Fed. R. Civ. P. 54(b).

D. **Challenging defaults and default judgments:** A party may challenge both the entry of default and the default judgment pursuant to Fed. R. Civ. P. 55(c) and 60(b).

   1. **Entry:** A party may have the entry of default set aside by showing *good cause* why it did not plead or otherwise defend. Examples of good cause include that the party never received notice of the suit or suffered a serious illness.

   2. **Default judgment:** A default judgment in some cases may be set aside if the party against whom it was entered can show procedural irregularities or other reasons to set aside the judgment.

      a. **Ordinary vs. sanction defaults:** It is often said that *default judgments are highly disfavored.* However, this maxim applies mainly to judgments rendered against a party who failed to defend. A default judgment rendered as a sanction is much more difficult to overturn than an ordinary default.

      b. **Procedural errors:** Procedural errors *do not always require setting aside* the judgment. The court instead evaluates whether the error affected the party's ability to defend himself.

         ★

         i. However, if the procedural defect is so significant that it results in a *denial of due process*, the defect is automatically grounds for reversal. Moreover, if the procedural defect is a denial of due process, a state cannot require the defaulting party to prove a ***meritorious defense*** as a precondition to opening a default. *Peralta v. Heights Medical Center,* 485 U.S. 80 (1988).

    ii. Similarly, the judgment may be set aside if the rendering court lacked ***subject matter*** or ***personal jurisdiction***. Improper venue is not grounds to set aside a default judgment.

c. Other reasons to reopen: A party may be able to set aside a default judgment even if the court followed the dictated procedure to the letter. Here, however, the party's chances of success turn on the reasons why default was entered.

    i. No notice of action: If a party can demonstrate that it never received notice of the action, a court will almost automatically set aside the default judgment. Recall that failure to receive notice does not necessarily constitute a procedural defect. As long as the claimant serves using authorized means, the default is procedurally proper regardless of whether the defendant actually receives the notice.

    ii. Other bases: If the party can show any of the grounds for reopening a judgment listed in Fed. R. Civ. P. 60(b), the court will set aside the default judgment. Rule 60(b) is discussed in Chapter 13, Part V.A. Although courts are normally very strict in applying this rule, the requirements are relaxed for default judgments.

III. INVOLUNTARY DISMISSAL

In some respects, the involuntary dismissal is the defendant's logical counterpart to the default judgment. A court may dismiss plaintiff's action (or one or more claims in that action) when the plaintiff fails to take an active role in the case or as a sanction.

A. Grounds: *Fed. Civ. P. 41(b)* allows a court to order dismissal for two reasons.

    1. Failure to prosecute: If the plaintiff fails to move the case along to completion, the court can dismiss it.

        a. Dismissal rare: Courts are very reluctant to grant a dismissal for failure to prosecute. A court typically warns the plaintiff and gives him a chance to rectify the delay.

        b. Prejudice: Although a defendant technically need not demonstrate that it is prejudiced by the delay, courts rarely grant a dismissal for failure to prosecute if the defendant is not injured or if the defendant is also responsible for the delay.

    2. Failure to comply with rules or court order: Dismissals for failure to comply with the rules or a court order can be divided into two categories.

        a. Defect: The first is where there is a defect in the claimant's case, including ***lack of jurisdiction***, any other ***Rule 12 defense***, ***res judicata***, and ***statute of limitations***.

        b. Sanction: In addition, a court may dismiss plaintiff's case as a sanction for violating a rule or court order during the case. However, because less drastic punishments are usually available, sanction dismissals are ***relatively rare***.

B. Effect of dismissal: Fed. R. Civ. P. 41(b) also specifies the effect of a dismissal on later litigation. In many cases, the dismissal will be an ***adjudication on the merits***, which prevents the plaintiff from suing the defendant again.

1. **Basic rule:** An involuntary dismissal operates as ***an adjudication on the merits*** unless one of the following is true:

   a. The court dismisses for lack of ***subject matter jurisdiction***, ***personal jurisdiction***, or ***venue***, or because of ***failure to join a necessary party*** under Fed. R. Civ. P. 19; or

   b. The ***court specifies*** in the dismissal order that the adjudication is ***not on the merits***.

   c. **Some dismissals never on the merits:** The judge has some discretion to alter the default rule of Rule 41(b). But that discretion is only one way. Although a judge may turn a dismissal that would ordinarily be on the merits into one that is not, the judge ***has no power to declare*** that a dismissal for lack of jurisdiction, venue, or failure to join a necessary party is on the merits.

      Example: *P* sues *D* for breach of contract. The court dismisses because of *P*'s failure to prosecute the case. The order of dismissal is silent as to whether it operates as an adjudication on the merits. *P* cannot sue *D* again for the same breach.

      Example: Same facts as prior example, except that the court dismissed for lack of personal jurisdiction. Now *P* is free to sue *D* again (in a court with personal jurisdiction).

2. **Important exception in federal courts:** The Supreme Court's decision in Semtek International, Inc. v. Lockheed Martin Corp., 531 U.S. 497 (2001), significantly limits the effect of a Fed. R. Civ. P. 41(b) dismissal by a federal court. *Semtek* is discussed in Chapter 5, Part IV.C.2.

   a. The Court in *Semtek* held that a Rule 41(b) dismissal based on expiration of the statute of limitations only bars a party from refiling in the ***same federal court*** that granted the dismissal.

   b. Although portions of the Court's discussion focus explicitly on statute of limitations dismissals, the Court never restricts its holding to those dismissals. It is therefore unclear whether the holding applies to dismissals based on other grounds, such as failure to prosecute.

   c. If *Semtek* applies, however, it requires a federal court to borrow the law of the state in which the federal court that dismissed the case sat to determine the effect of the dismissal. Because state rules often treat dismissals the same way as Rule 41(b), the practical effect of *Semtek* may be limited to a few issues.

3. **Application of rule:** The preclusion rules of Fed. R. Civ. P. 41(b) are applied strictly. For example, in federal court a dismissal for failure to state a claim upon which relief can be granted ***is an adjudication on the merits***, unless the court gives leave to amend or explicitly provides in its order that the dismissal is not on the merits. Federated Department Stores v. Moitie, 452 U.S. 394 (1981). In many states, by contrast, a dismissal for failure to state a claim does not operate as an adjudication on the merits.

IV. VOLUNTARY DISMISSAL

A plaintiff may voluntarily dismiss an action she had filed in a court. Although such dismissals often accompany settlements, a plaintiff may also choose to dismiss for tactical reasons, such as a need to spend more time marshaling evidence or to refile the action in a different court.

A. How case dismissed: A case can be dismissed in three ways. Whether each of these methods is available depends on the point in the case at which dismissal occurs.

1. **By notice:** If defendant has not yet served an *answer* or a motion for *summary judgment*, plaintiff may dismiss the case without approval of the court or consent of the other parties. Plaintiff effects the dismissal by filing a *notice of dismissal* with the court.

   a. Plaintiff's right to dismiss by notice is based on *actual service* of the answer, not on the time allowed for service. Thus, even if four months have expired since the complaint was served, plaintiff may still dismiss by notice if defendant has not yet served its answer or a motion for summary judgment. Conversely, if defendant answers the day after the complaint is served, plaintiff may no longer dismiss by notice.

   b. Dismissal by notice is also available for counterclaims, cross-claims, and third-party claims. In these cases, the period for unilateral dismissal expires when the adverse party *serves its responsive pleading*, or, if no response is required, when *evidence* on the claim is introduced at trial or at a hearing (including a hearing on a summary judgment motion). Fed. R. Civ. P. 41(c). Note that for these claims a motion for summary judgment does not terminate the claimant's right to dismiss by notice.

2. **By stipulation:** A plaintiff may also dismiss by filing a *written stipulation of dismissal* that has been signed by *all parties* who have *appeared* in the case. Dismissal by stipulation may occur at any point in the case, even during trial.

3. **By court order:** The plaintiff may also file a motion asking the court to dismiss his case. If the plaintiff cannot unilaterally dismiss by notice, and one or more parties refuses to sign the stipulation, dismissal by court order is the only option available to the plaintiff. Dismissal by order may occur at any point in the case. However, if a counterclaim has been filed in the action, and the defendant who filed that counterclaim objects to the dismissal, the court cannot dismiss the plaintiff's claim unless it can retain jurisdiction over the counterclaim.

B. Effect of dismissal on refiling: Whether plaintiff may refile its case after a voluntary dismissal depends on the type of the dismissal.

1. **By stipulation or court order:** Fed. R. Civ. P. 41(a)(1) and (2) provide that dismissals by stipulation or court order are *without prejudice*, *unless* the stipulation or order *provides otherwise*.

2. **By plaintiff:** A dismissal by notice filed by the plaintiff is usually *without prejudice*. Fed. R. Civ. P. 41(a)(1). However, a notice of dismissal is an adjudication on the merits if it is filed by a plaintiff who has *previously dismissed another action* based on the same claim.

   Example: *P* sues *D*. *P* dismisses the case by filing a notice of dismissal. *P* then refiles. *P* and *D* settle the case and file a signed stipulation of dismissal. The stipulation, however, is silent as to whether it bars later litigation. *P* now sues *D* a third time. Although *D* can use the settlement agreement to show the affirmative defense of accord and satisfaction, *P* is not barred by Fed. R. Civ. P. 41(a) from bringing the claim. The "prior dismissal" rule of Rule 41(a)(1) does not apply because the second case was dismissed by stipulation, and the rule specifically applies only when the second dismissal is by notice.

Quiz Yourself on
SETTLEMENTS, DEFAULTS, AND DISMISSALS

110. Porthos sues D'Artagnan in a federal district court in Virginia for injuries that Porthos sustained in a duel between the two. Porthos later learns that under governing law, neither party to a duel may recover damages for his injuries. Before D'Artagnan files a pleading or motion, Porthos files a notice of dismissal. In this notice, Porthos explicitly indicates that he is dismissing to enable him to file the case in a different state, where the law will allow recovery. D'Artagnan objects to this dismissal. Can D'Artagnan prevent Porthos from dismissing the case? _____

111. Same facts as Problem 110. Assume that Porthos successfully dismisses the case by a notice of dismissal. Porthos refiles in a Tennessee federal court, where governing law allows recovery for injuries sustained in a duel. D'Artagnan moves to dismiss, arguing that Porthos lost his right to sue again by voluntarily dismissing the case. Will D'Artagnan's motion succeed? _____

112. Tenant, a small business, leases its store from Landlord. Landlord brings an action against Tenant, stating two claims. First, Landlord sues for ejectment, claiming that Tenant has not paid its last several months of rent. Second, Landlord seeks damages for harm that Tenant allegedly caused to the leased premises.

    Tenant immediately files a motion to disqualify the judge for bias. Tenant's motion is denied. Tenant does not file an answer or take any further action in the case. Two months after the answer was due, Landlord moves for an entry of default. Will default be entered? _____

113. Same facts as Problem 112. Assume that the clerk enters a default against Tenant. Can Landlord immediately collect money from Tenant, or will it have to take additional steps to have an enforceable judgment? _____

114. Passenger sues Driver in federal court for injuries sustained in a one-car accident. The court grants Driver's motion to dismiss for lack of subject matter jurisdiction. The court's order of dismissal explicitly states that ''this dismissal for lack of subject matter jurisdiction shall operate as an adjudication on the merits.''

    A week later, Passenger sues Driver again in the same federal court. However, in his complaint Passenger states that he moved to an adjacent state last week and is now a citizen of that state. Driver moves to dismiss based on the explicit language in the earlier order of dismissal. Who wins? _____

Answers

110. D'Artagnan's objection is useless. Under Fed. R. Civ. P. 41(a), Porthos may dismiss by filing a notice of dismissal at any time before D'Artagnan serves either an answer or a motion for summary judgment. The facts specify that D'Artagnan has not served a pleading or motion. Porthos's motives for dismissing the case are irrelevant.

111. D'Artagnan loses again. Under Fed. R. Civ. P. 41(a)(1), a dismissal by notice is without prejudice unless the plaintiff has dismissed once before.

112. The clerk should enter default in this case. Under Fed. R. Civ. P. 55, default is entered against a party who fails to plead or otherwise defend. Tenant did not file an answer and so has not pled. Although Tenant did appear by filing its motion, that motion does not constitute a defense since it does not attack anything Landlord has done or alleged.

113. Obtaining a default judgment is a two-stage process. Entry of default is the first step. Getting the default judgment is the second. If damages are for a sum certain, the clerk issues the judgment. Here, however, although the rent is a sum certain (or a sum that can easily be calculated), the damages to the space are not a sum certain. Therefore, the judge has to enter the judgment.

The judge will hold a hearing at which Landlord can prove the amount of damage. Moreover, under Fed. R. Civ. P. 55(b)(2), Tenant will have to be served with written notice of the hearing. That rule requires notice to a defaulting defendant who appeared. Although Tenant failed to plead or otherwise defend, it appeared when it filed its motion to disqualify the judge.

114. Passenger will prevail. Fed. R. Civ. P. 41(b) explicitly says that an involuntary dismissal for lack of jurisdiction is not an adjudication on the merits. The judge has no authority to turn a dismissal for lack of jurisdiction into an adjudication on the merits.

V. SUMMARY JUDGMENT

Summary judgment is a frequently sought — although much less frequently granted — way to resolve a case before trial. Summary judgment gives the court a limited ability to look beyond the language in the pleadings to the actual facts that each side has marshaled to support its case. The governing rule is *Fed. R. Civ. P. 56*.

A. Other procedures distinguished: Summary judgment should be distinguished from other means of resolving a case before trial.

    1. Judgment on the pleadings: The *Fed. R. Civ. P. 12(c)* judgment on the pleadings allows a court to resolve a case based solely on the allegations in the pleadings. However, the court *must accept the factual allegations* in the pleadings as true. In a summary judgment motion, by contrast, the court looks at the evidence each side has.

    2. Judgment as a matter of law: A judgment as a matter of law under Fed. R. Civ. P. 50 occurs *during the trial*. A summary judgment motion, by contrast, must be made before the trial commences.

B. Procedure: A party requests a summary judgment by filing a motion. Fed. R. Civ. P. 56 contains certain rules governing the content, form, and timing of the motion.

    1. Types of summary judgment: A party may seek summary judgment on all claims in the case, or a *partial summary judgment* on one or more specific claims. Fed. R. Civ. P. 56(a). Claims include counterclaims, cross-claims, and third-party claims.

    2. Who can move: Both the claimant and the defending party may move for summary judgment on a particular claim. In fact, it is fairly common for *both* parties to move for summary judgment.

    3. Form of motion: Although a party requests summary judgment by filing a specific motion under Fed. R. Civ. P. 56, Rule 12 also provides that certain other motions can be ''converted'' to a motion for summary judgment. If a party files a motion to dismiss for *failure to state a claim* or a motion for *judgment on the pleadings* but includes facts outside the pleadings, the court must treat the motion as a motion for summary judgment. *Fed. R. Civ. P. 12(b)(6) and 12(c)*.

4. **Material accompanying motion:** A party moving for summary judgment usually includes supporting materials with the motion, such as affidavits, answers to interrogatories, and transcripts of depositions. The rule specifically provides that all affidavits must be based on *personal knowledge*, set forth facts that would be *admissible in evidence*, and affirmatively demonstrate that the person making the affidavit is competent to testify on the matters covered by the affidavit. Fed. R. Civ. P. 56(e). The movant also typically includes a *memorandum* in support of the motion.

5. **Timing:** A motion for summary judgment may be filed very early in the case.

   a. **By party defending against claim:** A party defending a claim may move for summary judgment *at any time*, even before it files its response to that claim. Fed. R. Civ. P. 56(b).

   b. **By claimant:** The claimant may serve a motion for summary judgment after the defending party makes its own motion for summary judgment, or after *20 days* following commencement of the action. Fed. R. Civ. P. 56(a).

   c. **Timing of hearing:** Regardless of who files the motion, the motion must be served at least *10 days* prior to the hearing on the motion. Fed. R. Civ. P. 56(c).

   d. **Disposition of early motions:** A motion for summary judgment presented at a very early stage of the case may present a problem for the other party. In such cases, the court may *delay the hearing* on the motion until the party has had adequate opportunity to *conduct discovery*. Fed. R. Civ. P. 56(f).

6. **Response by opposing party:** The party opposing the motion for summary judgment may submit its own evidence supporting its side of the argument, including *affidavits* and a *memorandum* opposing the motion.

C. **Hearing:** Once the motion and supporting evidence have been submitted, the court will hold a hearing on the motion. All parties may appear at this hearing and argue for or against the grant of summary judgment. Although a court has the power to take oral testimony at the hearing, in practice it will rely almost exclusively on the material submitted by the parties.

D. **Standard for summary judgment:** Fed. R. Civ. P. 56(c) provides that the court shall grant summary judgment if there is *no genuine question of material fact* and the movant is *entitled to judgment as a matter of law*.

1. **Basic principles:** Numerous cases establish guidelines for applying this standard.

   a. **Court does not weigh evidence:** The trial judge does not weigh the competing evidence. If there is conflicting evidence, the court must deny the motion for summary judgment.

   b. **Credibility:** Similarly, the court does not determine whether the evidence is credible. Determining credibility is the province of the factfinder (jury or judge) at trial.

   c. **Favor nonmoving party:** All evidence is to be viewed in the light most favorable to the nonmoving party.

d. **The problem of inferences:** If each party has direct testimony involving the crucial issue, the court's task is simple: Summary judgment must be denied. The more difficult cases are those where one or both parties offers evidence that requires the factfinder to draw an inference as to the crucial fact.

Example: *P* is trying to prove that *D* was intoxicated on the day the two got into an accident. *P* offers direct eyewitness evidence that *D* was seen walking into a bar on the day in question. This evidence calls for an inference: namely, that the defendant drank and became intoxicated.

i. As a general rule, inferences are considered *a matter for the jury*. Therefore, a court faced with evidence that calls for an inference typically denies summary judgment and lets the jury face the question.

ii. However, in some situations the inference is simply *too improbable* or farfetched to be allowed. In these cases, the court can grant summary judgment against the party who needs to rely on the inference.

Example: Consider the prior example. The eyewitness also testifies that *D* left the bar 30 seconds later and was not seen reentering. It would be improper for the finder of fact to infer that *D* became drunk in the bar. If this is *P*'s only evidence of intoxication, the court should grant summary judgment for *D*.

iii. **Competing inferences:** In many cases, more than one inference can be drawn from the evidence. Unless all possible inferences favor one party, the court *should grant summary judgment* for the party without the burden of production, as discussed below. However, if one inference is much more likely than the alternative, the court may conclude that it is the only viable alternative.

Example: While standing on the quadrangle minding his own business, Law Professor is hit in the head with a baseball. He immediately turns in the direction from which the ball came. He sees only two people, *A* and *B*. Law Professor sues *A* for battery. *A* moves for summary judgment and should prevail. Law Professor's case requires an inference: namely, that it was *A* rather than *B* who threw the ball. Because it is equally likely that *B* threw the ball, it is impossible to draw the inference that Law Professor needs. Without such proof, Law Professor cannot win.

Example: Same as prior example, except that *B* is sleeping on the quadrangle. Now *A*'s motion will be denied. Law Professor's inference that *A* threw the ball is far more likely than the alternative inference that *B* was the culprit. Note that the denial of summary judgment means only that the case goes to trial.

e. **Issues within the province of the jury:** Some issues are considered particularly appropriate for jury determination. One example is *negligence*. A court is much less likely to grant a summary judgment on the issue of whether defendant exercised reasonable care than it is on other issues in the case.

2. **No genuine issue of material fact:** Fed. R. Civ. P. 56 bars summary judgment only if there is a genuine issue of material fact. This standard allows the court to look beyond the pleadings and to evaluate the evidence in order to determine whether a real dispute exists.

a. Various views: Courts differ significantly in how rigorously they treat this requirement. In some states, it is virtually impossible to get summary judgment. As long as the nonmovant has some evidence supporting its side, the court will let the case go to trial even if the evidence is very weak. In other states, and in the federal courts, summary judgment is granted more frequently. Although these courts insist that they are not judging credibility or weighing the evidence, in truth they are doing both to a limited degree.

b. The importance of the burden of production: To understand how the ''no genuine issue'' standard is applied, it is necessary to understand the burden of production.

   i. Burden of production: The burden of production, sometimes called the burden of ''going forth with the evidence,'' dictates who must introduce evidence on an issue. *If neither party offers any evidence on an issue, the party with the burden of production loses.*

   (a) A *claimant* typically bears the burden of production on *every element* of its claim. Therefore, a plaintiff suing for breach of contract must introduce evidence that a contract existed, that it was breached, and that the plaintiff suffered damages as a result. Similarly, a defendant counterclaiming for battery must show an offensive contact, intent, and harm.

   (b) A party *defending against a claim* typically has the burden of production on all *affirmative defenses*. Therefore, a defendant who is defending a breach of contract action by arguing that the contract was procured by fraud must introduce evidence of a false representation by the plaintiff and reasonable reliance by the defendant to its detriment.

   (c) Switching burdens: If the party with the burden of production introduces overwhelming evidence in his support, the burden of production switches to the other side. If the other party fails to offer any evidence in her favor, the court, not the jury, will decide the issue.

   Example: *P* sues *D* for breach of contract. *D* denies both that a contract existed, and that it was breached. *D* does not offer any affirmative defenses. *P* introduces a deposition of *D* in which *D* admitted the contract, *D*'s breach, and *P*'s damages. The court will grant summary judgment for *P* unless *D* introduces other evidence that tends to negate at least one of the elements.

   ii. Interrelationship of burden of production and summary judgment: The burden of production plays a crucial role in summary judgment. Logically, there are two distinct categories of summary judgment cases.

   (a) Nonmovant has the burden: If the party moving for summary judgment does not have the burden of production, the court's task is to determine *whether the other party has satisfied the burden* of production by *introducing evidence on all elements*. If it has not satisfied the burden, summary judgment will be granted.

   (b) Movant has the burden: If the party moving for summary judgment has the burden of production, the court should grant summary judgment if:

   1. that party has introduced so much evidence that the burden has shifted to the other side, and

2. the other side has not introduced enough evidence to meet the burden that was shifted to it.

iii. **Effect of burden of persuasion:** The burden of persuasion is the standard applied by the finder of fact in determining who prevails at trial. In most civil matters, the party with the burden of persuasion must prove his case by a ***preponderance of the evidence***. However, for certain issues, most notably ***fraud***, the burden is ***clear and convincing evidence***. The burden of persuasion affects the burden of production. In a fraud case, for example, a plaintiff must produce more evidence to meet its burden of production than it would on a claim where the burden of persuasion was a mere preponderance of the evidence. Anderson v. Liberty Lobby, Inc., 477 U.S. 242 (1986).

c. **Application of standard in cases where defendant moves for summary judgment:** If defendant moves for summary judgment, the court must decide whether plaintiff has significant evidence supporting its claim.

Note on terminology: To simplify matters, the discussion in this part and Part d speaks in terms of plaintiffs and defendants. However, the analysis ***also applies to defenses, counterclaims, and other claims***. When dealing with affirmative defenses and other types of claims, *plaintiff* should be read to refer to the party with the burden of production, while *defendant* is the party without the burden of production.

i. **Every element:** Plaintiff must have significant evidence on ***every element of the claim***. If plaintiff lacks evidence on even one element, the court should grant summary judgment for defendant even if plaintiff has overwhelming evidence on all other elements.

ii. **"Mere scintilla" test:** Some courts will deny summary judgment if plaintiff has any evidence in its favor. However, the ***federal courts*** have ***rejected the mere scintilla approach*** and require plaintiff to have significant evidence.

iii. **Defendant's duty:** Defendant has the initial responsibility, or burden, of demonstrating to the court the absence of a genuine issue of fact.

★ (a) The U.S. Supreme Court elaborated on this duty in Celotex Corp. v. Catrett, 477 U.S. 317 (1986). It held that defendant ***need not offer proof that negates plaintiff's case***. It need only show that plaintiff has failed to meet the burden of production. (On the other hand, if defendant *does* have affirmative evidence that negates an element of plaintiff's claim, it is free to introduce it.)

(b) However, defendant cannot simply assert that plaintiff has no evidence. Instead, it must point out to the court those parts of the depositions, affidavits, and other evidence that demonstrate that plaintiff has no evidence on one or more elements of its claim.

★ **Example:** Bias v. Advantage International, Inc., 905 F.2d 1558 (D.C. Cir. 1990), illustrates how a defendant shows the absence of facts necessary to support plaintiff's claim. The plaintiff in that case was the estate of a college basketball star. The decedent died two days after being selected in the first round of the NBA draft. The estate claimed that defendant, decedent's agent, had breached its promise to procure life insurance covering decedent. Defendant admitted that it had breached this promise but countered by asserting that decedent's drug use would have made it impossible to procure a policy. Defendant supported this allegation with evidence showing that decedent used drugs regularly and that no life insurance company would issue a policy to a drug user. The court held that this evidence was enough to demonstrate no genuine issue of material fact. Moreover, because plaintiff had no real evidence suggesting to the contrary, summary judgment for defendant was appropriate.

    d. Application of standard in cases where plaintiff moves for summary judgment: A plaintiff may also seek summary judgment when she feels that her evidence completely overwhelms the evidence of the defendant.

        i. Logically, granting summary judgment to a plaintiff presents greater difficulties. Even if defendant has no evidence, the jury could always disbelieve the evidence proffered by the plaintiff and find for the defendant. Nevertheless, courts do occasionally enter summary judgment for plaintiffs.

        ii. For plaintiff to prevail on a summary judgment motion, it must have presented enough evidence to **switch the burden of production** to defendant. Plaintiff must have **substantial evidence** on each and every element of its claim. In addition, defendant must either have no conflicting evidence or evidence that is so completely overwhelmed by plaintiff's evidence that it cannot be believed. If defendant raises significant issues concerning the credibility of plaintiff's evidence, a court is less likely to grant summary judgment.

  3. Movant entitled to judgment: The second part of the summary judgment standard is that the movant must be entitled to judgment as a matter of law. This merely means that governing law allows the movant to prevail on the undisputed facts. In most cases, this part of the standard presents little difficulty. Nevertheless, a summary judgment motion can serve the same role as a motion to dismiss for failure to state a claim: Even if the evidence is exactly as plaintiff claims, if the law does not favor plaintiff, a court should not grant summary judgment for plaintiff.

E. The judgment: A summary judgment on the entire case is a **_final judgment_** and is treated like a judgment rendered after a full trial.

Quiz Yourself on
RESOLUTION BEFORE TRIAL

115. Paulette fancies herself a future Olympic equestrian. Hoping to work on her riding skills, she arranges a week-long visit to Darrell's Dude Ranch in Colorado. Once he hears that Paulette wants a challenge, Darrell puts her on F-5 Tornado, his meanest and strongest spirited horse. F-5 throws Paulette into the dirt, bruising both her ego and several of her ribs. Paulette sues Darrell in a federal district court for $150,000 in damages.

    Before filing his answer, Darrell meets with Paulette. The two agree to settle the case for $60,000. The parties file a stipulation of dismissal, and Darrell promptly pays the $60,000. Two weeks later, Paulette sues Darrell again on the same claim. Conceding that Darrell already paid her $60,000, Paulette asks for only $90,000 in damages. Darrell promptly moves to dismiss the case. However, Paulette correctly points out that the stipulation of dismissal had no explicit language preventing Paulette from suing for the remaining money. Will the court let Paulette sue for the remaining $90,000? _____

116. Same facts as Problem 115, except that Paulette and Darrell do not settle the case. After several months, Darrel has neither answered nor filed any papers with the court. Paulette therefore obtains an entry of default against Darrell. She now seeks a default judgment. However, she has three questions. First, she wants to know if the court will hold a hearing before entering the default judgment. Second, if the court does hold such a hearing, she is unsure whether Darrell is entitled to notice. Third, while she asked for $150,000 in damages in her complaint, she has since discovered that her injuries are more extensive than she thought and that her total damages are $300,000. Therefore, she wants to know if she can convince the court at the hearing to enter judgment in the larger amount. You are Paulette's attorney in this matter. How will you reply to her? _____

117. Art Luvver collects valuable paintings. After buying a masterpiece at auction, he arranges to have Van's Van Lines transport the painting to Art's home. While en route, the driver of the truck is involved in an accident with another vehicle. Both drivers perish, and the masterpiece is completely destroyed.

    Art sues Van, the owner of Van's Van lines, in a federal district court based on diversity jurisdiction. Van does not bother to answer or make a motion. Instead, he immediately moves for summary judgment, alleging that Art has no proof that Van's employee was in any way negligent. Under the law that this federal court would apply, Art would have to prove negligence in order to recover. Realizing that he has no evidence of negligence, Art elects to dismiss the case by filing a notice of dismissal. After dismissing, Art hopes to refile the case in another state, where the governing law would make Van strictly liable. May Art dismiss his case by filing a notice of dismissal? _____

118. Same facts as Problem 117, except that Art decides not to dismiss. Instead, Art contests Van's summary judgment motion. Art first argues that the motion is untimely because it was filed too early. Second, Art claims that even if the motion is timely, the court should not hold the hearing on the motion this early in the suit. Is either argument correct? _____

119. Same facts as Problems 117 and 118. Assume that the court refuses to hear the motion for summary judgment. Art and Van conduct discovery for four months. At the end of four months, both parties file their own motions for summary judgment.

    Although the parties engaged in extensive discovery, they learn very little as a result. They do learn that the accident took place at an intersection with a stop light. However, neither party has any evidence on one crucial point — whether Van's employee or the other driver ran a red light. There were no witnesses other than the two deceased drivers. The physical evidence provides no clues. Will the court grant either Art's or Van's motion for summary judgment? _____

120. Same facts as Problems 117 and 118. Assume that the court refuses to hear the motion for summary judgment. Art and Van conduct extensive discovery. At the end of the discovery phase, Art alone moves for summary judgment.

    Art hit the jackpot in discovery. As luck would have it, a photography class was being held near the intersection on the day of the accident. Five students happened to take photos at the very instant the two vehicles both entered the intersection. Art manages to obtain copies of four of these photos. These photos clearly reveal that the light facing Van's driver was red, while the light facing the other driver was green. All of the students are neutral third parties.

Even after exhaustive efforts, neither party manages to obtain the fifth photograph. However, Van does obtain an affidavit from the instructor of the photography class. In this affidavit, the instructor states that she spoke with the photographer of the missing photograph. Although the instructor has not actually seen the photograph, the photographer insists to her that his photo shows that the light facing Van's driver was green.

The affidavit includes hearsay evidence and, as such, cannot be used as evidence at trial. Aside from the photographs and the affidavit, neither party has any evidence showing the color of the light. Nevertheless, Van argues that summary judgment should be denied. He asserts that the affidavit alone is clearly enough to create a genuine issue of material fact for trial, especially given that it is Art, a plaintiff, who has made the motion. Is Van correct, or will Art be granted a summary judgment?

Answers

115. The court will not dismiss the action. A stipulation of dismissal bars a later action only if it specifies that the dismissal is on the merits. Here the stipulation was silent.

116. There will be a hearing in this matter. Because damages for personal injuries are not a sum certain, the court will need Paulette to prove that she actually suffered the alleged harm. However, Darrell is not entitled to notice of the hearing. Under Fed. R. Civ. P. 55(b)(2), a party receives notice of the hearing only if he has "appeared." The facts specify that Darrell has done nothing, so he has not appeared in the case. Finally, Paulette cannot recover the additional damages at the hearing. A default judgment is limited to the damages sought in the complaint. Of course, Paulette could still seek those damages. She could amend her complaint, but she would have to serve it on Darrell and give him another chance to respond.

117. Dismissal by notice is not available. Under Fed. R. Civ. P. 41(a), a party may dismiss by notice only before the defendant answers or files a motion for summary judgment.

118. Art is incorrect on timeliness, but correct on his second claim concerning the hearing. A defendant may file a motion for summary judgment at any time. Fed. R. Civ. P. 56(b). It does not matter that Van has not yet filed an answer. However, the court should not hold the hearing right away. Instead, Rule 56(f) indicates that the court should give Art time to collect evidence to bolster the assertions in his pleadings.

119. The court should grant Van's motion but deny Art's motion. This question involves the burden of production and inferences. Because Art is the plaintiff, he probably has the burden of production on the question of whether Van's driver was negligent. Thus, if neither party has any evidence on that crucial point, Art loses.

Art is not completely bereft of evidence. We do know that the accident happened at an intersection with a light. Art wins if Van's driver ran a red light. Although there is no evidence on that point, if the court can infer from the known facts that Van's driver ran the light, the court should deny summary judgment. However, a court will *not* draw the inference that Art suggests. The court would infer that Van's driver ran the light only if that inference is the only one likely to be true in these circumstances. Here, the competing inferences are at least as likely as the one Art needs to win. It is equally likely that the other driver ran a red light, in which case Van is not liable. (In fact, there is a *third* possible inference here, which if true would also result in no liability. It is possible that the light was malfunctioning, showing green both ways.)

Because the court will not draw an inference, there is no genuine issue of material fact here. *Neither* side has any evidence on the question of who ran the red light.

Here, both parties have filed a motion for summary judgment. Both are correct in saying that there is no genuine issue of material fact. However, applying the second part of the summary judgment standard, only Van is entitled to judgment as a matter of law. Because Art has the burden of production on the issue of negligence, he loses if there is no evidence of negligence.

120. The court should grant Art's motion for a summary judgment. True, courts do not often grant summary judgment for a plaintiff. After all, if the jury does not believe all of plaintiff's evidence, the defendant still wins.

Here, however, no one in her right mind could not be convinced by Art's four photographs. They were taken by people with no interest in the case and directly show the crucial fact. The photographs thus switch the burden of production to Van.

Van's affidavit does not offset Art's strong evidence because it cannot be used. Fed. R. Civ. P. 56(e) requires that affidavits state facts that are admissible in evidence. Therefore, Van has no evidence at all to support his side of the case. Given that Art's evidence is overwhelming, the court should grant summary judgment for Art.

Exam Tips on *RESOLUTION BEFORE TRIAL*

If an exam question deals with resolving a case in the pretrial stages, it is important to consider all the different ways a case may end prior to trial. Different methods have their own advantages and disadvantages.

- ☛ **Default:** Obtaining a default judgment involves several technical issues. Because default judgments are ***highly disfavored*** by courts, a party must be careful to follow Fed. R. Civ. P. 55.

  - ☞ The default process has ***two basic stages***: the ***entry of default*** and the ***default judgment***.

  - ☞ The court may hold a ***hearing*** before entering a default judgment to require the plaintiff to offer proof on damages and perhaps on other issues. If the defendant has ***appeared*** in any way, it is entitled to notice prior to this hearing.

  - ☞ It is relatively easy to reopen a default judgment, except for default judgments imposed as a sanction for failure to cooperate.

- ☛ **Involuntary dismissals:** Students sometimes do not recognize the ***tremendously broad scope*** of the involuntary dismissal rule. Most dismissals that result from a motion, spanning from subject matter jurisdiction to statute of limitations to failure to comply with discovery, are involuntary dismissals governed by Fed. R. Civ. P. 41(b).

  - ☞ It may help to think of the involuntary dismissal for ***failure to prosecute*** as defendant's version of the default judgment. Like a default judgment, a defendant must make a strong showing before a court will dismiss for failure to prosecute.

☞ Fed. R. Civ. P. 41(b) also treats most dismissals as *adjudications on the merits*, which means that they prevent the party from filing the same claim or claims again. However, the rule exempts certain types of dismissals and gives the dismissing judge the authority to exempt others.

☞ If a party dismisses a case in *federal court* and tries to refile in a different court, you should discuss the possible effects of the Supreme Court's *Semtek* decision.

☛ **Voluntary dismissals:** A plaintiff may dismiss her action in several different ways. Fed. R. Civ. P. 41(a) has provisions specifying whether the plaintiff may file again. Study these provisions carefully because they can be tricky.

☛ **Summary judgment:** Conceptually, summary judgment is the most difficult of the various means to resolve a case before trial. This difficulty arises in large part because summary judgment *considers both the law and the facts*.

☞ Although the *timing* rules of Rule 56 allow a summary judgment motion to be filed very early in the case, judges rarely agree to decide the motion until the parties have had adequate time to conduct discovery.

☞ **The standard for summary judgment:** The most difficult part of any summary judgment question is applying the ''no genuine issue of material fact'' standard.

☞ You may find it helpful to think of summary judgment as an earlier form of *judgment as a matter of law*. Although the standard for the two types of judgment is markedly different, they share certain basic similarities. In both forms of dismissal, you may face problems such as *burden of production* and *inference*.

☞ Although a judge is not supposed to gauge credibility, if one side's evidence is so overwhelming that the little bit of evidence offered by the other side cannot be believed, summary judgment may be appropriate.

☞ Understanding the *burden of production* is critical to understanding summary judgment. It is much easier for the party *without* the burden of production to prevail on a motion for summary judgment.

☞ One common type of test question involves a summary judgment motion by the party *without the burden*. In this case, first look to see if the party with the burden has introduced evidence on *each and every element of the claim*. If no evidence has been offered on even one element, the motion should be granted.

☞ Conversely, if the *party with the burden* is making the motion, summary judgment ordinarily is not granted. However, if the party with the burden has offered very strong evidence on every element, and the opposing party has offered little or no evidence to rebut it, summary judgment may be appropriate.

CHAPTER 10

DETERMINING THE TRIER

ChapterScope ▬▬▬▬▬▬▬▬▬▬▬▬▬▬▬▬▬▬▬▬▬▬▬▬▬▬▬▬▬▬▬

This chapter concerns jury trials and, to a lesser extent, bench trials. It explores the situations in which a party may be entitled to a jury, as well as the process by which jurors are selected and challenged. Finally, it covers the process of challenging the judge assigned to a case.

- In some cases, the *U.S. Constitution* guarantees a party a right to a jury.

    - The Seventh Amendment applies *only to the federal courts*, not the state courts.

    - Determining whether a party has a right to a jury requires a historic analysis. This focus makes applying the Seventh Amendment especially difficult in cases involving *new rights that did not exist at common law* and cases that involve a *mix of legal and equitable claims and defenses*.

- If a jury is impaneled, the jury decides *questions of fact* and the *application of law to fact*. Pure questions of law are decided by the judge even when the case is tried before a jury.

- Selection of the actual jurors who will sit in a case occurs through a two-step process.

    - First, the court draws a *jury pool* from the universe of available jurors.

    - Second, the parties select the actual panel through a process called *voir dire*. During *voir dire*, potential jurors may be challenged *for cause*, or a party may exclude a limited number of jurors without stating a reason by using a *peremptory* challenge.

    - A party may not use peremptory challenges as a back-door way to exclude jurors based on their race or gender.

- Parties may also challenge the judge assigned to sit in a case. In cases of bias or other difficulty, the judge should *recuse* himself from the matter.

I. RIGHT TO A JURY TRIAL IN FEDERAL COURT

The U.S. Constitution provides a right to a jury trial in certain civil cases.

A. Seventh Amendment: The Seventh Amendment to the U.S. Constitution provides in relevant part, ''In Suits at common law, where the value in controversy shall exceed twenty dollars, the right of trial by jury shall be preserved. . . .''

    1. Preserves, not creates, right: The Seventh Amendment is unique in that it does not create a right, but instead *preserves* a right that existed before the Constitution was enacted. Therefore, to determine if a party has a right to a jury today, a court must determine if the underlying action would have been heard by a jury in *1791*, the year the Seventh Amendment came into effect.

    2. Applies only to civil cases: The Seventh Amendment applies only to civil cases. In criminal cases, the Sixth Amendment creates a right to a jury trial. The two amendments are interpreted very differently.

3. **Applies to issues, not to entire case:** Although the Seventh Amendment on its face applies to "suits," it has been interpreted to apply only to those *issues* within a case that qualify for a jury. Thus, it is possible for a jury to decide some issues while the judge decides others.

4. **Not only source of right:** The Seventh Amendment is not the only source of a right to a jury trial in civil cases. In some situations, Congress gives litigants a right to a jury for causes of action that it creates.

5. **Amendment never *bars* jury:** The Seventh Amendment guarantees a right *to* a jury trial in certain cases. Neither the Seventh Amendment nor any other provision of the Constitution create the converse right *not* to have a jury in situations falling outside the Seventh Amendment.

6. **Amendment does not apply to states:** Unlike most of the other provisions of the Bill of Rights, the Seventh Amendment has *never been extended to the states*. Therefore, states are not required by the amendment to grant juries in any cases. However, many states do afford a right to a jury trial in their own constitutions or by statute.

B. **Features preserved by the amendment:** The Seventh Amendment does not require a jury exactly like the juries used in 1791. For example, in 1791 only men could serve on a jury. Certain features of the traditional jury have proven problematic.

1. **Size:** The jury at common law always comprised 12 members. However, the federal rules allow a court to seat a jury of "**not fewer than six and not more than twelve.**" *Fed. R. Civ. P. 48*. Rule 48 also provides that if the jury *falls below 6* members (due to illness, death, or disqualification), no verdict may be taken from the jury *unless the parties consent*.

    a. **Actual application:** In practice, federal courts rarely seat a 6-person jury. Far more common are 9- or 12-member juries.

    b. Although a jury of fewer than 6 members may not be constitutional, a 6-member jury has been found to satisfy the amendment.

2. **Unanimity:** At common law, the jury verdict had to be unanimous. The federal rules *preserve the requirement of unanimity*. Fed. R. Civ. P. 48. However, the parties may stipulate to a non-unanimous verdict. By contrast, a majority of states do not require a unanimous verdict.

3. **Demand:** The right to a jury is a personal right that can be waived by the parties.

    a. Under *Fed. R. Civ. P. 38(b)*, a party must serve on the other parties a *written demand* for a jury within *10 days* following service of the last pleading dealing with the issue for which a jury is demanded. That demand must also be filed with the court within a reasonable time. Fed. R. Civ. P. 5(d).

    b. *Any party may file* the demand.

    c. Unless the demand specifies particular issues, a party will be deemed to have demanded a jury trial on *all issues triable by a jury*. Fed. R. Civ. P. 38(c). If a party limits the demand to certain issues, *any other party* may demand a jury trial on *any or all remaining issues* triable by a jury by serving its own demand within 10 days after the initial service.

C. **Application of the Seventh Amendment — an overview:** The Seventh Amendment preserves a right that existed in 1791. As a general matter, in 1791 only actions that were tried in the *common law courts* were tried before a jury. Understanding this provision requires some understanding of how the English court system allocated jurisdiction among different courts.

1. **Different systems:** The English historically maintained several different court systems, each of which could hear only certain categories of cases. The main systems were ***Common Law***, ***Equity***, ***Exchequer***, and ***Admiralty***. Although this somewhat byzantine system was not followed in most of the North American colonies, it nevertheless was incorporated into the Seventh Amendment.

2. **Jury at law:** Of the four main systems, only Common Law (sometimes called simply Law) would employ a jury to decide a case.

3. **Exchequer and admiralty:** The historic roles of Exchequer and Admiralty involved, respectively, claims against the sovereign and suits involving vessels in navigable waters. There is ***no constitutional*** right to a jury in these cases even today.

4. **Law vs. Equity:** When dealing with the right to a jury trial, the most problematic distinction is that between Common Law and Equity. The problem arises from the fact that the authority of these courts overlapped to a significant extent. In many cases, a party could take a dispute either to Law or Equity, depending on how the case was structured.

   a. **Remedy:** In many cases, the remedy sought by the party dictated whether the case went to Law or Equity.

      i. **Remedies at Law:** The common law courts were limited to certain specific remedies. The most important remedy available in the common law courts was ***damages***. However, a common law court could also grant certain forms of specific relief, such as ***replevin*** and ***ejectment***.

      ii. **Remedies in Equity:** Equity was not confined to a fixed slate of remedies but could instead fashion an appropriate remedy for the occasion. Nevertheless, certain remedies were often used in Equity, including ***injunctions***, ***specific performance***, ***accounting***, ***rescission*** of a contract, ***reformation*** of a contract, and ***restitution***.

      iii. **Mutually exclusive:** In most respects, these remedies were available *only* in one system. Thus, Equity could not grant replevin. Similarly, Law could not enjoin the defendant or reform a contract.

   b. **Equitable claims and procedures:** Differences in remedy were not the only distinction between Law and Equity. Equity also recognized certain claims and allowed certain procedures that were not available in Law.

      i. **Claims:** Historically, only a court of Equity would hear certain claims for relief, including ***breach of a fiduciary duty***, ***subrogation***, ***contribution***, and ***indemnity***, and a debtor's claim to ***redeem a mortgage*** after foreclosure.

      ii. **Procedures:** Equity also demonstrated flexibility in procedure. Thus, a party who wanted to bring a case as a ***class action*** or who needed to use ***discovery*** could sue only in Equity, even if she sought damages.

      iii. **Remedy not controlling:** If a party used one of the equitable claims or procedures, Equity could hear the claim notwithstanding that the remedy sought was itself available only in Law. Thus, a party bringing a ***class action for money damages*** would historically sue in Equity.

c. Preference for Law: Because of the tremendous overlap, the English system eventually worked out a compromise that established Law as the "preferred" court. After this compromise, a party could sue in Equity only if he could establish that *the relief available in Law was inadequate*. That same rule carries forward to this day. In many systems, a party can obtain an equitable remedy only by showing that the legal remedy, usually damages, is insufficient to redress the problem.

Example: *P* wants to sue *D* to enforce a contract under which *D* agreed to repair and return an old watch that used to belong to *P*'s great-grandfather. Although the market value of the watch is not that high, the watch has tremendous sentimental value. *D* refuses to return the watch. Because damages would not adequately compensate *P*, *P* would sue in equity for specific performance.

D. Application of analysis to new claims: Since 1791, legislatures have created numerous new rights. Because these new statutory claims did not exist in 1791, applying the history-based approach of the Seventh Amendment can prove difficult.

1. Two-part test: In Tull v. United States, 481 U.S. 412 (1987), the Supreme Court established a two-part test to use in determining whether a statutory claim must be tried by a jury.

a. Step one: The first step is to identify the ***closest historic analogue*** to the action in eighteenth-century English practice and determine whether that historical analogue would be heard in Law or Equity.

b. Step two: The second step is to analyze the ***nature of the remedy*** sought and determine if it is ***legal or equitable in nature***.

c. Second step predominates: More recent decisions of the Court have made it clear that this second step predominates over the first. Thus, even if the closest analogue is an action in equity, if the remedy being sought is essentially legal in nature, the parties are entitled to a jury.

★   **Example:** An excellent example of how this two-part test applies is Chauffers, Teamsters & Helpers, Local No. 391 v. Terry, 494 U.S. 558 (1990). At issue in *Chauffers* was a claim against a union for breach of its duty to represent. Under the first step, the Court determined that the closest analogue was the equitable claim for breach of fiduciary duty. However, that equitable claim was not 100 percent analogous. The Court then applied the second step and found the remedy (back pay) to be a form of damages, a legal remedy. Because the second step is more important in the analysis, the Court held that there was a right to a jury.

i. Continued relevance of first step: A concurring opinion in *Chauffers* questions whether the first step has any continued relevance. However, if the statutory cause of action is a ***perfect analogue*** — that is, if the legislature has simply codified an action that existed in 1791 — the fact of codification should not affect whether the party gets a jury. In these cases, the first step may control.

ii. Applying the second step: The second step of the analysis can be difficult to apply in some cases. A remedy is not legal merely because it involves money. Curtis v. Loether, 415 U.S. 189, 196 (1974). If a monetary remedy is essentially restitutionary in nature — that is, if it forces the party to disgorge money in her possession that ***properly should have gone to the claimant*** — it will be treated as equitable. On the other hand, if the money compensates for a harm caused to the claimant, it is damages and is legal in nature.

E. Application of analysis to new procedures: Modern procedural innovations produce situations that did not exist in 1791 and that therefore cannot be resolved using a straightforward historical analysis.

   1. **New remedies:** In addition to creating new substantive rights, legislatures occasionally create new remedies unheard of in 1791. One example is the declaratory judgment. See Chapter 6, Part I.C. In determining whether to grant a jury in a declaratory judgment case, courts look to the underlying dispute in an attempt to determine *what action would eventually be brought* were the declaratory judgment option unavailable. If a party could demand a jury in that action, a jury is available in the declaratory judgment action. The analysis here parallels how courts analyze declaratory judgments for purposes of determining *federal question jurisdiction*. See Chapter 4, Part III.F.2.

   2. **Effects of the merger of Law and Equity:** Because of Fed. R. Civ. P. 2, federal courts no longer hold separate proceedings for actions in Law and in Equity, but allow all claims, legal and equitable, to be brought in a single suit. See also Fed. R. Civ. P. 18, which allows a party to join all claims, ''legal, equitable, or maritime,'' that the party may have against an opposing party. This merger of Law and Equity has a significant effect on the jury trial question.

      a. **Traditional equitable procedural devices:** As discussed above, certain procedural devices — such as the class action, interpleader, and discovery — were historically available only in Equity. Today, however, the federal rules make these devices available in all civil actions. Therefore, the mere fact that a case involves one of these procedural devices *does not affect whether the parties are entitled to a jury trial*. If the underlying claim is one that would otherwise be heard by a jury, the fact that the party prosecutes the claim using an equitable procedural device does not operate to deny the parties their right to a jury.

      Example: *P*, as representative of a class comprising all first-year law students at City University Law School, sues the university in federal court for failing to provide adequate parking space. *P* seeks damages. Although a class action is an equitable procedural device, either party may demand a jury in the case.

   ★ b. **Reclassification of equitable remedies:** In a few cases, the merger of Law and Equity results in traditional equitable claims being ''reclassified'' as legal claims for purposes of jury trial. The best-known example of this phenomenon is Dairy Queen, Inc. v. Wood, 369 U.S. 469 (1962).

      i. The plaintiff in *Dairy Queen* sued for trademark infringement. One of the remedies it sought was an *accounting*, traditionally an equitable remedy. An accounting would require defendant to examine its records to ascertain how much profit it had made by using plaintiff's mark.

      ii. The Court held that the amount that defendant would be required to calculate was essentially a measure of *damages*. The mere fact that the equitable remedy of accounting put the onus of calculating these damages on the defendant rather than the plaintiff did not change its essential character. Therefore, the Court held that the parties were entitled to a jury on the accounting claim, as it was essentially legal in nature.

   ★ c. **Joinder of legal and equitable claims in single action:** After the merger of Law and Equity, legal and equitable claims can both be presented in a single action, making it difficult to apply the historic test to the hybrid case. The Supreme Court set out the basic analysis for courts to use in this situation in Beacon Theatres, Inc. v. Westover, 359 U.S. 500 (1959). That decision held that a party is entitled to a jury on ***all issues that are relevant to the legal claims***, even if some of those issues are also relevant to equitable claims.

Example: *D* periodically visits an orchard and takes apples from the trees. *P* erects a barrier preventing *D* from entering the land. *P* then sues *D* for an order of ***replevin***, requiring *D* to return the apples already taken, and an ***injunction***, preventing *D* from trespassing again on *P*'s land. *D* defends by arguing that the city, not *P*, owns the land. *D* also files a counterclaim for ***damages*** for being excluded from the property. *P* demands a jury on all legal claims. A jury will hear ***all issues related to the replevin*** (recall that replevin is a legal remedy) ***and damages claims***. This means that the jury will also decide most of the issues relevant to the injunction claim, for that claim shares certain crucial issues — such as who owns the land — with the legal claims. The judge will decide only those few issues unique to the injunction claim, such as whether a grant of an injunction would be in the public interest.

★   **Example:** For an informative illustration of how this rule applies in a complex case involving both claims and counterclaims, see Amoco Oil Co. v. Torcomian, 722 F.2d 1099 (3d Cir. 1983) (jury hears legal issues in both the complaint and the counterclaim).

★   3. **Agency adjudication:** Another feature of modern life is the increased use of administrative agencies to deal with complex issues. Agencies may occasionally adjudicate the rights of individuals. However, administrative agencies historically ***do not use juries***. To prevent Congress from sidestepping the jury trial requirement by assigning cases to agencies, the Supreme Court has created a ***limited exception*** as to when an agency may decide a case involving a ***legal claim*** without a jury. Atlas Roofing v. Occupational Safety & Health Administration, 430 U.S. 442 (1977). The exception has three elements.

   a. The claim must be litigated before an ***agency tribunal***, not a court.

   b. The underlying claim must be one ***created by Congress.***

   c. The right being litigated must be a ***public right***. Although the concept of a public right cannot be defined with precision, it is something that affects the public interest, not merely the interests of an individual or small group.

      i. The vast majority of public rights are ***litigated by the government***. However, not all claims litigated by the government involve public rights. See Granfinanciera, S.A. v. Nordberg, 492 U.S. 33 (1989), in which the court held that a jury was required in a claim brought by a bankruptcy trustee, an officer of the federal government.

      Example: The Federal Aviation Administration brings an action under a new federal statute dealing with lost luggage. The statute allows actions to be tried before an FAA tribunal. The FAA seeks an order requiring airlines to reimburse passengers for luggage that has been lost. This action *cannot* be heard without a jury. Although the claim is brought by the government, the right being litigated is not a public right but is essentially the private right of each passenger.

      Example: Same facts as the prior example, except that the FAA seeks to recover fines specifically authorized by the federal statute. The action may be heard by the agency tribunal without a jury. The claim being litigated is a public right. Because the claim is being litigated before an agency tribunal, not a court, no jury is required.

★   **ii.** It may also be possible for an individual to sue to enforce a public right. For example, a claim by an environmental group objecting to wide-scale pollution may involve a public right. On the other hand, these sorts of claims are rarely litigated before agencies.

Quiz Yourself on
SEVENTH AMENDMENT RIGHT TO A JURY

121. Pamela sues David in federal district court for breach of contract and makes a timely demand for a jury. After some discussion, the parties stipulate to a nonunanimous verdict. The jury returns a 7-5 verdict for David. Pamela asks to have the jury verdict set aside. Although acknowledging that she agreed to a nonunanimous verdict, Pamela argues that both Fed. R. Civ. P. 48 and the Seventh Amendment to the U.S. Constitution require a unanimous verdict. What result? _____

122. Over the past 20 years, the United States has closed a number of military bases and related facilities. The government typically sells the land to private individuals, who are then free to develop the land as they see fit. In some cases, however, the government had leased or licensed small portions of certain military bases to private parties while the base was in operation. When someone buys the base, these lessees and licensees often refuse to leave voluntarily. This ''holdover'' problem makes buying military land less attractive and therefore has reduced the government's proceeds.

Congress enacts a new federal statute to remedy the holdover problem. Under this statute, the new owner of a former military base may ask the court for a judgment directing the holdover lessee or licensee to vacate the premises. The statute does not authorize damages or any other form of relief other than this order.

XYZ, Inc., recently purchased a former military base in Alabama. However, there are three holdovers on the property. XYZ sues the three holdovers under the new federal statute. One of the defendants files a timely demand for a jury trial. XYZ and the other two defendants do not want a jury trial. They claim that a jury should not be impaneled if a majority of the parties do not want it. They also claim that even if the demand was proper, there is no right to a jury. Will the court empanel a jury in the case? _____

123. Same facts as Problem 122, except that the new federal statute creates another option. The statute creates a new federal agency to deal with the sale of federal lands. In addition to (or in lieu of) suing in court for an order to vacate, the new owner may sue the holdover before the agency to recover any damages suffered by the owner because of the delay in taking possession. The statute specifically provides that the agency will try the case without a jury.

XYZ brings a claim before the agency against the three defendants. Notwithstanding the language in the statute, one defendant insists that the claim be tried before a jury. Is a jury required for this case? _____

124. Pollack and Degas enter into a contract in which Pollack agrees to sell a painting to Degas. The parties negotiate the contract over the phone. Pollack describes the painting to Degas as a ''Manet.'' However, Degas thinks Pollack said ''Monet.'' When Degas discovers that the painting is not what he thought, he refuses to perform under the contract.

Degas sues Pollack in federal court, asking that the contract be rescinded because of mistake. Pollack denies that there was a mistake. Pollack also counterclaims for breach of contract, seeking $300,000 in damages. Degas files a timely demand for a jury trial, which Pollack contests. Will a jury be impaneled? If so, will it hear all of the issues in the case? _____

Answers

121. The nonunanimous verdict will stand. Although Fed. R. Civ. P. 48 generally requires a unanimous verdict, the parties may stipulate to a mere majority. Courts have upheld nonunanimous verdicts against Seventh Amendment challenges.

122. The court will impanel a jury. First, Fed. R. Civ. P. 38(b) provides that "any party" may demand a jury by filing a timely demand. A majority of the parties is not required. The facts also specify that the demand here was timely.

Second, the Seventh Amendment right to a jury trial does apply to this claim. Because the claim was created by statute, it will be analyzed using the two-part test. Under the first part of the test, the closet analogue is an order of ejectment. Although ejectment is a form of specific relief, it was historically legal, not equitable. Second, the form of relief — an order requiring someone in possession to vacate — is also legal because it is exactly the form of relief provided in common law ejectment actions. Because the claim is legal, a jury is required.

123. The case probably must be tried by a jury. Congress may allow an agency to adjudicate without a jury only if the case involves public rights. The right in question here — the right to force people to vacate privately owned land — is almost certainly a private, not a public, right. That the land was formerly used as a government base does not make the private owner's right a public right. Because the underlying claim (a suit for money damages) is indisputably legal, the case must be heard by a jury.

124. A jury will be impaneled. Because this case involves a mix of legal (damages) and equitable (rescission) claims, the jury will decide all issues that are relevant to the legal claim, even if that same issue comes up in the equitable claim. In this case, the jury will decide all of the main issues, including whether there is a valid contract (which includes the question of whether the contract is voidable for mistake), whether the contract, if valid, is breached, and damages. There really are no remaining issues that are unique to the rescission claim.

II. SELECTING JURORS

In every jury trial, the court must identify and notify potential jurors, command them to come to court, and weed out those with unacceptable knowledge of or bias toward the given case. Although the notion of a "jury of one's peers" is often held out as the ideal, there is **no positive right** to a jury of people who are "like" a litigant. On the other hand, litigants and jurors alike may object if certain groups are **intentionally excluded** from serving on a jury.

A. Overview: The process of selecting a jury comprises **two main stages**.

    1. Selecting the pool: The court identifies the universe of potential jurors. From that universe, the court selects, usually at random, a pool of jurors who are to be available for **jury duty** on a given day or days.

2. **Selecting the panel:** The court, usually with the help of the attorneys for the parties, *questions* the jurors to uncover their views and any potential bias. Attorneys may exclude jurors by exercising *two different types of challenges*.

    a. **Challenge for cause:** An attorney may exercise a challenge for cause against a juror who holds a *bias* toward one of the parties or the subject matter, or who has too much *prior knowledge* of the facts of the underlying dispute. In most courts, there is *no limit* to the number of challenges for cause an attorney may exercise.

    b. **Peremptory challenge:** An attorney may exercise a peremptory challenge against a juror who the attorney wants to exclude for reasons that would not support a challenge for cause. Unlike challenges for cause, there is a *limit* to the number of peremptory challenges that may be exercised.

B. Selecting the jury pool: The process of selecting the pool of jurors varies in certain significant ways among the various court systems. However, all systems strive to achieve the same basic end: to achieve a *broad cross-section* of those people in the jurisdiction who are *qualified to serve as jurors*.

1. **State courts:** There are notable differences among the states in defining qualifications to serve as a juror. States also employ different means for identifying jurors.

    a. **Qualifications:** The most commonly used qualifications for jury duty in the state courts are residency in the area, ownership of property, payment of taxes, and good health.

    b. **Identification of qualified jurors:** States use a number of different methods to identify those parties who are capable of sitting on a jury, including voting registration lists, driver's license information, telephone directories, property tax records, and personal references. Many states use multiple sources in order to ensure that qualified jurors are not left out.

    c. **Exclusions:** States typically exempt certain people from jury duty.

        i. **Automatic exclusion:** Some people are automatically exempted from jury duty based on their health or the nature of their occupation. For example, military, police, and fire personnel are often excluded because of the demands of their work. In addition, some (but not all) states automatically exempt *judges* and *attorneys* from jury duty because it is feared that they will unduly influence the other jurors.

        ii. **Exclusion by request:** Other jurors may seek exemption if jury duty poses an *undue hardship*. For example, an employee who is paid by the hour may be released from jury duty if the lost income during a long case would prove difficult to absorb.

2. **Federal courts:** The jury selection system in the federal courts was completely revamped in 1968. *28 U.S.C. §§1861-1871* now dictate how the basic process operates.

    a. **Qualifications:** *28 U.S.C. §1865* provides that a person is qualified to serve as a federal juror if she:

        i. is *a U.S. citizen*;

        ii. is *18 years of age or older*;

        iii. has *resided* for *one year* or more within the judicial district in which she will serve as a juror;

    iv. can read, write, and understand the ***English language*** to a degree sufficient to complete the juror qualification form;

    v. can ***speak*** the English language;

    vi. suffers from ***no mental or physical infirmity*** that would preclude her from rendering satisfactory service;

    vii. has ***no charge pending*** against her for the commission of a crime punishable by imprisonment for more than one year; and

    viii. has ***not been convicted*** in state or federal court of a crime punishable by imprisonment for more than one year, unless her civil rights have been restored.

b. Identification of qualified jurors: *28 U.S.C. §1863(b)* requires that the universe of jurors shall be gleaned from either ***voter registrations lists*** or ***lists of those actually voting*** and, if necessary to ensure the underlying goal of a ***fair cross-section of the community*** (28 U.S.C. §1861), additional sources of names. The additional sources include many of the same lists as those used by state courts. Names of potential jurors are then placed on a ***master jury wheel***.

c. Exclusions: *28 U.S.C. §1863(c)* allows people with certain characteristics to be excluded from the jury pool, according to definite standards.

    i. Automatic exclusions: *28 U.S.C. §1863(b)(6)* automatically excludes from jury duty military personnel, members of police and fire departments, and government officials who are actively engaged in the performance of their official duties.

    ii. Exclusion by request: The statute allows other groups to be excluded by request.

        (a) *28 U.S.C. §1863(b)(5)(B)* allows members of volunteer firefighter groups, volunteer rescue squads, and volunteer ambulance crews to request exclusion ***without the need to show hardship***.

        (b) *28 U.S.C. §1863(b)(5)(A)* allows each district to identify ***other groups*** and occupational classes, the members of which will be excluded provided that they demonstrate ***undue hardship or extreme inconvenience***.

        (c) *28 U.S.C. §1866(c)(1)* allows a court to excuse ***individuals*** who do not otherwise fall into the other groups but who nevertheless can demonstrate undue hardship or extreme inconvenience. However, exclusion under this provision is ***temporary***, lasting only as long as the hardship or inconvenience remains.

3. Constitutional restrictions in determining universe of jurors: Several provisions of the U.S. Constitution restrict a court's ability to exclude classes or people from jury duty.

a. The ***Equal Protection Clause*** prevents the government from discriminating in jury selection based on race, religion, national origin, and, to a more limited extent, age and gender.

b. The ***Seventh Amendment*** not only guarantees litigants a jury in certain cases, but also guarantees that the jury will represent a ***fair cross-section*** of the community. Although this does not guarantee any party in an individual case a jury composed of particular categories of people, it does guarantee all litigants that groups will not be excluded from juries without good reason.

Note: Because the Seventh Amendment does not apply to the states, a state may exclude certain classes of people from juries as long as the classes used do not discriminate in a way forbidden by the Equal Protection Clause. For example, a state is free to create a jury of "experts" to decide a complex case. Exclusion of nonexperts would not violate the Equal Protection Clause.

4. **Selection of pool:** Periodically, the court will select a pool of jurors from the universe of potential jurors to serve in upcoming cases.

   a. In federal courts and in most states, the pool is selected at *random*.

   b. Note that the constitutional issues discussed above do not apply to a jury pool selected at random. Thus, if a jury pool drawn at random turns out to comprise all men and no women, the parties cannot challenge the composition of the pool.

C. **Excluding jurors, formation of the panel:** The pool of jurors is narrowed to the actual panel that will hear a case through a process called *voir dire*. *Voir dire* involves questioning the jurors to determine their qualifications to sit in the actual case at hand.

   1. **Stages:** *Voir dire* typically happens in two stages. First, the entire pool is asked a series of general questions to determine if they know the parties or have any sort of a personal bias toward or stake in the outcome of the case. Second, questions are posed to individual jurors to determine other possible bases for challenge.

   2. **Who conducts questioning:** The mechanics of *voir dire* vary from court to court. In some courts, the attorneys bear the primary responsibility for questioning the jurors. In others, the court asks questions.

   3. **Challenges for cause:** Each party usually has an ***unlimited number*** of challenges for cause. Grounds justifying a challenge for cause include:

      a. an existing ***personal relationship*** with, or in some cases even knowledge of, the parties, their attorneys, the major witnesses, or the judge;

      b. that the potential juror is ***employed*** by one of the parties, or in some cases a person or organization closely affiliated with a party;

      c. a strong ***predisposition*** for or against one side based on reasons other than the law.

      ★
      Example: In Thompson v. Altheimer & Gray, 248 F.3d 621 (7th Cir. 2003), a case involving a claim of racial discrimination, a small business owner in the jury pool indicated that her prior experience would affect her judgment and that she believed that some people filed spurious claims against their employers. The court held that her answers were not grounds for a challenge for cause.

   4. **Peremptory challenges:** Each party has a ***limited*** number of peremptory challenges, which in most cases allow an attorney to exclude a juror ***without stating a reason***.

      a. **Number:** The number of peremptory challenges available to a party varies from system to system. In the ***federal courts***, each party is limited to ***three*** peremptory challenges. However, the court may deem coplaintiffs or codefendants to be a single party or may allow additional challenges as it sees fit. 28 U.S.C. §1870.

★   **b. Race- or gender-based challenges:** The Supreme Court has created a limited exception to the traditional rule that a party exercising a peremptory challenge does not need to state a reason for the challenge. If the court detects a pattern of excluding jurors based on their race, national origin, religion, or gender, the party may be required to justify the challenge by providing other, nonobjectionable reasons for the exclusion. Edmonson v. Leesville Concrete Co., 500 U.S. 614 (1991).

   i. Excluding a juror based on that juror's race, national origin, religion, age, or gender violates the juror's rights to *equal protection* under the Fourteenth Amendment.

   ii. If a party exhibits a *pattern* of excluding jurors who share one of these characteristics, that party will be required to justify excluding each of the jurors for some reason other than the characteristic.

   (a) Demonstrating a pattern: A pattern of wrongful exclusion may be demonstrated if, for example, a party exercises two of its three peremptory challenges on people with the characteristic. What is necessary to establish a pattern also turns on other factors, such as the total number of people with that characteristic in the jury pool.

   (b) Justifying exclusion: The party who exhibited the pattern need not show that he could have challenged the juror for cause. Instead, he merely needs to provide a *rational basis* for wanting to exclude the juror. Intelligence, attentiveness, and the like may well justify exclusion.

   iii. Challenging party need not share characteristic: The party challenging the exclusion of jurors need not share the characteristic in question. Thus, for example, an atheist could challenge the exclusion of Lutherans from the jury.

Quiz Yourself on
JUROR SELECTION

125. The federal District of Carolina has recently amended its plans for jury selection. Under the new plan, practicing attorneys are automatically excluded from the jury pool. The rationale is that an attorney would wield far too much influence on the other members of a jury. A group of attorneys challenges this plan, arguing that it does not comply with the federal statutes governing jury selection. Are the attorneys correct? _____

126. Kim, who is of Korean heritage, sues Jones in state court for defamation. Kim demands a jury trial.
        As is its usual procedure, the state court compiles a pool of potential jurors by drawing names completely at random. The pool of 100 jurors includes 55 people of Korean heritage. Kim and Jones are both shocked to discover this because people of Korean heritage make up only 3 percent of the people both in the district's population and on the court's master list of potential jurors. Kim immediately files a motion asking the court to select a new jury pool. Jones opposes the motion. First, Jones claims that because Kim cannot show prejudice by the particular composition, he cannot challenge the

jury. Second, Jones argues that even if Kim can challenge, the jury pool is constitutionally acceptable. Who should prevail? _____

127. Sneezy sues Doc in federal court for medical malpractice after Doc fails to cure Sneezy's serious cold. As the case nears trial, the parties begin to conduct their *voir dire*. The questioning soon reveals that one of the potential jurors, Marcus Welby, is a retired physician. However, in response to questions from Doc's attorney, Welby states that he was never sued for malpractice. Welby also insists that he can judge the case fairly. Sneezy tries to challenge Welby for cause, arguing that Welby is biased. Will Sneezy be able to exclude Welby? _____

Answers

125. The new plan does not comport with the federal statutes. 28 U.S.C. §1863(b)(6) automatically excludes certain government officials, but not attorneys. In addition, §§1863(b)(5)(A) and 1866 allow a district to exclude other individuals, but only on request and only on a showing of hardship. Because the vast majority of attorneys otherwise meet the eligibility requirements, the district cannot exclude them as a class.

126. Jones should prevail. Jones is wrong when she argues that Kim cannot challenge the jury. Any party may challenge the composition of the jury pool, even if that party is not a member of the group being excluded.

    However, Kim's challenge will fail on the merits. The Constitution bars only systematic exclusion of jurors. Because the jurors were chosen at random from a list that fairly represented the makeup of the district, the exclusion of non-Koreans was not systematic.

    Note that it does not matter that this action was filed in a state court. A juror's right to be free from systematic exclusion is based on the Equal Protection Clause, not the Seventh Amendment. The Equal Protection Clause binds the states.

127. It is unclear whether Sneezy will be able to exclude Welby. Some courts would allow the exclusion, but most would not. The *potential* for bias is obvious since Welby may be sympathetic to another doctor. The problem is that other than the fact both Doc and Welby are doctors, there is no objective indication of bias. Because he himself was never sued for malpractice — and now that he is retired will not be — Welby has no reason to be sympathetic to Doc's cause. Moreover, Welby has insisted that he can judge the case fairly. Nevertheless, some courts will find the commonality of experience enough to sustain a challenge for cause.

III. DISQUALIFICATION OF JUDGES FOR BIAS AND OTHER GROUNDS

Like jurors, judges can be barred from hearing a case in situations where they might be biased. In addition to allowing the parties to challenge a judge, governing law often requires a judge to recuse herself without motion.

   A. Federal courts: Congress has enacted two separate statutes dealing with the question of when a judge will be disqualified from hearing a matter, ***28 U.S.C. §§144 and 455.***

1. **No significant differences:** On the surface, §§144 and 455 look very different. Section 144 speaks only in general terms, while §455 provides a detailed list of when a judge should not serve. Nevertheless, the courts have basically *interpreted the provisions in the same way*. Common features include the following.

   a. **Same bases for disqualification:** Courts have interpreted the general language in §144 as encompassing all of the detailed provisions in §455. Therefore, the grounds for recusing a judge under each provision are the same.

   b. **Procedure:** Although §455, unlike §144, seems to require the judge to recuse himself, parties frequently make a motion under §455 to the judge asking for recusal.

2. **Grounds for disqualification:** The standards justifying recusal are set out in §455, which, as noted just above, have been interpreted to apply equally to §144. Section 455 lists certain specific reasons for disqualification, as well as a general catchall provision.

   a. **Specific grounds:** The specific grounds are set out in *§455(b)*. They include situations where:

      i. the judge has a *personal bias* or *personal knowledge of a party*;

      ii. the judge has *personal knowledge of the underlying facts*;

      iii. while in private practice, the judge, or a lawyer with whom the judge practiced, *worked on the matter in controversy*;

      iv. the judge, or a lawyer with whom the judge practiced, has been a *material witness* concerning the matter in controversy;

      v. while working as a government employee, the judge participated as *counsel, adviser, or material witness* in the proceeding, or expressed an opinion concerning the merits of the controversy;

      vi. the judge, his spouse, or a minor child living in the judge's household has a *financial interest* in the subject matter of the proceeding or one of the parties (for example, owning stock in one of the parties), or *any other interest* that might be affected; or

      vii. the judge, her spouse, or someone closely related (as defined in the statute) is a *party, lawyer*, or *witness* in the proceeding, or has an *interest* that could be *substantially affected* by the proceeding.

   b. **General grounds:** Section 455(a) provides that a judge must recuse himself from any proceeding "in which his *impartiality might reasonably be questioned*." For example, if the judge wrote a law review article advocating the position taken by one of the parties, her impartiality is open to question.

   ★   **Example:** The court applied the general grounds of §455(a) in In re Boston's Children First, 244 F.3d 164 (1st Cir. 2001). The court held that a judge should recuse herself for stating in public that a case before her was "more complex" than an earlier case, even though the judge made that statement in response to criticism from one of the party's attorneys.

   c. **Waiver:** If the parties waive disqualification after full disclosure, a judge who would be disqualified only under the general grounds of *§455(a)* may continue to sit in the case. However, if any of the grounds of *§455(b)* apply, **waiver is not allowed** and the judge must recuse herself.

B. State courts: Although the procedure differs, the grounds for disqualification of judges in most state systems mirror the grounds that apply in federal court.

Quiz Yourself on DETERMINING THE TRIER

128. After a long and tempestuous relationship, Scarlett finally decides to break off her engagement with Rhett. Rhett sues Scarlett in a state court. Rhett asks for an order requiring Scarlett to return the engagement ring he gave her or, in the alternative, damages for the value of the ring. Rhett also demands a jury trial. The trial judge denies a jury. Rhett immediately files a special appeal of the trial judge's ruling to the court of appeals, arguing that the Seventh Amendment requires a jury in this case. Will Rhett prevail? _____

129. Same basic facts as Problem 128, except that Scarlett sues Rhett before Rhett can sue her. Scarlett files her claim in federal court. She seeks a declaratory judgment stating that the ring was a gift and that she is accordingly not liable if she sells it. Thirty days later, Rhett files an answer that argues that Scarlett would be liable if she sold the ring. Three days after serving the answer, Rhett files and serves a written demand for a jury trial.

Scarlett argues that the case should be tried without a jury. First, she claims that Rhett did not satisfy the procedural rules dealing with jury demands. Second, she claims that even if the demand was proper, there is no right to a jury in this case. Who will prevail? _____

130. The reputation of corporate America has been sullied in the last few years by a series of questionable, and often illegal, acts by corporate executives. As quickly as legislatures have responded to these problems, shady executives have dreamed up other equally devious schemes.

One scheme that has only recently appeared is the supplemental insurance plan. Corporate employees are presented with an option to purchase additional health insurance above and beyond the meager plans offered by the employer. Unbeknownst to the employees, however, this insurance does not protect the employees, but instead pays for corporate executives to take long ''rest and recuperation'' stays at posh resorts.

Congress reacts to this scheme by enacting a new federal statute. This statute gives employees the right to sue their employers for pushing a supplemental insurance plan that misleads the employees into thinking that they, instead of the executives, will benefit. An employee who proves that an employer marketed a deceptive plan may recover all money she paid into the plan.

Several employees of Megacorp, Inc., sue the company in federal court under the new statute, seeking return of the money they paid into an insurance plan. Some of the plaintiffs also appear on *Oprah* and other talk shows, talking at great length about how they have been ''had'' by the corporate executives.

One of the employees files a second claim against Megacorp. This employee claims that he was demoted for arriving at work late one day. If true, that demotion would be illegal under federal labor laws. The employee asks the court to grant him the money he would have received had he not been demoted.

Megacorp files an answer denying liability. It argues that its plan was not deceptive because it clearly spelled out that the funds would be used for ''Executive health care.'' Megacorp also denies that the demotion of the one employee was in any way wrongful. Finally, Megacorp files a counterclaim, asking the court to enjoin the employees from defaming the corporation on talk shows.

The employees demand a jury. Megacorp argues that no jury should be impaneled in the case. Who will prevail? _____

131. Morris sues Jaatinen in federal court for extensive damage caused to a home that Morris had leased to Jaatinen. Jaatinen, a Finnish citizen who is spending a year in the United States, denies liability, claiming that the damage was caused in a storm. During *voir dire*, Morris exercises two of his three peremptory challenges against two jurors who emigrated to the United States from Finland. These two jurors, Nuutila and Korolainen, are the only two ex-Finns in the pool. Unlike Jaatinen, however, Nuutila and Korolainen are U.S. citizens. Jaatinen challenges the use of the peremptory challenges, demanding that Morris justify the exclusion. Will Morris be required to provide a justification?

_____

132. Same facts as Problem 131. Roberts is another potential juror in the pool. Roberts was walking along the street on the day the damage to the home occurred. When asked whether she saw how the damage to the home occurred, Roberts said that she had seen the entire event. However, neither Morris nor Jaatinen ask the juror to disclose *how* the damage had happened, for fear that the information might affect the other jurors.

Jaatinen exercises a challenge for cause against Roberts. Morris argues that a challenge for cause is inappropriate here because there is no showing of bias. How should the court rule?

_____

133. Judge Judy has been assigned to hear a products liability class action suit against ACME, Inc. Several months into the case, the plaintiff's attorney discovers that Judge Judy's husband owns a few shares of stock in ACME. It is clear, however, that Judge Judy does not know of her husband's stock. The plaintiff is considering asking Judge Judy to recuse herself from the case. However, plaintiff is not sure that the husband's stock is grounds for recusal and does not want to take the chance of irritating Judge Judy. If the plaintiff asks Judge Judy to recuse herself, is he likely to succeed?

_____

━━━━━━━

Answers

128. Rhett has not only lost Scarlett, but he will lose his appeal. Rhett's case is in a state court. The Seventh Amendment requires a jury only in federal court. Although the state constitution may also require a jury, Rhett relied only on the Seventh Amendment in his appeal.

129. Rhett will prevail. First, the Seventh Amendment provides a right to a jury in this case. Scarlett seeks the remedy of declaratory judgment, which by itself is neither legal nor equitable. To determine if there is a right to a jury in a case involving a declaratory judgment, one must ask what suit would

eventually occur if the suit for declaratory judgment was never filed. Here, had Scarlett not sued for a declaratory judgment, Rhett would have sued her after she sold the ring. Once the ring is gone, Rhett could ask only for damages. A suit for damages for wrongfully disposing of property is clearly legal. Therefore, Scarlett's suit for a declaratory judgment will be treated as a legal claim, and the Seventh Amendment will afford a right to a jury.

Second, Rhett's demand for a jury is procedurally proper. It is in writing, as required by Fed. R. Civ. P. 38. Moreover, Rhett filed and served his demand within 10 days of the answer. Rule 38 requires that the demand be served within 10 days after service of the "last pleading directed to the issue" that will be tried by a jury. Rhett's answer, which denies the allegations of Scarlett's complaint, is the last pleading directed to the legal issue.

130. A jury will be impaneled, but only on the wrongful demotion issue. To begin, it is important to note that the right to a jury trial applies to issues and claims, not necessarily the entire case. This case involves three basic claims.

Megacorp's injunction is the easiest claim. This claim is purely equitable, and by itself does not create a right to a jury.

The federal statutory claim is also equitable. There is no clear historical analogue. The closest analogue would be fraud, which could be heard in law or equity depending on the relief sought. Under part 2 of the test, however, the nature of the remedy is equitable. In essence, the employees are seeking restitution of the money they paid into the plan. The employees had the money and turned it over to the employer for a particular purpose. Restitution is an equitable remedy. Therefore, the statutory claim, by itself, does not require a jury.

The wrongful demotion claim is legal. Again, there is no clear analogue. However, the employee is clearly seeking damages — the money that he would have received had the employer not acted improperly. Therefore, the parties have a right to a jury trial on the wrongful demotion claim.

Because this case involves a mix of legal and equitable claims, the court must provide a jury for all issues involved in the legal claims. Therefore, a jury must hear all of the issues relating to the wrongful demotion claim. The jury will hear those issues even if they also arise in the equitable claims. Here, however, it is unlikely that the wrongful demotion claim shares any common issues with the two equitable claims. Therefore, the judge will decide all issues relating to the equitable claims.

131. Morris should be required to provide a justification. Morris's exclusion of the only two immigrants from Finland makes a *prima facie* case of discrimination based on national origin. Jaatinen can challenge that exclusion even though he is not necessarily in the same "class" as Nuutila and Korolainen. Morris should be required to come up with a colorable, national-origin-neutral reason for excluding the jurors.

132. Roberts will be excluded from the jury for cause. Any potential juror with personal knowledge of the facts of the case can be challenged for cause. The challenging party need not show that the juror is biased for or against him.

133. Judge Judy should recuse herself. The statutes make it clear that a financial interest of the judge or a spouse in the subject matter of the litigation is grounds for recusal. That Judge Judy does not know of the interest does not matter. The rule is designed to prevent not only actual bias but also the appearance of bias. Besides, once the plaintiff makes the motion, Judge Judy will learn of the interest.

Exam Tips on *DETERMINING THE TRIER*

☛ If a question asks whether a case will be tried before a jury, you should always consider both the *procedural* and the *constitutional* aspects.

☛ Do not forget that the Seventh Amendment applies only in federal court.

☛ Even if the Seventh Amendment guarantees a right to a jury in a particular case, a party must still make a timely demand for a jury trial. The time period for demanding a jury is fairly short: only 10 days following the service of the last pleading directed to the issue.

☛ When analyzing a problem under the Seventh Amendment, it is crucial to have a solid understanding of the various types of remedies, as well as the various equitable claims and procedural devices.

  ☞ First, you must know which remedies, claims, and devices are legal and which are equitable. The only way to learn this is by rote. Be especially careful of ejectment and replevin, which look like equitable remedies but are legal.

  ☞ To apply the test for statutory remedies, you must also understand the general characteristics of each of the remedies.

☛ **Statutory rights:** Although the test for new statutory rights has two parts, the second, which looks to the nature of the remedy, is more important than the first.

☛ **Equitable procedures:** If a case involves a procedure that historically existed only in equity, your analysis should ignore the procedure at first. If the party is bringing a legal claim, but brings it using an equitable procedural device, there is a right to a jury trial.

☛ **Joinder of legal and equitable claims in single action:** When legal and equitable claims are joined in a single case, it is important to remember that the Seventh Amendment requires a jury on *issues*, not for the entire case. The basic rule is that the party receives a jury on all issues relevant to all the legal claims. Only any residual issues that relate solely to the equitable claim or claims will be decided by the judge.

☛ Congress can sometimes bypass the jury trial requirement by sending a case involving legal claims to an agency. However, before concluding that the case can be tried without a jury, make sure that all three parts of the test are satisfied.

☛ When dealing with *selection of the jury*, recall that there are two distinct phases.

  ☞ In the first phase, narrowing the universe to the pool, the primary considerations are to identify as many potential jurors as possible and to select the actual pool in a way that limits systematic exclusion of people based on their characteristics.

  ☞ In the second phase, selecting the actual panel, make sure you have a solid grasp of the reasons a juror may be excluded for cause.

    ☞ Because peremptory challenges usually do not require a reason, it is difficult to craft an exam question dealing with them. However, a peremptory challenge can be questioned if it appears to be done for improper reasons. Therefore, if a question involves a peremptory challenge, you should consider whether it deals with exclusion of jurors based on race, national origin, religion, gender, or other objectionable characteristics.

☞ The rules governing disqualification of judges are fairly detailed. In addition to the specific grounds for objection, do not forget that 28 U.S.C. §455(a) allows a judge to be excluded in any case in which her impartiality might be called into question.

Chapter 11

THE TRIAL

ChapterScope ──────────────────────────────

This chapter explores various issues that may arise during the trial of a civil case. The main focus is on *jury trials*, which present special complications. The chapter discusses ways for the court to deal with improper influences on the jury and erroneous jury verdicts.

- Courts have a number of tools at their disposal to prevent the jury from being influenced by *untrustworthy evidence* or *improper argument*. In addition to the *rules of evidence*, there are rules dealing with attorneys who make *prejudicial arguments* and jurors who attempt to conduct their own *investigation*.

- Before sending the jury out to decide the case, the court provides detailed *jury instructions* that inform the jury of the governing legal rules. Some states and the federal courts also give the judge some leeway to *comment* on the evidence.

- If the evidence presented at trial overwhelmingly favors one side, the court may decide the case itself by entering *judgment as a matter of law* rather than sending the case to the jury. In the alternative, the judge may decide to let the jury go ahead and decide the case, but render judgment as a matter of law *after the verdict* if the jury reaches the incorrect result.

- If the trial goes awry, the judge may also grant a *new trial*. New trials are available in two basic situations:

  - in situations where a verdict is against the *great weight of the evidence* (this gives the judge a less drastic option than rendering judgment as a matter of law); and

  - in situations where a *procedural error* occurred that may have prejudiced the outcome of the case.

- In some jurisdictions, it can be difficult for a party seeking a new trial to *use juror testimony* to attack a verdict.

I. PREVENTING IMPROPER INFLUENCE ON THE JURY

Although a jury in theory represents the "voice of the community," it decides cases in a very controlled environment. The jury may consider only the evidence submitted to it at trial. Restrictions control what sort of evidence can be submitted to the jury. After hearing the evidence, the jury is then instructed in the legal principles that should be used to decide the case.

A. Rules of Evidence: The Rules of Evidence significantly limit the sorts of information that may be presented to a jury. As Evidence is its own course, a detailed discussion of the Rules of Evidence is beyond the scope of this outline. However, a few general principles may be useful.

1. **Relevant evidence:** A party may use only relevant evidence. Whether information is relevant depends on the form of the evidence and the purpose for which it is to be used. See Fed. R. Evid. 401 et seq.

2. **Hearsay evidence:** The Rules of Evidence place significant limits on the use of hearsay evidence. Generally speaking, hearsay is an *extrajudicial statement* that is offered *to prove the truth of the matter asserted*. Fed. R. Evid. 801(c). Although as a general rule hearsay evidence is not admissible, there are many situations in which it may be used. Fed. R. Evid. 803 and 804.

3. **Judicial notice:** A court may take judicial notice of certain matters that are either generally known or capable of being determined with relative ease. If a court takes judicial notice of a fact, no evidence need be introduced concerning that fact.

B. **Juror experimentation:** One of the jury's roles is to determine whether evidence is *credible*. However, the jury cannot conduct its own tests to determine whether testimony is accurate. Juror investigation is grounds for a new trial. On the other hand, a juror is expected to use his or her own life experience in evaluating evidence. *When the knowledge was acquired* distinguishes permissible knowledge from impermissible knowledge.

1. **Before trial:** A juror may use knowledge acquired before trial. To the extent that the knowledge produces a bias in the juror, it is up to the parties to discover that bias during *voir dire*.

2. **During trial:** On the other hand, all information that the jury acquires during trial must come from the parties. If one side introduces false or misleading evidence, it is up to the other side to counter it.

   Example: While sitting on his patio, *P* is injured by a flying rock. *P* concludes that the rock was ejected by his neighbor's lawn mower. *P* sues *D*, the lawn mower manufacturer, for his injuries. *D* offers the testimony of an expert witness, who asserts that the particular model of lawn mower could not possibly have propelled the rock that great a distance. Two jurors have knowledge that contradicts this testimony. Juror *X* recalls an article discussing the dangers of lawn mowers that she read in a magazine several months prior to trial. *X* recalls that several lawn mowers were capable of propelling rocks a distance at least as great as that in question. However, *X* cannot recall whether *D*'s lawn mower was one of those tested. During a break in the trial, *Y* goes home and performs his own test with his lawn mower, which is the same model as that which caused *P*'s injury. Only juror *Y*'s conduct is grounds for a new trial. Even though *Y*'s knowledge may be more reliable, it was acquired during trial.

C. **Attorney misconduct:** Although an attorney is supposed to represent her client, certain conduct goes too far and may result in a new trial. An attorney cannot supplement the testimony with her own facts or comment on the evidence. Nor may an attorney make an *improper appeal to sympathy*, or ask the jurors to *picture themselves in the party's situation*.

D. **Instructions:** Once the evidence is presented, the court instructs the jury as to the law to use in deciding the case. The instructions state both the legal standards that apply to the various claims and defenses and the logical sequence that the jury should follow in deciding the case. For example, in a case where the plaintiff alleges negligence and the defendant contributory negligence, the judge will describe both the standard for determining negligence and the consequences of finding one or both parties negligent.

1. **Drafting the instructions:** Although the judge actually delivers the instructions to the jury, she usually solicits proposed instructions from the parties. Many jurisdictions have adopted *form instructions* for use in standard types of cases.

2. **Objections:** The parties may review the proposed instructions before they are submitted to the jury and may object to any items in the instructions. Fed. R. Civ. P. 51.

E. **Judicial commentary:** Some jurisdictions give the judge a limited authority to comment on the evidence. Federal courts, in particular, give the judge considerable leeway in this regard.

II. JUDGMENT AS A MATTER OF LAW

A jury has a role to play only when the facts are in dispute. When it is clear from the evidence that one side should prevail, the judge may effectively take the case from the jury by entering judgment as a matter of law (JML). *Fed. R. Civ. P. 50.*

A. **When available:** A party may move for JML either *before the case is submitted to the jury* or *after a verdict is returned*.

1. **Terminology:** Current Fed. R. Civ. P. 50 uses the term "judgment as a matter of law" to describe *both the preverdict and postverdict judgments*. Prior to 1991, different terms were used for the two motions. Many states still use the old terminology.

   a. The **preverdict** JML is sometimes referred to as a *directed verdict*. Notwithstanding the term, the judge does not "direct" the jury how to decide the case, but simply enters judgment.

   b. The **postverdict** JML is sometimes referred to as a *judgment notwithstanding the verdict* or *JNOV* (from the Latin "judgment *non obstante veredicto.*") As the name suggests, the judge enters a judgment that ignores the jury verdict.

2. **Timing of preverdict JML motion:** Although Fed. R. Civ. P. 50(a) allows a motion for preverdict JML to be made "at any time" before the case is submitted to the jury (Fed. R. Civ. P. 50(a)(2)), it also specifies that JML cannot be granted on a particular claim or defense unless the opposing party *has been fully heard* on that issue. Fed. R. Civ. P. 50(a)(1). Therefore, in practice such motions are filed at two stages.

   a. A *defendant* often files a motion for JML at the *close of plaintiff's case*.

   b. *Both parties* may file a motion for JML at the *close of all the evidence*.

3. **Timing of postverdict JML motion:** A motion for JML after the verdict must be filed within *10 days after entry of judgment*. Fed. R. Civ. P. 50(b).

   a. This 10-day period *cannot be extended.* Fed. R. Civ. P. 6(b).

   b. A party cannot take action to collect or enforce a judgment until after this 10-day period expires. Fed. R. Civ. P. 62(a).

   c. The reason the motion occurs "after entry of judgment" is Fed. R. Civ. P. 58, which requires the clerk to enter judgment "forthwith" following receipt of the verdict.

4. **Preverdict JML motion as prerequisite to postverdict JML:** In the federal courts, and in most of the states whose rules are based on the Federal Rules of Civil Procedure, a party may

not seek a postverdict JML unless she filed a motion for JML ***at the close of all the evidence***. Fed. R. Civ. P. 50(b).

    a. "Renewed" motion: The rule creates a legal fiction: Even if the judge explicitly denies the preverdict motion, she is "considered" to have reserved decision on the motion. The party then "renews" the motion after the verdict and judgment.

    b. Rationale: This technical rule evolved because of the Seventh Amendment right to a jury trial. The common law courts allowed directed verdicts but did not permit a judge to overturn a verdict. Treating the judgment notwithstanding the verdict as a "delayed" ruling on the directed verdict motion avoids this constitutional problem.

  5. New trial motion as alternative: Fed. R. Civ. P. 50(b) allows a party moving for a postverdict JML to join a motion for new trial in the alternative. How the court deals with these alternate motions is discussed in Part III.

B. Standard: The standard for granting a JML is that ***no rational jury*** could find for the party opposing the motion.

  1. Preverdict and postverdict compared: Although the ***standard is identical*** for a preverdict and a postverdict JML motion, in practice it is more difficult to prevail on a postjudgment JML. After all, the judge in that case is faced with a jury verdict that decides precisely what a party is claiming "no reasonable jury" could decide.

  2. Summary judgment compared: Logically, the "no reasonable jury" standard used for JML motions is similar to the "no genuine issue of material fact" standard used for summary judgment (which is discussed in Chapter 9). However, there is one crucial practical difference. Because the judge considering a JML has ***seen and heard live witnesses***, she is allowed more leeway to ***weigh the evidence*** and ***gauge credibility***. Even if there is evidence on both sides, it may be that no reasonable jury could decide for one of the parties if the evidence is overwhelmingly one-sided.

C. Applying the standard: Although a full appreciation for how courts apply the "no reasonable jury" standard can come only from a review of the case law, certain themes appear in the cases.

  1. Basic principles: Courts have established basic guidelines for applying this "no reasonable jury" standard.

    a. Court's power limited: Although the court may ***weigh evidence***, its power is limited. If there is substantial evidence on both sides, the court must deny the motion for JML and let the jury weigh the evidence.

★   **b. Jury determines credibility:** Similarly, the judge should leave most ***credibility determinations*** to the jury. A judge may disbelieve a witness's testimony only if the witness is completely unbelievable, either because his tale is internally inconsistent or because he was completely contradicted in cross-examination or by the testimony of other witnesses. See Pennsylvania Railroad v. Chamberlain, 288 U.S. 333 (1933) (although plaintiff's eyewitness's testimony was directly on point, it was impossible to believe given the distance and angle from which the witness viewed the event; therefore, given that the defendant had a number of witnesses who contradicted the testimony, JML for defendant was appropriate).

    c. Issues within the province of the jury: Some issues are considered particularly appropriate for jury determination. One example is ***negligence***. A court is much less likely to grant JML on the issue of whether defendant acted reasonably than it is on other issues in the case.

  2. The problem of inferences: As in summary judgment, one of the more difficult issues is when proffered evidence does not directly establish a crucial fact but instead asks the factfinder to draw an inference. The basic principles are the same in JML as in summary judgment. See Chapter 9, Part V.D.1 for a discussion of these issues.

  3. The importance of the burden of production: Applying the "no reasonable jury" standard requires consideration of the burden of production. Again, the basic issues are the same in JML as in summary judgment. See Chapter 9, Part V.D.2.b for a detailed discussion. However, application of these principles differs slightly in JML. Because a judge has more authority to weigh evidence and gauge credibility in JML, she has somewhat more authority to rule that a party has failed to meet his burden of production.

★   **Example:** Reid v. San Pedro, Los Angeles & Salt Lake R.R., 39 Utah 617 (1911), is a classic illustration of an inference problem. Plaintiff sued the railroad when her cow was killed on railroad tracks. There were three possible ways the cow could have gone from the pasture to the tracks: through one of two open gates (in which case the owner would bear the loss) or through a break in the fence (in which case the railroad would be liable). The cow was closer to the gates than the break. The court held that because the inference that the cow came through the gates was just as likely — if not more likely — than the inference that she came through the break, JML for defendant was appropriate. *P* had the burden of production and had failed to provide any evidence from which a jury could reasonably infer that the cow came through the break.

III. NEW TRIALS

In certain situations, a judge has the authority to order a case to be tried again before a new jury. A new trial can serve as a less drastic alternative to a JML. In addition, a new trial can cure a case that was tainted by procedural defects or misconduct.

  A. Basic principles: Most new trials are obtained pursuant to ***Fed. R. Civ. P. 59***.

    1. Timing: A motion for a new trial under Rule 59 must be filed within ***10 days after entry of the judgment***.

      a. This 10-day period ***cannot be extended.*** Fed. R. Civ. P. 6(b).

      b. A party cannot collect or enforce a judgment until this 10-day period expires. Fed. R. Civ. P. 62(a).

      c. A party may move for JML and a new trial in the alternative. How a court deals with such a motion is discussed below.

    2. New trials under Rule 60(b): In addition to Fed. R. Civ. P. 59, a party may also be able to obtain a new trial under Rule 60(b). The time limit for obtaining relief under Fed. R. Civ. P. 60(b) is at least a year, and more in some situations. However, Rule 60 motions are rarely granted. Rule 60 relief is discussed in Chapter 13, Part V.A.

  B. Two categories of new trial: Fed. R. Civ. P. 59 allows a court to grant a new trial "for any of the reasons for which new trials have heretofore been granted in actions at law in the courts of the

United States.'' Logically, there are two distinct categories of situations in which courts will grant a new trial.

1. The first category is when the jury clearly **reached the wrong conclusion**.

2. The second category is when a **serious procedural error** occurred during the trial.

C. New trial to cure erroneous jury verdicts: If a judge is convinced that the jury has reached the wrong result, he can order a new trial.

    1. Standard: A judge may grant a new trial when she determines that a jury verdict is **against the great weight of the evidence**.

    2. JML compared: This standard is **significantly easier to satisfy** than the ''no reasonable jury'' standard that applies in JML cases. The new trial standard by its very nature envisions that the judge can weigh the evidence. By the same token, the judge may **evaluate credibility** to a certain extent. A court is therefore more likely to grant a new trial than a JML.

★   **Caveat:** Nevertheless, the standard is **great weight** of the evidence. If the evidence is close, or even somewhat in favor of the party who lost the jury verdict, the court should deny the new trial motion and let the verdict stand. See Lind v. Schenley Industries, 278 F.2d 79 (3d Cir. 1960), where the court of appeals reversed the trial judge's grant of a new trial, finding that the judge had improperly substituted his interpretation for that of the jury.

    3. Combined JML/new trial motion: Because the new trial based on the weight of the evidence attempts to deal with the same basic problem as a JML, a party may want to bring both motions: hoping for a judgment in his favor, but willing to settle for a new trial as a second-best alternative. Fed. R. Civ. P. 50(b) accordingly allows a party to ask for both a JML and a new trial in a single motion. The new trial motion is a motion in the **alternative**.

        a. Court must decide both: Although granting a JML makes the new trial motion moot, **Fed. R. Civ. P. 50(c) requires the judge to rule on both**, even if the judge grants the JML. In such a case, the ruling on the new trial is treated as **conditional**.

        Note: The purpose of this requirement is to save time on appeal. If the appellate court reverses the JML, it is inefficient to remand, have the judge rule on the new trial motion, and possibly have another appeal. Requiring the conditional ruling on the new trial motion allows the court of appeals to deal with both.

        b. Application of standards: Because the ''great weight of the evidence'' standard that applies to new trials is easier to satisfy than the standard used for JML, a judge who grants a JML will also **ordinarily grant the conditional new trial**. However, this is **not always the case**. If the judge finds, for example, that plaintiff's only evidence on a certain point calls for an impermissible inference, she will grant a JML. However, if the court of appeals determines that the inference *is* permissible, the evidence that was presented at trial would be enough to sustain the verdict, and a new trial would be unnecessary.

        c. New trial sought by winner: Fed. R. Civ. P. 50(d) allows a party who survives his opponent's JML motion to ask for a new trial if his opponent appeals. Thus, if the court of appeals decides that the evidence overwhelmingly favored the opponent, it may nevertheless grant a new trial to the winner because of procedural problems that occurred at trial.

D. New trial to cure procedural defects: The second main reason for granting a new trial is because procedural errors occurred at trial.

    1. Prejudice required: No trial is ever perfect. Minor errors that occur during the trial process are not grounds for a new trial. Instead, the party must show that the error *prejudiced* him by possibly changing the outcome of the case.

    2. Objection usually required: In addition, a party who fails to make a *timely objection* to the court waives the error. However, in rare cases of "clear error," a party need not object. A clear error is an error committed by the court that is so blatant that it suggests the judge is biased.

    3. Common situations: New trials are often granted for:

        a. improper admission or exclusion of *testimony or other evidence*;

        b. outside influences on the jury, including news stories that discuss the case in depth and juror experimentation;

        c. prejudicial or improper arguments by one or both attorneys;

        d. improper commentary on the evidence by the judge; and

        e. improper deliberations, including failure to reach a unanimous decision (when required) or a "quotient verdict," where the jurors derive the damage figure by agreeing to the average of the amounts submitted by the jurors.

    4. Use of juror testimony to prove procedural error: Many procedural errors occur in the courtroom and therefore are easily demonstrated. Showing outside influence on the jury or errors in the deliberation process, however, usually requires the use of juror testimony. To protect jurors from harassment after the trial, many jurisdictions limit the use of juror testimony to challenge a verdict.

        a. Most courts allow the attorneys for the parties to *poll* the jury by asking questions of individual jurors. However, the attorneys may not harass or criticize the jurors.

        b. Obtaining the information from the jurors is not the same as being able to use it. Courts differ significantly in the extent to which a party may *use juror testimony to impeach a verdict*. There are three main approaches.

            i. Common law rule: Under the common law rule, a party cannot use a juror's testimony to impeach the verdict under any circumstances.

            ii. Federal rule: In the federal courts and some states, a party cannot use juror testimony to impeach except to the extent the testimony deals with *extraneous prejudicial information* or *outside influence*. Fed. R. Evid. 606(b).

            ★   **Example:** In Peterson v. Wilson, 141 F.3d 573 (5th Cir. 1998), the court applied the federal rule and held that juror testimony could not be used to prove that the jury had ignored the judge's instructions.

            iii. Iowa rule: Under the so-called Iowa rule, which is in force in a number of states, juror testimony can be used to prove *overt acts* but not matters that cannot be perceived through the senses.

Example: During polling, the attorney for *D* discovers that the damages award was the product of a quotient verdict. Under the common law and federal rules, the party cannot use the juror's testimony to impeach the verdict on that basis. Under the Iowa rule, by contrast, the party can use the juror's testimony because the use of the quotient verdict is something that can be perceived through the senses. Under any of the approaches, the attorney can use other evidence (such as slips of paper in the wastebasket) to prove the quotient verdict.

E. Partial and conditional new trials: Courts may limit a new trial to one or more issues instead of the entire case. In addition, a court may grant a conditional new trial, in which case no new trial is held if the verdict winner agrees to a modification of the verdict.

1. **Partial new trials:** In many cases, the defect at trial does not affect all of the issues in the case. For example, the improper introduction of evidence may affect one claim but not others in the case. Or it may be that although the evidence supporting liability is overwhelming, the damages award is against the great weight of the evidence. In these cases, the court may limit the new trial to the affected issues.

   Caveat: Some courts are unwilling to grant a new trial on the issue of liability alone, under the theory that the juror's determination of damages invariably affected its decision as to laibility. See, e.g., Doutre v. Niec, 2 Mich. App. 88 (1965).

2. **Conditional new trials:** A court may also make its grant of a new trial conditional. In some cases, if the verdict winner agrees to a modification of the judgment, the court dispenses with a new trial and enters a judgment for the modified amount.

   a. **When used:** Conditional new trials are most often used when the *damages* awarded by the jury are against the great weight of the evidence.

   b. **Remittitur and additur:** Courts often distinguish between cases of remittitur and additur.

      i. *Remittitur:* Remittitur occurs when the jury returns an *excessive* award. The jury grants defendant's motion for a new trial unless plaintiff agrees to reduce the damages award.

      ii. *Additur:* Additur is the logical converse of remittitur. It occurs when the verdict is *too low*. If defendant agrees to an augmented damages figure, no new trial will occur.

         Note: *Additur is unavailable in a federal court*. It has been found to violate the Seventh Amendment right to a jury trial. Remittitur, however, is available in federal court.

      iii. **The modified verdict:** Courts differ on how to calculate the proper damages figure in additur and remittitur. For example, in cases of remittitur, most courts hold that the damages should be the *highest figure* that does not go against the great weight of the evidence. Other judges determine for themselves what a reasonable award is.

   c. **Appeal:** A verdict winner who accepts the condition, and thereby avoids a new trial, normally may not appeal the modified judgment. The verdict loser may appeal, however, because her new trial motion was denied.

Quiz Yourself on
THE TRIAL

134. Chris Client sues Barry Sterr in federal court for attorney malpractice. Chris calls five experts, all of who are experienced and well-known in the field. The experts uniformly agree that Barry acted unreasonably. Barry calls only one expert, who is not nearly as experienced. The witness contradicts himself several times on the stand and is unable to answer several simple questions.

   Before the judge sends the jury out to deliberate, she talks to the jury about Barry's expert. The judge points out the many inconsistencies in the expert's testimony. The judge closes by saying, "Personally, were I on the jury, I'd be much more inclined to believe plaintiff's witnesses than defendant's." Barry fumes but says nothing. The jury returns a verdict for Chris, and Barry files immediately for a new trial. Will the court grant Barry's motion for a new trial? _____

135. Same facts as Problem 134, except that Barry objects to the judge's comment when it is made. The objection is denied. Will the court grant Barry's motion for a new trial? _____

136. You are the attorney for the plaintiff in a case in federal court. Your client's office building burned to the ground in a fire, and you brought suit on his behalf against the company that produced the sprinklers for the building. After a long trial, you are disappointed when the jury returns a verdict in favor of the other side.

   Less than one-half hour after you leave the courtroom, you run into one of the jurors in the courthouse coffee shop. In casual conversation, you learn that one of the other jurors was confused by the expert testimony offered in the case. Therefore, during a recess in trial, this other juror researched the matter further on the Internet. The juror shared what he learned with the other members, which turned many of them to defendant's side.

   Armed with this information, you immediately ask the court for a new trial. Defendant opposes your motion. Defendant claims that this casual conversation cannot be used as grounds for a new trial. In addition, defendant claims that you acted unethically in talking to the juror without the judge's permission after the trial. Is your motion for a new trial likely to succeed? _____

137. Norton and Kramden are neighbors in a large apartment building. Norton sues Kramden for nuisance, claiming that Kramden makes far too much noise. At trial, Norton introduces only one witness, a person who lives in an apartment building across the street. Although this person has never been in the building where Norton and Kramden live, she testifies that she has on many occasions heard loud voices emanating from their building.

   When Norton is done presenting his case, Kramden moves for judgment as a matter of law. The judge denies the motion. Kramden then introduces several witnesses who testify that he is as silent as a church mouse. The jury returns a verdict for Norton, and Kramden immediately moves for judgment as a matter of law. How should the court rule? _____

138. Same facts as Problem 137, except that Kramden makes another motion for judgment as a matter of law at the close of his own case. That second motion is also denied. Three days after judgment is entered for Norton on the verdict, Kramden files yet again for JML. How should the court rule? _____

139. Consider again the basic dispute in Problem 137. This time, however, Norton does not call any third-party witnesses. Instead, he himself takes the stand. Norton testifies that on certain specified dates he heard Kramden making loud noises in his apartment. Kramden calls a dozen witnesses, all of whom testify that on the dates in question Kramden was either not at home or was as quiet as a church mouse.

Kramden moves for judgment as a matter of law at the close of all the evidence. The court denies the motion and sends the case to the jury. The jury returns a verdict for Norton and judgment is entered. Three days later, Kramden moves for judgment as a matter of law, or in the alternative a new trial. Norton responds by arguing that the jury verdict should stand. Norton also argues that the motion for new trial is not procedurally proper. Although Norton admits that the motion for judgment as a matter of law is timely, he argues that Kramden may not move for a new trial because he did not make such a motion before the case was submitted to the jury.

How is the court likely to rule?¨ _____

140. Rita is a meter maid with the city police force. Although her evaluations have been excellent, Rita is fired from the force during a round of budget cuts. Rita sues Connie Stable, the chief of police, claiming that state civil rights laws give her the right to a hearing prior to termination.

The state civil rights law provides a ''good faith immunity'' in cases like this. According to the statute, ''an official can be held liable for a civil rights violation only if he or she knew that his or her actions were illegal.'' At trial, Rita proves beyond a doubt that she did not receive a hearing. However, neither party offers any evidence concerning whether Connie knew that firing Rita without notice and a hearing was illegal.

Rita and Connie both move for judgment as a matter of law at the close of all the evidence. Will the court grant either motion? _____

━━━━━━━━━━

Answers

134. The court will deny Barry's motion because he did not object to the judge's statement when it was made.

135. Although Barry has now preserved his objection, he is not likely to win a new trial. A judge in a federal case has a limited power to comment on the evidence. Admittedly, the judge may have gone too far by telling the jury how she would decide. On the other hand, the comment was likely harmless error. Given Chris's strong evidence, the jury probably would have found for him notwithstanding the judge's comment.

136. The motion for a new trial is likely to succeed. First, there is nothing wrong with talking to a juror after trial, provided that you do not harass the juror. This casual conversation certainly is not harassment. Second, the information that the juror conveyed to you is grounds for a new trial. It is reversible error for a juror to conduct his or her own research on the matters being litigated. Third, although the only way you can prove the research is through juror testimony, you will be able to use juror testimony in this situation. The case was litigated in federal court. Under Fed. R. Evid. 606(b), a party can use juror testimony to prove extraneous outside information.

137. Kramden's motion should be denied. In order to move for JML after the verdict, a party must have moved for JML at the close of all the evidence. Kramden made his motion at the close of plaintiff's case.

138. Now Kramden will prevail. He made a motion for JML at the close of all the evidence, preserving his right to move again after the verdict. He made the motion within 10 days following entry of judgment. Fed. R. Civ. P. 50 does not set a limit on the number of times a party may move for JML.

The court should also overturn the jury verdict. Norton has the burden of production. He does have evidence of loud noises. But that evidence requires an inference: namely, that it was Kramden making the noise. Given that the parties live in a "large apartment building," it is much more likely that the loud noises came from someone else. Therefore, because the inference that Kramden made the noise cannot be allowed, Norton has no evidence on a crucial element of his claim.

139. The court will probably deny JML but grant the new trial. First, the new trial motion is timely. Although a party cannot move for a postverdict JML without a prior motion at the close of all the evidence, Fed. R. Civ. P. 59 does not impose a similar requirement for new trial motions.

The court should deny JML. True, the evidence is fairly one-sided. There is also strong reason to doubt the veracity of Norton's self-serving testimony. Nevertheless, the evidence is inherently believable and calls for no inferences. The court has only a limited power to judge credibility when considering JML. A reasonable jury could believe Norton and disbelieve the twelve opposing witnesses.

However, the court should grant a new trial. The verdict, although within the realm of reason, is against the great weight of the evidence. Here, the judge has a greater authority to gauge credibility and can consider the self-serving nature of Norton's testimony.

140. Judgment as a matter of law is appropriate. However, it is not clear in whose favor judgment will be entered. The outcome depends on the burden of production. If Rita had the burden of coming forth with evidence to show that Connie knew her acts were illegal, then the court should grant the motion because Rita has no evidence on a crucial element. However, if Connie has the burden of coming forth with evidence showing that she did *not* know, then JML for Rita is appropriate because the facts indicate that she has conclusive evidence on the other elements of her claim. From the quoted language, it is not clear which party has the burden of production on this issue.

Exam Tips on
THE TRIAL

☞ If an exam question deals with ***procedural errors***, make sure the alleged error could have had an impact on the trial. A harmless error is not grounds for reversal.

☞ The issue of outside juror knowledge is one of the most vexing in juror qualification. Generally, only outside knowledge obtained during the proceeding is grounds for a new trial. Knowledge obtained before the proceeding may be grounds for a challenge for cause, but usually does not result in a new trial.

☞ When dealing with ***judgments as a matter of law***, you must determine who has the burden of production on the claim or defense. The analysis differs depending on whether the movant has the burden.

☞ A party must have made a motion for JML at the ***close of all the evidence*** in order to move for JML after the jury returns with a verdict.

☞ Problems involving inferences are common on law school examinations. Although there are rarely absolute right or wrong answers, make sure that you are being reasonable when you determine whether an inference can be allowed.

☞ One issue that students tend to find particularly difficult is the ***combined motion for judgment as a matter of law and new trial motion***. Many students try to memorize all the possible outcomes (for example, denying JML but granting NT). You will find the issue much easier if you simply work through each of the four possibilities and determine what the court of appeals would do.

☞ A judge who is considering a motion to grant a new trial because the verdict is against the great weight of the evidence has some ability to weigh the evidence presented in the case. However, she should not simply substitute her opinion for that of the jury.

☞ Recall that the 10-day limits for a postverdict motion for JML and new trial cannot be extended.

CHAPTER 12

APPEALS

ChapterScope ━━

This chapter deals with appeals, the process by which court decisions are reviewed by a higher court. The discussion focuses almost exclusively on appeals in the ***federal system***.

- Not every trial court ruling can be reviewed. There are firm limits on what issues can be appealed, when an appeal may take place, and how much deference the appellate court must give to the lower court's decision.

- In the federal courts, an appellate court's power to hear a case is defined by statute. There is also a separate set of rules, the ***Federal Rules of Appellate Procedure***, that apply to appeals.

- Only someone who lost in the court below may appeal. However, the concept of "losing" a suit is quite flexible. Even a party who prevails may be able to appeal if the victory is not as complete as she would have liked.

- A party may waive the right to appeal a particular issue.

- The most significant limitation on appeals from the federal trial courts is the ***final judgment rule***. Generally speaking, a party may not appeal until the lower court has completely resolved the case.

  - However, there are several ***exceptions*** to the final judgment rule. Some of these exceptions are set out in the statutes and rules, while one is court-created.

  - A party may also be able to avoid the final judgment rule by seeking review under a special writ such as ***mandamus*** or ***prohibition***.

- Once a case is properly presented to the appellate court, that court must consider its ***scope of review***. The appellate court's power to upset a trial court's ruling depends on whether the issue being reviewed is one of ***fact*** or one of ***law***.

I. DETERMINING WHAT ISSUES MAY BE APPEALED

Appeals courts do not exist to ensure a perfect result in every case. Instead, their role is to correct any mistakes made by the trial court that negatively affected one or more parties. Therefore, a party cannot appeal an issue unless that issue was resolved *adversely* to the party's interests. In addition, a party who fails to give the trial court the chance to rectify the problem ordinarily cannot appeal.

- **A. Adversity:** Of course, a party who loses the case may appeal. But even a party who technically "wins" a judgment may appeal, provided the judgment affords that party less relief, or relief that is different in nature, than the party requested. In fact, it is fairly common for both the plaintiff and defendant to appeal a judgment. Situations in which both parties appeal are called *cross appeals*.

Example: *P* sues *D* for breach of a contract in which *D* agreed to deliver a chair to *P*. *P* seeks specific performance of the contract. The trial court finds for *P*. However, finding that the chair is not unique, the court denies the request for specific performance and instead awards damages to *P* in the amount of the value of the chair. Because the judgment did not give *P* what she requested, *P* can appeal.

B. Need to raise issue to trial court: If a party does not give the trial judge the chance to consider and rule on an issue, the party generally cannot appeal that issue.

   1. Legal theories: An appealing party cannot raise a claim or defense for the first time on appeal. In addition, even if a party did present a legal theory at trial, he can *waive* that theory.

   a. Exception: One very important exception to this principle is *subject matter jurisdiction*. Either party (including the plaintiff, who chose the court) may raise subject matter jurisdiction at any time, including on appeal.

   b. Use of rejected theories by appellee: The party who *won* at trial may use any legal theory that *appears in the record* to support the judgment, even if the trial court rejected that theory and the party did not pursue the theory any further at trial.

   2. Objections to procedural mistakes: With respect to matters other than legal theories, a party presents the matter to the trial court by lodging an objection. Failure to object prevents a party from raising that issue on appeal.

   a. Timeliness: If an objection is not timely, the grounds for the objection are waived. A party must challenge evidence, for example, by objecting when the other side tries to introduce that evidence.

   b. "Renewing" an objection: If a mistake made at one stage of the trial has an impact at a later stage, the party may be required to object again at that later stage.

   Example: *P* sues *D* for negligent infliction of emotional distress after *D* accidentally destroys *P*'s family heirloom. *D* moves to dismiss for failure to state a claim, claiming that the tort is not available for the destruction of property. The trial court denies the motion. Later, the trial court proposes jury instructions setting out the elements of negligent infliction. Even though *D* has already tried to convince the trial court that the tort does not exist, it must object to the instructions in order to appeal the issue.

   c. Exception: Some jurisdictions do not require an objection in the case of "*plain error*." An error is plain when it is so blatantly incorrect that it draws into question the competence or partiality of the judge. Findings of plain error are very rare.

C. Harmless error: An error that does not "affect the substantial rights of the parties" cannot be the basis of a reversal on appeal. *28 U.S.C. §2111*. Such errors — mistakes that did not affect the outcome below — are called *harmless errors*. For example, if the lower court erroneously admitted evidence on a certain issue, but the party also had a considerable amount of other admissible evidence tending to show the same thing, the admission of the improper evidence might be harmless.

II. TIMING OF THE APPEAL

In the federal courts, and in many states, a party may appeal only ***final judgments*** of the trial court. The following discussion discusses the final judgment rule in the federal courts only. State practice may differ significantly.

A. Final decision rule: The final decision rule is set out in ***28 U.S.C. §1291***, which allows appeals from all "***final decisions***" of the federal district courts.

1. **Jurisdictional:** Section 1291 is a jurisdictional statute. If an appeal does not meet the requirements of §1291, the appellate courts ***lack subject matter jurisdiction***.

2. **Appeals not covered by §1291:** Not all appeals from the district courts fall within §1291. Certain cases go to the ***Federal Circuit***. 28 U.S.C. §§1292, 1295. A handful of cases go directly from the district courts to the U.S. Supreme Court under 28 U.S.C. §1253.

3. ***Final decision* defined:** The Supreme Court has defined a final decision as "one which ends the litigation on the merits and leaves nothing to do but execute the judgment." Catlin v. United States, 324 U.S. 229, 233 (1945). In other words, the court hearing the case must have resolved all issues necessary to wrap up the dispute.

   a. **Interlocutory rulings:** Most of a trial judge's rulings during the course of pretrial proceedings and the trial do not completely resolve the case and therefore are not final. These decisions are called *interlocutory rulings*.

   b. **Examples:** Examples of rulings that are not final within the meaning of §1291 include:

      i.   most ***discovery*** rulings;

      ii. grant or denial of a ***request for a jury***;

      iii. ***denial*** of a motion to ***dismiss*** or a motion for ***summary judgment***;

      iv. ***grant*** of a motion to dismiss or summary judgment on ***some, but not all, claims or defenses*** (but see the discussion of Fed. R. Civ. P. 54 below); and

      v.   orders granting a ***new trial***.

★
           Example: In Liberty Mutual Insurance Co. v. Wetzel, 424 U.S. 737 (1976), the Court held that a trial court's grant of summary judgment on the issue of liability, but not relief, was not a final decision for purposes of §1291.

4. **Practical importance of finality:** Section 1291 clearly prevents a party from filing an appeal too early. But it also determines whether a party has filed its appeal too late. Once a judgment becomes final, a party has only a limited period to file its appeal.

   a. In ***federal courts***, a party usually has only ***30 days*** to file an appeal. This time limitation is jurisdictional, so that an appeal filed too late cannot be heard by the appellate court. Fed. R. App. P. 4(a)(1).

   b. The 30-day period may be extended if a party makes certain motions. See Fed. R. App. P. 4(a)(4)(A) and 4(a)(5).

B. Exceptions to the final decision rule: There are several exceptions to the final decision rule in the statutes dealing with federal jurisdiction, the Federal Rules of Civil Procedure, and case law.

1. **Final resolution of discrete portion of case under Rule 54(b):** In a case involving multiple claims, it is possible that some of the claims will be resolved prior to others. If the trial court enters judgment on some but not all of the claims, Fed. R. Civ. P. 54(b) may allow the parties to appeal the ruling without waiting for a final decision on the entire case. Rule 54(b) has two basic requirements: that the judge enter judgment on a discrete "claim for relief" and that she expressly indicate that there is no reason to delay entry of the judgment.

   a. **"Claim for relief":** The Fed. R. Civ. P. 54(b) term "claim for relief" is broader than it may appear. If a party sets forth a single basic wrong but seeks recovery for that wrong under several different theories, the different theories are all part of the same "claim for relief." Therefore, if the court resolves only one of the theories of relief, no immediate appeal of that ruling is possible under Fed. R. Civ. P. 54(b). Liberty Mutual Insurance Co. v. Wetzel, 424 U.S. 737 (1976).

      i. On the other hand, merely because two claims are related or share considerable overlapping facts does not mean that they comprise the same claim for relief. Sears, Roebuck & Co. v. Mackey, 351 U.S. 427 (1956).

         Example: *P* and *D* are neighbors. *P* is upset because *D* has frequent cookouts at her house, and the smoke bothers *P*'s allergies. Moreover, at one of these parties, a guest threw a baseball through *P*'s window. *P* sues *D*. *P*'s complaint raises three claims: (a) nuisance, based on the frequent cookouts; (b) trespass, based on the smoke from the cookout entering *P*'s property; and (c) negligence, based on the broken window. The trial court grants a summary judgment for *D* on the trespass claim, holding that the movement of smoke particles cannot qualify as a trespass. The judge expressly certifies that there is no reason to delay entry of the summary judgment. *P* cannot appeal the summary judgment at this time. The trespass claim was merely one of two alternate claims for recovery arising out of the frequent cookouts.

         Example: Same facts as prior example, except that the judge grants summary judgment for *P* on the negligence claim. The judge certifies that there is no reason to delay entry of the judgment. *D* can appeal the judgment immediately. (In fact, if *D* does not appeal within 30 days, she loses her right to appeal.)

      ii. A *counterclaim, cross-claim*, or *third-party claim* is *separate* from the plaintiff's original claim even if it arises out of the same transaction or occurrence. Therefore, judgment on a counterclaim can be appealed under Fed. R. Civ. P. 54(b) even if the original claim remains pending.

      iii. Claims by or against *separate parties* are separate claims under Fed. R. Civ. P. 54(b). For example, if a court dismisses plaintiff's claim against one of two joint tortfeasors, the court has resolved a discrete "claim for relief."

   b. **Express determination:** In addition to the "single claim" requirement, Fed. R. Civ. P. 54(b) also requires that the trial judge expressly determine that there is *no reason to delay entry* of judgment.

      i. The purpose of this express determination requirement is to provide notice to the parties that the time for appeal has commenced.

    ii. However, a court of appeals is not bound by the trial judge's determination. Even if the trial judge certifies that immediate appeal is available, the court of appeals can determine for itself whether the single claim requirement was satisfied.

2. Injunctions and other orders: *28 U.S.C. §1292(a)* provides that certain orders are not subject to the final judgment rule of §1291. These interlocutory orders may be appealed immediately. The orders covered are the following three.

    a. Injunctions: The most important of the §1292(a) exceptions deals with injunctions. Any order of the trial court that *grants or refuses, continues, modifies, or dissolves* an injunction may be appealed immediately. 28 U.S.C. §1292(a)(1). Although a *preliminary injunction* qualifies as an injunction under this rule, a *temporary restraining order* does not and therefore cannot be immediately appealed.

    b. Receivers: Any order appointing or refusing to appoint a receiver, or facilitating a receivership, may be appealed immediately. 28 U.S.C. §1292(a)(2).

    c. Admiralty: Parties may also appeal any order in an admiralty case that finally determines the rights and liabilities of the parties. 28 U.S.C. §1292(a)(3).

3. Certification under §1292(b): 28 U.S.C. §1292(b) allows certain issues to be appealed when both the trial judge and the appellate court agree that an immediate appeal is proper.

    a. Criteria: However, the statute places several conditions on such appeals.

        i. The order must involve a *controlling question of law* about which there is *substantial ground for difference of opinion*. Contested questions of fact cannot be appealed under the section no matter how important they are.

        ii. The trial judge must determine that allowing an immediate appeal might materially *advance the ultimate termination of the litigation*.

        iii. The trial judge must *certify in writing* that both (i) and (ii) are satisfied. The decision whether to certify lies *within the discretion* of the trial judge.

        iv. The party who wants to appeal must apply to the appellate court within *10 days* of entry of the order.

        v. The appellate court must *agree to hear the issue on appeal*. The decision whether to hear the appeal lies totally *within the discretion* of the appellate court.

    b. Rarely granted: Courts of appeal rarely agree to hear appeals under §1292(b).

4. Certification of class actions: A recent amendment to Fed. R. Civ. P. 23 allows for immediate review of the *grant or denial* of class certification. The court of appeals has *discretion* whether to hear the appeal. Fed. R. Civ. P. 23(f).

5. Mandamus and prohibition: Writs of mandamus and prohibition are other ways to obtain review of an interlocutory order in a compelling case. However, they differ from ordinary appeals in certain important ways.

    a. Definitions: Mandamus and prohibition are *original proceedings* that are brought against a public official. Because a judge is a public official, both writs are available as a way of challenging a judge's decision in a case. *Mandamus* orders the trial judge to *do something*. *Prohibition* orders the judge to *refrain* from doing something.

b. Extraordinary relief: Mandamus and prohibition are both ''extraordinary writs,'' available only in ''exceptional circumstances amounting to a judicial 'usurpation of power.' . . .'' Kerr v. United States District Court, 426 U.S. 394 (1976). Therefore, review under these writs is not frequently granted. However, *mandamus* is frequently granted in federal court when a trial judge improperly refuses to *impanel a jury*.

6. Practical finality: In addition to the exceptions set out in the Federal Rules of Civil Procedure and statutes discussed above, the court-created *''collateral order'' doctrine* allows appeal of certain interlocutory orders.

a. Basic test: An order may be appealed under the collateral order doctrine if:

i. the trial judge makes a ruling on an *important issue* that is *separate from the merits* of the case,

ii. the issue is *conclusively settled*, and

iii. the ruling would be *effectively unreviewable* if it cannot be appealed until after final judgment. Coopers & Lybrand v. Livesay, 437 U.S. 463 (1978).

b. Important issue separate from the merits: If the issue is tied up with the merits of the action, review under the collateral order doctrine is unavailable. This restriction saves the court of appeals from having to deal with the merits more than once.

Example: A trial court denies a motion for summary judgment. The order is not appealable as a collateral order because it requires the court to consider the merits of the case.

i. Fact or law: Unlike appeals under §1292(b), the ''important issue'' may be either an issue of fact or a combined issue of law and fact.

ii. Important: The courts have given little guidance on what makes an issue important. Instead, they tend to focus on the ''separate from the merits'' language.

c. Conclusively determined: The trial court's decision must be one that is unlikely to be revised later in the suit.

d. Effectively unreviewable: The final element is that the decision be ''effectively unreviewable'' if the party is forced to wait to appeal until after final judgment. This is the *most difficult* part of the test to satisfy.

i. The court must determine if the ruling will cause damage that cannot be repaired if the losing party must wait until an appeal following a final judgment.

ii. In most cases, however, a *new trial* can cure the problem. Thus, collateral order appeals are limited to cases where a *new trial cannot repair the damage* done.

e. Application of test: Because this three-part test is very difficult to satisfy, most attempts to invoke the doctrine fail. Several cases help to illustrate when the doctrine applies.

★   **i.** *Cohen*: **denial of bond in shareholder's derivative action:** The Supreme Court opinion in Cohen v. Beneficial Industrial Loan Corp., 337 U.S. 541 (1949), allowed appeal of a trial court's order refusing to require the plaintiff in a shareholder's derivative action to file a bond as security for costs. The Court found the issue to be important (because it involved a question under the *Erie* doctrine) and completely separate from the merits (because the question turned solely on an interpretation of Fed. R. Civ. P. 23.1, not on the facts of the case). Moreover, although it would have been possible for the court to change its mind, that was not likely. Finally, the decision could not be effectively reviewed after final judgment. The purpose of the bond was to protect the defendant from the *expenses of defending a frivolous case*. By denying the bond, the court took away that protection. Moreover, if the defendant were forced to litigate the case to completion before appealing, it would suffer the very harm that the bond was designed to deal with, namely, the expenses of litigation.

★

    ii. ***Eisen*: order to pay cost of notice:** Similarly, in Eisen v. Carlisle & Jacquelin, 417 U.S. 156 (1974), the Court held that an order requiring the defendant to pay most of the costs of serving the members of the plaintiff class in a class action could be appealed under the collateral order doctrine. The decision turned on an interpretation of the class action rule (Fed. R. Civ. P. 23) and had nothing to do with the merits of the case. Nor was the decision effectively reviewable through normal avenues of appeal. Granting a new trial after final judgment in the case would not remedy the harm because defendant would already have paid the costs of service.

   iii. **Immunity:** The law provides immunities for certain categories of defendants. To the extent an immunity is a ''right'' not to be dragged into court at all, a ruling denying an immunity may fit within the collateral order exception doctrine.

      (a) However, the judge's ruling must deny the immunity as a matter of law, not based upon a determination of whether certain facts alleged by plaintiff are in fact true. Thus, if the immunity is a *qualified immunity* that can be overcome by a showing that the defendant acted in bad faith, a decision denying the immunity based on a finding that the defendant did act in bad faith could not be appealed as a collateral order.

★

      (b) An order refusing to enforce a forum selection clause in a contract is not a decision denying ''immunity.'' The forum selection clause does not prevent litigation but merely defines where that litigation must take place. Lauro Lines s.r.l. v. Chasser, 490 U.S. 495 (1989).

   iv. **Discovery orders:** The collateral order exception is almost never used for orders concerning discovery. The rationale for this is not entirely clear. It may be that such issues are not deemed important, or that a party subject to a discovery order can ''appeal'' the order by refusing to comply, being declared in contempt, and immediately appealing the contempt order.

   v. **''Death knell'' doctrine rejected:** The Supreme Court has refused to expand the collateral order doctrine. It explicitly rejected the so-called death knell doctrine, which some courts had used to allow appeals of a decision that had such a great impact on the losing party that it effectively ended the litigation. Coopers & Lybrand v. Livesay, 437 U.S. 463 (1978).

Quiz Yourself on
APPEALABILITY, THE FINAL JUDGMENT RULE, AND EXCEPTIONS

141. Landowner sues Neighbor for trespass. At trial, Landowner calls a witness who testifies that she saw Neighbor on Landowner's land on the date in question. Because Landowner did not disclose the name of the witness in either the initial or pretrial mandatory discovery disclosures, this witness proves to be a complete surprise to Neighbor's attorney. Nevertheless, the attorney regains his composure and conducts an effective cross-examination.

    The trial continues for another day. Because Landowner has no other evidence showing that Neighbor trespassed, Neighbor moves for judgment as a matter of law. Neighbor correctly points out that the Federal Rules of Civil Procedure prevent Landowner from using the witness's testimony because Landowner failed to turn over the name in discovery. The judge denies the motion and submits the case to the jury. The jury rules for Landowner, and judgment is entered accordingly.

    Neighbor appeals, arguing that the judge erred in submitting the case to the jury. Assuming that Neighbor would be entitled to judgment as a matter of law without the evidence of this one witness, will Neighbor prevail in this appeal? _____

142. Cousteau, an ocean biologist, recently bought a new research ship from ACME Shipbuilding Co. The ship sinks on its maiden voyage, causing serious injury to Cousteau. Cousteau sues ACME in a federal district court, alleging two separate claims. Cousteau first alleges that ACME breached an express warranty set out in the purchase contract. Cousteau's second claim is a products liability claim, which asserts that the ship was negligently designed. The trial judge grants ACME's motion for partial summary judgment on the express warranty claim. Cousteau immediately files an appeal. May Cousteau appeal this summary judgment? _____

143. Drake Yoola is a third-year law student who has a terrible aversion to the sun. He is accordingly quite upset when he learns that the Dean has arranged for the school's graduation ceremony to be held outdoors in the early afternoon. Drake sues the Dean in a federal district court. Because the graduation is in two weeks, Drake asks for a preliminary injunction requiring the Dean to hold the ceremony indoors. The court denies the request. May Drake appeal at this time, or must he wait until after the trial on damages? _____

Answers

141. Neighbor will not prevail because he did not object to the evidence in a timely fashion. Objections to the introduction of evidence usually must be made when the evidence is offered.

142. Cousteau may not appeal at this time. The summary judgment is not a final judgment because it resolved only one of the two claims in the case. Nor does this situation fit into the Fed. R. Civ. P. 54(b) exception. Even if the judge's order had specified that there was no reason to delay appeal on the ruling, the judge did not resolve a complete ''claim for relief.'' The warranty and products liability claims are both based on a single injury and therefore are both part of the same ''claim for relief'' under that rule.

143. Drake may appeal immediately. 28 U.S.C. §1292(a)(1) allows a party an immediate appeal from an order either granting or refusing an injunction.

III. SCOPE OF APPELLATE REVIEW

An appeal is not a new trial. An appellate court gives a certain amount of ***deference*** to the decisions of a trial court. How critically it reviews the lower court's decision ***depends on the nature of the issues involved***.

A. Issues of law: Issues of law are reviewed ***de novo***. Under *de novo* review, the court gives no deference whatsoever to the trial court's decision as to the rule of law, but instead determines for itself what the proper rule should be.

　　Note: In certain cases dealing with appeals from ***agencies***, courts indicate that they give deference to the agency's interpretation of the law. This principle is unique to ***administrative law*** and does not apply to an appeal from a trial court.

B. Issues of fact: Issues of fact are reviewed under a "***clearly erroneous***" standard. The Supreme Court defined this standard: "A finding is 'clearly erroneous' when although there is evidence to support it, the reviewing court on the entire evidence is left with the definite and firm conviction that a mistake has been committed." United States v. U.S. Gypsum Co., 333 U.S. 364 (1948).

　　1. Clearly erroneous standard applied: Clearly erroneous review is very limited. The court of appeals may reverse only if it is convinced the trial court is incorrect.

　　　　a. The court of appeals should not reevaluate the ***credibility*** of the witnesses.

　　　　b. If there is ***significant evidence on both sides*** of the issue, the lower court's finding ***cannot be clearly erroneous***.

　　　　c. If the findings of fact are made by a ***jury***, the standard is ***even more difficult*** to satisfy. Although often referred to as the clearly erroneous standard, in practice the court of appeals applies the ***no reasonable jury standard*** that applies in judgments as a matter of law under Fed. R. Civ. P. 50. See Chapter 11.

★　　　　**Example:** For an illustration of how these principles apply in actual practice, see Anderson v. Bessemer City, 470 U.S. 564 (1985), where the Court held that a trial judge's finding of discriminatory intent was not clearly erroneous, even though it was based on minimal evidence and even though the judge had asked the parties to submit proposed findings of fact that the judge used in the opinion.

　　2. Mixed fact and law: Many issues are mixed questions of law and fact. For example, whether a party breached a contract or acted negligently requires the factfinder to determine not only what happened, but also how the law applies to the situation that occurred.

　　　　a. In the federal system, a mixed question of law and fact is ***treated just like a question of fact*** and is subject to the clearly erroneous standard.

　　　　b. However, if the trial court's ruling on a mixed question was based on an error in law, the appellate court hears the issue *de novo*.

3. **Documentary evidence:** Sometimes, the only evidence pertaining to an issue at trial is set out in documents. For example, a court interpreting a written contract must read the contract itself. In such cases, much of the rationale for deferring to the trial court disappears because the court of appeals is every bit as capable of reading and interpreting the documentary evidence as the trial court.

    a. **Federal view:** Nevertheless, in the federal courts the ***clearly erroneous standard applies*** even when the evidence is comprised completely of documents and physical evidence. Anderson v. City of Bessemer City, 470 U.S. 564 (1985).

    b. **Applying standard to instruments:** As a practical matter, however, it is easier for a court of appeals to find a lower court's interpretation of a contract or other legal document clearly erroneous. Because interpretation of a legal document does not involve issues of credibility, the lower court's findings can be overturned if they are clearly at odds with the written words.

C. **Issues within discretion of the trial judge:** Certain issues, such as the decision whether to grant a new trial, are deemed particularly within the province of the trial judge. A court of appeals reviews these decisions under an ***abuse of discretion standard***. As the name implies, a court of appeals will reverse only if it concludes that there is ***no possible reasonable basis*** for the decision. The standard is sometimes referred to as ***arbitrary and capricious***.

Quiz Yourself on *APPEALS*

144. Lars, a citizen of Denmark, is on an extended driving trip in the United States. While in a very remote part of the country, Lars is stopped by Sheriff Smith. Hearing Lars's accent, Smith concludes that Lars must be a spy and locks him in the local hoosegow. After considerable effort, Lars finally obtains his release. Lars sues Smith in federal district court, seeking recovery under the state's civil rights laws.

    Smith immediately files a motion to dismiss, citing a state statute that provides an immunity to officers acting within the line of duty. Under this statute, Smith is liable only if it is shown that he acted with "wanton disregard for someone's rights." The trial court, however, rules that the immunity does not apply to claims brought under the particular civil rights statute that Lars is using. Smith files an immediate appeal to the court of appeals. Can the court of appeals hear Smith's appeal at this time? _____

145. Same facts as Problem 144, except that Smith does not seek an immediate appeal of the trial judge's ruling. The case proceeds through discovery. After discovery is complete, Smith files a motion for summary judgment. Smith argues that he can be held liable under the civil rights law only if he *knew* that his actions were wrongful. Although Lars has evidence of negligence, he has no evidence that Smith knew his actions were wrongful. The trial judge disagrees with Smith and denies the summary judgment motion, finding that an officer such as Smith can be held liable even if he was negligent.

    However, the judge is unsure of her ruling on the standard of care. Therefore, she certifies the question of the applicable standard of care for review. In this certification, the judge states that because there is considerable doubt on the issue, allowing an appeal at this time might speed up the resolution of the case. Before the court of appeals, Lars argues that the appellate court cannot review the trial judge's ruling at this time even if it wanted to hear the issue.

Does the appellate court have the authority to review the judge's findings concerning the standard of care at this time? _____

146. Same facts as Problem 144, except that Smith does not seek an immediate appeal of the trial judge's ruling. The case proceeds to trial, where Smith wins a judgment completely exonerating him from all liability. Lars appeals, based upon a number of alleged procedural errors made by the trial judge in the case. Smith is still sore about the trial judge's rejection of his immunity defense and is considering bringing that issue before the court of appeals. May Smith, as the party who won at trial, nevertheless challenge the trial judge's ruling on the immunity defense? _____

147. Until recently, Walter was a pastry chef at an upscale restaurant. Walter was fired when Paulette, the head chef, found Walter with his "fingers in the pot." Walter immediately sues Paulette in a federal district court, bringing two claims. The first is a wrongful termination claim, based on the firing. The second is a defamation claim. In this second claim, Walter claims that Paulette spoke badly of him to his ex-coworkers, harming his reputation.

After discovery, the trial judge grants Paulette's request for summary judgment on the defamation claim. The trial judge's written opinion states, "The evidence is clear that plaintiff was dipping into the restaurant's livelihood. Therefore, everything defendant said about plaintiff was completely true and cannot give rise to a claim for defamation. Because there is no reason to delay the entry of summary judgment on the defamation claim, I hereby grant summary judgment to Paulette on that claim."

Four months later, the case goes to trial, where Paulette wins a judgment on the remaining wrongful termination claim. Walter immediately files an appeal. However, because the case was tried by a jury, Walter has little confidence that he can prevail on the wrongful termination claim. Instead, he bases his appeal only on the defamation claim. Can Walter appeal on the defamation claim? _____

Answers

144. Smith's appeal is timely. Although none of the other exceptions apply, his case fits within the collateral order exception. That exception has been applied in cases involving an immunity, for in those situations the very fact of exposing the protected person to a trial is the sort of irremediable harm that the doctrine is designed to prevent. The base issue of whether the immunity is available to this type of defendant as a matter of law does not turn on the merits of the underlying dispute. The issue of immunity is also extremely important. Therefore, appeal is possible under the collateral order doctrine.

145. The final judgment rule is a rule that defines the jurisdiction of the courts of appeal. Therefore, unless the case fits within one of the exceptions, the appellate court cannot hear this case merely because it wants to hear it. The denial of summary judgment is not a final judgment because the trial judge must still conduct a trial on the merits.

The trial judge's certification of the question, however, raises the possibility that the issue can be reviewed under §1292(b). The trial judge used proper language in the certification. In addition, the case meets the other requirements of §1292(b). The issue being appealed is one of law, as required by

§1292(b). Although the judge evaluated the facts in making the ruling, the actual question of standard of care is one of law. In addition, allowing an immediate appeal might advance the termination of the case. If the trial judge was incorrect and the standard of care is the ''knowing'' standard argued by Smith, the case is essentially over because Lars has no evidence of knowledge. Therefore, if the court of appeals elects to hear the case at this time, it has the authority.

146. Smith is free to raise the immunity defense. A party who prevailed at trial may ask the appellate court to affirm the trial court's judgment on any grounds it chooses, including grounds rejected by the trial court.

147. Walter probably cannot appeal because he filed his appeal too late. The Federal Rules of Appellate Procedure give Walter 30 days following final judgment to appeal. He did file an appeal within 30 days of the trial judge's last ruling. However, he needed to file the appeal within 30 days of the grant of summary judgment. Under Fed. R. Civ. P. 54(b), the trial judge's ruling was *probably* a final judgment on the defamation claim. Moreover, the judge included the ''magic language'' about how there was no reason to delay entry of judgment. The ruling was accordingly a final judgment, commencing the 30-day period for appeal on that issue. Because the trial itself did not commence until four months after the ruling, we know that he did not meet this 30-day deadline. Walter did not move to extend the 30-day period for filing an appeal.

   The only open issue is whether the trial judge's ruling actually qualified as a final judgment under Fed. R. Civ. P. 54(b). In order for that rule to apply, the judge must entirely resolve a separate and distinct claim for relief. The firing and defamation are probably separate claims because they involve distinct injuries caused by separate acts. On the other hand, they *do* overlap to some extent. Most notably, the key issue in each case is the same — whether Walter did what Paulette claims he did. If the two claims are part of the same overall claim for relief, then Walter could not appeal until after the entire case was resolved, and his appeal would be timely.

 Exam Tips on
APPEALS

☞ When dealing with a question concerning appeals, always consider three subissues: may ***this party*** appeal, may they appeal on ***these grounds***, and is the appeal ***timely***?

☞ **Who may appeal:** Recall that a party can ''win'' a suit and still be able to appeal.

☞ **Grounds for appeal:** Always make sure that a party ***has not waived*** the grounds it is asserting for the appeal. In many cases, a party must ask the trial court to correct its own mistake when the mistake is made.

☞ **Time for appeal:** The final judgment rule is admittedly difficult. However, do not focus so much on that rule that you forget the other main limitation on appeal: the ***30-day time limit***.

☞ When dealing with the final judgment rule, be sure that you understand the various exceptions. Some of the exceptions, such as the provision allowing immediate appeal of either the grant or denial of an injunction, are relatively straightforward. Spotting one of these exceptions can save you valuable time, and if they apply you do not need to deal with the more difficult exceptions such as the collateral order rule.

☞ Before concluding that appeal is possible under Fed. R. Civ. P. 54(b), make sure that the trial judge's ruling contains language about ''no just reason to delay'' entry of the judgment.

☞ The most difficult issue in the ***collateral order doctrine*** is determining whether the issue is effectively reviewable. In the vast majority of situations, the erroneous ruling can be effectively cured by a new trial. It is only when the fact of the trial is *itself* the problem that the doctrine is likely to apply.

☛ **Scope of review:** The two main issues in scope of review are determining whether the issue in question is one of law or fact and how the various standards of review apply.

☛ Recall that a mixed question of law and fact — such as whether a party was negligent — is treated as a question of fact for purposes of review.

☛ Be very sure of yourself before you conclude that a court of appeals may overturn a jury verdict. Jury verdicts are entitled to a very high degree of deference.

CHAPTER 13

RESPECT FOR JUDGMENTS

ChapterScope _____

This chapter deals with the effect a judgment in one case has on later litigation involving one or more of the parties. A judgment can affect later cases in three main ways. The first is as ***precedent***, a topic not covered in this chapter. Second, a judgment can completely bar the litigation of certain ***claims or defenses***, even those that were not raised in the first case. Finally, it can prevent relitigation of certain ***issues*** that actually were litigated and decided in the first action.

- The doctrine of ***claim preclusion*** (sometimes called ***res judicata***) prevents parties from raising certain claims that were litigated or should have been litigated in the first action.

  - In certain cases, ***defenses*** will also be precluded. Both Fed. R. Civ. P. 13(a) and the common law compulsory counterclaim rule can bar defenses.

  - Claim preclusion applies only to later disputes between the ***same parties*** or those who are in ***privity*** with parties to the first action.

- The doctrine of ***issue preclusion*** (sometimes called ***collateral estoppel***) prevents parties from relitigating certain issues that were actually litigated in the first case.

  - Determining precisely what the first court decided is not always obvious from the judgment. Instead, it is necessary to dissect the judgment logically to determine what findings were actually made and necessary to the decision.

  - Unlike claim preclusion, courts increasingly allow people who were not parties to the first action to use issue preclusion. Whether such ***nonmutual use*** is allowed often depends on whether the use is ***offensive*** or ***defensive***.

- Claim and issue preclusion apply only to findings of either pure ***fact*** or ***mixed questions*** of law and fact. They do not apply to pure rulings of law.

- Courts have recognized certain ***limits*** on the reach of both claim and issue preclusion because of a concern for fairness and other policy considerations.

- Two other doctrines look similar to claim and issue preclusion.

  - The ***law of the case doctrine*** prevents a court from reopening a legal issue that was decided earlier in the case.

  - The notion of ***judicial estoppel*** may prevent a party who advances a position in one case from taking an inconsistent position in a later case.

I. CLAIM PRECLUSION

Claim preclusion forces parties to litigate in a single action all claims arising from a single basic event.

A. Overview

1. **Policies:** Claim preclusion serves two main policy ends.

    a. **Efficiency:** First, by requiring parties to join all closely related claims in a single suit, it helps ensure the most efficient use of scarce judicial resources.

    b. **Consistency:** Claim preclusion also helps to ensure consistency in litigation.

2. **Terminology:** Courts sometimes refer to claim preclusion as *res judicata*.

    a. Somewhat confusingly, at other times the phrase *res judicata* is used as a collective term to refer to the entire doctrine of preclusion, including both claim and issue preclusion.

    b. The terms *bar* and *merger* reflect two different aspects of claim preclusion.

        i. *Bar* means simply that someone who actually raises a particular claim in a case is barred from raising it again in later litigation.

        ii. *Merger*, by contrast, deals with claims (and sometimes defenses), that were *not raised* in the prior case. If such claims arise from the same basic set of events, the party may be precluded from raising them in the later case. A party who attempts to litigate the same basic claim in two actions is said to have *split* the action.

3. **Basic standard:** Generally, claim preclusion applies when:

    a. the first action resulted in a *final judgment on the merits*, and

    b. the party raises a claim that was previously litigated or a claim that arises from the same basic events as one that was previously litigated.

4. **Plaintiffs barred:** Generally, claim preclusion applies only to claims by parties who were *plaintiffs in the first action*. If a party was not a plaintiff (or in certain narrow circumstances to be discussed below, a defendant), claim preclusion does not require the party to litigate its claim in the first action. One reason justifying the disparate treatment of plaintiffs and other parties is that the plaintiff has the luxury of selecting the court.

B. Barring claims: A claim is barred if it either *was or should have been* raised by a party who was a plaintiff in the prior action.

1. **Claims brought in action #1:** A party who litigates a claim in one suit can never again raise the *same claim* against the *same defendant*.

    a. **Same claim:** Two cases involve the same claim if the party uses the *same legal theory* to recover against the *same party* based on the *same underlying facts*.

        Example: *P*, a football quarterback, is injured when his blockers fail to prevent the defense from tackling him. *P* sues *Tackle* for his injuries, claiming that *Tackle* was negligent in performing his duties. *P* loses. *P* now sues *Guard* for negligence, seeking recovery for the same basic injury. Claim preclusion does not bar the claim. Even though the legal theory is the same and the same basic facts are involved, *P*'s claim against *Guard* is not the same claim as *P*'s claim against *Tackle*.

    b. A claim is barred only if it was *resolved* by the court in the first action. The final judgment requirement is discussed in Part I.D.2.

c. Note that it is ***irrelevant how the first case is resolved***. Plaintiff is barred from bringing a claim regardless of whether she won or lost in the first case.

2. **Claims that were not brought in action #1:** Claim preclusion also prevents a party who was a plaintiff in the first action from relitigating claims that were not brought in the first action but are factually related to claims presented in that action. ***Courts differ significantly*** on the test used to determine whether a claim is sufficiently related to a claim raised in the first action to be barred by claim preclusion.

   a. **Majority view:** Most courts look to see if the two claims arise from the ***same transaction or occurrence***, or ***series of transactions or occurrences***. This is for all intents and purposes the same test used in the Federal Rules of Civil Procedure joinder rules. This is also the view favored by the ***Restatement (Second) of Judgments***.

      i. Courts usually find the standard satisfied only if the claims share some of the ***same relevant evidence***. Unlike the standard often used in joinder, a mere logical relationship between the claims ordinarily does not suffice.

      ii. As long as the claims share some of the same evidence, however, the legal theories can be completely different.

         Example: *P* sells ground coffee under the trademark CONNOISSEUR. *D* starts to sell ground coffee under the trademark CONNISUER. *P* sues *D* for trademark infringement. Once that suit is complete, *P* sues *D* for false advertising, based on certain claims that *D* made in its advertisements. *P*'s second claim is barred. Both claims arise from the same occurrence, namely, *D*'s sale of its coffee.

   b. **Same cause of action approach:** A minority of courts use the ''same cause of action'' test. This test is much narrower; that is, it bars significantly fewer claims. It looks for a ***high degree of overlap in the evidence*** required to prove both claims. This test is satisfied only if the claims share many of the same basic elements, so that the evidence necessary to prevail on the second claim is by and large the same evidence that should have been presented in the first action.

      Example: Consider the example discussed just above. Under the same cause of action test, the false advertising claim is not part of the same cause of action as the trademark infringement claim. The trademark claim requires *P* to prove that *D* used a similar mark in a way that caused customer confusion as to the source of the coffee. *P* need not offer evidence of the quality of the goods or other statements made in *D*'s advertising. The false advertising claim, by contrast, focuses on what *D* said about the coffee, whether those statements gave consumers an impression concerning the quality of the coffee, and whether the statements were true.

   ★ **Example:** For a real case applying this approach, see Frier v. City of Vandalia, 770 F.2d 699 (7th Cir. 1985) (because the claims shared a significant overlap in evidence, the new claims were barred under Illinois law, which uses the same cause of action approach).

   c. **Same primary right test:** A few courts use the older ''primary right'' approach, which carries over some of the concepts of common law pleading. Under this approach, the court must determine if the claim in the second action attempts to protect the same primary legally protected right of the plaintiff. If so, it is barred.

Example: Again consider the trademark/false advertising example. Under the same primary right test, the false advertising right is barred. Both claims, trademark infringement and false advertising, protect the same basic interest of *P*, namely, *P*'s right to sell its coffee to customers without unfair interference by others.

d. Installment contracts: Contracts that are to be performed in installments, such as a loan or lease, present special issues in claim preclusion. Generally, each installment is considered a *separate transaction*. Therefore, once one breach occurs, a party may bring an action for that breach without losing the right to sue for later breaches. However, this general principle is qualified by three important exceptions.

i. Acceleration clause: If the contract in question contains a clause under which breach of one installment *automatically* makes all installments due and owing immediately, the party must sue for the entire contract. However, few acceleration clauses are automatic. Most are at the option of the nondefaulting party.

ii. Material breach: If, as a matter of contract law, breach of a particular installment is so significant that it destroys the essential value of the contract, the party must sue for breach of the entire contract, not merely the installment.

iii. Rule of accumulated breaches: Although each installment is a separate transaction, the rule of accumulated breaches requires a party to join all breaches that have *already occurred* as of the moment he brings suit. However, the rule of accumulated breaches *does not apply to negotiable instruments*, such as a basic check.

C. Barring defenses: In most cases, the common law doctrine of claim preclusion bars claims, not defenses. In certain narrow circumstances, however, the doctrine may also prevent a party from bringing a claim based on the same basic elements as a defense that the party should have raised in the prior action. The Federal Rules of Civil Procedure significantly expand the scope of defense preclusion in federal courts.

1. Compulsory counterclaims: The starting point in any analysis of whether a party who was a defendant is barred from raising a claim is to determine whether there is a *compulsory counterclaim provision* in the governing Rules of Civil Procedure. If the jurisdiction in which the *first action* was litigated had such a rule, it is likely to control the issue. *Fed. R. Civ. P. 13(a)*, the compulsory counterclaim rule in the federal courts, is discussed in Chapter 14, Part I.B. Note that the rule contains several exceptions.

★   **2. Common law rule:** If the rules do not require a defendant to bring a particular counterclaim in suit one, the party who was the defendant is free to bring the claim in suit two unless it falls within the narrow common law compulsory counterclaim rule. The common law rule asks whether the claim in the second case would have been a *defense* in the first case. If the claim would have been a defense, it is barred. However, if the claim was a pure counterclaim, not a defense to the claim in the first case, the common law rule allows the party to bring it in the second case. Martino v. McDonald's System, Inc., 598 F.2d 1079 (7th Cir.), cert. denied, 444 U.S. 966 (1979).

Example: Smith hires Jones to install a new roof on Smith's house. Jones completes the project in satisfactory fashion. However, as Jones drives away from Smith's house, he negligently drives his truck through Smith's prize rose garden. When Smith refuses to pay, Jones sues Smith for breach of contract. Jones sues in a state that has no compulsory counterclaim provision in its Rules of Civil Procedure. Smith prevails in the suit.

Smith then sues Jones, seeking recovery on two separate claims. First, Smith alleges that Jones committed fraud when the two were negotiating the roofing contract. Second, Smith sues Jones for negligence, for the damage to the rose garden.

The fraud claim is barred. In addition to being an affirmative claim, fraud would also have been a defense on the contract claim since fraud in the inducement makes a contract void. (Note that it is irrelevant that Smith won the first case without invoking the fraud defense.) However, Smith is free to bring the negligence claim. That claim is a pure counterclaim. Jones's negligence is not a defense to Jones's breach of contract claim.

Note: Do not forget that most jurisdictions have some sort of compulsory counterclaim rule. Thus, had the case in the prior example been subject to Fed. R. Civ. P. 13, Smith would also be barred from bringing the negligence claim because it arose from the same transaction or occurrence.

D. Other issues in claim preclusion: Other difficult issues may also arise in claim preclusion.

   1. Same parties—the problem of privity: In most cases, claim preclusion applies only to claims between the same parties. Therefore, a plaintiff is free to sue two defendants for the same injury in different actions, even if those two defendants could easily have been joined in the same suit. Similarly, if two people are injured by the exact same act of the defendant, each can sue separately. However, an important exception to the "same party" rule arises in cases of privity.

     a. Effect of privity: If *X* and *Y* are in privity, claim preclusion applies to both equally. Thus, if *X* is barred from bringing a claim against another, *Y* is also barred from bringing the claim against that person. Similarly, in any situation where *X* could use claim preclusion to prevent another person from bringing a claim, *Y* can also use claim preclusion against that person.

     b. When privity exists: Privity exists when, because of the relationship between the parties, the two are litigating the *same legal right*.

       i. One situation where privity exists is when a party sues as the *legal representative* of another. Examples include a *guardian-ward* relationship and the class representative in a properly crafted *class action*.

       ii. A second category of cases involving privity is where the two parties have a *mutual* or *successive interest* in the same property of contract.

         (a) This notion underlies the concept of "running with the land" in property law. Thus, if a person who regularly walks across land successfully sues the landowner and establishes an easement by adverse possession, anyone who buys the land from the landowner is bound by that judgment and takes the land subject to the easement. The landowner and buyer have successive interests.

         (b) An example of a mutual interest is a landlord and a tenant. If a tenant sues a nearby factory for nuisance, the outcome also binds the landlord.

       iii. Caveat: Situations involving privity are relatively rare. Before finding privity, it is crucial to ensure that the two parties are indeed litigating the exact same legal right. For example, *joint tortfeasors* are not in privity. Similarly, parties with a *joint undivided interest in land* are not in privity.

★   **Example:** The case of Searle Brothers v. Searle, 588 P.2d 689 (Utah 1978), provides an excellent illustration of a situation that at first glance may look like one of privity but is not. In that case, a wife sued her husband for divorce. In dividing the marital property, the court had to deal with a piece of property. The husband claimed that he owned the property jointly with a partnership. The partnership comprised the husband and two sons. The court rejected the claim and awarded the property to the wife.

The partnership then sued to protect its one-half interest in the same property. The wife claimed that the husband was in privity with the partnership and that the partnership therefore was bound by the judgment. The court rejected the argument. Because the husband and the partnership owned the property jointly, they had neither mutual nor successive interests. Moreover, the fact that the husband was managing partner of the partnership did not change the result.

2. Final judgment on the merits: Not all court decisions have claim and issue preclusion effect. *Only final judgments on the merits qualify* for claim and issue preclusion.

  a. Final judgment: A final judgment is one that completely wraps up the matter in question, leaving the trial court nothing more to do. In most jurisdictions, a judgment has claim preclusion effect even though it is currently on appeal.

  b. On the merits: Claim preclusion bars all claims arising from the same core of facts. The doctrine applies only if the court actually *resolved one or more claims* involving those facts.

  i. On the merits: All jurisdictions agree that certain rulings are on the merits, including a judgment after trial and a summary judgment.

  ii. Not on the merits: Other final determinations are clearly not on the merits, including a dismissal for lack of *jurisdiction*.

  iii. Statute of limitations: A judgment based on the expiration of the statute of limitations is not considered a judgment on the merits by most courts. If a court grants judgment based on the statute of limitations, a party may still be able to sue in a different forum and gain advantage of that forum's longer limitations period.

  iv. Issues where courts differ: Other rulings are not as clear, including dismissal for failure to prosecute and dismissal for failure to state a claim upon which relief can be granted.

  v. Effect of Rule 41(a) and (b): Fed. R. Civ. P. 41(a) and (b), and similar rules in force in many states, deal with whether dismissals are on the merits. Fed. R. Civ. P. 41(a) is discussed in Chapter 9, Part IV. Fed. R. Civ. P. 41(b) is discussed in Chapter 9, Part III. Several Supreme Court decisions have interpreted how these rules apply to federal dismissals.

  (a) The Court has made it clear that a Rule 12(b)(6) dismissal for failure to state a claim has claim preclusion effect. Federated Department Stores v. Moitie, 452 U.S. 394, 399 n.3 (1981).

  (b) Because of the Supreme Court's *Semtek* opinion, certain Rule 41(b) dismissals may apply only in the federal court that issued the dismissal. See Chapter 5, Part IV. In other courts, the preclusive effect of the dismissal will be governed by the law of the state where the federal court that issued the order sits.

3. **Jurisdictional issues:** Claim preclusion tries to avoid inefficiency by encouraging a party to join all claims arising from the same basic facts. But joinder may not be possible in all cases. For example, federal courts have ***exclusive jurisdiction*** over certain claims arising under federal law. The issue is whether claim preclusion applies when a party ***could not litigate*** a particular claim in the first action because of lack of jurisdiction.

   a. **Majority view:** Most state courts hold that a claim that could not be presented in the first case because of lack of jurisdiction is not barred by claim preclusion. This is also the view of the Restatement (Second) of Judgments. It does not matter that the party could have filed the first action in a different court that could have heard both claims.

★   b. **No special federal rule:** The Supreme Court has refused to create a uniform federal common law rule governing whether a state court judgment precludes a claim over which the federal courts have exclusive jurisdiction. Instead, whether the claim is precluded turns on the law of the state that heard the state court claim. Marrese v. American Academy of Orthopaedic Surgeons, 470 U.S. 373 (1985); Gargallo v. Merrill, Lynch, Pierce, Fenner & Smith, 918 F.2d 658 (6th Cir. 1990).

Quiz Yourself on
CLAIM PRECLUSION

148. Carol is the managing partner of a large law firm. The law firm has two offices in the metropolitan area: a main office located in the city center and small satellite office in the suburbs. Carol enters into a contract with SpickandSpan, a janitorial service, under which SpickandSpan agrees to clean the firm's main office. The contract requires SpickandSpan to clean the office every night after normal business hours.

After a few months, Carol is so impressed with SpickandSpan's work that she enters into another contract with SpickandSpan for the satellite office. The terms of this contract are virtually identical to the contract for the main office.

Three of the firm's largest clients have huge deals scheduled to close near the end of the year. Client *A* has scheduled its closing for December 30, at the main office. Client *B* has a closing scheduled for December 31, also at the main office. Client *C* is also scheduled to close on December 31, but at the satellite office.

Unbeknownst to Carol, SpickandSpan has its annual New Year's Eve soiree on the afternoon of December 29. The liquor flows a bit too freely, and as a result, SpickandSpan's employees do not clean either of the offices on the 29th. Long-term hangovers cause the employees to do a very poor job of cleaning on the evening of the 30th. Client's *A*, *B*, and *C* are mortified at the condition of the firm's office and immediately take their business elsewhere.

On January 22, Carol brings an action on behalf of the firm against SpickandSpan to recover for the loss of client *A*. Carol wins a judgment of $10,000 for the firm.

Buoyed by her success, Carol brings another action against SpickandSpan in which she seeks recovery for the loss of clients *B* and *C*. SpickandSpan brings a motion for summary judgment, alleging claim preclusion. How will the court rule? _____

149. Della, a law student, slips on the floor in the law school and falls, resulting in serious injury. Della learns that Jan Itor and Cass Todian, the law school's maintenance workers, had waxed the floors of the hallway a mere 30 minutes before Della's unfortunate accident. Della brings a negligence action against Jan. Although Della wins a judgment for $50,000, Jan has no assets to pay the judgment.

    The next day, Cass wins the lottery. Della therefore brings a new action against Cass. Della alleges in her complaint that because Jan and Cass were working together, they are jointly and severally liable for Della's injuries. In his answer, Cass argues that Della's claim is barred by claim preclusion. Is Cass correct? _____

150. Radio Shanty sells radios and other electronic devices at bargain-basement prices. For big purchases, Radio Shanty has its own in-house financing system. Karl takes advantage of this financing system to buy a large stereo system from Radio Shanty. Karl signs a note payable to Radio Shanty and gives Radio Shanty a security interest in the stereo.

    When Karl later fails to make the October payment under the note, Radio Shanty sues. The court enters judgment in favor of Karl, holding that Radio Shanty failed to introduce evidence of a loan agreement. Several weeks later, Monolith, Inc., buys Radio Shanty in a corporate takeover. Radio Shanty is dissolved as a corporation, and all of its corporate assets are absorbed by Monolith, including all of the debts owed under the in-house financing program.

    When Monolith discovers that Karl missed the October payment, it sues Karl. Unlike Radio Shanty, Monolith can prove that Karl owes the money. Karl moves for summary judgment based on claim preclusion. Monolith argues that claim preclusion cannot apply to it because it had no chance to represent itself in the prior action. Does claim preclusion apply here? _____

Answers

148. The action dealing with client *B* is barred, but the action dealing with client *C* may proceed. With respect to client *B*, Carol is suing for breach of an installment contract. Each nightly cleaning is a separate installment. Although each installment is a separate obligation, when multiple breaches have occurred at the time the first action is filed, the rule of accumulated breaches requires the party to include all breaches that have already occurred. By omitting the December 30 breach when she sued in January, Carol has lost the right to recover on that claim.

    The claim relating to client *C*, however, is not part of the same cause of action. Carol entered into two contracts on two different dates. Although the wording of each is very similar, they are still separate agreements. Therefore, Carol need not join breaches under the two contracts.

149. Della's claim is not barred. Even though Jan and Cass were acting in concert and accordingly may be jointly and severally liable for her injury, Della's claim against each of the maintenance workers is a separate and distinct claim.

150. Monolith's claim is barred by claim preclusion. It is suing for the exact same legal right as that involved in the prior case brought by Radio Shanty. Monolith and Radio Shanty are in privity with respect to this right because Monolith is a successor in interest to Radio Shanty. Given that the parties are in privity, Monolith is barred from bringing a second action to the same extent that Radio Shanty would be barred.

II. ISSUE PRECLUSION

Issue preclusion, or ***collateral estoppel***, is a companion doctrine to claim preclusion. Even when a party can bring a particular claim in the second court, certain issues relevant to that claim may be controlled by the outcome of prior litigation.

A. Overview: The analysis of issue preclusion differs significantly from the analysis of claim preclusion.

1. **Basic analysis:** Issue preclusion applies in a case if:

   a. the ***same issue*** is involved in the two actions;

   b. that issue was ***actually litigated***;

   c. that issue was ***actually decided***; and

   d. a ruling on the issue was ***necessary to the decision***.

2. **No merger:** Issue preclusion almost never applies if the issue was not actually litigated in the first case. Therefore, there is no doctrine of merger in issue preclusion. The ***primary exception is jurisdiction***. A party who litigates a case to completion without challenging subject matter jurisdiction usually is barred from claiming in a second action that the first court's judgment is invalid for lack of subject matter or personal jurisdiction.

B. Same issue: Issue preclusion applies only if the second action involves exactly the same issue as the first. Although this is often a relatively straightforward determination, certain situations can prove troubling.

1. **Differences in burden of persuasion:** Differences in the burden of persuasion on a particular issue in two cases can result in the same basic facts being treated as two separate issues for purposes of issue preclusion. A party who ***fails*** to meet a ***higher burden*** in the first case is ***not precluded*** from relitigating that same issue in a later case in which the ***burden is lower***.

   Example: *D* destroys property belonging to State. Convinced that *D* acted intentionally, State prosecutes *D* for vandalism. In this state, any intentional destruction of property constitutes vandalism unless *D* proves a justification. Although *D* offers no justification, the jury finds for *D*.

   State now brings a civil action against *D*, claiming conversion. Like vandalism, a claim for conversion requires that the plaintiff prove the intentional destruction of property. *D* argues issue preclusion, claiming that the prior case found that *D* did not intentionally destroy the property. Issue preclusion does not apply. The issue in the criminal case was whether State could prove intentional destruction ***beyond a reasonable doubt***. In the civil case, however, the State need only show by a ***preponderance of the evidence*** that *D* intentionally destroyed the property.

   Example: Same as prior example, except reverse the order of the suits. State loses the civil suit for conversion. Now, State is precluded from prosecuting *D* for vandalism. If State could not prove intentional destruction under the lower standard, it logically should not be able to prove it under the more rigorous standard that applies in a criminal prosecution.

2. **Series of related obligations or events:** Another situation in which it can be difficult to determine if two cases involve the same issue is when a similar question of law arises in connection with separate but related obligations or events.

a. **When issue arises:** This problem often arises in an ***installment contract***, when parties enter into a ***series of contracts*** using identical language, or when parties deal with each other repeatedly in the same way, giving rise to a tort or property claim.

b. **General rule:** In most cases, the issues are ***not considered the same issue*** for purposes of issue preclusion, no matter how similar they seem. Notwithstanding the facial similarity, each obligation or event is technically a separate legal situation, and each requires an independent legal determination.

Example: *L* leases an apartment to *T* for a term of two years pursuant to an oral lease. Rent is to be paid monthly. When *T* does not pay rent in January, *L* sues. *T* claims that he need not pay rent because (a) the roof leaks, and (b) the oral lease is invalid under the statute of frauds. *L* prevails.

When *T* does not pay again in May, *L* brings a second action. (Claim preclusion does not apply because this is an installment contract.) *T* raises the same two defenses. Issue preclusion does not apply to the roof-leaking defense. Merely because the roof did not leak in January does not mean it does not leak now. However, issue preclusion does apply to the statute of frauds question. Although this is an installment contract, the issue of whether the lease is valid applies with equal force to all installments. See Cromwell v. County of Sac, 94 U.S. (4 Otto) 351 (1876).

C. **Actually litigated:** Unlike claim preclusion, issue preclusion applies only to issues that were actually presented to the court in the first action.

1. Because of this requirement, ***default judgments*** and ***dismissals*** do not have any issue preclusion effect.

2. Again, there is no concept of merger in issue preclusion.

D. **Actually decided:** Perhaps the most difficult question in issue preclusion is determining how an issue was actually decided in the first case. Plaintiffs frequently rely on ***alternate theories*** of recovery, and defendants frequently impose one or more defenses to a claim. If the court simply declares who wins without clearly stating *why* that party won, it may be difficult to ascertain precisely what the court found.

1. **Analysis:** To determine what a case actually decided, it is necessary to dissect the case logically. If a particular fact ***must have been decided in a particular way*** for the court to reach the result, issue preclusion will apply to that question. Conversely, if the court could reach the result in two or more different ways, and it is not clear which path the court chose, issue preclusion will not apply.

★ **Example:** Illinois Central Gulf R.R. v. Parks, 181 Ind. App. 141 (1979), sets out a relatively straightforward application of this rule. *P* and his wife were injured by a train at a grade crossing. In suit 1, both sued the railroad, the wife for her own injuries and *P* for loss of consortium. The wife won, but *P* lost.

P then sued the railroad for his own injuries (under state law, *P*'s consortium claim and personal injury claim involved different legal "rights" and accordingly were not barred by claim preclusion). The railroad argued that issue preclusion should prevent *P* from recovering.

The court disagreed and let the case proceed. The court reasoned that *P* could have lost either because he was contributorily negligent or because he suffered no damages. Although the contributory negligence issue was the same in both suits, damages would differ for the different claims.

Example: *P* has a copyright in a valuable computer program. When *D* begins to sell a similar program, *P* sues for copyright infringement. *D* denies that her program is similar enough to *P*'s to infringe the copyright and, in the alternative, argues that *P*'s copyright is invalid. The case is tried to a jury, and *D* wins a general verdict.

Later, *D* begins to sell a different program, which is even more similar to *P*'s. *P* sues again for copyright infringement. *D* claims that she is not liable because the first case established that *P*'s copyright is invalid. Issue preclusion does not apply. It is impossible to tell how the court ruled on copyright validity. Even if the copyright was found valid, *D* would prevail if the earlier program did not infringe the copyright.

Example: Same as prior example, except that *P* wins the first suit. Now, *P* claims that issue preclusion prevents *D* from arguing that the copyright is invalid. Issue preclusion does apply, and the question of copyright validity is resolved in *P*'s favor. For the court to find for *P*, it was logically necessary for it to find the copyright valid and that *D* infringed. Of course, issue preclusion does not apply to the question of whether *D*'s acts infringed because that issue is not the same as the one litigated in the first action.

2. **Types of decisions:** The "actually decided" issue frequently arises in the context of a ***jury trial*** because of the predominance of the ***general verdict***. In a bench trial, by contrast, the judge is supposed to discuss in detail all of the various claims and defenses in her judgment. Similarly, in a jury trial involving a special verdict, the jury specifies what it decides on each individual question in the case.

E. **Necessary to the judgment:** The final requirement for issue preclusion is that resolution of the issue in question was necessary to the judgment. Obviously, mere dictum is not necessary. But the "necessary to the judgment" requirement may also prevent issue preclusion from applying to many findings that were actual issues in dispute at the first trial.

Note: Courts and commentators often treat "actually decided" and "necessary to the judgment" as a single question. However, logically each presents its own unique issues, and the two are best thought of separately.

1. **When problem arises:** The issue of whether a factual determination was necessary to the judgment arises whenever a judgment ***explicitly*** sets out ***alternate bases for the holding***. Examples include:

   a. when a plaintiff seeks recovery for the same injury on ***alternate claims***, and the court finds that ***plaintiff should prevail*** on two or more of those claims;

   b. when a defendant defends using ***alternate defenses***, and the court finds that ***defendant should prevail*** on two or more of those defenses; and

   c. when a defendant asserts a ***defense*** to plaintiff's claim, and the court finds that ***defendant should prevail*** both on the defense and because plaintiff failed to prove its claim.

2. **Different from "actually decided":** Because the "necessary to the judgment" issue arises when the court explicitly states the reasons for its holding, the problem is conceptually distin-

guishable from the question of how an issue was actually decided in a case involving a general verdict.

3. **No clear rule:** Courts are *split fairly evenly* as to whether any of the alternate holdings is entitled to issue preclusion effect. About half follow the view of the Restatement (First) of Judgments, under which *all* of the alternate rulings have issue preclusion effect. Others follow the view of the Restatement (Second) of Judgments, under which *none* of the alternate rulings have issue preclusion effect.

   Example: *P* sues *D* for specific performance of a contract. *D* defends in the alternative, first denying that there was a contract, and second arguing that because *P* waited so long to seek enforcement, the defense of laches should apply. The court conducts a bench trial and eventually holds for *D*, explicitly finding both that there was no contract and that *P*'s claim is barred by laches. A month later, *D* takes another act that *P* considers to be a new breach of the contract. *P* immediately sues *D* again. *D* argues that the prior judgment established that there was no contract. Under the view of the Restatement (First), the court would apply issue preclusion. Under the view of the Restatement (Second), issue preclusion would not apply.

F. **Parties benefited and burdened:** Historically, both claim and issue preclusion applied only between those who were parties to the first suit or those in privity with the parties. Today, however, most jurisdictions have relaxed that requirement in issue preclusion.

   1. **Traditional rule:** The traditional rule required "*full mutuality*" before collateral estoppel could apply. In other words, the rule was the same as in claim preclusion: Preclusion applied only as between those who were parties in the first suit (and those in privity with parties).

   2. **"Indemnity circle" exception:** Many jurisdictions recognize an exception to the requirement of full mutuality, which is commonly called the *indemnity circle*. If a plaintiff sues someone who is *primarily liable* for an injury and *loses* that suit, that same plaintiff is precluded from arguing in a later action that another party is *secondarily liable* for that tort if that other party has a right to *indemnity* from the primarily liable party.

      Example: *P* is injured in a collision with a city bus. *P* sues the bus driver and loses. *P* then sues City, alleging that it is vicariously liable for the driver's negligence. Under the state law, an employer who is held vicariously liable has a right to indemnity from the employee. Issue preclusion prevents *P* from arguing that City is liable for the driver's negligence. However, *P* can still claim that City was affirmatively negligent in other ways.

   3. **Relaxation of mutuality requirement:** Most jurisdictions have abandoned the full mutuality requirement and allow *nonmutual use of issue preclusion*. However, whether nonmutual use is available may turn on whether the use is *offensive* or *defensive*.

      a. *Offensive* and *defensive use* **defined:** Whether a particular use is offensive or defensive depends on the procedural posture of the party in the *second suit*.

         i. *Offensive use* is use by a party who is *trying to recover on a claim* in the second suit.

         ii. *Defensive use* is use by a party who is *defending on a claim* in the second suit.

      b. **When nonmutual defensive use allowed:** Most courts have completely abandoned the mutuality requirement in cases of defensive use. A person who was not a party to the prior action may freely use issue preclusion against someone who was a party to that first suit and is now bringing a claim against the person invoking preclusion.

Example: *X* sues *Y* for trespass on certain land. *Y* argues that a prior judgment has issue preclusion effect in this case and prevents *X* from prevailing on the trespass claim. In this prior action, *Z* had sued *X* for trespass on the same land. The court entered judgment for *Z*. *Y* correctly argues that the prior judgment established that *Z*, not *X*, owned the land in question, which means *X* cannot sue *Y* for trespass. Most courts would allow *Y* to use issue preclusion in this defensive way, even though *Y* was not a party to the prior suit.

c. **When nonmutual offensive use allowed:** Offensive nonmutual use has proven more problematic, and accordingly its use is subject to greater limitations.

★

    i. **Problems with offensive nonmutual use:** The Supreme Court's decision in Parklane Hosiery Co. v. Shore, 439 U.S. 322 (1979), discusses the problems with offensive use. The two main problems are the ***free rider*** and ***inconsistent judgment*** problems.

       (a) Free rider: Because potential plaintiffs can only benefit from an earlier suit, they have an incentive to "sit and wait." If another plaintiff wins, they can take advantage of the victory. If the other plaintiff loses, they can still bring their action and not suffer any ill effects from the earlier loss.

       (b) Efficiency concerns: Second, nonmutual offensive use presents the risk of ***inconsistent judgments***. If plaintiffs sue in separate actions, and none of the plaintiffs are affected by the prior results, different courts could reach different conclusions concerning the same basic issue.

    ii. **Different rules:** Because of these concerns, jurisdictions differ as to the extent to which they allow nonmutual offensive use. A few do not allow nonmutual offensive use at all. However, many jurisdictions allow nonmutual offensive use with certain limits designed to account for these policy concerns. The ***federal approach***, which is set out in *Parklane* and has been adopted by many states, allows nonmutual offensive use ***unless such use is unfair because***:

       (a) there are ***prior inconsistent judgments*** (although one or two judgments in favor of the defendant do not prevent issue preclusion if those are outweighed by many judgments against the defendant);

       (b) it would have been ***easy*** for the party seeking to use offensive nonmutual preclusion ***to join in the prior action***; or

       (c) there are ***other reasons*** making it unfair to use preclusion.

★

       Example: For an illustration of how this test applies, see State Farm Fire & Casualty Co. v. Century Home Components, 275 Or. 97 (1976), where the court refused to allow offensive use given the inconsistent results in prior cases against the defendant.

d. **Use against person who was not a party:** It is important to remember that the relaxation of the mutuality requirement applies only against people who were ***parties in both actions***. It is a ***violation of due process*** to use claim or issue preclusion ***against someone who was not a party*** in the first case.

Example: *P* sues *D*, a large factory that emits noxious fumes, for nuisance. *D* attempts to use issue preclusion, relying on a judgment in *D*'s favor in a case filed by a different plaintiff. This other judgment held that *D*'s factory did not constitute a nuisance. Even though this is a defensive nonmutual use, *D* cannot use issue preclusion against *P*. Because *P* was not a party to the prior action, the due process clause entitles him to his day in court.

Note on privity: A person in privity with a party to the prior case not only may take advantage of preclusion, but also may have ***both claim and issue preclusion used against her*** without limitation. Privity ensures that the person's rights were fully and fairly represented.

Quiz Yourself on
ISSUE PRECLUSION

151. Landlord hires Attorney to sue several of the tenants in Landlord's shopping mall. Attorney first sues tenant *A*. Attorney serves process in the case by taping the summons and complaint to the door of *A*'s store. Because this form of service is ineffective under state law, tenant *A* moves for and obtains dismissal of the case based on ineffective service. After the dismissal, Attorney sues tenant *B*. He serves the same way. Tenant *B* likewise obtains dismissal of the case.

     Because Attorney's mistakes cause Landlord to lose a great deal of money, Landlord brings a malpractice action against Attorney, based on the error made in the suit against tenant *A*. Following a bench trial, the trial judge grants judgment for Attorney. The trial judge explicitly finds that Attorney was not negligent for failing to realize that service in this fashion was improper.

     Landlord now brings a second malpractice action against Attorney, based on the error made in the suit against tenant *B*. This second action is not barred by claim preclusion. However, Attorney moves for summary judgment based on issue preclusion. Does issue preclusion apply in this case? _____

152. Jake is rudely awakened one morning when the engine from a jet airplane crashes through his ceiling. The engine extensively damages the home and causes Jake serious bodily injury. Jake sues the airline for the injuries to his person. The airline's answer denies responsibility. After a short trial, the jury renders a general verdict for the airline, and judgment is entered accordingly.

     Jake brings another suit against the airline, seeking damages for the harm to the house. Under the minority rule applied in this state, Jake is not barred by claim preclusion from seeking recovery for the property damage in a separate action. The airline nevertheless argues that issue preclusion prevents Jake from asserting that the airline was negligent. Will the airline prevail on its issue preclusion argument? _____

153. Moe, Larry, and Curly are partners in a home repair service. While on a repair job at Schemp's house, all three are injured when Schemp's vicious pet Pomeranian attacks them. Larry and Curly bring separate actions against Schemp, the owner of the home, for their injuries. Larry and Curly each allege that Schemp was negligent in failing to restrain the dog. Larry's case reaches trial first, and Schemp prevails. The court enters judgment for Schemp. A few days later, the court in Curly's case enters a $3,000 judgment for Curly.

     Moe now sues Schemp. Moe similarly argues that Schemp was negligent for failing to restrain the dog. Moe further argues that issue preclusion prevents Schemp from arguing that he was not negligent in failing to restrain the dog. Will issue preclusion apply? _____

154. McDougal's, Inc., operates a nationwide chain of fast-food restaurants. McDougal's has entered into franchise agreements with individuals across the nation. Each of the franchisees signs a contract containing detailed terms. One of the terms requires the franchisee to purchase ''all ingredients used in preparing the food products'' directly from McDougal's.

     Fran operates a McDougal's franchise in New Mexico. To please her customers, Fran includes a small tray of condiments on every table. Fran does not purchase these condiments from McDougal's. McDougal's sues Fran for breach of the franchise agreement. Fran answers, claiming that condiments are not used in the ''preparation'' of the food. The parties eventually iron out a settlement under which Fran agrees to pay $2,000 to McDougal's. The parties agree on a consent judgment, which the court then enters.

     One year later, McDougal's triples the price of its condiments. Fran therefore reverts to purchasing the condiments from a third party. McDougal's again sues her for breach of the franchise agreement. Fran again argues that condiments are not used in the ''preparation'' of the food. McDougal's argues that issue preclusion prevents Fran from bringing up that issue in this suit. Is McDougal's correct? _____

Answers

151. Issue preclusion does not apply. In order for issue preclusion to apply, the two cases must involve the *same issue*. The basic legal question in both cases is the same, namely, whether Attorney's mistaken belief that he could serve by taping notice to the store door was negligent. However, although the legal question is the same, the issue of negligence requires the application of law to fact. Although it might not have been negligent to think that service by taping to the door was proper in the first case, the circumstances are different in the second case. Most importantly, the result of the Landlord v. tenant *A* decision should have put Attorney on notice that this form of service was ineffective. Therefore, the cases do not involve the same issue, and issue preclusion does not apply.

152. Issue preclusion does not apply. Because the case was decided by a general verdict, we do not know why the jury reached the result it reached. It could have found that Jake failed to prove that the airline was negligent. In the alternative, the jury could have found that Jake suffered no personal injuries in the action. In the latter case, there would be nothing inconsistent about letting Jake prevail in the second case, where he seeks damages for harm to his property. Because we cannot be sure what was actually decided in the first case, issue preclusion does not apply.

153. Issue preclusion probably does not apply. Moe is trying to use offensive nonmutual collateral estoppel. Most courts apply a test akin to that in *Parklane Hosiery* when dealing with offensive nonmutual use. Under this test, the court allows offensive nonmutual use unless the current party could easily have joined in the prior action or unless allowing issue preclusion is unfair because of prior inconsistent judgments.

     Here, Moe quite easily could have joined in the prior action. More importantly, it is unfair to Schemp to apply issue preclusion. Schemp has won one suit and lost another. It is unfair to let Moe take advantage of Curly v. Schemp while at the same time not be hindered by Larry v. Schemp.

154. McDougal's is not correct. Issue preclusion does not apply here because the issue was not fully litigated in the earlier case and the court did not actually decide the crucial issue. Consent judgments do have claim preclusion effect but have no issue preclusion effect.

III. LIMITS ON PRECLUSION

The policies underlying claim and issue preclusion sometimes conflict with other concerns in the civil litigation process. As a result, courts have developed several exceptions to the preclusion doctrines.

   A. Exceptions to claim preclusion: There are relatively few exceptions to claim preclusion. The most commonly recognized are the following four exceptions.

   1. A suit in another state to collect on a judgment: When a party obtains a judgment in one state, he may take that judgment to another state in order to obtain assets owned by the judgment debtor in that other state. Historically, it was necessary to bring a suit in the second state to enforce the judgment. Claim preclusion *does not bar* the judgment victor from suing on the judgment in other states in order to collect the judgment.

   2. First court lacked subject matter jurisdiction over an omitted claim: This situation is discussed in Part I.D.3 of this chapter.

   3. By agreement: Claim preclusion does not apply where the *parties agree* to allow claim-splitting or the court in the first action *expressly indicates* that the party is free to bring one or more claims in a later action.

   4. Fairness requires: In exceedingly rare situations, because of *overwhelming concerns for fairness*, certain claims may be brought in a later action.

   B. Exceptions to issue preclusion: Restatement (Second) of Judgments §28 lists the more numerous exceptions to issue preclusion.

   Note: Although the Restatement lists these situations as "exceptions," many of them could also be dealt with under the "same issue" requirement.

   1. No review available: Issue preclusion does not apply if *no review of the judgment was available*. However, issue preclusion does apply if review is available but, for whatever reason, is not sought by the judgment loser.

   2. Intervening change in law: Issue preclusion does not apply if the issue involves the application of law to fact and there has been an *intervening change in the law or the interpretation of the law*.

   3. Procedural advantages: Issue preclusion may not apply if there are *procedural advantages* available in the second suit that were not available in the first action. For example, if the first action did not allow for *discovery* or *cross-examination*, issue preclusion may well not apply. Similarly, cases in *small claims* or similar tribunals usually are not entitled to preclusive effect because of the significant limitations on procedure.

4. **Burden of persuasion greater:** Issue preclusion does not apply if the *burden of persuasion* on the party who is to be burdened by issue preclusion was more rigorous in the first action than in the second. This issue is discussed at length in Part II.B.1 above.

5. **Against public interest:** Issue preclusion does not apply if it goes against the *public interest*. This rationale supports the general rule that *offensive* nonmutual issue preclusion is *not available against the federal government*. United States v. Mendoza, 464 U.S. 154 (1984).

6. **No incentive:** Issue preclusion does not apply if the party to be bound did not have an *incentive to litigate* the first case fully and fairly, either because of the actions of others or because he could not appreciate the ramifications of the first action on later litigation.

IV. FULL FAITH AND CREDIT

To this point, the discussion has assumed that the courts hearing the first and second actions are located in the same jurisdiction. However, the U.S. Constitution and federal statute law also require courts to apply claim and issue preclusion to decisions rendered by other jurisdictions. Although a full discussion of full faith and credit is beyond the scope of a first-year Procedure course, it is important to understand the basics.

A. **Governing law:** Both Article IV of the U.S. Constitution and federal statutes impose a full faith and credit requirement. The most important statute is *28 U.S.C. §1738*. There are also specialized statutes governing the full faith and credit effect of child custody determinations, *28 U.S.C. §1738A*, and child support orders, *28 U.S.C. §1738B*.

1. **State-federal issues:** The full faith and credit statutes have been interpreted to apply between state and federal courts. State courts must give full faith and credit to federal courts and vice versa.

2. **Foreign judgments:** Neither the constitution nor the statutes apply to judgments of foreign courts. Nevertheless, under the doctrine of *comity*, courts in the United States may afford claim and issue preclusion effect to judgments of foreign tribunals that result from a fair process.

B. **What full faith and credit requires:** In essence, full faith and credit *makes claim and issue preclusion apply across state lines*. A court must afford preclusive effect to the decisions of other courts.

Example: *P* sues *D* in a state court in State *A*. The court enters judgment for *D*. *P* sues *D* again in a federal court in State *B*, raising a slightly different claim arising from the same facts. The federal court will grant *D*'s motion to dismiss the action based on claim preclusion.

1. **Governing law:** The rules governing claim and issue preclusion vary among different jurisdictions. When applying full faith and credit, the court in the second action must look to *the law of the jurisdiction that decided the first action* to determine whether the claim or issue is precluded.

Example: *P1* is a passenger on a City bus that is involved in an accident. *P1* sues City for negligence in a state court in State *A*. *P1* prevails. *P2*, another passenger on the same bus, sues City for her injuries, again based on a theory of negligence. *P2* sues in a state court in State *B*. *P2* argues that the prior judgment should be given issue preclusion effect on the question of whether City was negligent. The law of State *B* forbids nonmutual offensive use of collateral estoppel in these circumstances. However, the court in *B* must look to the law of State *A*. If under the law of *A* a party such as *P2* could make offensive nonmutual use, *B* is required by full faith and credit to apply issue preclusion to the issue of negligence. To refuse preclusive effect is to give "less than full" faith and credit.

2. **Giving *more* preclusive effect:** In some situations, a state might want to give preclusive effect to a judgment even though the court that issued the judgment would not.

    a. **State courts:** Under both the Constitution and the full faith and credit statute, a state court is *free to apply preclusion* even though the first court would not.

        Example: Same as prior example, except that the laws of *A* and *B* are reversed. *A* does not allow *P2* to use issue preclusion offensively. *B* is nevertheless free to apply the law of *B* and to prevent City from relitigating the question of its negligence.

    b. **Federal courts:** A federal court *may not* give more preclusive effect to a state court judgment than the rendering court would give. Migra v. Warren City School District Board of Education, 465 U.S. 75 (1984).

C. **Scope of full faith and credit:** The requirement of full faith and credit is ***very strict***. A judgment is entitled to full faith and credit even though the court clearly made an error. A court must enforce the judgment of another state or federal court even though the underlying claim is illegal or violates the public policy of the enforcing jurisdiction. Fauntleroy v. Lum, 210 U.S. 230 (1908). However, there are some exceptions.

1. **Orders affecting title to real property:** A court in one state cannot decree property rights in real property situated in another state. Fall v. Eastin, 215 U.S. 1 (1909). Therefore, such an order is not entitled to full faith and credit.

2. **Lack of jurisdiction:** A judgment rendered without jurisdiction is void and therefore not entitled to full faith and credit. In theory, then, a party may ***collaterally attack*** a judgment in the courts of another state by showing lack of jurisdiction. The limits on collateral attack are discussed in Chapters 2 and 4.

★   **Example:** The Supreme Court's decision in Durfee v. Duke, 375 U.S. 106 (1963), provides a classic example of the limits on collateral attack. The case involved ownership of land. The court's jurisdiction turned on whether the land was in Nebraska or Missouri, which was not clear. The parties had litigated the question of jurisdiction before the Nebraska courts in the first action. Duke then tried to bring a second action in Missouri. The Court held that Duke was precluded from arguing that the land was in Missouri because he had appeared in the first case. However, the court's decision also makes it clear that other parties would be free to bring an action in Missouri and assert their rights to the same property.

3. **Divorce:** In order for a state to grant a divorce, one of the spouses to the marriage must be domiciled in that state. If a state grants a divorce when neither spouse lives there, the decree is not entitled to full faith and credit.

V. OTHER ISSUES IN PRECLUSION

Certain other rules affect how the doctrines of claim and issue preclusion apply.

A. Reopening judgments: Most procedural systems place strict time limits on motions to amend the judgment or to file an appeal. The Federal Rules of Civil Procedure, for example, allow a party only 10 days to move to overturn or amend a judgment, and that time period cannot be extended. A party also has only 30 days to appeal in the federal system. However, the Federal Rules of Civil Procedure, and some states, provide a safety valve that allows judgments to be reopened. In the federal courts, the governing rule is ***Fed. R. Civ. P. 60(b)***, which allows a party to obtain ***relief from a judgment*** — typically a new trial — in certain situations.

1. **Grounds for reopening judgment:** Fed. R. Civ. P. 60(b) allows a federal court to reopen a judgment in the following situations:

   a. When the judgment was the result of ***mistake, inadvertence, surprise, or excusable neglect***. Fed. R. Civ. P. 60(b)(1). Aside from default judgments without notice, courts apply this rule very strictly. Simple oversights and mistakes do not suffice.

   b. When the party seeking relief discovered ***new evidence*** that a diligent search would not have uncovered in time to move for a new trial under Rule 59. Fed. R. Civ. P. 60(b)(2).

   c. When the judgment resulted from ***fraud, misrepresentation, or other misconduct*** of an adverse party. Fed. R. Civ. P. 60(b)(3). Here, the party must also show that the fraud or other misconduct was ***prejudicial*** to the party's chances to win the case.

   d. If the judgment is ***void***. Fed. R. Civ. P. 60(b)(4).

   e. If the judgment has been ***satisfied, released, or discharged***. Fed. R. Civ. P. 60(b)(5).

   f. If the judgment is ***based on an earlier judgment*** that was reversed or otherwise vacated. Fed. R. Civ. P. 60(b)(5). This language deals with the situation where a court applied claim or issue preclusion but the judgment given preclusive effect was reversed.

   g. If it is ***no longer equitable*** to apply the judgment prospectively. Fed. R. Civ. P. 60(b)(5).

   h. *For any other reason justifying relief*. Fed. R. Civ. P. 60(b)(6). Most courts interpret Rule 60(b)(6) so it does not overlap with the other provisions. Therefore, if the situation fits within Rule 60(b)(1) to (3) — and is therefore subject to the one-year limit — the party cannot use Rule 60(b)(6) to bring the same claim after the one year expires.

2. **Relief very rare:** Other than default judgments, courts rarely grant relief under Fed. R. Civ. P. 60(b).

3. **Time limits:** Motions seeking relief under Fed. R. Civ. P. 60(b)(1), (2), or (3) must be made within ***one year*** of the judgment. This time ***cannot be extended***. Fed. R. Civ. P. 6(b). Motions under Rule 60(b)(4), (5), and (6) have no fixed deadline but must be brought within a ***reasonable time***.

★ 4. **Independent action for relief:** Rule 60 also preserves the historic independent action for relief from a judgment, which is a ***new action*** brought to set aside a prior judgment. However, in United States v. Beggerly, 524 U.S. 38 (1998), the Supreme Court held that if the grounds for relief asserted in an independent action parallel the grounds listed in Rule 60(b)(i) to (iii), the independent action is subject to the same one-year time limit.

B. Law of the case: Claim and issue preclusion apply between two or more separate judicial proceedings. The doctrine of "law of the case," by contrast, applies at ***different stages of the same action***.

1. **Basic rule:** The basic rule of the law of the case is that a court's interpretation of the law at one stage of the proceeding will bind that court, and all lower courts, at further stages in the proceeding.

    Example: *P* sues *D*. The trial court dismisses the action, finding that *P* has no legal claim. *P* appeals, and the court of appeals reverses, finding that *P* does have a viable claim. The court of appeals remands the case for trial. Obviously, the trial court must apply the court of appeals' ruling. At trial, *P* prevails, and *D* appeals. *D* attempts to argue that *P* has no legal claim. The court of appeals will apply the law of the case and rely on its prior determination.

2. **Limits:** The law of the case applies only to ***rulings of law***, not findings of fact. Moreover, the earlier ruling ***only binds courts in the actual case***. A court may ignore its ruling (although not the ruling of a higher court) in a different proceeding, even if the legal issue is identical.

C. **Judicial estoppel:** Judicial estoppel is a somewhat amorphous doctrine that, like claim and issue preclusion, applies when a party is involved in two cases that overlap to some extent. Basically, the doctrine prevents a party who has taken a ***sworn position*** in the first case from taking an inconsistent position in the second. Courts typically apply judicial estoppel when the party being estopped *prevailed* on the issue in the first action. In issue preclusion, by contrast, the party usually either *lost* on the issue, or won less than what she now seeks.

Quiz Yourself on
RESPECT FOR JUDGMENTS

155. On Monday, Lucky Louie, a law student, is walking from the parking lot to the school when he is hit by a city bus. The mishap breaks Louie's arm. On Wednesday, while Lucky Louie is walking across the same street at the same time of day, he is again hit by a city bus. This accident leaves him physically intact but breaks the priceless heirloom watch that he keeps in his pocket. The same driver was operating the bus on both dates.

      Lucky Louie first sues the driver and the City for the Monday accident. Lucky Louie alleges that the driver operated the bus negligently and that the City was negligent in the way it trained its bus drivers. The court grants summary judgment for Lucky Louie against the driver but grants summary judgment against Louie on his claim against the City.

      Lucky Louie now brings a second action against the same defendants, based on the Wednesday incident. Lucky Louie again alleges that the driver was operating the bus carelessly and the City was negligent in the way it trained its bus drivers.

      Both defendants move for summary judgment, this time based on claim and issue preclusion. Will Lucky Louie's case be affected by claim and/or issue preclusion? _____

156. Pomum, Inc., and Fenster, Inc., both produce and sell tiny watch-sized computers. Because their products are so small, the companies rely on a special computer chip produced by Chip's Chips, Ltd. Fenster enters into a contract with Chip under which Chip agrees to sell his entire output to Fenster. When Pomum learns of this, it sues Fenster in state court, alleging unfair competition. Fenster wins a judgment.

After this judgment is entered, Pomum sues Fenster again in federal district court, alleging that Fenster's exclusive contract also violates federal antitrust laws. Fenster files a motion for summary judgment based on claim preclusion. Pomum responds by correctly pointing out that the federal courts have exclusive subject matter jurisdiction over antitrust claims, so that Pomum could not have filed its antitrust claim in the first case. How is the court likely to rule on Fenster's motion? _____

157. Ann Ternett runs an Internet survey firm. She has a contract with USA Online, a major Internet service provider, for Internet access. Under this contract, Ann pays USA a monthly fee of $3,000, which gives all of her employees unlimited access. USA sues Ann in March 2003 for $6,000, claiming that she did not pay the fee for January and February of that year. Ann's answer denies liability. First, she argues that she did pay the fee. Second, and in the alternative, she asserts that she was not obligated to pay the monthly fee because USA made false representations to her when the parties negotiated the contract. The case is tried to a jury in September 2003. The jury returns a special verdict in which it explicitly finds that (i) Ann had paid the $6,000 fee, and (ii) that Ann was not obligated to pay anyway because of the false representations. Judgment is entered for Ann in conformance with this verdict.

After the case is complete, USA files another action against Ann in which it claims that Ann did not pay the fee for May, June, and July 2003. Ann moves for summary judgment based on both claim and issue preclusion. How should the court rule? _____

158. One extremely hot day, a number of passengers board a flight operated by Daisy Airways. When the plane pulls away from the gate, the pilot notices that one engine is malfunctioning. Instead of returning to the gate, however, the pilot keeps the passengers on the plane while the mechanics try to deal with the problem. The passengers remain in the plane for over five hours in stifling 100° F outside temperatures.

Pamela, a passenger on the plane, sues Deena, the pilot of the airplane, in a state court for damages. Pamela claims that she suffered heatstroke on the flight. After a short bench trial, judgment is entered for Deena. The trial judge's ruling explicitly finds that Pamela failed to prove that Deena acted negligently in trying to deal with the problem on the tarmac.

Pamela now sues Deena a second time, this time in a federal court. When Deena raises claim preclusion, Pamela responds by arguing that the state court judgment was invalid for two reasons. First, a federal statute provides that the federal courts have exclusive jurisdiction over claims arising out of injuries caused on airplanes. Second, a different federal statute provides that a pilot is liable for all injuries suffered by passengers if he or she keeps the passengers on the tarmac for more than one hour in temperatures higher than 85° F. Although Pamela relied on that federal statute in her first case, the state court simply disregarded it, stating that it was a "stupid law."

Deena acknowledges that both of the federal statutes apply to Pamela's claim. She nevertheless argues that Pamela's claim is still barred by claim preclusion. What result? _____

159. Husband and Wife are traveling in an automobile. Husband is driving. Distracted for a moment by something on the side of the road, Husband drives the car into a ditch, seriously injuring Wife. Wife sues Husband for her injuries. The trial court grants Husband's motion for summary judgment, holding that a common law spousal immunity prevents Wife from suing Husband in tort. Wife appeals. The court of appeals reverses, holding that a new statute abrogates the common law immunity. The appellate court remands the case for a trial.

The trial results in a judgment for Wife. Husband appeals. Husband has done additional research and has discovered language in the statute that makes it clear that it was *not* intended to override the prior common law spousal immunity. Wife argues that Husband is precluded from making that argument. How is the court of appeals likely to rule? _____

Answers

155. This problem presents questions of both claim and issue preclusion. As a preliminary matter, that the first case was decided by summary judgment does not affect claim preclusion. Nor does it affect issue preclusion in this case, for Lucky Louie had a full chance to present his evidence.

Claim preclusion could be an issue for Lucky Louie's claim against the driver. If the two accidents arose from the same primary event, the claims would comprise a single cause of action under the majority approach. However, the two injuries did not occur from the same event. Notwithstanding their similarity, the two accidents are two distinct events. If the court applied the minority ''same primary right'' test, it would reach the same result. Louie would clearly have two separate injuries, which he could sue for separately.

With respect to the City, it may appear at first glance that claim preclusion would apply. Unlike the driver, the same negligence of the City — the policy of defective training — was the cause of both injuries. Nevertheless, because Louie still suffered two distinct injuries, claim preclusion does not apply.

However, although claim preclusion does not apply to the claim against the City, the City can use issue preclusion. We know that Louie lost the first suit against the City. Ordinarily, we could not be sure whether he lost because he failed to prove negligence or because he failed to prove harm. In this case, however, we know that Louie proved harm because he recovered against the driver. Therefore, the summary judgment for the City in the first case must have been based on a finding that Louie failed to prove a negligent training policy. Because that issue is the same issue as involved in this case, issue preclusion applies.

156. Fenster's motion is likely to fail, although there are not enough facts to form a definite answer. First, there is an issue of full faith and credit. A federal court is required by 28 U.S.C. §1738 to afford full faith and credit to the judgments of a state court.

However, the federal court will bar the claim only if the claim would be barred under the law of the state that rendered the judgment. If the state will bar a claim that could not have been brought in the first court because of lack of jurisdiction, then the federal antitrust claim here is barred. Although we do not know state law, most states will *not* bar a claim over which the court in the first action had no jurisdiction.

157. Although Ann is not likely to prevail on claim preclusion, she may prevail on issue preclusion depending on the law in effect in this jurisdiction.

The contract is an installment contract. Therefore, as a general matter, USA is free to sue for each month's payment separately. Although the rule of accumulated breaches requires USA to join the claims for all installments already overdue, the majority rule is that the party need not include breaches that occur after suit is filed. Because USA filed suit in March, it did not need to include the May, June, and July breaches and is free to sue for them in this separate action.

However, issue preclusion may apply. Although each installment is a separate claim, they share issues. The problem is that the first case was decided on alternate bases. The first basis (nonpayment) is not the same issue as present in this case. That Ann paid for January and February does not mean she paid during May, June, and July. The second basis (misrepresentation) *may* be the same in the two cases. To the extent that USA has evidence that it now provides what it claimed it would provide, then the issue is different and issue preclusion does not apply. If the service has not changed, however, then the issue is the same and issue preclusion may apply.

Whether issue preclusion applies depends on whether the state follows the view of the Restatement (First) of Judgments, under which the finding would have preclusive effect, or the Restatement (Second), under which the alternate ruling would have no effect. Courts are roughly evenly split, and there is no way to tell which rule this jurisdiction follows.

158. Pamela's claim is almost certainly barred by claim preclusion. 28 U.S.C. §1738 requires federal courts to give full faith and credit to state court judgments. The federal court must bar the claim to the same extent that the courts of that state bar the claim.

As a general matter, a judgment rendered by a court without jurisdiction is void and accordingly not entitled to full faith and credit. However, to challenge a prior judgment on this basis, the party raising the challenge cannot have appeared in the prior case. Pamela not only appeared, but she selected the state court.

In addition, a court cannot refuse full faith and credit to a judgment merely because the first court erred or even because the second court strongly disagrees with the policy underlying the law used in the first case. Therefore, the federal court cannot refuse full faith and credit based on the fact that the state court blatantly disregarded the federal liability statute.

159. Wife is likely to prevail. Neither claim nor issue preclusion apply because this is not a collateral attack on a final judgment. However, the doctrine of law of the case provides that once a court decides a legal issue, all courts at the same or lower level cannot overturn that ruling in later proceedings in the case, even if the ruling is erroneous.

 Exam Tips on
RESPECT FOR JUDGMENTS

☛ You should consider claim and issue preclusion whenever you are presented with an exam question setting forth two separate suits.

☛ Do not forget that claim and issue preclusion are related concepts. Therefore, unless a problem makes it clear that you are to consider only one, analyze both.

    ☞ Consider *claim preclusion first*. If it applies, it has a much broader sweep, barring complete claims.

    ☞ If claim preclusion does not apply, consider whether individual issues involved in both of the suits might nonetheless be barred.

☛ **Claim preclusion:** Do not forget that states apply different tests to determine if two claims are sufficiently related to qualify for claim preclusion.

    ☞ When dealing with counterclaims, recall that in most cases you will apply Fed. R. Civ. P. 13 rather than the more complicated common law compulsory counterclaim rule. As long as there was an answer filed in the first case, Rule 13 trumps.

    ☞ A plaintiff is generally free to sue two or more defendants in separate cases, even if the defendants would be jointly and severally liable.

    ☞ Make sure that you have a solid grasp of the sorts of rulings that qualify as a judgment on the merits for purposes of claim preclusion.

☛ *Privity* is a conceptually difficult doctrine. As a rule of thumb, however, privity does *not* exist between joint tortfeasors or between co-owners of property.

☛ When dealing with *issue preclusion*, first identify all the issues that should logically arise in each of the two cases. In addition, make sure you know whether the first case was a bench trial or jury trial and, if a jury trial, the form of the verdict.

☞ In the case of a *general verdict*, analyze the first case very carefully in order to determine what must have been decided. If there are alternate theories under which the jury could have reached the same result and only one of those theories is relevant in the second case, issue preclusion does not apply.

☞ In a *bench trial* or *special verdict*, by contrast, you may well have to deal with the problem of alternate holdings.

☞ In either of these situations, be on the lookout for a situation where *all of* the issues from the first case reappear in the second. In this case, it does not matter which theory the factfinder used in the first case.

☛ Lack of *mutuality* is an issue only in issue preclusion, not in claim preclusion. In claim preclusion, the two cases must involve the same parties.

☛ You should discuss *full faith and credit* in your answer whenever the two courts are in different jurisdictions. Although it may be obvious that the second court has to enforce the first judgment, you should at least mention the full faith and credit obligation in your answer.

☞ When dealing with full faith and credit, always recall that the preclusion law of the first court sets the floor.

☞ No matter how much the facts cry for a different result, recall that a state cannot refuse to enforce another state's judgment because it disagrees with the underlying claim.

☛ Be very hesitant before concluding that a party may reopen any judgment other than a default judgment using Fed. R. Civ. P. 60(b).

CHAPTER 14

JOINDER OF CLAIMS AND PARTIES

ChapterScope

This chapter takes Procedure beyond the single plaintiff-defendant-claim case to situations involving multiple claims and parties. The chapter focuses almost exclusively on joinder under the Federal Rules of Civil Procedure.

- Parties have tremendous freedom in adding claims. Joining additional parties to the suit is, however, more limited.

- Plaintiff is not the only party who may join claims and parties to the case.

  - Defendants may file *counterclaims* against plaintiffs and *cross-claims* against each other.

  - Defendants (and in some cases plaintiffs) may *implead third parties* to the action for purposes of indemnity or contribution.

  - In some cases, third parties may *intervene* in existing cases to protect their rights.

- Many of the Federal Rules of Civil Procedure dealing with joinder use the *same transaction or occurrence* test.

- When a claim involving multiple claims and parties is litigated in *federal court*, it is crucial to deal with whether the federal court has jurisdiction over the joined claims and/or parties.

  - Joinder and jurisdiction are separate issues. Although the analyses of the two often will dovetail, it is important to deal with each separately.

- Joinder of claims and parties is usually at the discretion of the parties. However, in certain cases joinder of parties is required by FRCP 19.

I. JOINDER OF CLAIMS AGAINST CURRENT PARTIES

Fed. R. Civ. P. 13 and *18* allow plaintiffs and defendants who are already in a lawsuit to file additional claims against the other. In most cases, these claims are optional; however, *certain counterclaims are compulsory*.

A. Adding claims to original claim, counterclaim, or cross-claim: *Fed. R. Civ. P. 18(a)* provides that "A party asserting a claim to relief as an original claim, counterclaim, cross-claim, or third-party claim, may join . . . as many claims . . . as the party has against an opposing party." Note that the rule applies to "any party," not merely plaintiffs.

1. Not applicable to first claim: Fed. R. Civ. P. 18 applies only when the party *already has one claim* that he has brought against the other party *under some other rule*. In essence, then, Rule 18 applies only to claims two and higher.

2. **No relationship required:** Rule 18 *does not use the same transaction test*. A party may join additional claims regardless of whether the claims have anything to do with each other.

3. **Jurisdictional limits:** In federal court, a party's ability to join unrelated claims is significantly restricted by the requirement that a federal court have *subject matter jurisdiction over all claims*. See Part V.B.

4. **Alternate claims allowable:** Rule 18 allows a party to join claims even if those claims are inconsistent with each other.

B. **Counterclaims:** *Fed. R. Civ. P. 13* allows a defendant to bring any claims that she may have against the opposing party. In some cases, however, a defendant *must* bring certain claims or risk losing them.

1. **Permissive counterclaims:** *Fed. R. Civ. P. 13(b)* allows a defendant to bring any claim he has against the plaintiff, regardless of whether it is related in any way to the plaintiff's claim.

2. **Compulsory counterclaims:** If defendant has a claim that *arises from the same transaction or occurrence* as the plaintiff's claim, defendant *must raise* the claim in his responsive pleading, unless one of the exceptions apply.

a. **Same transaction or occurrence:** Rule 13(a) is one of several rules that make joinder turn on whether the claims arise from the same transaction or occurrence.

i. **Rationale:** In interpreting this phrase, it is important to keep in mind the policy underlying joinder under the Federal Rules of Civil Procedure. The liberal rules of joinder serve two basic ends: *efficiency* and *consistency*. If two claims overlap to a significant extent, it is inefficient to have two courts decide the same issues in two separate cases. Similarly, if two courts adjudicate the same key facts, they may reach *inconsistent results*.

ii. **Tests:** Several tests are used to measure whether a claim and counterclaim meet the "same transaction or occurrence" standard.

(a) **Logical relationship test:** This test asks if the two claims are logically related in any significant way. This is the *majority rule*. The relationship need not be logical in the strict sense. In other words, the outcome of one claim need not turn on the outcome of the other. Instead, they must derive from the same underlying set of facts, even if the subset of facts relevant to each claim differs.

(b) **Same evidence test:** This test asks if there is a significant overlap between the *disputed elements* of the two claims. A *significant minority* of courts use this analysis. The test is *narrower* than the logical relationship test. It is not enough that the claims arise from the same identifiable event; rather, the *core facts* giving rise to the claims must overlap to some degree.

(c) **Other tests:** A few courts use other tests. For example, some ask whether the *issues of law and fact* raised by the two claims are largely the same. It is not entirely clear how this test differs from the same evidence test. Others ask whether *res judicata* (discussed in Chapter 13) would bar the claim if it was not brought with the other.

    b. Excepted claims: Even if a counterclaim arises from the same transaction or occurrence, a defendant need not assert it if:

        i. defendant has ***not filed an answer*** (Fed. R. Civ. P. 13(a) requires the counterclaim to appear in the answer);

        ii. the claim ***has not yet arisen*** when the defendant files his answer;

        iii. adjudication of the claim requires the presence of ***third parties*** who would destroy diversity jurisdiction or over whom the court cannot obtain personal jurisdiction;

        iv. at the time the answer is served the counterclaim is ***already being litigated*** in another state or federal action; or

        v. the plaintiff's suit is based on ***in rem*** or ***quasi-in-rem*** jurisdiction.

    c. Failing to plead compulsory counterclaim: Although the Federal Rules of Civil Procedure do not clearly specify this result, a defendant who fails to plead a compulsory counterclaim loses that claim and cannot assert it in later litigation.

3. Counterclaims by plaintiffs and others: Fed. R. Civ. P. 13(a) and (b) permit counterclaims to be brought not only by defendants but by any party against an "opposing party."

    a. By plaintiff: Thus, if defendant files a counterclaim against the plaintiff, plaintiff may add additional claims against the defendant as counterclaims. If plaintiff's additional claim arises from the ***same transaction or occurrence*** as defendant's counterclaim and does not fall into one of the Rule 13(a) exceptions, it is a compulsory counterclaim.

    b. By other parties: Counterclaims may — and in some cases *must* — also be filed by third parties who have been added to the suit under Fed. R. Civ. P. 14 (impleader) or 13(h). These rules are discussed in Parts II.B and C below.

C. Cross-claims: Cross-claims are filed by one ***co-party*** against another, for example, by one defendant against another defendant. ***Fed. R. Civ. P. 13(g)*** governs cross-claims.

1. Same transaction test: A party may file any claim against a co-party arising from the same transaction or occurrence as ***either*** the ***original complaint*** or a ***counterclaim***, or that relates to property that is the subject matter of the transaction. The "same transaction or occurrence" analysis is discussed in Part I.B. of this chapter.

    Example: *P1* and *P2* sue *D* in a federal court. *D* files a counterclaim against both *P*s that does not arise from the same transaction or occurrence as the *P*s' original claim. *P1* wants to file a cross-claim against *P2*, seeking indemnity from *P2* should *D* prevail on the counterclaim. Because the cross-claim arises from the same transaction as the counterclaim, *P1* may file the cross-claim in this action.

2. Always voluntary: Fed. R. Civ. P. 13(g) specifies that a party "may" file a cross-claim. Cross-claims are always optional, never required.

3. Cross-claims vs. counterclaims: On the other hand, once a party is served with a cross-claim, she and the claiming party become "opposing parties," and she is required by Rule 13(a) to file any factually related counterclaims she has against the serving party.

Example: In the prior example, suppose that *P1* does file the cross-claim against *P2*. *P2* has a claim against *P1* that arises from the same occurrence as the cross-claim filed by *P1*. Rule 13(a) requires *P2* to file her claim against *P1* in this case.

II. JOINDER OF PARTIES

Many real-life disputes involve more than a single plaintiff and a single defendant. The Federal Rules of Civil Procedure are fairly liberal in allowing additional parties to be joined in the action.

A. Multiple plaintiffs and defendants: *Fed. R. Civ. P. 20* allows multiple parties to join as plaintiffs in the action and allows the plaintiff or plaintiffs to sue more than one defendant.

   1. Parties joining as plaintiffs: The first sentence of Rule 20 provides: "All persons may join in one action as plaintiffs if they assert any right to relief jointly, severally, or in the alternative in respect of or arising out of the same transaction, occurrence, or series of transactions or occurrences and if any question of law or fact common to all these persons will arise in the action."

      a. Joint, several, or in the alternative: Plaintiffs sue ***jointly*** when they share a right, such as when they sue to collect for damage to a chattel in which they own an undivided interest. Plaintiffs sue ***severally*** when each has an individual right to recover, such as when a passenger and driver who were injured in an automobile accident sue for their respective individual injuries. When plaintiffs sue ***in the alternative***, they allege that one of them, but not both, is entitled to recover. Taken together, these three situations cover all the ways in which plaintiffs might be entitled to recover.

      Example: Testator leaves property in her will to "my favorite daughter." After Testator dies, two of her daughters, *P1* and *P2*, each claim to be Testator's favorite. *P1* and *P2* may sue the executor of Testator's estate in the alternative. Only one of the two will prevail.

      b. Same transaction or occurrence: The second requirement is that the claims arise from the same transaction or occurrence or ***series of transactions or occurrences***.

         i. The "same transaction or occurrence" analysis is discussed in Part I.B of this chapter.

         ii. Series of transactions or occurrences: Unlike Fed. R. Civ. P. 13, Rule 20 allows joinder either if the claims arise from the same transaction or occurrence or a ***series of transactions or occurrences***. Although this language seems broader, courts have interpreted the language in Rule 20 no differently than they have in Rule 13.

★   **Example:** Mosley v. General Motors Corp., 497 F.2d 1330 (8th Cir. 1974), illustrates the reach of the same transaction or occurrence test under Fed. R. Civ. P. 20. In that case, 10 plaintiffs sued their employer, alleging that they had been the victims of race and sex discrimination. The court allowed the 10 to join. Even though the plaintiffs were subject to individualized acts of discrimination, the court relied on the fact that the plaintiffs had alleged a "general policy of discrimination" within the company. All the claims arose from that general policy.

      c. Common question: Finally, the claims must share a ***common question of law or fact***.

         i. Significance: The common question must bear a ***significant relationship*** to the action in order to qualify.

    ii. Not redundant: Merely because two claims arise from the same transaction or occurrence does not guarantee that they involve a common question of law or fact. Under the majority "logical relationship" test for same transaction or occurrence, it is possible for two claims to arise from the same basic facts but be based on entirely discrete subsets of that general fact pattern. In that case, there may be no question of law or fact common to the claims.

2. Parties joined as defendants: Fed. R. Civ. P. 20 also allows a plaintiff to sue multiple defendants. The analysis is parallel to that used for multiple plaintiffs, using essentially the same three-part test.

    a. Jointly, severally or in the alternative: Plaintiff must allege that the defendants are liable to him jointly, severally, or in the alternative. These three cover all possible bases of liability.

        i. Joint and several: In many states, two defendants are held jointly and severally liable for torts in which they both play a role. Joint and several liability meets the first requirement of Fed. R. Civ. P. 20.

        ii. Alternative: Defendants are liable in the alternative when plaintiff alleges that one of the defendants is responsible, but it is not sure which one.

    b. Same transaction or occurrence: The "same transaction or occurrence" analysis is discussed in Part I.B of this chapter.

B. Adding parties to counterclaims and cross-claims: If a party files a valid counterclaim or cross-claim, ***Fed. R. Civ. P. 13(h)*** allows her to add additional parties to the claim under the conditions specified in Rule 20. When dealing with the addition of parties under Rule 13(h), think of the claim against the existing and additional parties as a separate suit and determine whether the claimant could sue the parties as codefendants under Rule 20.

Example: *P* sues *D. D* has a claim against both *P* and a party who acted in concert with *P. D* can counterclaim against *P*. Because Rule 20 allows *D* to sue both *P* and the other party as codefendants in an original action, *D* can add the other party to the counterclaim pursuant to Rule 13(h).

C. Third party claims (impleader): In many situations, the law holds multiple parties responsible for an injury. Typically, parties who are jointly liable have a right to seek ***contribution*** or ***indemnity*** from other responsible parties. If plaintiff does not (or cannot) sue all of the responsible parties, ***Fed. R. Civ. P. 14*** preserves defendant's right to seek contribution or indemnity by allowing defendant to bring the other responsible parties into the suit.

1. Terminology: Joinder of an additional party in this fashion typically goes by the name ***impleader***. The person joined is called a ***third-party defendant*** (3PD). The party joining the third-party defendant is called a ***third-party plaintiff*** (3PP).

Note on multiple names: Often, a court dealing with impleader refers to a party by its original role in the suit as well as its role in the impleader. Thus, a defendant who impleads another party may be called ***defendant/third-party plaintiff***.

2. When impleader available: Fed. R. Civ. P. 14 allows a party to implead a 3PD "who is or may be liable to the third-party plaintiff for all or part of" ***another party's existing claim against the 3PP***.

a. **Who may use:** *Fed. R. Civ. P. 14(a)* speaks in terms of a defendant using impleader, and that is far and away the most common situation. However, *Fed. R. Civ. P. 14(b)* specifically allows a plaintiff to use impleader if that plaintiff has been sued for affirmative relief in a counterclaim.

b. **Permission of court:** A party need not obtain the court's permission to implead if she files the third-party complaint within *10 days* of filing the original answer (or in the case of an impleading plaintiff, the reply) to the claim. After that, court permission is required. Fed. R. Civ. P. 14(a).

c. **Common situations:** Impleader is available only when the third party is derivatively liable *to the 3PP* for all or part of what it has to pay the plaintiff.

   i. **Joint and vicarious liability:** In cases where two defendants are both liable, the law usually (but not always) provides a right to seek *contribution* (in the case of joint liability) or *indemnity* (in the case of vicarious liability). If plaintiff sues only one of the defendants, the defendant may join the other(s) to assert the contribution or indemnity claim as part of the same suit, thereby providing for more efficient litigation.

   ii. **Contractual duty to indemnify:** The other main category of case in which a party uses impleader is when the 3PD has agreed by contract to indemnify the 3PP for sums it has to pay the claimant. *Insurance* falls into this category.

d. **Importance of substantive law:** A party can use impleader only if the substantive law allows the 3PP to recover against the 3PD. Absent a tort or contractual right to contribution or indemnity, impleader is unavailable.

★   **Example:** In Price v. CTB, Inc., 168 F. Supp. 2d 1299 (M.D. Ala. 2001), the court reviewed Alabama law to determine whether it afforded defendant a cause of action against the third-party defendant. Finding that Alabama law allowed a claim for implied contractual indemnity, the court held that the impleader was proper.

   i. **Claim need not be matured:** However, the 3PP's right to contribution or indemnity need not yet be matured. Fed. R. Civ. P. 14 allows impleader if the 3PD is *or may be* liable to the 3PP.

      Example: *P* sues *D* for a tort claim. *D* has an insurance policy with InsCo covering just the sort of situation set out in *P*'s complaint. However, the policy makes it clear that InsCo's duty to pay does not arise until a claimant actually recovers a judgment against *D*. Notwithstanding this language, *D* may implead InsCo into the case. Of course, the court will determine whether *D* must pay *P* before entering judgment against InsCo. In essence, then, *impleader accelerates a lawsuit that ordinarily would not occur until later*.

      Note: Many jurisdictions do not allow evidence of insurance coverage to be introduced. Although the Federal Rules of Civil Procedure would still allow impleader, a court in such a jurisdiction has the discretion to deny impleader of the insurance company in order to keep the fact of insurance from the jury.

ii. **"Him not me":** Impleader is proper only if the ***3PD is liable to the 3PP*** for all or part of the ***3PP's liability to plaintiff***. A defendant cannot use impleader by arguing that it is not liable to plaintiff at all and that plaintiff has sued the wrong defendant. However, a defendant who joins a 3PD may allege ***in the alternative*** that she is not liable to the plaintiff and that the 3PD is solely responsible.

e. **Unavailable against existing parties:** Fed. R. Civ. P. 14(a) makes it clear that the 3PD must be someone who is ***"not a party to the action."*** Thus, a party cannot use impleader to assert a contribution or indemnity claim against a codefendant or plaintiff.

3. **Additional impleader:** Multiple levels of impleader are possible. A 3PD can itself bring a third-party complaint if it alleges some other party is liable to it for all or part of its liability to the defendant-3PP. Fed. R. Civ. P. 14(a).

4. **Special service rules:** In order to hear a third-party claim, a court must have ***personal jurisdiction*** over the new 3PD. However, ***Fed. R. Civ. P. 4(k)(1)(B)*** contains a special provision designed to facilitate impleader. That rule provides that service is effective to create jurisdiction on ***any party joined under Rule 14*** who is served at any place within the United States that is ***within 100 miles of the court that issued the summons***. Service under this provision is effective regardless of whether the state long-arm statute would reach the party or whether there are any minimum contacts between the 3PD and the state.

5. **Venue:** Addition of third parties under Rule 14 does not affect venue under §1391 or 1392.

6. **Procedure after successful impleader:** An impleader essentially creates a "suit within a suit." The 3PD must respond to the third-party complaint just as if it were an original complaint. Any counterclaims that arise from the ***same transaction*** as the third-party complaint must be brought or they are lost.

a. **Defenses to plaintiff's claim:** Since the liability of the 3PD turns on the validity of the plaintiff's original claim, Rule 14 also allows the 3PD to assert any defenses it has to the plaintiff's claim.

b. **Plaintiff-3PD claims:** Rule 14 also allows the plaintiff and third-party defendant to file claims against each other.

i. **Same transaction:** However, the plaintiff and 3PD may file a claim against the other only if that claim arises from the transaction or occurrence that is the subject of an ***original claim by plaintiff against the original defendant***. The factors that enter into the same transaction test are discussed in Part I.B of this chapter.

ii. **Compulsory counterclaims:** Nothing requires either the plaintiff or 3PD to file these related claims against each other. However, once the plaintiff files a claim against the 3PD, the 3PD *must* file any claims that she has against the plaintiff that meet the requirements of Fed. R. Civ. P. 13(a) (the compulsory counterclaim rule). The rule is not clear if the compulsory counterclaim rule applies when the 3PD files a claim against the plaintiff.

Quiz Yourself on
BASIC JOINDER OF CLAIMS AND PARTIES

160. Saccharine Soft Drinks produces a variety of overly sweet beverages that are sold in glass bottles. Pamela and Peter are seriously injured when they each drink a Saccharine beverage containing small shards of glass. Pamela and Peter drink different types of beverages that they buy from different stores on different dates. Pamela notices the shards in the bottle but drinks the beverage anyway.

Can Pamela and Peter join as plaintiffs to sue Saccharine? _____

161. Same basic facts as Problem 160. Saccharine obtains its bottles from two different manufacturers, ACME and General. It is impossible to tell from an inspection of the bottle which of the two manufacturers supplied the bottle. Under governing law, Saccharine and the manufacturer of the bottle are liable for any injuries caused to unsuspecting consumers because of glass shards in the bottle. However, they are not liable if the consumer knows the risk but drinks the beverage anyway.

Pamela tries to sue Saccharine, ACME, and General as codefendants in a single action. Both ACME and General object, pointing out that it is logically impossible for *both* of them to have produced the bottle in question. Is joinder proper? _____

162. Same basic facts as Problems 160 and 161. The court rejects the defendants' objection and allows Pamela's suit against Saccharine, ACME, and General to proceed.

Saccharine tests its products on live animals. When word of this animal testing becomes public, Pamela and other animal rights activists raid the laboratory and free all the animals. This raid occurs well before Pamela is injured by the glass shards.

Saccharine tries to file a claim for the raid as a counterclaim in Pamela's action. Pamela objects, arguing that the counterclaim does not arise from the same occurrence as her claim against Saccharine. Will Pamela prevail? _____

163. Same facts as Problems 160-162. Saccharine also files two claims against its codefendant ACME. First, Saccharine alleges that ACME has revealed some of Saccharine's valuable trade secrets to one of Saccharine's competitors. If that is correct, ACME violated a crucial term of its contract with Saccharine. Second, Saccharine alleges that if it is held liable for Pamela's injuries, ACME must indemnify Saccharine for any damages it must pay. Saccharine argues that if the bottle does prove to be defective, it was ACME's fault, not Saccharine's.

ACME files a timely objection to joinder of both claims. How will the court rule? _____

164. Same facts as Problems 160-162, except that Pamela sues only Saccharine and ACME. In her complaint, Pamela specifically alleges that ACME produced the bottle in question.

ACME denies liability. In the alternative, it decides to implead General, arguing that the bottle in question came from General's plant instead of ACME's.

General and Pamela both object to the impleader. How should the court rule? _____

Answers

160. Pamela and Peter probably can join, but it depends on how they phrase their complaint. Fed. R. Civ. P. 20 sets out a three-part test. Under the first part, they are suing ''severally,'' one of the three allowable forms (this part of the test is always met, but it is worth addressing anyway).

The second part of the test is the most difficult hurdle. The injuries are two unrelated occurrences. However, if Pamela and Peter allege that the shards were due to some defect in the bottling process, then they should be able to join. That bottling process defect clearly meets the ''logical relationship'' test because both injuries are tied to the defect. The allegation should even meet the stricter same evidence test since Pamela and Peter would need to prove a defect to prevail.

If Pamela and Peter cannot allege in good faith that the shards were due to a common manufacturing defect, they have a more difficult case. If the shards were due to, say, the fault of the respective shippers, then the claims do not arise from the same occurrence or connected series of occurrences.

With respect to the third part, the cases share common questions of law (what standard of care applies to Saccharine?) and, if they phrase the complaint correctly, fact (what is wrong with Saccharine's bottling operations?). That Pamela has an additional unique fact does not matter. The claims need only share some significant common issues.

161. Joinder of the defendants is clearly proper. True, only one of the two manufacturers can be responsible. But Fed. R. Civ. P. 20 allows a plaintiff to sue defendants in the *alternative*, which Pamela seeks to do here.

The claims against the defendants clearly arise from the same transaction — the injury to Pamela gave rise to the claims.

Finally, the claims share a crucial common issue of fact: How did the shards end up in the bottle?

162. Pamela will lose. She is correct that the counterclaim does not arise out of the same transaction as the original claim. But Fed. R. Civ. P. 13(b) allows a party to file any claim, even those that are unrelated, as permissive counterclaims.

163. Both claims should be allowed. These are cross-claims governed by Fed. R. Civ. P. 13(g). Under that rule, a cross-claim must arise out of the same transaction as the original claim or a counterclaim. The trade secret claim does not arise out of the same transaction, even under the liberal ''logical relationship'' test. However, the indemnity claim clearly does arise from the same transaction and is therefore a proper cross-claim.

Should the court dismiss the trade secret claim? No. Recall that Fed. R. Civ. P. 18 allows a party to join additional claims to a cross-claim, even though the claim is completely unrelated. Therefore, Saccharine can join its trade secret claim to the proper cross-claim under Rule 18.

164. The court should not allow the impleader. Pamela is specifically alleging that ACME made the bottle. By claiming that General made the bottle, ACME is attempting to absolve itself from all liability, not to seek contribution or indemnity from General as required by Fed. R. Civ. P. 14.

D. Compulsory joinder: All of the joinder methods discussed so far allow, but do not *require*, joinder of new parties. In some situations, however, people **must** be joined to the action. Federal Rule of Civil Procedure 19 governs compulsory joinder in the federal courts.

1. Primarily a defense: Compulsory joinder is primarily a *defense*, not a joinder method. Fed. R. Civ. P. 19 comes into play only when a party **moves to dismiss** the action because of the absence of one or more interested people.

    a. How raised: Fed. R. Civ. P. 19 is usually invoked by defendant raising a ***Fed. R. Civ. P. 12(b)(7) motion*** or by raising the defense in the ***answer***.

    b. Result of successful motion: If the court concludes that the missing party should have been joined, it ***orders the nonmovant to join the person***. If the person cannot be joined (usually because of lack of subject matter or personal jurisdiction), the court then considers whether the action should be dismissed.

2. Development of doctrine: The necessary party rule was originally a court-created doctrine. Many states use the historic approach.

    a. The historic approach determines whether the absent person is "necessary" or "indispensable." An ***indispensable party*** was one who had an interest in the outcome of the pending litigation that would invariably be affected by the final decree in the litigation. A ***necessary party*** also had an interest in the case, but that interest was separable from those of the parties, allowing the court to issue a final judgment that would not affect the party.

    b. If the party was ***indispensable*** and could not be joined, the court would ***dismiss***. However, if the party was merely ***necessary***, the court would ***retain the case***.

3. Rule 19: The federal rule preserves the basic principles of the historical rule but significantly refines — and to some extent changes — the analysis.

    a. Different approach: Under Fed. R. Civ. P. 19, there are not separate categories of "necessary" and "indispensable" parties. Instead, there is only one category: ***persons to be joined if feasible***. If a court determines that a party should be joined but the person cannot be joined, the court then decides whether to dismiss. Therefore, there is no need to use the labels "necessary" and "indispensable" when applying Fed. R. Civ. P. 19.

    b. Three steps: Application of Rule 19 may involve up to three separate steps.

        i. Should the party be joined? ***Fed. R. Civ. P. 19(a)*** establishes the criteria for determining whether a person should be joined.

        ii. May the party be joined? If the court determines that the person should be joined, the next step is to determine whether the party can add the missing person. Although the rules always allow for joinder of the missing person, ***personal*** and ***subject matter jurisdiction*** may prevent joinder.

        iii. Consequences of nonjoinder: If the person cannot be joined, the court must decide whether to dismiss the case, based on its evaluation of the factors listed in ***Fed. R. Civ. P. 19(b)***.

    c. Persons to be joined if feasible: Fed. R. Civ. P. 19(a) lists ***three situations*** where a person should be joined if feasible.

        i. Absence precludes complete relief: Clause (1) specifies that a person should be joined if "in the person's absence complete relief cannot be accorded among those already parties."

        Example: *P*, a law student, is upset because her law school has not offered the course Advanced Civil Procedure for 10 years. *P* sues Professor *D*, the professor who used to teach the course, and asks the court to order the professor to offer the course during the next academic term. At this law school, however, scheduling is the sole prerogative of the dean. The dean should be joined to this action if feasible, for even if *P* were to obtain an order against *D*, there is no guarantee that the course would be offered.

ii. Absence prejudices missing person: Clause 2(i) provides that a person should be joined if that person "claims an interest relating to the subject of the action and is so situated that the disposition of the action in the person's absence may (i) as a practical matter impair or impede the person's ability to protect that interest. . . ."

(a) Interest: The absent person must have an interest in the action that is both ***direct*** and ***legally protectable***. Note that although the language of the two rules is highly similar, the concept of an interest under Fed. R. Civ. P. 19 is much narrower than it is under Fed. R. Civ. P. 24(a). See Part E.

Example: *P*, a competitor of *D*, sues *D* for false advertising, based on claims that *D* made about its own product. *X* is another competitor of *D*. *X* is not a necessary party. Although *X* is interested in the outcome of the case because of the *stare decisis* effect it might have on any false advertising claim *X* might bring, *X* has no direct interest in the outcome of this dispute.

Example: *P* is a tenant in a shopping mall owned by *D*. In the lease, *D* agrees that it will not lease any other space in the mall to a tenant who would compete with *P*. *D* nevertheless signs a lease with *X*, a company that sells the same goods as *P*. *P* sues to enjoin *D* from delivering possession of the store to *X*. *X* satisfies Rule 19(a)(2)(i). If *P* prevails, the outcome will directly affect *X*'s interest in the space. Helzberg's Diamond Shops v. Valley West Des Moines Shopping Center, 564 F.2d 816 (8th Cir. 1977).

Note: If *P* had sued for damages rather than an injunction, *X* would not be necessary because regardless of who won the suit, *X* would be able to take possession.

(b) Practical impairment: In addition to showing that the absent party has an interest, the movant must demonstrate that the pending lawsuit will "impair or impede" that interest.

1. Likelihood enough: The movant need not demonstrate that impairment is certain or even likely. It need merely demonstrate that there is a distinct possibility that the case could be resolved in a way that would impair or impede the absent person's interest.

2. "As a practical matter": Fed. R. Civ. P. 19(a)(2)(i) requires only that the interest of the absent person be impaired ***as a practical matter***. Therefore, it is not necessary to show that the judgment would absolutely foreclose the interest. If the judgment would make it ***significantly more difficult*** for the absent person to protect her interest, she may need to be joined.

Example: Consider the shopping mall situation discussed in the prior example. If *P* were to prevail in its suit, *X* would not be absolutely foreclosed from protecting its interest. *X* could bring a suit for specific performance against *D*. However, because there would already be an injunction against *D* preventing performance under the lease, it would be extremely difficult for *X* to obtain an order directing *D* to deliver possession to *X*.

iii. Absence prejudices parties: Clause 2(ii) provides that a person should be joined if that person "claims an interest relating to the subject of the action and is so situated that the disposition of the action in the person's absence may . . . (ii) leave any of the persons already parties subject to a substantial risk of incurring *double, multiple or otherwise inconsistent obligations* by reason of the claimed interest.

  (a) Interest: Analysis of whether the absent person has an "interest" is the same as it is under clause 2(i), discussed above.

  (b) Multiple or inconsistent obligations: There are two categories of cases where the "double, multiple, or inconsistent obligations" standard is likely to be satisfied. The first is where the existing party and the absent person both claim rights in the same property but only one of them by law is entitled to receive it. The second is when a party to the suit is insisting that the law requires another party to act one way, while the absent party claims that the other party is *required* by law to act in an inconsistent manner.

  Example: A group of minority firefighters sues City, claiming that City illegally discriminated against them in promotion decisions based on their race. The plaintiffs seek an order requiring City to give them preference in future promotion decisions. A group of nonminority firefighters, upon hearing of the suit, threaten a suit of their own, arguing that the law forbids preferences based on race. Assuming that the interest in being promoted is legally protectable, the nonminority firefighters should be joined if feasible because failure to join them could leave City facing inconsistent legal obligations. Cf. Martin v. Wilks, 490 U.S. 755 (1989).

  Example: In Temple v. Synthes Corp., 498 U.S. 5, reh'g denied, 498 U.S. 1092 (1990), the Supreme Court reaffirmed that nothing in Fed. R. Civ. P. 19 requires a plaintiff to join all joint tortfeasors. Although a judgment for the full amount might be entered against the named defendants, those defendants can seek contribution or indemnity from the missing defendants in a separate action.

d. Adding the missing person to the case: If application of Fed. R. Civ. P. 19(a) demonstrates that the person should be joined, the opposing party must join the person to the suit if possible.

  i. Absent person properly a defendant: If the absent person should be a defendant, the plaintiff will join the party under *Fed. R. Civ. P. 20*. Someone who should be joined under Fed. R. Civ. P. 19(a) will always satisfy the requirements of Rule 20.

  ii. Absent person properly a plaintiff: Often a plaintiff is required to join an absent person as an additional plaintiff. Because Rule 20 does not authorize making a person a plaintiff against her will, Rule 19(a) explicitly allows the court to make the person a *defendant* or, in the proper case, an *involuntary plaintiff*. Note that this is the only case where Rule 19 operates as a joinder rule.

  iii. Potential problems with joinder: Joinder of the missing person may be impossible because the court lacks *personal jurisdiction* over the party or because addition of the party would destroy *venue*. In a federal court hearing a case based on diversity jurisdiction, addition of the missing person may also serve to destroy *diversity jurisdiction*.

e. **Consequences of inability to join:** If a person who should be joined is not brought into the case, there is a chance the court will dismiss the case. ***Fed. R. Civ. P. 19(b)*** covers this situation.

    i. **Plaintiff refuses to join:** If a plaintiff is ordered to join another person but refuses to, the court will ordinarily dismiss the case.

    ii. **Plaintiff cannot join:** If a plaintiff cannot join the missing person because of jurisdiction or venue limits, Fed. R. Civ. P. 19(b) requires the court to consider four factors in determining whether to dismiss the case:

        (a) the extent to which a judgment rendered in the person's absence would prejudice the absent person or the parties (this factor is similar to the analysis under Rule 19(a), but looks to the ***degree of prejudice***);

        (b) whether any prejudice could be reduced by protective provisions in the judgment, the shaping of relief, or other measures;

        (c) whether a judgment rendered in the person's absence will be adequate (this factor is already met if the absent person is indispensable because of Rule 19(a)(i)); and

        (d) whether the plaintiff will have an adequate remedy if the case is dismissed.

    iii. **Dismissal not favored:** Courts will usually go to great lengths to avoid dismissing an action under Fed. R. Civ. P. 19. They instead will try to minimize the prejudice by limiting or shaping the judgment in the case.

Quiz Yourself on
COMPULSORY JOINDER

165. Darla Decedent dies in 2003. Darla's last will and testament is dated August 9, 1995. The will leaves her entire estate to "my husband." From 1971 to 1999, Darla was married to Andrew. In 2001, however, Darla divorced Andrew and married Ben.

    The executor of Darla's estate is convinced that she meant to leave her estate to Andrew. The executor accordingly delivers all of the property in the estate to Andrew. When Ben learns of this, he brings a suit against the executor. Ben asks for damages, claiming that he should have received the estate. The court agrees with Ben and awards him $50,000 in damages. When Ben attempts to collect this judgment, the executor argues that the judgment is void because Ben failed to join Andrew in the action. Is the judgment void? _____

166. Same facts as Problem 165, except that the executor moves to dismiss Ben's suit for failure to join Andrew while the suit is still pending. Because of lack of personal jurisdiction, it is impossible to join Andrew to the action. Will the court dismiss Ben's suit? _____

167. Same facts as Problem 165, except that Ben brings his suit before the executor distributes the property. Ben seeks an order requiring the executor to distribute the property to him. The executor moves to dismiss Ben's suit for failure to join Andrew. Because of lack of personal jurisdiction, it is impossible to join Andrew to the action. Will the court dismiss Ben's suit? _____

Answers

165. The judgment is not void. The necessary party rule is simply a defense that the executor could have asserted while Ben's case was pending. Once that case is complete, the defense no longer has any effect. It certainly does not affect the court's power to decide the case.

166. The court will not dismiss Ben's suit because Andrew is not a necessary party. The test is set out in Fed. R. Civ. P. 19(a), which lists three situations in which a person is deemed necessary. First, Andrew's presence is not necessary to afford complete relief. Ben is not asking for the estate itself but merely for damages. The executor does not need Andrew as a party to pay damages. Second, the suit in no way prejudices Andrew. Again, Ben seeks only damages. Third, there is no prejudice to existing parties. Although it looks as if the executor faces double liability, any liability would actually result only from her wrongful decision to give the property to Andrew rather than to Ben.

167. Now the court probably will dismiss. Andrew is a necessary party. Although Andrew's presence is not necessary to afford complete relief, failure to join Andrew not only results in prejudice to Andrew but also exposes the executor to double liability. Andrew is prejudiced, of course, because he would not receive the estate. The risk of double liability arises because Andrew could then turn around and sue the executor. Although the executor delivered the property to Ben only because of the court order, Andrew — who was not a party to Ben's suit — is not bound by that judgment and could still prevail in his suit against the executor.

Once it is determined that Andrew is necessary, Ben must join him if feasible. The problem specifies, however, that the court has no personal jurisdiction over Andrew.

If Andrew cannot be joined, the court needs to determine whether to dismiss or let the case proceed without Andrew. Here, it considers the factors in Rule 19(b). A judgment without Andrew would prove highly prejudicial to Andrew and possibly to the executor. Second, there *are* measures the court could take to reduce the prejudice. The court, for example, could order the executor to *interplead* Andrew and Ben. Or the court could refuse to order the executor actually to convey the assets but could simply require the trustee to hold the assets in trust until Andrew's claim is resolved.

Third, a judgment rendered without Andrew would not be completely adequate because it would leave the executor exposed to a later suit by Andrew. Finally, if the case is dismissed, Ben will have no adequate remedy. Although he could sue again in a forum that could exercise personal jurisdiction over Andrew, there is no guarantee that forum could exercise personal jurisdiction over the executor or the estate.

E. Intervention: Intervention allows strangers to the lawsuit to join as parties in order to protect their rights or interests. Intervention is governed by ***Fed. R. Civ. P. 24***. In some cases, a party may intervene as of right; in others, court permission is required.

   1. Permissive intervention: Permissive intervention is governed by ***Fed. R. Civ. P. 24(b)***.

      a. Timely application: Although no strict deadline is set forth, a request to intervene is more likely to be granted early in the lawsuit.

      b. Grounds: A party may seek permission to intervene ***either*** when a ***federal statute*** grants a conditional right to intervene or when the applicant's claim or defense shares a ***common question of law or fact*** with the existing suit.

      c. Discretion: The decision to allow or deny intervention is rarely reversed on appeal.

2. **Intervention by right:** *Fed. R. Civ. P. 24(a)* gives a party the right to intervene without court permission in certain situations.

   a. **Timely application:** The timely application requirement assumes a more important role in a case of intervention by right because it is the sole issue on which the court may exercise discretion. Whether the application is timely turns on whether delay in applying to intervene would *prejudice* the parties in preparing their suit.

   b. **Grounds:** A party has a right to intervene when *either* of the following conditions are met.

      i. A *federal statute* grants an unconditional right to intervene. Several federal statutes give the United States the right to intervene in actions challenging federal law or acts of the federal government.

      ii. The applicant (A) "*claims an interest* relating to the property or transaction that is the subject of the action" *and* (B) the applicant "is so situated that the disposition of the action *may as a practical matter impair or impede the applicant's ability to protect that interest, unless* (C) the applicant's interest is *adequately protected by existing parties*.

         (a) **Interest:** Historically, the requirement of an interest required applicant to show a *proprietary interest* or some other *significantly protectable legal interest*. However, the trend today is to relax the requirement.

            1. **Need not be economic:** The interest in question need not be a property interest or other economic interest.

            2. **Public interest:** The requirement of a legally protectable interest is often relaxed when the suit involves a matter of public interest or when a public interest group seeks intervention.

            3. **Broader than Rule 19(a):** The notion of an interest is significantly broader under Fed. R. Civ. P. 24(a) than it is under Fed. R. Civ. P. 19(a).

         (b) **Practical impairment:** The applicant must also demonstrate that its interest may be "impaired or impeded" by the ongoing litigation.

            1. **Practical, not legal:** The impairment need be only practical. Therefore, the applicant need not show that the suit would operate as *res judicata* to any future attempt by applicant to protect its right.

            2. **May be impaired:** The applicant need not show that impairment is certain, merely that it could occur if the lawsuit is resolved in a particular way.

            3. Recent decisions make it clear that there is a tendency for courts to *merge the interest and impairment elements* of the analysis. The greater the level of impairment, the broader the scope of interests that courts will protect.

         (c) **Unless adequate representation:** Even if the interest and impairment standards are satisfied, a party cannot intervene of right if the existing parties already protect the applicant's interest. However, it is fairly easy to show lack of adequate representation. An applicant need show only that the existing parties have a *definite incentive* not to represent the interests of applicant.

★

      Example: NRDC v. U.S. Nuclear Regulatory Commission, 578 F.2d 1341 (10th Cir. 1978), demonstrates a typical application of Rule 24(a). An environmental group sues the U.S. Nuclear Regulatory Commission, challenging the Commission's decision not to conduct an environmental study before issuing a license to operate a uranium mill to Company *X*. Company *Y*, which also has filed an application for a license, seeks to intervene in the action as of right. The court allowed Company *Y* to intervene. First, the court found that Company *Y*'s interest in its own license was sufficient to allow intervention even though the suit did not directly involve *Y*'s application.

      Second, the court found that Company *Y*'s interest was impaired even though the lawsuit technically would not foreclose Company *Y* from making any arguments it deemed appropriate when its license application was considered. If the environmental group were to prevail in its suit dealing with Company *X*'s application, that ruling likely would affect how the agency handled all other applications, including that of Company *Y*.

      Finally, the court found that Company *X* did not adequately represent the interests of Company *Y*. It hypothesized that Company *X* might have an incentive to argue for a ruling that would apply *prospectively only*, thereby leading the agency to undertake a full environmental study for Company *Y*'s application but not for Company *X*'s.

F. Interpleader: Interpleader is a special type of joinder designed to deal with the situation where a party faces ***multiple, inconsistent claims***. Instead of waiting for the claimants to bring suit, and possibly to obtain inconsistent judgments, the process of interpleader allows the party who owes the obligation to bring an action against all of the claimants and let the claimants fight it out amongst themselves.

    1. Overview: Interpleader typically is used by a party who is liable to someone but is not completely sure to *whom*. For example, the executor of an estate may face conflicting claims for certain assets of that estate. Interpleader allows a party in this position to bring all the claimants into a single action so that the party knows to whom to deliver the asset. Because of the nature of the joinder device, the statutes and rules use a unique terminology to describe the parties and subject matter of an interpleader case.

        a. The ***stake*** is the thing that is being claimed by two or more people. It can be property (as in the example of the executor posed just above) or an obligation (such as the obligation of an insurance company to pay money to someone).

        b. The ***stakeholder*** is the person who is in possession of the stake.

        c. The ***claimants*** are the parties who seek to obtain the property or performance of the obligation.

    2. Two types of interpleader: The federal system recognizes two separate forms of interpleader. The first, ***rule interpleader***, is governed by ***Fed. R. Civ. P. 22***. The second, ***statutory interpleader***, is governed mainly by ***28 U.S.C. §1335***. Statutory interpleader is far more useful because of certain special rules dealing with subject matter jurisdiction, personal jurisdiction, and venue.

3. Common features of rule and statutory interpleader: Although there are important practical differences between rule and statutory interpleader, both share certain fundamental characteristics.

    a. How action initiated: The stakeholder may initiate an interpleader action by naming the claimants as defendants in an *original action*. In the alternative, if one or more of the claimants sues the stakeholder, the interpleader action may be initiated by *counterclaim* or *cross-claim*.

    b. When interpleader available: Interpleader is not available merely because a party is faced with multiple claims. Instead, the claims must be inconsistent, leaving the stakeholder "exposed to *double or multiple liability*." Fed. R. Civ. P. 22(1).

    Example: A truck driver collides with a bus, seriously injuring 25 people. The driver has only $30,000 in assets to her name, plus a liability insurance policy with a maximum of $50,000 in coverage for a single incident such as this wreck. The injured passengers sue the driver and the insurance company in a series of separate actions, asking for total damages in excess of $500,000. The *driver cannot interplead*. Even though the claims exceed her total assets, her liability is legally unlimited. Therefore, judgments against her do not present double or multiple liability. However, the *insurance company can interplead*. Its liability is limited by law to $50,000. Because the several plaintiffs seek more than that amount, there is a risk of multiple, inconsistent liability.

4. Rule interpleader: *Fed. R. Civ. P. 22* allows a stakeholder to commence an interpleader action in a federal court. Notwithstanding the special terminology, a rule interpleader action is analyzed like any other federal action for purposes of determining jurisdiction and venue. This is the most significant difference between rule and statutory interpleader.

    a. Subject matter jurisdiction: The court must have a basis for jurisdiction over every separate claim by the stakeholder against each claimant. The *complete diversity* rule can pose a special problem in these cases. For diversity jurisdiction to exist under 28 U.S.C. §1332, the stakeholder must be *diverse from all claimants* and the value of the stake must exceed $75,000.

    b. Personal jurisdiction: For a court to hear the interpleader case, there must be personal jurisdiction over *all claimants*.

    Note: Although an interpleader action essentially adjudicates who "owns" the stake, the Supreme Court held in New York Life Insurance Co. v. Dunlevy, 241 U.S. 518 (1916), that a court *cannot use quasi-in-rem jurisdiction* in interpleader. Personal jurisdiction over the claimants is required.

    c. Venue: In a federal court, venue is proper either where all the "defendants" reside or where a substantial portion of the events or omissions giving rise to the cause of action occurred. 28 U.S.C. §1391(a) and (b). If the stakeholder brings the interpleader as an original action, the claimants are the defendants. If the stakeholder brings the interpleader by counterclaim, it may be the sole defendant, and therefore venue would also be proper in the district where the stakeholder resides.

5. Statutory interpleader: Although phrased as a jurisdictional statute, *28 U.S.C. §1335* has been interpreted to give federal courts authority to grant a remedy in interpleader cases. This "statutory interpleader" is *separate and distinct from rule interpleader*. Congress also enacted special rules governing subject matter jurisdiction, personal jurisdiction, and venue in cases brought under §1335.

a. **Subject matter jurisdiction:** As with rule interpleader, the federal court must have subject matter jurisdiction over every claim in the case. However, 28 U.S.C. §1335 makes it much easier to obtain jurisdiction in diversity cases. It requires only *minimal diversity among the claimants* and an amount in controversy of only *$500*.

    i.   **Minimal diversity among claimants:** Unlike the complete diversity requirement in rule interpleader, §1335 allows jurisdiction whenever at least one of the claimants is *diverse from any other claimant*. The citizenship of the stakeholder is usually not considered. However, some courts consider the citizenship of the stakeholder when the stakeholder denies liability to all claimants.

    ii. **Amount in controversy:** As compared to the $75,000 amount in controversy requirement in rule interpleader, diversity jurisdiction exists in statutory interpleader whenever the *stake is worth $500 or more*.

        Example: *P* files a statutory interpleader action against *D1*, *D2*, and *D3*. *P*, *D1*, and *D2* are all citizens of Ohio. *D3* is a citizen of South Dakota. The stake is worth $600. Diversity jurisdiction exists under §1335.

b. **Personal jurisdiction:** *28 U.S.C. §2361* complements §1335 by allowing the court to serve process *anywhere in the United States*. Therefore, as long as all the claimants reside or can be found anywhere in the country, the federal court can exercise personal jurisdiction over them.

c. **Venue:** *28 U.S.C. §1397* similarly sets out a special venue rule for statutory interpleader. Venue is proper in any judicial district where *one or more of the claimants resides*. Unlike rule interpleader cases, the statute does *not* look to where a substantial portion of the events or omissions occurred.

Quiz Yourself on
INTERVENTION AND INTERPLEADER

168. Jippy, Skiff, and Smackers are the nation's three largest producers of peanut butter. As most people know, not all peanut butter is the same. Jippy and Skiff add sugar and nonpeanut oils to their products, which makes them more appealing to children. Smackers, by contrast, takes the purist approach. Its peanut butter contains only ground peanuts and salt.

    Smackers sues Jippy under federal false advertising laws in federal district court. Smackers claims that Jippy is misleading the public by calling its product "peanut butter," when in truth it contains many extra ingredients.

    Because Skiff uses many of the same extra ingredients, it is concerned about Smackers's suit against Jippy. Skiff fears that if Smackers prevails, the decision will have the effect of defining what

''peanut butter'' is in the U.S. market. Skiff therefore wants to join the action. The federal false advertising laws, however, do not give Skiff a right to intervene. Will Skiff succeed in joining the lawsuit? _____

169. Horizon Communications operates a cellular telephone service. Recently, however, it has found itself
in somewhat of a bind. Two of Horizon's customers, Alice and Bob, both claim that a Horizon representative promised them the valuable phone number 345-6789. However, when the representative set
up the phones for Alice and Bob, she programmed a different number in each of the phones. Because
Alice and Bob had business cards and stationery printed up with the 345-6789 number on them, they
are threatening a suit against Horizon. However, Horizon's computers still show that the number has
not been assigned to anyone.

Horizon's troubles worsen when it receives a phone call from Callous Bank. Callous loaned
money to Bob. In return, Callous claims, Bob gave the bank a security interest in all of his assets, including his cell phone account. When Bob failed to pay the loan, Callous foreclosed and now claims
that it owns the 345-6789 number.

Horizon is considering bringing an interpleader action to determine who really owns the number
345-6789. If it does bring such an action, it wants to be able to argue that *it* still retains the phone number. Is interpleader a proper way to deal with Horizon's dilemma? _____

_____

Answers

168. Skiff may be able to intervene if the judge allows permissive intervention. However, it will not be able
to intervene as of right.

The judge may well grant permissive intervention under Fed. R. Civ. P. 24(b). There are common questions of law or fact. The case may have some effect on Skiff, and allowing Skiff in would not
unduly complicate matters. On the other hand, permissive intervention is up to the discretion of the
trial judge.

If the trial judge denies permissive intervention, Skiff will not be able to intervene as of right.
First, it must file a timely application. That hurdle will not be difficult to clear. Second, because the
false advertising laws do not give Skiff a right to intervene, Skiff must demonstrate that it has an interest that will be impaired. Skiff is definitely ''interested'' in the suit. However, it has no legally recognized interest in the dispute between Smackers and Jippy. On the other hand, a legally recognized interest is not always necessary — if the impairment is great enough, lesser interests may suffice.

Skiff could be affected in that a judgment in favor of Smackers would be *stare decisis* in a later
suit by Smackers against Skiff. In some situations, courts will allow *stare decisis* alone to qualify for
intervention of right. However, in those cases (see, for example, the *NRDC* case discussed in the text),
the party had a legally protected interest that was directly threatened. Skiff has no such interest. It has
not been sued and does not need a ''license'' to sell peanut butter.

169. Interpleader will deal only partially with Horizon's problems. Horizon can file an interpleader action
against Callous and Bob. Those two parties have competing claims to the same basic right — the number that Horizon ostensibly assigned to Bob. It does not matter that Horizon claims it did not assign
that number to either claimant. Under modern interpleader practice, the stakeholder (Horizon) can use
interpleader even though it denies liability to anyone.

However, Horizon cannot use interpleader to join Alice to the suit. Alice's claim is not *logically*
inconsistent with that of Bob/Callous. It is possible that the representative did promise the number to

two different people. Although Horizon obviously cannot give the same number to both, there is nothing inconsistent with holding it liable for making inconsistent promises.

III. SEVERANCE

In some cases, joinder of claims and parties results in a lawsuit that is unwieldy. Two Federal Rules of Civil Procedure, *20(b)* and *42(b)*, give the court the power to *sever* the lawsuit into subsuits.

A. No real difference: Although the wording of the two rules differs slightly, there is no appreciable difference in how they apply.

B. When severance granted: Courts typically rely on two main arguments to justify severing claims under Fed. R. Civ. P. 20(b) and 42(b). First, a court may sever when the case is *unmanageable or unduly complex*. The second main justification is when the presence of one claim may *prejudice* another claim. For example, if *P* sues two *D*s, alleging fraud against one and breach of contract against the other, the allegation of fraud may prejudice the breach of contract claim.

C. Effect of severance: Severance divides an existing case into two or more new cases. The plaintiff(s) need not serve the defendant(s) a second time. Moreover, unless the court orders additional pleadings, the existing pleadings will be used in all the new cases.

IV. CONSOLIDATION OF ACTIONS

Fed. R. Civ. P. 42(a) allows a court to consolidate existing actions that are currently pending before it if those actions involve a ''common question of law or fact.'' Although consolidation may occur at the initiative of the court, it usually is the result of a motion filed by a party in one of the actions.

V. JURISDICTION ISSUES IN JOINDER

Joinder of additional claims and parties raises issues of subject matter jurisdiction and personal jurisdiction. With the exception of interpleader, which has its own special rules that are discussed above, the basic principles of Chapters 2 and 4 apply in joinder. However, a brief review of those principles may be useful in this chapter.

A. Personal jurisdiction: A court must have personal jurisdiction over every party to the action, except plaintiffs and any other party who waives his right to contest jurisdiction. Thus, the court needs to be able to establish jurisdiction over *all defendants* and any other party *joined to the action against his will*.

B. Subject matter jurisdiction: For litigation in a federal court, subject matter jurisdiction may also bar an attempted joinder.

  1. Basic rule: As discussed in Chapter 4, subject matter jurisdiction must exist over *every claim in the proceeding*.

  2. Federal question and diversity: An individual claim can involve federal question or diversity jurisdiction if, standing on its own, it meets the requirement for jurisdiction.

3. **Supplemental jurisdiction:** If any of the claims do not qualify for either federal question or diversity jurisdiction in its own right, a federal court may be able to exercise supplemental jurisdiction over the claim. The basics of supplemental jurisdiction are discussed in Chapter 4. However, because the test for supplemental jurisdiction parallels the test for certain forms of joinder, some types of joinder are likely to qualify for supplemental jurisdiction.

    a. **Similarity in analysis:** The first step in the supplemental jurisdiction analysis is to determine whether the claim arises out of a ***common nucleus of operative fact*** as another claim over which the federal court has an independent basis for jurisdiction. 28 U.S.C. §1367(a). This test is for all practical purposes identical to the ***same transaction or occurrence test*** used in certain joinder rules.

    b. **Rules that will satisfy §1367(a):** Therefore, if a claim is joined to a suit on the grounds that it arises from the ***same transaction or occurrence as a claim filed by plaintiff***, and there is an independent basis for federal jurisdiction over the claim filed by the plaintiff, the joined claim will automatically meet the requirements of §1367(a). Examples of such claims include:

       i. ***compulsory counterclaims*** under Fed. R. Civ. P. 13(a);

       ii. ***cross-claims*** under Fed. R. Civ. P. 13(g) that arise out of the same transaction as the original claim by plaintiff (cross-claims are also proper if they arise out of the same transaction as a counterclaim; §1367(a) may not be satisfied in these cases);

       iii. ***joinder of plaintiffs or defendants*** under Fed. R. Civ. P. 20 (however, see Part f.i for a very important limitation);

       iv. ***parties joined to counterclaims or cross-claims*** under Fed. R. Civ. P. 13(h);

       v. claims by a ***third-party defendant against the plaintiff*** under Fed. R. Civ. P. 14(a); and

       vi. claims by a ***plaintiff against a third-party defendant*** under Fed. R. Civ. P. 14(a) (however, see Part f.i for a very important limitation).

       Note: As discussed below, joinder under these rules does not automatically qualify for supplemental jurisdiction. It merely satisfies the first element, the "common nucleus" test.

       Example: *P* sues *D1* and *D2* for negligence. The suit arises under state law. However, because both defendants are diverse from *P* and the case meets the amount in controversy requirement, *P* sues in a federal court. *D1* files a proper cross-claim against *D2*. *D2* files a compulsory counterclaim against *P* for an amount less than $75,000. Even though neither of the *D*s' claims has an independent basis for jurisdiction, both satisfy §1367(a), and therefore possibly qualify for supplemental jurisdiction, because they share a common nucleus of operative fact with *P*'s federal claims.

    c. **Impleader:** Proper ***impleader*** claims ***also satisfy §1367(a)***. Although Fed. R. Civ. P. 14(a) does not use the same transaction test, a proper impleader claim also ***automatically meets the requirements*** of §1367(a) since the liability of the third-party defendant ultimately traces back to the same event as the claim by the plaintiff.

    d. **Permissive counterclaims:** Because Fed. R. Civ. P. 13(b) defines permissive counterclaims as those that ***do not arise from the same transaction or occurrence***, permissive counterclaims ordinarily do not qualify for supplemental jurisdiction. However, some counterclaims do arise from the same transaction or occurrence but are not compulsory because they fall into one of Rule 13(a)'s listed exceptions. Courts treat these excepted counterclaims as permissive even though they do not literally fall within Fed. R. Civ. P. 13(b). These "excepted" counterclaims **satisfy §1367(a)** because they arise out of the same transaction or occurrence as the original claim.

e. **Claims joined under Rule 18 may not qualify:** Fed. R. Civ. P. 18 allows joinder of additional claims regardless of whether they are related to the original claim. Because Rule 18 does not use the same transaction test, the "automatic" rules discussed in Parts b and c do not apply to these claims.

Example: *P* sues *D1* and *D2* in federal court, based on a federal question. All the parties are citizens of Indiana. *D1* brings a state law cross-claim against *D2* that arises from the same transaction or occurrence as *P*'s claim. *D1* adds another state law cross-claim against *D2* that does not arise from the same transaction as the original claim by *P*. Although the original cross-claim satisfies §1367(a), the second cross-claim does not because it does not arise from a common nucleus of operative fact.

f. **Remainder of §1367 must be satisfied:** It is crucial to remember that meeting the same transaction or occurrence test **does not mean that the claim automatically qualifies for supplemental jurisdiction**. Instead, it means only that the claim satisfies §1367(a), which is merely the first hurdle. The requirements of §1367(b) and (c) must also be satisfied. Section 1367(b) in particular prevents certain joinder claims for qualifying for supplemental jurisdiction.

   i. **Section 1367(b) and claims by plaintiffs:** Section 1367(b) prevents a court from exercising supplemental jurisdiction over certain claims **by plaintiffs** when jurisdiction over the original claim is based on **diversity**. This provision defeats many joinder attempts by plaintiffs in diversity actions. See Chapter 4, Part IV for a detailed analysis of this provision.

   Example: *P* sues *D1* and *D2* in a federal court, claiming that under state law the *D*s are jointly liable to *P* for $200,000. Jurisdiction is based on diversity. *P* and *D1* are diverse, but *P* and *D2* are citizens of the same state. Even if the joinder of the two defendants satisfies the same transaction requirement of Fed. R. Civ. P. 20, **P cannot join D2** into this suit. There is no independent basis for subject matter jurisdiction. Because a plaintiff joins defendants under Rule 20, one of the rules listed in §1367(b), supplemental jurisdiction is not allowed.

   Example: Same as the prior example, except that *P*'s claim against *D1* is based on federal law. *P*'s claim against *D2* is a state law claim. **P may use supplemental jurisdiction** (unless the court dismisses because of §1367(c)) because §1367(b) does not apply to situations where *P*'s federal claim is a federal question.

   Example: *P*, a citizen of California, sues *D*, a citizen of Oregon, in a federal court based on diversity. *D* impleads *3PD*, a citizen of Nevada. *P* wants to add a claim against *3PD* for $50,000. **P cannot bring the claim** because there is no independent basis for jurisdiction (because the amount in controversy is not satisfied), and §1367(b) bars supplemental jurisdiction against *3PD*, a person joined under Fed. R. Civ. P. 14.

    ii. **Section 1367(c):** Even if a joined claim meets §1367(a) and (b), a court may still refuse to exercise supplemental jurisdiction over the claim based on the factors listed in §1367(c).

Quiz Yourself on
JOINDER

170. Willard and Rosie, both citizens of Kentucky, are canoodling during a romantic horse-drawn carriage ride when the carriage wheel suddenly falls off. The frightened horse drags the carriage down the street with the couple inside, seriously injuring both. The horse and carriage are operated and owned by Ash Company, a citizen of both Delaware and Kentucky. Lea Company, a citizen of North Carolina, is the carriage manufacturer. Willard and Rosie join as plaintiffs in a federal court diversity action, charging Ash Co. with negligent operation and Lea Co. with strict products liability. Defendants object in timely fashion to both joinder and subject matter jurisdiction. How should the court rule? _____

171. The federal "lemon law" requires the seller of an automobile to disclose to a potential purchaser any defects of which the seller was aware. If the seller fails to disclose a defect, the seller must repair the defect without cost to the injured purchaser. However, the statute also makes it clear that sale of a "lemon" is not grounds for canceling the sales contract.

    Gail purchases a used car from Honest John. When she buys the car, Gail also takes advantage of Honest John's "on the lot credit" program where Honest John himself lends the purchaser the money to buy the car. A week later, Gail discovers a defect and immediately asks Honest John to fix the car, citing the lemon law. Honest John refuses, so Gail quits making payments under her loan. Two months later, after repeated efforts to get the car repaired, Gail sues Honest John in federal court for $200, the estimated cost of repair. Honest John denies liability, claiming that the statute applies only to the sale of *new* automobiles. The court agrees with Honest John and enters judgment for him.

    Now, Honest John has filed suit against Gail to recover on the loan. Gail has not made any payments. Does she nevertheless have a way to prevent Honest John from bringing all or part of his claim? Is this strategy likely to work? _____

172. Gary, Jeff, Heather, and Sarah have just completed their first year of law school. During the past year, the four worked together in a study group. This group prepared joint outlines for its members to use in reviewing the material in each course.

    Gary and Sarah discover that Jeff, the entrepreneur, sold the group's Civil Procedure outline to Bar None Corp., a company that conducts bar reviews. Gary and Sarah, both citizens of Indiana, immediately sue Jeff, a citizen of Wisconsin, in federal court. Gary and Sarah allege that Jeff's actions infringe their copyright in the outlines.

    Jeff immediately files a counterclaim in the action. Jeff alleges that during the spring semester interview season, Gary and Heather secretly suggested to the interviewers that Jeff and Sarah conspired to cheat on their examinations. Jeff claims that these statements defamed him and kept him from obtaining a high-paying job. Jeff's counterclaim names not only Gary, but also attempts to join

Heather, who is a citizen of Montana, into the action. Jeff seeks $300,000 in damages from Gary and Heather based on the tort theory of defamation.

Gary and Heather both object to Jeff's counterclaim, arguing that neither the joinder rules nor jurisdictional requirements are met. How should the court rule? _____

173. Same facts as Problem 172. Jeff files a timely third-party complaint against Bar None. This complaint contains two separate claims. First, Jeff correctly points out that under federal copyright laws, a copyright infringement occurs only when a party makes a copy of a protected work. Jeff claims that he did not make a copy of the outline but instead merely sold the original to Bar None. Because only Bar None made a copy, Jeff's argument continues, only Bar None committed infringement. Therefore, Jeff concludes, only Bar None can be held liable to Gary and Sarah. Second, Jeff's third-party complaint also includes a federal antitrust claim against Bar None. Jeff argues that Bar None has established a monopoly in the bar preparation business.

Bar None objects to joinder, arguing that Jeff cannot join these two claims in the copyright action. Is Bar None correct? _____

174. Caterpillar Tractor Company, an Illinois company with its principal place of business in Peoria, Illinois, manufactures bulldozers and other heavy-duty earthmoving equipment. Faced with slumping demand due to a decrease in construction, Caterpillar decides to diversify its offerings. Caterpillar chooses to tap into the current craze for sports utility vehicles. Caterpillar's engineers design the ultimate SUV: a bulldozer, with the blade removed, but equipped with a luxurious cabin replete with every creature comfort. Although the Catsplorer costs $335,000, uses three gallons of fuel for every mile traveled, and, with its treads, can obtain a maximum speed of only 6 miles an hour, demand for the product exceeds Caterpillar's wildest expectations. In fact, two buyers — Tommy and Courtney — pay an extra $10,000 for the honor of owning the very *first* production Catsplorer.

When Tommy learns of Courtney's involvement, he sues Caterpillar. Tommy asks the court for an order of specific performance, requiring Caterpillar to deliver the first production Catsplorer to him.

Courtney reacts with lightning speed once she learns of Tommy's suit. Courtney files a petition to intervene in the action. When the court denies her petition, Courtney claims that the federal rules give her a right to intervene in the suit. The court has subject matter jurisdiction over Courtney's claim. Does Courtney have a right to intervene? _____

175. Reva, a citizen of Kentucky, is an ardent "mall walker." While doing her laps early one morning, she stumbles over a diamond of approximately one carat in size. Reva takes the diamond to mall security. While she is there, three separate people — Mary, a citizen of Maryland, Ken, a citizen of Kentucky, and George, a citizen of Georgia — come to the mall security booth. Each claims to have lost a similar diamond.

The diamond is worth at least $90,000. Reva is unsure what to do. Mary, however, is less patient than Reva. Mary sues Reva in a federal district court in Kentucky. Although it is clear that subject matter jurisdiction, personal jurisdiction, and venue requirements are satisfied, Reva wants to find a way to get the court to dismiss the action. What is her best strategy? _____

176. Same facts as Problem 175. Rather than dismiss the federal action, Reva wants to take this opportunity to interplead Ken and George and let the three claimants argue about who owns the diamond. Can Reva use interpleader to avoid multiple liabilities? Assuming *arguendo* that interpleader is available, can Reva bring it in Mary's federal action? If Reva brings the interpleader as a separate suit, where can the case be heard? _____

Answers

170. Under Fed. R. Civ. P. 20, multiple plaintiffs can join, and multiple defendants can be joined, as long as the claims and liability are joint, several, or in the alternative and there is a common question of law or fact. Here the plaintiffs sue severally and are suing the defendants jointly. The claim arises from a single occurrence: the accident. The common question of law or fact is who is responsible for causing the accident.

However, before the case may proceed, it must also be established that the court has subject matter jurisdiction. The action involves no federal question. Therefore, diversity is the only option. Because Willard and Rosie are citizens of Kentucky, they are diverse from Lea. However, Ash Co. is a citizen of Kentucky. Because Willard and Rosie are also citizens of Kentucky, complete diversity is absent.

The only other option is supplemental jurisdiction (28 U.S.C. §1367). The claim against Ash does arise out of a common nucleus of operative fact, as does the claim against Lea. However, supplemental jurisdiction does not apply in this case because subsection §1367(b) states that the court shall not have jurisdiction over claims by plaintiffs against persons made by parties under Fed. R. Civ. P. 20 if jurisdiction over the "federal" claim is based on diversity. Although Willard and Rosie may sue Lea Co., Ash Co. will have to be dismissed from the action.

171. Gail's best strategy is to argue that Honest John's claim was a *compulsory counterclaim* in the first action. Fed. R. Civ. P. 13(a) requires a defendant to allege in its answer all claims that arise from the same transaction or occurrence as the plaintiff's original claim. Failure to bring a compulsory counterclaim means that the claim is lost.

Whether Gail will succeed in her attempt depends on which of the two tests the court uses to determine same transaction. Under the same evidence test, the counterclaim is not compulsory because there is no relationship between the claims. John's counterclaim is based on the loan, while Gail's claim is based on the sale. The disputed elements are different and would involve the presentation of different evidence. Note that the facts specify that a violation of the lemon law *does not affect the underlying sales contract*.

However, if the logical relationship test is used, John's counterclaim is probably compulsory. Both claims arise from the same general "transaction" — the sales/financing "deal" that was made on a single day.

Note that even under the logical relationship test, not all of Honest John's claims will be barred. Fed. R. Civ. P. 13(a) requires him only to bring claims that he had at the time he filed his answer. Therefore, he would lose only installments that were due on or before the date Honest John filed his answer. He would be free to sue for later-accruing payments.

172. The court will allow the counterclaim against Gary and will allow Jeff to join Heather to that counterclaim.

Gary: This claim is a counterclaim. Fed. R. Civ. P. 13(b) allows a defendant to bring any claim he might have against the plaintiff, regardless of whether it relates in any way to the plaintiff's original claim. Joinder accordingly is not a problem here.

Jurisdiction is also easily satisfied for Jeff's claim. Because Jeff and Gary are of diverse citizenship and the claim exceeds $75,000, diversity jurisdiction is satisfied.

Heather: Fed. R. Civ. P. 13(h) allows a defendant to join additional parties to an action by way of a counterclaim if Fed. R. Civ. P. 20 would have allowed the defendant to sue the plaintiff and the additional party as codefendants in a single action. Jeff clearly could have sued both Gary and Heather in a single case, and so Rule 13(h) is satisfied.

Again, diversity is present between Jeff and Heather and the amount in controversy is satisfied, so jurisdiction is no problem.

173. Bar None is correct. The copyright claim is not a proper impleader claim. By arguing that only Bar None is liable for infringing the copyright, Jeff has made an improper "him, not me" argument. Impleader is proper only when the defendant claims that the third-party defendant must reimburse the defendant for all or part of the defendant's liability to the plaintiff.

Because the copyright claim fails, Jeff cannot use Fed. R. Civ. P. 18 to join the antitrust claim. Both claims should be severed from the main case.

174. Courtney may intervene as of right. The governing rule is Fed. R. Civ. P. 24(a). First, Courtney has an interest in the first production Catsplorer based upon her contract. Moreover, that interest is very likely to be impaired by Tommy's suit. If Tommy prevails, he gets the vehicle. Courtney may still recover damages for breach of contract, but that is less desirable to her than getting the vehicle itself.

True, if Courtney does not join the suit, she is not barred from suing for the vehicle itself. But the very fact that she would have to sue to obtain the vehicle qualifies as impairment.

175. Reva's best strategy is to move to dismiss the case for failure to join a necessary party.

First, it is clear that both Ken and George are parties who should be joined under Fed. R. Civ. P. 19(a). Each of them claims an interest in the diamond. That interest could well be impaired as a result of Mary's suit. In addition, if the court orders Reva to deliver the diamond to Mary, Reva could still be sued in separate actions by Ken and George, raising the threat of multiple liability for Reva.

Given that Ken and George are necessary, they must be joined if feasible. Their claims are in the alternative with that of Mary, so they should be joined as involuntary plaintiffs pursuant to the provisions of Rule 19.

Personal jurisdiction is clearly no problem with Ken since he resides in the forum state. It also seems that George is present in the state, so there may also be personal jurisdiction over him.

Subject matter jurisdiction, however, is clearly a problem. Although George is diverse from Reva, Ken is not. And since Ken can only logically "fit" in the case as a plaintiff, he cannot be joined to the action without destroying complete diversity.

The analysis then turns to Rule 19(b). A judgment rendered in Ken's absence will significantly prejudice him and, as noted above, pose a threat to Reva. Second, there are no clear protective measures that can be used here. Third, a judgment without Ken is not really adequate because additional litigation may well be necessary. Finally, if the case is dismissed for nonjoinder, Mary would have an adequate remedy in that she could sue in state court. All in all, a court should order the case dismissed because of the inability to join Ken.

176. Interpleader is certainly proper here. Legally, only one of the claimants can truly be entitled to the diamond. If the three sue Reva in separate actions, however, the courts could reach inconsistent results, holding her liable to two or all three of the claimants.

Reva can file her interpleader action as a counterclaim in Mary's suit. In the alternative, she can file a new action in interpleader as a plaintiff.

If Reva chooses to bring the claim in a federal court (either in Mary's suit or in a new action), however, she will have to use statutory rather than rule interpleader. Under rule interpleader, there

would have to be complete diversity between Reva on the one hand and all the claimants on the other. As noted in Problem 175, Reva and Ken are not diverse.

Statutory interpleader (28 U.S.C. §1335), by contrast, requires only that at least one of the claimants be diverse from any other claimant. Therefore, Reva may easily bring her action in the federal court against all the parties because all of the claimants are diverse from each other and the amount in controversy is met (statutory interpleader also lowers the amount in controversy requirement to $500, but that is not an issue here).

Personal jurisdiction is not an issue. In statutory interpleader, nationwide service of process to all the claimants is available under 28 U.S.C. §2361.

Finally, venue is easy to satisfy. For statutory interpleader, 28 U.S.C. §1397 states that venue is proper in any judicial district where one or more claimants reside. Therefore, venue could be in Kentucky, Maryland, and Georgia because at least one claimant resides in each of those states.

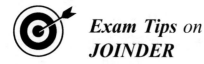

Exam Tips on *JOINDER*

☛ **Learn the terminology:** One of the problems with joinder is the confusing terminology. The Federal Rules of Civil Procedure have separate rules dealing with cross-claims and counterclaims. Worse still, you have to learn the difference between the similar-sounding devices *impleader*, *interpleader*, and *intervention*. Mastering the terminology can help you avoid misreading the question and discussing a joinder device not mentioned in the problem.

☛ **Joinder and jurisdiction:** Joinder is intimately tied to subject matter jurisdiction. Therefore, it is quite common for a joinder question to deal both with the joinder rules and jurisdiction. But this is not always the case. Therefore, read the question carefully. Does it involve both joinder and jurisdiction, or only one or the other?

　☞ If a problem does raise issues of both subject matter jurisdiction and joinder, make sure your answer deals with each as a separate issue. Although the tests can be similar (especially when supplemental jurisdiction is an issue), you need to show that you recognize that the two are discrete parts of the total problem.

☛ **Same transaction or occurrence test:** Many of the joinder rules turn on whether the additional claim arises from the ''same transaction or occurrence'' (STO) as some other claim. Be adept at applying this test.

　☞ Remember that courts differ on the standard to apply in determining whether claims arise from the STO. Most use the *logical relationship test*. A significant minority of courts, however, use the more restrictive *same evidence test*.

　☞ Unless the problem tells you which approach is used in the particular forum (or unless your professor tells you otherwise), analyze every STO issue using *both* tests.

☛ **Quirks in individual joinder rules:** Many of the joinder rules have their own particular ''red flag'' issues.

　☞ **Joinder of *P*s and *D*s under Rule 20:** When applying this rule, don't forget that there are *three parts* to the test. In addition to your STO discussion, point out whether the claims involve a common issue of law or fact and whether the claims or liability are joint, several, or in the alternative.

☞ **Impleader:** The biggest issue in impleader is to determine whether the claim by the third-party plaintiff is really one in the nature of impleader. The third-party plaintiff *must* be seeking damages from the third-party defendant to **reimburse the third-party plaintiff** for damages it must pay the original plaintiff.

   ☞ Be on the lookout for the "*him, not me*" situation where the third-party plaintiff is trying to avoid liability altogether. Impleader is not proper in this situation.

☞ **Intervention:** First, **do not forget permissive intervention**. If the party is merely seeking to intervene, make sure to discuss why the judge might be inclined merely to allow the third party into the case.

   ☞ If the problem involves intervention by right, recall that the Fed. R. Civ. P. 24(a) notion of interest is more loosely defined than under Fed. R. Civ. P. 19.

☞ **Interpleader:** Recall that there are **two types** of interpleader, **statutory** and **rule**. The main differences between the two relate to jurisdiction and venue.

   ☞ Make sure the case is a proper one for the use of interpleader.

☛ **Compulsory joinder:** In most cases, joinder is **optional, not mandatory**. However, there are two important exceptions to this basic principle.

   ☞ **Compulsory counterclaims:** Counterclaims that arise from the STO as the original claim must be brought or they are lost.

      ☞ **Hint:** If a test question presents a situation where a party has **already filed a counterclaim**, it really does not matter that the counterclaim is compulsory. All counterclaims are permissive under Fed. R. Civ. P. 13(b). The real effect of concluding that something is a compulsory counterclaim arises **after the case** if the party should try to file the omitted claim in a new action.

   ☞ **Necessary parties:** Fed. R. Civ. P. 19 also allows a party to object to another party's failure to join someone to the case. Because Rule 19 is primarily a defense, do not discuss it when dealing with parties who are attempting on their own to join someone to a case. You should discuss Rule 19 only when someone has **moved to dismiss** the case because someone is missing or if the problem somehow hints that a party is looking for a way to dismiss or get rid of the case.

☛ **Joinder and subject matter jurisdiction:** As discussed above, joinder and subject matter jurisdiction are separate issues, and you should discuss them separately in your answer. Nevertheless, there is a clear logical connection between some forms of joinder and the doctrine of supplemental jurisdiction.

   ☞ However, do not make your life any more difficult than it needs to be. Instead of jumping right into supplemental jurisdiction, **first consider whether diversity or federal question jurisdiction exists**. Only if neither of these is available (or if there is some doubt as to their availability) do you need to avail yourself of the more complex supplemental jurisdiction analysis.

   ☞ If you do need to consider supplemental jurisdiction, your analysis will often dovetail in some ways with your discussion of joinder. Basically, the **same Article III case test used in §1367(a) is functionally equivalent to the STO analysis** used in the Federal Rules of Civil Procedure.

      ☞ However, avoid bald statements like "supplemental jurisdiction is available because this is a compulsory counterclaim." Such statements are not always true because they fail to consider 28 U.S.C. §1367(b) and (c). In addition, even if they are correct in the case, such statements are so conclusory that you may lose points for failure to analyze the issue sufficiently.

☞ Instead, you might consider something like, ''As discussed above, this claim is a proper cross-claim under Fed. R. Civ. P. 13(g) because it arises out of the STO as plaintiff's claim. Because the same Article III case analysis used in 28 U.S.C. §1367(a) is for all intents and purposes the same as the STO analysis, this claim forms part of the same Article III case as the plaintiff's federal claim. Therefore, §1367(a) is satisfied.''

☞ **Personal jurisdiction:** If a party is joined to a case, the court must be able to exercise personal jurisdiction over that party. In addition to the normal personal jurisdiction analysis discussed in Chapter 2, recall that there are two special rules that apply to joinder: the *100-mile bulge* rule of Fed. R. Civ. P. 4(k)(1)(B), which applies to impleader under Fed. R. Civ. P. 14 and to involuntary plaintiffs joined under Fed. R. Civ. P. 19, and the *nationwide service* available in *statutory interpleader* actions.

CHAPTER 15

CLASS ACTIONS

ChapterScope

This chapter deals with class actions, where a representative litigates her rights as well as the rights of others. Although the chapter focuses on the class action rules in federal court, many of the principles also apply in state court.

- A class action is a proceeding in which the rights or duties of every member of the class are litigated by a class representative.

- Because the **Due Process Clause** of the U.S. Constitution prevents government from taking away certain rights without notice and an opportunity to be heard, class actions present constitutional concerns. Nevertheless, the Supreme Court has held that a class action does not violate the Due Process Clause if the representation is fully adequate.

- **Fed. R. Civ. P. 23** is designed to deal with these constitutional concerns. The rule places a number of strict controls on class actions.

  - The trial court must *certify* the case as appropriate for class action treatment.

  - The court must also determine that the case fits one of *three categories* of class actions.

  - Rule 23 has strict controls on who can be a representative and, in some cases, requires that notice and a chance to opt out be provided to the members of the class.

- Class actions also present unique **personal jurisdiction** concerns. As long as representation is adequate, however, a court in a typical class action can adjudicate the rights of the absent members even if there are no minimum contacts between those members and the forum.

- **Settlement** is another tricky issue in class action cases. There is a real risk of a conflict of interest if the defendant offers a settlement that benefits the representative personally but not the class. To avoid this, Rule 23 places strict limitations on settlement.

- Class actions are not the only example of a case where a representative litigates the rights of others. Two other situations covered by the Federal Rules of Civil Procedure are **shareholder derivative actions** and suits against members of an **unincorporated association**.

I. OVERVIEW OF THE CLASS ACTION

In a class action, one or more *representatives* litigates not only his personal rights, but also the rights of others who are similarly situated. The class action device offers the promise of judicial economy but also creates unique problems.

A. Governing rule: Fed. R. Civ. P. 23 governs class actions in the federal courts. The rule has been amended many times since it was first enacted.

B. Judicial control: One of the unique features of class actions is the extent to which the court plays a role in overseeing the case.

   1. Need judicial approval to proceed: A case cannot proceed as a class action without judicial approval. In many cases, the battle over whether the suit will proceed as a class action is the most hotly contested issue in the entire case.

   2. Need judicial approval to settle: Similarly, a class action cannot be settled without the approval of the court.

C. Variations: The typical class action involves a *single class* of people who would otherwise be *plaintiffs*, with one or more representatives representing the class. However, variations on this theme are possible.

   1. Defendant class: It is also possible for a plaintiff to sue a defendant class if the members of that class all acted in the same way toward the plaintiff.

   2. Subclasses: At times, the interests of people, although similar, are different enough to preclude them from being members of a single class. In these situations, it may be possible to divide the group into subclasses. Each subclass is treated as a separate class and must be separately certified.

   3. Class action limited to particular issues: It is also possible for the court to certify a case as a class action only with respect to certain issues. For example, in a products liability case, a court could certify the case as a class action on the question of liability only. If the court determines that the manufacturer is liable, the damages recoverable by each victim are litigated in separate, individual actions.

II. CONSTITUTIONAL CONCERNS WITH REPRESENTATIONAL LITIGATION

The key feature of a class action — that one party litigates the rights of others — raises significant constitutional concerns.

A. Due process: Class actions present concerns under the Due Process Clauses of the Fifth and Fourteenth Amendments to the U.S. Constitution. These clauses prevent government from depriving a person of *property* without *due process of law*.

   1. Property: Clearly, a judgment that requires a defendant to pay money to another person constitutes a deprivation of property. Although not as obvious, a plaintiff's right to recover money or specific relief against another person qualifies as property for purposes of due process.

   2. Providing due process: The constitutional requirement of due process of law has several different facets. With regards to class actions, however, there are two important, but separate, parts of the due process requirement.

   a. First, due process usually requires government to provide the person in possession of the property with *notice* and an *opportunity to be heard* by a tribunal.

   b. Second, due process also forms the constitutional basis for the requirement of *personal jurisdiction*.

B. Notice and opportunity to be heard: Even though members of a class can lose property without the chance to protect themselves at a hearing, a properly conducted class action satisfies the requirements of due process. The Supreme Court's watershed opinion in Hansberry v. Lee, 311 U.S. 32 (1940), both validated the basic concept of a class action and defined when a class action is constitutionally acceptable.

★   1. **Facts of *Hansberry*:** *Hansberry* involved a racially restrictive covenant on property, in the days before such clauses were ruled invalid. The clause in question, however, had a provision stating that it was not valid unless 95 percent of the landowners in the affected region signed it. In truth, only 54 percent of the landowners had actually signed.

   a. **Earlier action:** Before the *Hansberry* case arose, the validity of the covenant had been litigated in another action, which we can call A v. B. Both *A* and *B* had signed the covenant.

   i. When landowner *B* tried to sell his property to another in violation of the covenant, landowner *A* sued both *B* and the buyers. *A* designated her suit as a class action, with *A* representing a class comprising all property owners who had signed the covenant.

   ii. Even though only 54 percent of the homeowners had signed the covenant, *A* and *B* stipulated that the requisite 95 percent of owners had signed.

   iii. The court in A v. B found for *A*, upholding the validity of the covenant.

   b. ***Hansberry* case:** After this judgment, a different owner tried to sell to the Hansberrys, again in violation of the covenant. Yet another owner, Lee, sued the Hansberrys and their seller in state court to enjoin the sale.

   i. The defendants argued that the covenant was invalid by its own terms because too few people had signed it.

   ii. However, the state court held that the party who had agreed to sell to the Hansberrys was a member of the class in A v. B and accordingly was bound by the judgment in that case upholding the validity of the covenant.

   2. **Supreme Court holding:** The Supreme Court disagreed with the state court and held that the defendants were not bound by the ruling in A v. B. The Court held that the defendants' right to ***due process*** would be violated if they were bound by a suit in which their interests were not really represented.

   a. **Lack of adequate representation bars class action:** The Court noted that although the class representative in A v. B ostensibly represented the Hansberrys' seller, such representation was not constitutionally adequate.

   i. *A*'s interest — which was to enforce the covenant — was at odds with the interests of the Hansberrys' seller and the Hansberrys — which was not to enforce the covenant.

   ii. If the interests of the members were not adequately represented, then it ***violated due process*** for the court to issue a judgment adjudicating their rights or obligations.

   iii. In fact, the Court suggested that a class member would be free to "change her mind."

   b. **When class action proper:** On the other hand, the Court also made it clear that a class action could constitutionally adjudicate the rights of absent members provided there was ***adequate representation***. One key to adequate representation is the lack of any ***divergent inter-***

ests like those in *Hansberry*. In essence, a proper class action involves a situation where the interests of the representative and the class members are so closely aligned that the representative, by looking out for his own best interests, automatically also looks out for interests of the class members.

Note: This reasoning suggests that the parties in the original A v. B suit in *Hansberry* chose the wrong approach. Instead of a class of plaintiffs suing a single defendant, the plaintiff should have named a ***defendant class action*** comprised of all people who signed the covenant but did not want it enforced.

C. **Personal jurisdiction:** The Supreme Court has also dealt with the issue of personal jurisdiction in class actions. In Phillips Petroleum v. Shutts, 472 U.S. 797 (1985), the Court held that in the typical class action, a forum can adjudicate the claims of the absent members even absent minimum contacts between the members and the forum.

★   1. **Facts:** *Phillips* was a plaintiff class action in a Kansas state court in which a representative sued an oil company on behalf of a class of 33,000 people who, plaintiff claimed, were owed royalties by Phillips under oil well leases. Phillips argued that because in many cases neither the owner nor the oil well was in Kansas, there were no minimum contacts sufficient to allow Kansas to adjudicate the claims.

   Note: Although a party usually may not challenge a court's lack of jurisdiction over *other* parties, the Court allowed Phillips to assert the defense. After all, if Phillips were to prevail in the case, it would want the judgment to bind all members of the class. However, the judgment could bind the absent members only if the court had personal jurisdiction.

   2. **Supreme Court holding:** The Supreme Court held that the Kansas court ***could exercise jurisdiction*** over the absent members of the class. Although due process usually requires minimum contacts, the Court held that ***certain protections afforded by the class action*** device served as a ***substitute*** for minimum contacts. The Court noted the following features of class actions:

   a. the lack of any ***burden on the member*** to travel; instead, the burden of litigating the claim would be borne entirely by the representative;

   b. the guarantee of ***adequate representation*** of the members' interests;

   c. the provisions in Fed. R. Civ. P. 23 guaranteeing the members ***notice*** and the opportunity to ***opt out of*** the class;

   d. because courts would rarely allow a defendant to file a counterclaim against members of the class, the class action would result in ***no money judgment against*** the members.

   Note: The Court did remand the case to the Kansas courts, but for another reason. The Kansas courts had applied Kansas law to every claim. The Court held that Kansas could not constitutionally apply Kansas law to claims that had no connection whatsoever with that state.

   3. **Limits of holding:** Broadly read, *Phillips* could make personal jurisdiction a nonissue in class actions. However, the Court's opinion contains several significant limitations.

   a. **Defendant class action:** *Phillips* was a plaintiff class action. In theory, the rationale could apply to cases where a plaintiff sues a class of defendants. On the other hand, members of a defendant class would be subject to a money judgment. The Court specifically refused to deal with this question, stating in footnote 3 of the opinion that the opinion ''does not address'' defendant class actions.

b. **Nondamages class actions:** Nor did the Court express an opinion concerning other types of class actions, such as those seeking specific relief. Again in footnote 3, the Court suggested that the result in those cases could be different. This limitation is especially important because, as discussed below, *Fed. R. Civ. P. 23 does not guarantee* members of a 23(b)(1) or (b)(2) class either *notice or the right to opt out*, two features of class actions that were important to the rationale of *Phillips*.

Quiz Yourself on
CONSTITUTIONAL ISSUES IN CLASS ACTIONS

177. Major League Baseball has developed a bad reputation over the past two decades, in no small part because of the lack of player loyalty to their teams. Fans have grown increasingly frustrated by the annual parade of players leaving their favorite teams for higher salaries in other cities. To combat this, all the players in Major League Baseball sign a contract in which each promises not to take another position without the approval of at least 70 percent of the other players.

Soon after the contract is signed, Antoneres announces that he is taking a position with another team. Ballou, one of his teammates, immediately brings an action in a federal court in California for damages. Ballou manages to have the case certified as a plaintiff class action, with the class comprised of all players in Major League Baseball. All the players are served with notice. A few weeks later, however, the judge dismisses the case for failure to state a claim, holding that the players' contract violates federal antitrust laws and is unenforceable.

After final judgment is entered, Couture announces that he too is leaving his team for greener pastures. Dexter, one of Couture's teammates, sues Couture to enforce the contract. Couture defends by arguing that the class action judgment bars Dexter from suing. Dexter counters by arguing that he cannot be bound by the prior judgment because his interests were not represented. How should the court rule? _____

178. Same facts as Problem 177, except that rather than argue that his interests were not represented, Dexter argues that the California judgment does not bind him because of lack of personal jurisdiction. Dexter points out that he has no contacts whatsoever with California. How should the court rule? _____

Answers

177. Couture should prevail. Dexter is bound by the class action judgment because, unlike in *Hansberry*, his interests were represented. Dexter is a member of the plaintiff class. The interest of that class was to enforce the contract. Here too Dexter seeks enforcement. The only way Dexter would not be bound is if he can show that Ballou compromised the case or otherwise did a poor job representing the interests of those who wanted to enforce the contract.

178. Couture again prevails. According to *Phillips*, absent members of a plaintiff class need not have contacts with a state to be bound by the judgment in a class action litigated in that state. The facts here specify that the class members received notice. Because the protections afforded by Fed. R. Civ. P. 23 provide all the process that is due, minimum contacts are unnecessary.

III. REQUIREMENTS OF RULE 23

Understanding the constitutional limits established by *Hansberry* helps one to understand many of the requirements of Fed. R. Civ. P. 23. Most of the rule's requirements represent ways to ensure that the class representative adequately represents the interests of the class members.

A. Overview of Rule 23: Fed. R. Civ. P. 23 requires the court to *certify* the case as a class action by applying detailed standards. The certification decision is supposed to be made *as soon as practicable* after commencement of the action as a class action. Fed. R. Civ. P. 23(c)(1). In practice, the decision to certify can take months, or even years in a large complex case.

  1. Absent certification: Without certification, any judgment in the action will bind only the *named parties*.

  2. Two-step process: FRCP 23 establishes a two-step process for certification.

   a. Appropriateness: First, the court must determine whether the case is appropriate for a class action.

   b. Which category: Second, if the case is appropriate, the court must determine which category of class action is appropriate. Choosing the category is crucial because the rule sets out different procedural requirements for different types of actions.

  3. Appeal: *Fed. R. Civ. P. 23(f)* gives the appellate court the discretion to hear an immediate appeal of a decision granting or denying class certification, provided that application is made to the court of appeals within 10 days of entry of the order.

B. Is dispute appropriate for class action? *Fed. R. Civ. P. 23(a)* contains the standards for determining whether a given dispute is appropriate for use of the class action device. The rule sets out four basic requirements: *numerosity, commonality, typicality,* and *adequacy*.

  1. Numerosity: *Fed. R. Civ. P. 23(a)(1)* requires that the class be "so numerous that joinder of all members is impracticable." Because of the complicated procedural requirements that attach to a class action, the device makes sense only if the dispute involves enough class members to allow for economies of scale.

   a. There is *no fixed number* that will meet this requirement in every case. The minimum number turns on the particular features of the case. One key feature is the *amount of each claim*. If the claims are large in amount, either individual suits or ordinary joinder is more likely to be workable because each party has an incentive to litigate her own rights. Another factor is how *widely dispersed* the members are.

b. A few courts have allowed class actions with as few as 30 class members. However, in most cases, the threshold is significantly higher.

2. **Commonality:** *Fed. R. Civ. P. 23(a)(2)* allows a class action to be certified only if ''there are questions of law or fact common to the class.'' This notion of commonality defines the boundaries of the class.

   a. The commonality can concern *either law or fact*. Thus, unlike many other forms of joinder, the claims involved in a class action need not arise from the same transaction or occurrence.

   b. Commonality does not mean that all, or even most, questions of law and/or fact be shared. However, if there is a significant difference between the individual claims, a class action will not prove efficient because the court will have to spend too much time dealing with the individual elements of the claims.

3. **Typicality:** *Fed. R. Civ. P. 23(a)(3)* mandates that ''the claims or defenses of the representative parties are typical of the claims or defenses of the class.'' Typicality turns on several factors, including the size of the claim, the legal source of the claim, and whether the representatives or members are subject to any defenses. Most courts find the requirement is satisfied unless there is a major difference between the representatives' and members' claims.

4. **Adequacy:** *Fed. R. Civ. P. 23(a)(4)* requires that ''the representative parties will fairly and adequately protect the interests of the class.''

   a. Policy: This requirement attempts to deal with the constitutional problems identified in *Hansberry*. However, there is a significant overlap between the adequacy and typicality requirements. In fact, because adequacy more directly addresses the due process issues, it is unclear what separate role the typicality requirement serves.

   b. Determining adequacy: Courts consider several factors when determining adequacy of representation.

      i. Parallel interests: It is crucial to ensure that the interests of the representative are closely aligned with those of the class. If there is any sort of *conflict of interest*, actual or potential, representation may not be adequate.

      ii. Counsel for the representative: Another factor that courts closely scrutinize is the competence of the attorneys for the representative. Although this is not always possible, courts prefer that counsel be both competent in the subject matter of the litigation and have experience dealing with class actions.

      iii. Financial considerations: Because a class action is a complicated case that can take years to complete, the court also considers the representative's ability to *fund the litigation*.

   ★

      Example: For an illustration of how these standards apply in actual litigation, see Communities for Equity v. Michigan High School Athletic Assn., 1999 U.S. Dist. LEXIS 5780 (W.D. Mich. 1999). The court in that case held that the requirements of Rule 23(a) were satisfied.

C. **Which category of class action?** If Fed. R. Civ. P. 23(a) is satisfied, the court applies *Fed. R. Civ. P. 23(b)* to determine whether the case fits into one of the *three acceptable categories* of class actions. If the case does not fit into any of the three categories, the case cannot be certified as a class action.

1. **Rule 23(b)(1) — numerous necessary parties:** The first category of class action covers situations where there are many absent parties, each of whom, generally speaking, meets the test for a "necessary party" under Fed. R. Civ. P. 19(a). The rule allows a class action when *individual actions* involving the class members pose a risk of either:

   a. *inconsistent or varying outcomes* with respect to the individual members that would expose the *party opposing the class* to *incompatible standards of conduct* (Fed. R. Civ. P. 23(b)(1)(A)), or

   b. results that as a practical matter would *dispose of the interests of the other members, or impair or impede their ability to protect* those interests (Fed. R. Civ. P. 23(b)(1)(B)).

      Example: *D* manufactures an automobile. A number of drivers are injured when the airbags in their automobiles deploy prematurely. One of these drivers sues *D* for damages. *D* moves to certify the case as a class action, with the driver representing the class members. *D* argues that because it is by no means clear that the airbag was defective, *D* faces inconsistent outcomes if the various injured parties are allowed to bring individual suits. The court will not certify the case under Fed. R. Civ. P. 23(b)(1). Although individual suits may result in inconsistent outcomes, those outcomes do not result in inconsistent standards of conduct. *D* can simply pay any plaintiffs who win and not pay those who lose. (*Note*: This case might be certified under Rule 23(b)(3), which is discussed below.)

      Example: Same as the preceding example, except that the plaintiff sues *D*'s insurance carrier. The insurance policy has a limit of $1 million. Plaintiff moves to have the case certified as a class action. Plaintiff has proof that hundreds of people have been injured by the airbags in *D*'s cars and that those people have claims well in excess of $5 million. The class action meets the requirements of both Fed. R. Civ. P. 23(b)(1)(A) and (B). Under (b)(1)(A), the plaintiffs might all prevail in their separate lawsuits, resulting in total judgments above the policy limit. Under (b)(1)(B), plaintiffs who obtain their judgments first might exhaust the policy, leaving later claimants with nothing from which to recover.

2. **Rule 23(b)(2) — injunctive or declaratory relief:** Fed. R. Civ. P. 23(b)(2) allows class actions in situations where "the party opposing the class has acted or refused to act on grounds generally applicable to the class, thereby making appropriate final injunctive or corresponding declaratory relief with respect to the class as a whole."

   Example: A city routinely captures stray dogs without providing notice and a hearing to the owners. A dog owner sues the city, claiming that the practice violates due process. The owner sues for an injunction requiring the city to afford notice and a hearing before capturing a stray dog whose owner is known to the city. The case is proper for certification of a (b)(2) class comprising all dog owners in the city.

3. **Rule 23(b)(3) — the "damages" class action:** The (b)(1) and (2) class actions apply only in certain relatively narrow and clearly defined situations. The Rule 23(b)(3) class action, by contrast, is a sort of catchall category designed to deal with situations where class actions might still be appropriate but where the *claims are not as intertwined* as in the other two cases. Because the relationship between the various members is somewhat looser, Fed. R. Civ. P. 23 imposes additional restrictions on the Rule 23(b)(3) class action.

Note: Some courts, especially in older cases, refer to the Rule 23(b)(3) class action as a ***spurious*** class action. This reflects how significant an expansion of the class action device the rule represented.

a. Basic standard: A Rule 23(b)(3) class action is appropriate when:

    i. the ***common questions of law or fact predominate*** over questions affecting only individual members of the class, and

    ii. a ***class action is superior*** to either individual actions or a combined suit using other joinder devices for fairly and efficiently resolving the underlying controversy.

b. Determining superiority: The rule also specifies the factors to be considered in determining whether a class action is the optimal method.

    i. The first factor is the extent to which the ***individual members*** have an ***interest*** in controlling the prosecution or defense of their own actions. Fed. R. Civ. P. 23(b)(3)(A). An individual member is more likely to litigate her own case if the amount at stake is large or if her claim or defense has features that are not present in the claims or defenses of other members of the class.

    ii. The second factor is whether ***litigation*** involving claims by or against members of the class is ***already pending***. Fed. R. Civ. P. 23(b)(3)(B).

    iii. The third factor is whether the chosen forum is a ***desirable place*** to concentrate litigation of the various claims. This factor focuses primarily on practical issues that may arise, such as the ease of discovery and personal jurisdiction.

    Example: In Heaven v. Trust Company Bank, 18 F.3d 735 (11th Cir. 1997), the court held that Fed. R. Civ. P. 23(b)(3) was not satisfied, in large part because the defendant had counterclaims against many of the class members.

    iv. The fourth factor is what other difficulties may arise in ***managing the class action***.

c. Application of the standard: The certification decision in every Rule 23(b)(3) class action depends on the idiosyncratic features of the particular case. However, there are a few themes that commonly arise in these cases.

    i. Damages: In ***personal injury*** and ***misrepresentation/fraud*** cases, the damages suffered by each member of the class may differ significantly. If there is a wide discrepancy, the individualized issues of damages may outweigh the common issues in the cases and thereby prevent certification. One remedy for a court in this situation is to certify the case as a class action ***only for purposes of liability***.

    ii. Defenses: In many cases, the defendant may have defenses to the claims of some of the members of the class. For example, some of the members may have signed waivers of liability or waited so long to bring their claims that they may be precluded by the statute of limitations or laches. These individualized issues may prevent certification of the case as a class action.

    iii. Choice of law: Class actions often involve members scattered across the country or in different nations. Depending on the circumstances, claims by or against these scattered parties may be governed by different substantive laws. Similarly, different states may recognize different defenses. Differences in governing law often preclude certification of a Rule 23(b)(3) class action because the individual issues of law are likely to predominate over the common issues.

Example: A representative moves for certification of a Rule 23(b)(3) class action comprising every person who was hurt by a drug produced by *D*. The victims purchased and used the product in dozens of different states. Certification is unlikely because different state laws are likely to apply to determine whether *D* is liable.

D. Procedure after certification: If the judge certifies the case as a class action, Fed. R. Civ. P. 23 imposes additional procedural requirements. However, the procedure differs depending upon the type of class action involved.

1. **Notice and opt-out:** In *Fed. R. Civ. P. 23(b)(3)* class actions, the class representative(s) must give notice to all members of the class and afford those members the right to opt out of the class action.

   a. **Notice:** Rule 23(c) requires individual notice to *all class members*. If a member cannot be found, the court excludes the member from the class, and the judgment will not bind that person. In this regard, the notice requirements of Rule 23 go beyond the minimum requirements of due process.

   i.   The notice must specify that:

   (a) the court will exclude from the class any member who requests exclusion by the date indicated in the notice;

   (b) if a member does not request exclusion, he will be bound by the judgment, regardless of whether the judgment is in his favor; and

   (c) a member who does not ask to be excluded may enter an individual appearance through counsel.

   ii. The requirement of individual notice to all members *cannot be ignored or modified*. Notice by publication, for example, is not acceptable. Eisen v. Carlisle & Jacquelin, 417 U.S. 156 (1974).

   iii. **Cost:** The *representative must bear the cost* of notice. *Eisen.* In addition, the representative must bear the burden of ascertaining the identity of the class members. Oppenheimer Fund, Inc. v. Sanders, 437 U.S. 340 (1978).

   b. **Opt-out:** As indicated above, the notice must indicate that the member may request exclusion from the class. A member who so requests is said to opt out of the class action. In most cases, the class action notice provides a simple form that the members can use to request exclusion from the class.

   c. **Notice and opt-out in Rule 23(b)(1) and (b)(2) actions:** Note that Rule 23(c) requires notice and the right to opt out *only in Rule 23(b)(3) class actions*. By negative implication, they are *not required by Rule 23 in (b)(1) and (b)(2) actions*.

   i.   Nevertheless, on occasion courts *do* require notice in (b)(1) and (b)(2) actions. Fed. R. Civ. P. 23(d) gives a court the authority to require notice even in (b)(1) and (b)(2) actions.

ii. However, courts *rarely* give members the right to opt out of Rule 23(b)(1) and (b)(2) actions. This tendency reflects the nature of those types of class actions.

(a) In a Fed. R. Civ. P. 23(b)(1) class action, the members, for all practical purposes, are *necessary parties*. If their presence in the action is necessary to prevent prejudice to their interests or the interests of the litigants, it is counterproductive to allow them to opt out.

(b) A Fed. R. Civ. P. 23(b)(2) class action seeks injunctive or declaratory relief. If such relief is granted, it benefits the class members regardless of whether they are parties to the action. Therefore, it makes little sense to allow them to opt out of the action.

2. **Additional procedures:** *Fed. R. Civ. P. 23(d)* allows the judge in a class action to issue any additional orders that she deems necessary.

E. **Settlement of class action:** Settlement presents a special problem in class actions. If the party opposing the class can strike a favorable personal deal with the representative, the representative might settle the suit even though settlement is not in the best interests of the class as a whole. Because of this risk, *Fed. R. Civ. P. 23(e)* places significant restrictions on settlement of a class action.

1. **Notice:** Notice of any proposed settlement must be provided to all members of the class to give them a chance to challenge the proposed settlement. Unlike the notice required for class certification, notice of a settlement must be provided *in all categories of class actions*.

2. **Court approval:** No settlement is effective without court approval. This is a *unique feature of class actions* since courts do not approve settlements in other cases. In determining whether to approve a settlement, the court must ensure that it is fair for all members of the class. The court also carefully scrutinizes the allocation of *attorneys' fees* in the settlement agreement.

3. **The "settlement class action":** At times, attorneys attempt to certify a class solely for the purposes of forcing settlement. Such cases often involve mass torts, and the class may be comprised of thousands or even millions of members. The attempt to certify may be made *after* an individual plaintiff or group of plaintiffs has negotiated a settlement with the defendant. The defendant favors certification of a class as a way to resolve the dispute once and for all.

★   **a.** *Anchem:* The Supreme Court, however, significantly limited the use of settlement class actions in Anchem Products, Inc. v. Windsor, 521 U.S. 591 (1997). *Anchem* held that in a settlement class action where the class was defined as everyone who had ever been exposed to asbestos — regardless of whether any disease had yet manifested itself — it would be impossible to achieve adequate representation.

b. *Anchem* does not completely prevent the use of settlement class actions. Indeed, the Court in the case explicitly recognized that the fact that a settlement had been previously negotiated is a factor to consider in the certification decision. As long as the claims are sufficiently similar that typicality and adequate representation are met, a settlement class action is still possible.

F. **Judgment in class action:** The judgment in a class action must identify the members of the class. Such identification is necessary to determine who is bound by the judgment. In a *Fed. R. Civ. P. 23(b)(1) or (b)(2)* case, the judgment should name every person who is a member of the class. In a *Fed. R. Civ. P. 23(b)(3)* case, the judgment should include only those members who *received notice* and *did not opt out*.

Quiz Yourself on
APPLICATION OF RULE 23

180. Peter Plaintiff is seriously injured by a food processor. Peter sues Kit's Kitchenwares, the manufacturer of the food processor, for damages. Peter argues that Kit's was negligent in failing to put a warning label on the food processor. In addition to damages, Peter wants an order requiring Kit's to recall the food processors and add a warning label.

Kit's and Peter seek to have the case certified as a class action, with the class comprised of everyone who has been injured by this model of food processor. Peter will serve as representative. Kit's joins in the request for certification because it has already won four individual cases in which the plaintiffs argued that the lack of a warning label was negligence. Therefore, Kit's wants to know whether such labels are required so it can decide how to act in the future. The 2,000 people who have been injured by the food processor live all across the country, and each purchased the product in his or her home state. Which Fed. R. Civ. P. 23(b) category of class action best fits this situation?

_____

181. Same facts as Problem 180. The people who have been injured by the food processor work in a variety of occupations, from computer operators to law professors to concert pianists. However, because the product was sold only in the stores of a major national retail store, they all bought the product from that retailer. All of the people suffered injuries to their hands in operating the food processor, but the injuries vary significantly. Peter's injury is fairly typical. Peter works as a singer who provides voice-overs for radio commercials.

Is the proposed class likely to satisfy the Rule 23(a) requirements for a class action?

_____

182. Same facts as Problems 180 and 181, except assume that the court certifies a Rule 23(b)(3) class action. Notice is provided to all the members, and 70 opt out of the case. Judgment is entered for Kit's in the class action. Shortly thereafter, one of the people who opted out brings her own individual suit against Kit's. Kit's argues that the plaintiff is barred by the judgment in the class action from bringing an individual suit. How should the court rule?   _____

Answers

180. This most likely is a Rule 23(b)(3) class action. Although Peter seeks a form of injunctive relief (the recall order), that relief is merely incidental to the damages request. Rule 23(b)(2) is therefore inappropriate.

The situation also resembles the Rule 23(b)(1) situation in that Kit's is unsure how to act in the future. However, there is no risk of an inconsistent standard of behavior. Kit's may not know whether a label is required. On the other hand, nothing legally prevents Kit's from adding the label. Therefore, it will not expose itself to any liability by adding a label.

Therefore, only Rule 23(b)(3) is an option. Note that the case may not fit even this category. On the surface, the common questions of law and fact would seem to predominate — namely, the question of whether failure to have a warning label is a defect. However, given that the victims live all over the country, the different claims likely are governed by different laws. Although the issue of whether the lack of a label is a defect arises in all the claims, the governing legal standard could be different.

Finally, if the other members of the class also suffered serious injury, a class action might not be the best way to resolve this dispute. Each of the members might have a sufficient incentive to sue on his or her own behalf.

181. The judge is unlikely to certify this case as a class action. Numerosity is met because there are 2,000 potential class members. Commonality, however, presents an issue. Because the victims are located all across the country and purchased their products in their home state, different laws may govern the various claims.

Another problem here is the disparity among the plaintiffs, presenting problems with typicality and adequacy. First, the injuries suffered by the class members differ widely, even though all involve their hands. Second, the *consequences* of such injuries also differ. A computer operator and concert pianist might have much higher damages than a law professor for the same sort of injury. Moreover, because Peter, the class representative, is a singer on radio, the impaired use of his hand might not be as devastating. As a result, his claim is not typical.

One option might be to certify the case as a Rule 23(b)(3) class action for purposes of determining liability only, leaving it to individual cases to prove up damages. This limited approach could take care of the typicality and adequacy problems. On the other hand, with the difference in governing laws, commonality still remains a problem.

182. The suit is not barred. Although Rule 23 does not specifically say so, a party who opts out is not bound by the class action judgment.

IV. OTHER ISSUES IN CLASS ACTIONS

Class actions present a number of other unique problems.

A. Subject matter jurisdiction in federal court: No special statutes deal with federal subject matter jurisdiction in class actions. Therefore, a class action can be heard in federal court only if it involves a federal question, meets the requirements for diversity, or qualifies for supplemental jurisdiction.

1. **Federal question:** Many class actions are brought under federal statutes such as the securities or civil rights laws. Determining whether the claims involved "arise under" federal law involves the same considerations in class actions as in any other case.

2. **Diversity:** Diversity jurisdiction has proven much more problematic. Supreme Court interpretations of 28 U.S.C. §1332 (the diversity statute) have made it extremely difficult to file a class action based on state law in federal court.

    a. **Citizenship:** In determining the citizenship of the class, courts consider *only the class representatives*. The citizenship of the absent members is ignored. Supreme Tribe of Ben-Hur v. Cauble, 255 U.S. 356 (1921).

    b. **Amount in controversy:** However, *every member of the class* must independently meet the amount in controversy. Zahn v. International Paper Co., 414 U.S. 291 (1973). Claims of the members cannot be aggregated to satisfy the requirement. Snyder v. Harris, 394 U.S. 332 (1969).

Example: *P*, a citizen of North Dakota, sues *D*, a citizen of Oklahoma, for a state law tort claim. Because the parties are diverse, and because *P* claims $100,000 in damages, *P* brings the case as a class action on behalf of a class of everyone who was injured in the same way by *D*'s product. Members of the class live all across the country, including many who live in Oklahoma. Members have suffered damages ranging from $20,000 to $140,000. Result: A federal court cannot exercise jurisdiction over the class action. Although diversity is met because only *P*'s citizenship matters, not all of the claims meet the amount in controversy requirement.

Note: On these facts, the federal court might be able to certify a class comprising only those members whose claims exceed the amount in controversy. However, the court might refuse to certify because more complete relief could be had in state court.

3. **Supplemental jurisdiction:** *28 U.S.C. §1367* also may prove useful to a party attempting to bring a class action in federal court based on diversity jurisdiction.

   a. **When supplemental jurisdiction might apply:** In theory, the doctrine of supplemental jurisdiction proves useful when some of the members' claims independently qualify for federal subject matter jurisdiction, while others do not. If the claims arise from a *common nucleus of operative fact*, the basic requirements of §1367(a) are satisfied. See Chapter 4.

   b. Supplemental jurisdiction may apply in diversity cases when some of the claims meet the amount in controversy and others do not.

      i. **§1367(b):** As discussed in Chapter 2, §1367(b) bars virtually all claims by plaintiffs against other parties in cases where jurisdiction is based solely on diversity. However, it does not bar all claims. Instead, it bars only claims by plaintiffs against parties joined *under certain listed rules*.

      ii. *Rule 23* is *not one of the rules listed* in §1367(b). Therefore, some courts have concluded that supplemental jurisdiction can be used to get around the amount in controversy requirements in class action cases. Other courts disagree, concluding that the real purpose of §1367(b) is to preserve the complete diversity requirement.

      Example: In the prior example, courts that allow supplemental jurisdiction would allow the entire class action to be heard in federal court. As long as all the claims were factually related, those where the amount in controversy was less than $75,000 could be "attached" to those in excess of $75,000.

   c. **Caveat:** Even if a court concludes that, in principle, supplemental jurisdiction applies in class actions, the requirements of the doctrine are not always satisfied. Section 1367(a) requires that the federal and supplemental claims arise from a *common nucleus of operative fact*. The commonality requirement in Rule 23(a), however, merely requires that the claims share *common questions of law or fact*. If claims share an issue of law but do not arise from the same event or series of events, then they do not qualify for supplemental jurisdiction even if they can be combined into a class action.

B. Attorneys' fees: Attorneys' fees are an important consideration in class actions. Because of the procedural complexity and sheer size of a class action, the attorneys' fees are likely to be quite large.

    1. Paid from fund: If the class action results in a cash settlement or money judgment for the class, the attorneys' fees are paid out of the fund. It is not uncommon for the fees to exhaust the lion's share of the amount recovered, leaving the members of the class with little or nothing.

    2. Court approval: The requirement of court approval for class action settlements gives the court considerable control over the amount of the fee. If the court ascertains that the attorneys charged more than a reasonable amount, the settlement is denied.

V. OTHER EXAMPLES OF REPRESENTATIONAL LITIGATION

Class actions are not the only form of representational litigation. ***Fed. R. Civ. P. 23.1 and 23.2*** authorize federal courts to hear shareholder derivative actions, as well as actions involving unincorporated associations.

A. Shareholder derivative actions: A shareholders' derivative action is usually brought against the ***officers and/or directors of a corporation***. It seeks compensation for harm caused to the corporation by improper decisions of the officers and directors.

    1. Corporation as plaintiff: In theory, because the harm is suffered by the corporation, the action should be brought by the corporation itself.

    2. Not through officers or directors: However, a corporation acts only through its officers and directors. It is foolish to expect the officers and directors to sue themselves.

    3. Stockholder sues instead: To resolve this dilemma, the shareholders' derivative action allows a person who ***owns stock*** in the corporation to sue the officers and/or directors on behalf of the corporation. Rule 23.1 allows federal courts to hear these cases, provided the requirements for jurisdiction are satisfied.

    4. Action by member of unincorporated association: Rule 23.1 also allows an action *by* a member of an unincorporated association against the association's officers or directors, which is conceptually similar to a shareholders' derivative action.

    5. Requirements of Rule 23.1: Rule 23.1 places several restrictions on shareholders' derivative actions and actions by members of unincorporated associations. The ***complaint*** in the action must be ***verified*** and must make certain specific allegations. In addition, the plaintiff must ***fairly and adequately represent*** the interests of similarly situated shareholders or members. Finally, ***court approval*** must be obtained before the action can be dismissed or settled.

B. Unincorporated associations: In most cases, suits by or against unincorporated associations (clubs and other groups) must be filed by or against all the members of that association. However, ***Fed. R. Civ. P. 23.2*** allows suits involving these organizations to take a form similar to class actions.

Note: Suits involving unincorporated associations under Fed. R. Civ. P. 23.2 differ from those under Rule 23.1. In the case of Rule 23.1, the suit is ***against the association's officers or directors***. In Rule 23.2, by contrast, the ***association is suing or being sued*** by a third party.

1. **One or more representative parties:** The rule allows a suit by an unincorporated association to be brought by one or more representative parties. Similarly, a party suing the association may sue one or more representatives.

2. **Fairly and adequately protect interests:** However, Rule 23.2 allows the representative suit only if the court finds that the representatives will fairly and adequately protect the interests of both the association and its members.

3. **Other protections:** Rule 23.2 also adopts certain protections from the class action procedure. For example, *settlement* of the class action must meet the standards of Fed. R. Civ. P. 23(e), including the requirement of *court approval*.

Quiz Yourself on *CLASS ACTIONS*

183. Paulette sues Drugco, a major pharmaceutical company, in federal district court. Paulette seeks to recover damages for a serious allergic reaction that she suffered when taking one of Drugco's products. Paulette wants to have the case certified as a class action, with a class comprising all people who suffered the same allergic reaction. Paulette, who would be the class representative, is a citizen of a different state than Drugco, and her claim is well in excess of $75,000. However, a number of members of the class cannot bring individual diversity actions against Drugco, either because they are from the same state or because their injuries involve damages of less than $75,000. Assuming the case can be certified as a class action, does the federal court have jurisdiction over the entire action?

---

184. Same facts as Problem 183, except that assume the court certifies the case as a Fed. R. Civ. P. 23(b)(3) class action. Notice and a chance to opt out are given to all the class members. A few months later, Paulette receives what she feels is an excellent settlement offer from Drugco. The trial judge agrees and is willing to approve the settlement. Is Paulette free to go ahead and settle the case?

---

185. John "Jack" Russell absolutely loves the breed of small terrier that shares his name. A rich and somewhat eccentric man, Jack decides not to leave any of his vast estate to his relatives. Instead, his will specifies that his money is to be divided equally among "everyone who owns a purebred Jack Russell terrier on the date of my death."

After Jack dies, Ed Executor, the executor of Jack's estate, finds himself in an intractable situation. Thousands of people have written to Ed claiming a share of the estate. However, it is difficult for Ed to determine whether the claims are valid and whether there are others out there who have not asked for a share of the money. To solve this problem, Ed brings a class action in a North Carolina state court. He names four of the claimants as the representatives of a defendant class. The judge certifies the class under the appropriate Rule 23(b) category, concluding that to allow each of the owners to sue Ed separately would present a risk of multiple liability to Ed, as well as imperil the interests of the other owners. After a long and difficult trial, in which the parties diligently seek to find all of the people entitled to funds, the court enters a judgment and the estate is distributed.

After the case is complete, Russell Jackson sues Ed. Russell claims he is entitled to a share of the estate. Although the court did consider Russell's claim in the class action proceeding, it eventually determined that Russell did not buy his dog until after Jack had died. Therefore, Russell received nothing. Russell nevertheless claims that he is not bound by the class action judgment. First, he points out that he received no notice of the case. Second, he correctly notes that he has no contacts whatsoever with North Carolina. Because of these issues, Russell claims, it violates his due process rights if the judgment binds him.

Is Russell free to seek additional funds? _____

186. The Wolf Network (TWN) is the newest entrant on the national broadcasting scene. TWN takes an unapologetically arch-conservative viewpoint. Much of its so-called news is spent bashing politicians whose views do not comport with those of TWN's staff. In addition, TWN refuses to air campaign advertisements from politicians who do not have TWN's arch-conservative views. Many of the politicians complain to the Federal Communications Commission, to no avail.

One of the politicians takes a different course. He sues TWN in a state court, seeking an injunction requiring TWN to accept and air the campaign ads of all politicians willing to pay TWN's fees. The politician then seeks to have the case certified as a class action, with a class comprising all politicians who will be running for office in the future and would like to advertise on TWN, but are likely to have their ads rejected because of their views. As described, this class includes thousands of members who will be running for national, state, and local offices on different dates. The case nevertheless satisfies the requirements of Rule 23(a). Will the court certify it as a class action?

_____

Answers

183. The federal court probably does have jurisdiction. The citizenship issue is not a problem. For purposes of applying 28 U.S.C. §1332 to class action cases, it has long been the rule that the court considers only the citizenship of the named representative. Because Paulette is diverse, this requirement is met.

The amount in controversy presents a more serious problem. The traditional rule was that *all* members had to have claims in excess of $75,000. Several courts, however, have applied the supplemental jurisdiction statute to this situation. Even though the main claim is a diversity claim, these courts reason that §1367(b) does not bar claims of less than $75,000 because Fed. R. Civ. P. 23 is not among the rules listed in § 1367(b). If the court applies this rationale, it can hear Paulette's class action. Paulette's claim and those of the absent class members do arise out of the same transaction, namely, the design and marketing of the drug in question.

184. Before settling the case, Paulette needs to give notice to all the class members. Fed. R. Civ. P. 23(e). Notice is provided in the manner dictated by the court. If Paulette does not give notice, a member might not be bound by the settlement.

185. Russell's suit probably is barred, but the precedent is not entirely clear. His first claim of lack of notice probably will not succeed. The case as described would have been certified as a Rule 23(b)(1) class action. The reasons given by the trial judge describe the Rule 23(b)(1) necessary party class. Class members in a Rule 23(b)(1) case are not entitled to notice. Although *Phillips* casts some doubt as to whether this is constitutional, the lower courts typically have followed the rule and not ordered notice.

The lack of contacts argument stands a stronger chance of succeeding. *Phillips* is again the most important case. That case held that the protections afforded by the class action device satisfied due process, and, as a result, minimum contacts between the absent class members and the forum were not required. However, *Phillips* was a Rule 23(b)(3) plaintiff class action, and the Court explicitly limited its holding to plaintiff class actions. In most respects, there is no appreciable difference between a plaintiff and defendant class action. Nevertheless, because the *Phillips* Court did not decide the issue, the rule of that case may not apply, and minimum contacts could be necessary.

186. The court should certify this as a Rule 23(b)(2) class action. TWN has acted the same way toward everyone in the class. An injunction would remedy the claims of everyone in the class. The disparity in the claims is not a factor under Rule 23(b)(2).

Note that unless federal law governs the claims, the case might not satisfy the commonality requirement of Rule 23(a). However, the facts state that Rule 23(a) is satisfied.

Exam Tips on CLASS ACTIONS

☞ Do not overlook the serious constitutional concerns lurking beneath the surface of the class action device. By understanding these core concerns, you can better understand the many technical provisions in Fed. R. Civ. P. 23.

☞ With respect to personal jurisdiction, do not forget that the holding in the *Phillips* case is explicitly limited to plaintiff class actions under Fed. R. Civ. P. 23(b)(3). Although the rationale might seem to apply to other class actions, the precedent is not clear.

☞ When dealing with the question of certification, be sure to treat the Fed. R. Civ. P. 23(a) and 23(b) analyses as two separate steps.

☞ When dealing with Rule 23(a), the following hints may prove helpful.

   ☞ Commonality may be destroyed when the claims arise under state law and the parties are from different states. In these situations, different laws may govern the different claims.

   ☞ Typicality and adequacy are interrelated to some extent. A case will present a typicality or adequacy problem when the representative's claim is different in kind from those of the members or significantly different in degree.

☞ When dealing with Rule 23(b), remember that some situations do not fit any of the three categories and accordingly may not be brought as a class action.

   ☞ Although Fed. R. Civ. P. 23(b)(3) is a catchall category, remember that it applies only when the common questions predominate.

☞ As a general matter, hesitate before concluding that a class action is proper in the following cases:

   ☞ mass tort cases involving serious injuries (because the parties have the incentive to bring individual cases), and

   ☞ cases where parties scattered across the nation would be bringing state law claims (because of choice-of-law problems).

☛ Recall that notice and opt-out are required only in Rule 23(b)(3) cases.

   ☞ On the other hand, Rule 23(e) requires an additional notice should there be a proposed settlement. This additional notice must be provided in all cases.

☛ Recall that subject matter jurisdiction presents special concerns in the class action context. One of the special considerations is that as long as some of the member's claims meet the amount in controversy requirements for diversity, supplemental jurisdiction may be available for the other claims.

Essay Exam Questions

QUESTION 1 (Suggested time: 100 minutes):   Several years ago, Axel Greiss, a citizen of Germany, left his homeland and moved to Eau Claire, Wisconsin. A mechanic by trade, Axel set up a small automobile repair shop in Eau Claire. This operation has developed into a thriving business. Although he has not yet acquired U.S. citizenship, Axel enjoys Wisconsin and fully intends to remain there for many years.

While driving through Eau Claire one day, Carol Ina, a citizen of the state of South Carolina, notices that her automobile is having brake problems. Carol stops in Axel's shop for repairs. Axel sees the South Carolina license plates and, because he has never been to that state, strikes up a lively conversation with Carol as he fixes the brakes. Carol thinks her brake problems are solved. However, when she returns to South Carolina, her brakes fail at an intersection. Unable to stop, Carol runs over a pedestrian, Charles Ton. Charles, another South Carolina citizen, is seriously injured in this accident. Charles promptly sues Carol in a federal court in South Carolina. His complaint alleges that Carol was negligent in failing properly to maintain her car and seeks damages in the amount of $300,000. Charles asks Carol to waive service of process, and she agrees to waive.

Carol files an answer denying liability but raising no other defenses. She then files a timely third-party complaint against Axel, which alleges that Axel's negligence was the primary cause of the brake failure. Arguing that she did nothing wrong, Carol's third-party complaint asks the court to require Axel to reimburse her for any damages she is required to pay Charles. Carol serves this third-party complaint on Axel in Eau Claire by using the South Carolina long-arm statute, which allows for service under these circumstances. Charles also files a claim against third-party defendant Axel. Charles alleges that he is a third-party beneficiary of the contract between Axel and Carol and therefore can recover for Axel's shoddy work. Charles arranges to have a process server serve Axel in-hand in Eau Claire, Wisconsin.

Axel immediately files and serves a pre-answer motion to sever the claims against him from Charles's claim against Carol. Axel alleges that Fed. R. Civ. P. 14 does not allow either party to join a claim against him with the original plaintiff-defendant claim. Three days after that motion, Axel files a second pre-answer motion to dismiss the claims against him for lack of both subject matter and personal jurisdiction. Axel's motions cause Carol to reevaluate her own position. Therefore, although three weeks have expired since she served her answer, she attempts to amend her answer to add the defense of lack of subject matter jurisdiction.

Charles contests both Axel's motions and Carol's new defense. First, he argues that Axel and Carol have waived the jurisdictional defenses by failing to include them in their earlier filings. Second, Charles argues that even if the defenses were raised in a timely fashion, he should win on the merits. Carol also contests Axel's motion to sever, arguing that Fed. R. Civ. P. 14 allows her to implead Axel under these circumstances.

You are a clerk for the federal district judge assigned to hear this case. Your judge wants you to write her a short memorandum addressing the following questions:

1. Should the judge sever the claims against Axel?

2. Did Axel and Carol waive the personal and subject matter jurisdiction defenses?

3. Assuming (without affecting your answer to Question 2) that the jurisdictional defenses were raised in timely fashion, how should the judge rule on the merits?

Discuss each issue separately.

QUESTION 2 (Suggested time: 75 minutes):   Smith and Jones are co-employees at ACME, Inc. Although both started with the company at roughly the same time, Jones has a much larger and nicer office than Smith. During the three-odd years that the two have worked at the company, this fact has made Smith increasingly jealous.

Unable to take it any more, Smith sues Jones and Olson (ACME's office manager, who assigns offices to all new employees). Smith brings his case in a federal court that has subject matter jurisdiction, personal jurisdiction, and venue over the action. Smith claims that he is legally entitled to the office currently occupied by Jones. ACME company policy provides that when two or more employees join ACME during the same time period, the person who "first began to work for the company" gets first choice among the vacant offices. Smith's first day on the job was July 10, 2000. However, Smith was not given a choice of offices but was merely assigned to his current small office by Olson. Smith asserts that Jones's first day on the job was not until August 1, 2000. In his complaint, Smith asks the court to grant an injunction requiring Olson to reassign Jones's office to him. With respect to Jones, Smith asks for a writ of ejectment requiring her to vacate her current office.

Olson files and serves his answer 3 days after receiving the complaint. Jones, a procrastinator, does not file her answer until December 1, 2003 — a full 45 days after the answer was due. Both defendants deny that Smith is entitled to relief. Although they agree that the company policy is enforceable in court, they argue that Jones actually "began to work for the company" before Smith within the meaning of the company policy. The defendants assert that Jones *accepted* her offer of employment before Smith, even though her first day of work was later. Jones also argues in the alternative that even if "beginning to work" is measured by one's first day on the job, she had worked at ACME one day in June 2000 before taking an extended vacation.

You are the attorney representing Smith in this action. It is now early on the morning of December 12, 2003. Smith has left you a message indicating that he wants to meet with you later in the day to discuss the next steps in the lawsuit. In this message, Smith first asks you whether it is possible to have the action tried before a jury.

Second, Smith has several questions about discovery. He has in his possession two tangible items that he fears must be disclosed to the defendants in the initial mandatory disclosures. One is a letter that he received from Pearson, who was ACME's director of personnel at the time Smith and Jones were hired. Because this letter makes it clear that Smith received his offer before Jones, Smith would rather not reveal it now, but instead save it to surprise Jones and Olson at trial. The other item is a transcript of a telephone call. When Smith called Pearson to accept the offer of employment, he recorded the call, and then typed up a verbatim transcript of the tape. The tape has since been accidentally destroyed, but Smith still has the transcript. Although the transcript shows that Smith accepted his offer before Jones, Smith does not want to disclose it at this point, again because he would rather use it to surprise Jones and Olson. Smith's next discovery question involves a different matter. Smith is convinced that Jones is lying when she claims that she actually worked one day in June. Based on that statement, Smith suspects Jones is a pathological liar. Smith therefore wants to know whether it is possible to force Jones to submit to a mental examination to determine if she is, in fact, a pathological liar.

Finally, Smith wants to talk to Pearson, who he feels will support his argument that he, not Jones, actually began to work for ACME first. However, as Pearson has now retired and moved to Hawaii, Smith would rather not bother taking Pearson's deposition. Instead, Smith wonders if you can simply send Pearson a set of interrogatories to obtain the information.

How will you respond to Smith's questions concerning the jury trial, letter, transcript, mental examination, and interrogatories? Discuss.

QUESTION 3 (Suggested time: 45 minutes):   One day, Jay Walker decides to cross a busy street in the middle of the block rather than at the crosswalk. Shortly after reaching the other side, Walker is accosted by Lou Tennant, a police officer who works for Seksintha City in the state of Dakota. Tennant throws Walker to the ground, beats him severely, and then arrests him — all for the minor offense of jaywalking.

Infuriated, Walker sues Tennant in a federal district court in the state of Dakota. His complaint contains two counts. The first is under 42 U.S.C. §1983, a federal civil rights statute. To state a claim under §1983, a party must allege (a) that the person who engaged in the objectionable behavior was acting under "color of state law," and (b) that the objectionable behavior deprived plaintiff of a right guaranteed by the U.S. Constitution or federal law. Count I of Walker's complaint attempts to meet these requirements by using the following language:

Count I

2. Defendant works for, and at the time of the incident described in paragraphs 3 and 4 below was acting on behalf of, the City of Seksintha, State of Dakota.
3. On October 4, 2003, Defendant committed the tort of false arrest against plaintiff in connection with an alleged jaywalking.
4. In the course of the arrest, Defendant committed assault and battery on Plaintiff without any justification.
5. These actions denied Plaintiff his right to due process of law as guaranteed by the Fourteenth Amendment to the U.S. Constitution.

Walker's second count is based on title 12, §123 of the Dakota statutes. This section creates a cause of action against police officers who abuse their authority. The portion of Walker's complaint that deals with this count states:

Count II

6. Plaintiff repeats the allegations of paragraphs 2 through 4.
7. Said acts also violated title 12, §123 of the Dakota statutes.

The complaint also contains a jurisdictional statement and a prayer for damages.

Defendant Tennant realizes that the Dakota federal court has jurisdiction and venue. However, he files a timely motion to dismiss the complaint for failure to state a claim. His motion cites two provisions of the Dakota Pleading Rules. The first is the basic provision setting forth Dakota's system of Code pleading, which requires a pleader to set forth "a statement of the facts constituting the cause of action, in ordinary and concise language.'' The second provision is a specific pleading statute that applies only to actions under title 12, §123. This provision reads as follows:

> In any civil action brought under title 12, §123, the plaintiff must certify that he or she has met with the defendant(s) prior to filing suit in an attempt to reach an amicable, nonlitigated settlement, and that such meeting failed to produce such a settlement.

Walker's complaint contains no such statement. In fact, Walker never tried to meet with Tennant because he feared that Tennant would again cause him physical harm.

How should the court rule on Tennant's motion to dismiss? Discuss.

QUESTION 4 (Suggested time: 35 minutes):   Clampett recently sued his banker, Drysdale, in the federal district court for the Southern District of California. Clampett alleges that Drysdale negligently invested Clampett's funds in pork bellies. Drysdale immediately files a timely motion to dismiss Clampett's case. Drysdale bases his motion on the deposit agreement that Clampett signed when he turned his funds over to the bank. Not only does that agreement explicitly authorize Drysdale to invest the funds in pork bellies, but it also requires that all disputes concerning the bank's management of the money be settled by binding arbitration. Drysdale argues in his motion that the arbitration clause divests the federal court of its power to hear the case and that accordingly the court should dismiss the action.

The trial judge disagrees with Drysdale and denies the motion. Although recognizing that as a general rule agreements to arbitrate are enforceable in federal court, the judge finds that the clause in the Clampett-Drysdale agreement is unenforceable because Drysdale had lied to Clampett about the contents of the agreement before it was signed. Hoping to forestall Drysdale's inevitable request to reconsider, the trial judge includes the following language in her opinion denying Drysdale's motion:

> This ruling is the absolute final judgment of this court on the issue of whether this dispute will be arbitrated. If defendant Drysdale disagrees with this court's ruling, he is encouraged to appeal. In fact, this court sees no reason why such an appeal cannot occur immediately.

Drysdale takes the hint and immediately files an appeal in the proper court of appeals. May the court of appeals hear the case at the present time? Discuss.

Essay Exam Answers

SAMPLE ANSWER TO QUESTION 1

1. Motion to sever: Axel will lose the motion. The governing rule is Fed. R. Civ. P. 14 because Carol added Axel as a third-party defendant (3PD). Although that rule places a time limit on joining 3PDs, the facts specify that the impleader was timely.

Rule 14 allows a defendant to join as a 3PD anyone who is or may be liable to the defendant for all or part of the defendant's liability to the plaintiff. Carol's claim meets this test. Admittedly, she claims that she "did nothing wrong." However, her impleader claim recognizes that even without culpability, she can be held liable for the negligent actions of Axel. By asking Axel to reimburse her for any liability, her claim meets the requirements of Fed. R. Civ. P. 14.

The court should also keep Charles's claim against Axel. Because Charles has filed a claim against a third-party defendant, this issue is likewise governed by Rule 14 rather than by Rule 20. (Rule 20 would apply if Charles had sued the two as defendants originally.) Rule 14(a) allows a plaintiff to file a claim against a third-party defendant as long as the claim arises from the same transaction or occurrence as the plaintiff's claim against the defendant. Charles's claim certainly meets this criterion. His claim against both Carol and Axel arise out of a single occurrence: the defect in the car and the resulting injury.

2. Axel's motion to dismiss — timeliness: Axel filed a pre-answer motion before his motion to dismiss for lack of subject matter and personal jurisdiction. Under Fed. R. Civ. P. 12(g), a party may waive certain Rule 12(b) defenses by omitting them from a pre-answer motion. Therefore, we must first address whether Axel waived the jurisdictional defenses by failing to include them in the motion to sever.

Subject matter jurisdiction is not one of the defenses that are waived by failure to include it in a pre-answer motion. Pursuant to Fed. R. Civ. P. 12(h)(3), a party may raise lack of subject matter jurisdiction at any time and in any manner. Axel's challenge to subject matter jurisdiction is therefore timely.

The personal jurisdiction defense is a closer case. Personal jurisdiction *is* a defense that can be waived by failure to include it in a pre-answer motion. However, Axel's motion to sever did not constitute a waiver. Under Rule 12(g), the only pre-answer motions that result in waiver are motions raising a defense that "this rule" (that is, Rule 12) permits to be raised by motion. Severance based on improper joinder is not a defense listed in Rule 12 and therefore does not trigger the waiver rule of Fed. R. Civ. P. 12(g).

3. Axel's motion to dismiss — subject matter jurisdiction: Axel's motion to dismiss for lack of subject matter jurisdiction will be denied because the court has diversity jurisdiction over both claims against him. Carol and Charles are both citizens of South Carolina. Axel is a citizen of Germany because the facts say that he has not yet acquired U.S. citizenship. Although the problem does not state whether he has acquired permanent resident alien status, that fact will not make a difference. If he has not, he is a citizen of Germany for purposes of §1332, and alienage jurisdiction will exist. If he has acquired permanent resident alien status, he will be treated as a citizen of the state of his domicile. Because the facts state that Axel currently resides in Wisconsin and intends to remain there "for many years," his domicile is Wisconsin. Therefore, if Axel has acquired permanent resident alien status, he will be treated as a citizen of Wisconsin, and diversity exists. The amount in controversy for both claims is $300,000, which clearly satisfies §1332.

4. Axel's motion to dismiss — personal jurisdiction: As noted above, the motion is timely. And Axel should prevail on the merits. *Service* is not an issue. Under Fed. R. Civ. P. 4, a party suing in federal court may either use the service methods listed in Rule 4 or borrow the service methods of the state in which it sits or the state in which service occurs. Fed. R. Civ. P. 4(e). Charles's use of a process server to serve Axel in-hand is explicitly authorized by Fed. R. Civ. P. 4(c)(2). Carol used the state long-arm statute.

Although service was proper, the South Carolina federal court may not exercise personal jurisdiction over Axel. Because of Fed. R. Civ. P. 4(k), service in a federal action is sufficient to establish jurisdiction only if a state court could exercise jurisdiction over that same defendant. Here, it would violate due process for a South Carolina state court to exercise jurisdiction over Axel. Axel has no contacts with South Carolina sufficient to establish jurisdiction. Although he did intentionally deal with a citizen of that state, that transaction is not sufficient to establish jurisdiction. A connection with a state constitutes a contact only if it constitutes purposeful availment of the benefits and protections of a state's law. By repairing an automobile in Wisconsin, Axel did nothing to gain the benefits and protections of South Carolina law. Therefore, because he has no contacts with South Carolina, the Due Process Clause would prevent South Carolina from exercising jurisdiction. Because the state court could not exercise jurisdiction over Axel, Fed. R. Civ. P. 4(k) likewise prevents a federal court from exercising jurisdiction.

If Axel had had purposeful contacts with South Carolina, the "fairness" side of the test would not preclude the exercise of jurisdiction. Although there is a significant burden on Axel to travel to South Carolina, both the plaintiff and that state clearly have an interest in the outcome of the case.

5. Carol's motion to dismiss: Because Carol filed her motion after serving her answer, there is again an issue of timeliness. As noted above, however, Fed. R. Civ. P. 12(h) allows a party to raise the defense of subject matter jurisdiction at any time. She did not waive the defense by failure to include it in her answer.

There is a possibility, however, that Carol may not be allowed to file an amendment to her answer. Under Fed. R. Civ. P. 15(a), a party may amend her answer once without court permission. However, there is a time limit. There is no indication that Carol's answer contained a counterclaim. Therefore, under Rule 7(a), Charles will not be required to file a reply to the answer. Because the pleadings will end at the answer, Rule 15(a) allows Carol only 20 days after serving her answer to amend without court permission. The problem specifies that three weeks — 21 days — have expired. Because the time period is more than 10 days, intervening weekends and holidays are included. Fed. R. Civ. P. 6. Accordingly, Carol's absolute right to amend has expired.

She can still amend her answer if she can obtain the court's permission. In this situation, it is highly likely that a court would allow the amendment. Fed. R. Civ. P. 15(a) specifies that leave to amend shall be freely given if justice so requires. Given the importance of the defense, the high probability of success (see below), the lack of any prejudice to Charles by the slight delay in amending, and the fact that Carol could raise the defense in some other manner even if she cannot amend, a court almost certainly will allow her to amend to raise this defense.

Finally, a court will grant Carol's motion to dismiss for lack of subject matter jurisdiction. The claim is a common law tort claim, which is not a federal question. Jurisdiction is proper only if diversity is present. Here, although the amount in controversy is satisfied, there is no diversity. Both Charles and Carol are citizens of South Carolina and therefore fail the test under 28 U.S.C. §1332(a).

Note that dismissal of Charles's claim against Carol will also result in dismissal of Carol's impleader claim against Axel. However, because an independent basis of jurisdiction exists, the court could retain Charles's claim against Axel.

SAMPLE ANSWER TO QUESTION 2

1. Jury trial: The Seventh Amendment preserves a right to a jury trial (a) in cases in federal courts, and (b) for any claims and issues that would have been heard by a jury at common law. Smith's action is in federal court, so the first criterion is satisfied. However, his case presents a mix of legal and equitable claims. Smith's claim against Olson seeks only an injunction. Because an injunction is purely an equitable remedy, the Seventh Amendment would not require a jury on that claim.

Smith's claim against Jones seeking ejectment presents a claim at common law. Although ejectment is specific relief, historically it was a common law remedy, and a jury would be impaneled.

In cases presenting a mix of legal and equitable claims, a party is entitled to a jury on all *issues* relating to the legal claims, even if those same issues are also relevant to the equitable claims. Thus, Smith is entitled to a jury on all issues relevant to the ejectment. Because his claims against Jones and Olson are so intertwined, this also means that a jury could decide all of the common issues arising in the claim against Olson (which will constitute virtually all of the issues in that claim too).

Even when a party has a constitutional right to a jury trial, she must demand a jury in timely fashion. Fed. R. Civ. P. 38(b) requires Smith to file his demand within 10 days from service of "the last pleading directed to . . . any issue triable of right by a jury." In this case, the last pleading directed to the legal claim was Jones's answer. The fact that the answer was served late does not matter. Assuming the demand can be filed immediately, you can make a timely demand for a jury. Under Fed. R. Civ. P. 6, a time period of 10 days or less *excludes* intervening weekends and holidays. Since there is one weekend between December 1 and December 12, there is still time to file a demand.

2. Disclosing the letter: The letter need not be disclosed. Under Fed. R. Civ. P. 26(a)(1)(B), Smith must disclose the letter only if he may use it to support his claim. This letter is not relevant to Smith's claim. Although he and Jones disagree on what it means to "begin to work for ACME," no one is claiming that the term means the date of the *offer*, which is what the letter covers. (On the other hand, Smith really will not be able to use the letter to "surprise" Jones unless she happens to testify about the date of the offer, a trivial point.)

3. Disclosing the transcript: The transcript should be disclosed since Smith will almost certainly use it to support his case in one way or another. Even if it contains hearsay evidence, Smith can use the statements to find other supporting information that he can use at trial.

That Smith wants to use the information to "surprise" the defendants at trial is not a sufficient excuse. The purpose of the mandatory disclosure rules is to prevent just this sort of surprise. The only exception is when a party has information that it will use solely for impeachment. Here, Smith almost certainly will present this information as part of his case, not merely in response to testimony by Jones or Olson.

Nor does the transcript qualify for the word product qualified privilege. Although it is a document, it was not prepared in anticipation of litigation. Smith had no reason to anticipate that he would go to court over a claim concerning his office.

4. Mental examination: Smith cannot obtain a mental examination of Jones. The issue of Jones's mental condition has not been placed into controversy. Although a party can place her own condition into controversy in her pleadings, nothing in Jones's pleadings raises a question as to her veracity. For an opposing party to place a party's condition into controversy, *Schlagenhauf* requires more than the "suspicion" that Smith has. Smith would need to file affidavits or other real evidence providing facts that tend to show that Jones has a problem with the truth.

5. Interrogatories: Only a party to a suit is required to answer interrogatories. Because Pearson is not a party, he is under no obligation to respond to interrogatories in this case. On the other hand, if Pearson willingly answers the interrogatories, nothing prevents Smith from using the information.

SAMPLE ANSWER TO QUESTION 3

This question actually involves two separate *Erie* issues.

1. Code pleading: First, there is a question as to whether the federal court must follow the Dakota Code pleading rules. Note that *Erie* is an issue even when, as here, the federal court is exercising federal question jurisdiction.

The Dakota rule probably does conflict with federal law. Fed. R. Civ. P. 8(a) requires only a short, plain statement of the cause of action. Walker's complaint meets this standard because it sets out the legal theory coupled with the basic facts. However, the complaint does not contain sufficient facts to satisfy Dakota's Code pleading standard. If state law applies, the suit could be dismissed for failure to state a claim.

Because the federal law is a Federal Rule of Civil Procedure, the *Erie* analysis turns on whether Fed. R. Civ. P. 8(a) is "procedural" within the meaning of the Rules Enabling Act (28 U.S.C. §2072). The rule meets this test. It is not meant to make it easier or more difficult for a party to recover but merely controls how the plaintiff apprises the court and other parties of the claims it is asserting. Nor does Rule 8(a) abridge, enlarge, or modify the rights or defenses in any way.

2. Certification: On the surface, there is a conflict between the Dakota rule and the Federal Rules of Civil Procedure because the rules do not require a party to certify that he met with the defendant. However, that conflict actually proves to be fairly narrow. The Federal Rules of Civil Procedure do not deal with the issue of *whether* the plaintiff must actually meet. (Indeed, the defendant's right to negotiate might be deemed a substantive right that could not be impaired by the Federal Rules of Civil Procedure.) The rules deal only with whether the complaint must *specify* that a meeting occurred. A rule, such as Rule 8, that does not require a statement does not infringe the defendant's right to have such a meeting. Therefore, Rule 8 is procedural, and Walker need not specify that a meeting occurred. However, because the Federal Rules of Civil Procedure do not affect the state law requirement of meeting, Tennant will still be able to dismiss the case on other grounds because no meeting occurred.

SAMPLE ANSWER TO QUESTION 4

As a general rule, a federal appellate court may hear appeals only of "final" judgments. 28 U.S.C. §1291. The decision here is not final within the meaning of §1291 because it does not wrap up Clampett's claim. The suit for misuse of funds remains to be resolved.

There are, however, several exceptions to §1291. Many of these are obviously inapplicable. The order did not grant or deny an injunction or receivership and therefore does not qualify under §1292(a). Nor is discretionary review under §1292(b) available because the trial judge did not properly certify the decision as indicated in that section. Moreover, Drysdale's appeal is not a mandamus or prohibition.

Two other exceptions remain a possibility. The first is appeal of a "discrete part" of a case under Fed. R. Civ. P. 54(b). Although the trial judge's language looks like a proper certification under Rule 54(b), the case cannot be appealed under that section. Rule 54(b) applies only when the trial court enters a final judgment on one or more discrete *claims*. As indicated above, the decision here did not wrap up any claims, merely the arbitration issue.

The only other possible exception is the collateral order doctrine. This exception applies when the court (i) conclusively determines, (ii) an important issue, (iii) that is completely separate from the merits, and (iv) the decision would be effectively unreviewable if the loser must wait for an ordinary appeal. The first two requirements are met. The judge is certainly done with this issue. Moreover, the issue of arbitration is important, especially because federal statutes may require the court to honor this arbitration agreement.

It is unclear whether the issue is separate from the merits. The basis for the judge's decision — unconscionability — might also be an issue in the underlying dispute. Clampett must deal with the term in the deposit agreement explicitly authorizing investments in pork bellies. One way to accomplish that goal is to argue that the contract was entered into by fraud.

Finally, even if the other requirements are met, appeal under the collateral order doctrine should not be allowed because the decision would be effectively reviewable if Drysdale appeals after final judgment. The court of appeals could simply vacate any judgment in favor of Clampett and order the parties to arbitrate the dispute. Note, however, that a court could conclude that the right to arbitrate is a right not to be sued at all in a court (like the immunity issue discussed in *Lauro Lines*). This result is unlikely because binding arbitration, unlike immunity, does allow a third party to adjudicate the defendant's rights. However, if the court of appeals treats arbitration like an immunity, the decision denying arbitration *would not* be effectively reviewable via an ordinary appeal. Requiring a full trial prior to appeal would violate Drysdale's ''right'' not to have to go to court. Again, however, this result is unlikely.

Table of Cases

Table of Statutes and Rules

Subject Matter Index